THE CHOSEN
FOLKS

JEWISH HISTORY, LIFE, AND CULTURE
Michael Neiditch, Series Editor

THE CHOSEN FOLKS

Jews on the Frontiers of Texas

Bryan Edward Stone

UNIVERSITY OF TEXAS PRESS, AUSTIN

Requests for permission to reproduce material
from this work should be sent to:
    Permissions
    University of Texas Press
    P.O. Box 7819
    Austin, TX 78713–7819
    www.utexas.edu/utpress/about/bpermission.html

∞ The paper used in this book meets the minimum requirements
of ANSI/NISO z39.48–1992 (R1997) (Permanence of Paper).

Library of Congress Cataloging-in-Publication Data

Stone, Bryan Edward, 1967–
    The chosen folks : Jews on the frontiers of Texas / Bryan
Edward Stone. — 1st ed.
    p.   cm. — (Jewish history, life, and culture)
    Includes bibliographical references and index.
    ISBN 978-0-292-72897-4
    1. Jews—Texas—History. 2. Texas—Ethnic relations. I. Title.
    F395.J5S76 2010
    976.4'004924—dc22   2009036213

FOR MY
GRANDPARENTS

CONTENTS

Headstone in the Hebrew Cemetery in Corsicana, Texas.
Photograph by Barbara G. Stone © 2008.

Rope Walker, A True Story

On a warm, still afternoon in 1884, the citizens of Corsicana, Texas, gathered in the center of town for Trades Day.[1] Merchants from Navarro and nearby counties set up displays of their goods along Beaton Street, and a crowd came out to take advantage of the bargains and to enjoy the food—baked, fried, and barbecued—offered from stalls and shop windows. Normally a quiet stop along the Houston and Texas Central Railroad, Corsicana came alive for a brief time to celebrate its commercial success and, just as importantly, to break the monotony of life in an East Texas town of only a few thousand people.

Beaton Street was bustling with visitors—itinerant peddlers, shopkeepers from nearby towns, wholesalers in to drum up business with local stores, farmers and their families come to see the newest implements and to stock up on supplies. In that crowd the stranger could have blended in easily. Even the wooden peg leg where his right calf and foot had once been would not have drawn attention among people so accustomed to the sight of Confederate war veterans. His intention, however, was not to go unnoticed.

Later tellers of the story disagree on whether he was working for someone wishing to make a lasting advertising impression or had dreamed up the stunt on his own. Some have suggested that he was a former circus performer plying the only trade he knew for scattered nickels and dimes from the crowd. Few disagree, though, on the particulars of what he did.

As the people moved among the stalls, a heavy rope, one end securely tied to a rooftop, flew overhead to another rooftop across the intersection with Collin Street. They watched as the stranger came down from the first building, hobbled across the street, vanished into the second building, and reappeared on the roof to pull the line taut and tie it off. As they looked curiously up at him, he stepped back from the edge of the roof, out of their view. After a few dramatic moments, he reappeared, brandishing a pole several feet long. A cast-iron cookstove was attached firmly to his back with leather straps. Struggling only a little under the weight of the stove, the stranger stepped to the end of the roof, the balancing pole stretched out away from him on either side. He had tied his trouser legs over his knees, revealing the wooden leg, which he slid carefully out onto the line. People in the crowd saw that the bottom of the peg was notched to fit snugly over the rope.

Pushing the peg leg out before him, he followed with his good foot, stood a moment to secure his balance on the rope, waggled the pole a bit—for dramatic effect, surely—then slid the peg forward another step. The crowd fell to a tense hush and quickly cleared a swath below him as if rushing from a fire—far enough for safety but still close enough to watch. They stared upward as he worked his way along the rope, his face marked with intense concentration, his back straining forward under the weight of the stove. Even from two stories down, they could hear his strong and deliberate breathing, which settled into a mechanical pattern with the shifting of his weight and the inching of his body—slide the peg, step the foot—over the middle of the street.

He had his first trouble where the rope reached its lowest point and began its slight uphill incline toward home. He tipped a bit to one side, the crowd gasped, but he righted himself easily. With the next step he made another sideslip, dipping the pole opposite to recover his balance. The stove on his back gave him an unnatural inertia and he overcompensated, pulling too hard against the fall. Leaning more heavily now, he flung his shoulders again to the opposite side, the pole flailing uselessly in his hands, the quivering of his legs giving the rope first a barely controlled then a violent oscillation. He rode it there for a moment, then tumbled from the line. As the crowd watched in horror, he landed in a heap under the stove, a cloud of dust rising around him.

Someone confirmed that he was breathing, but barely. They carefully unstrapped the stove from his body and the strongest among them pushed it aside. Someone hoisted him over a shoulder and carried him to a nearby hotel, where they laid him in a bed and called for the town physician. Dr. J. T. Gulick arrived quickly and found the stranger hovering on the edge of consciousness. Gulick asked the stranger his name but got no response. A brief examination showed that death was imminent. Unsure if the stranger could even understand, the doctor gently told him the bad news and asked if he wanted a preacher. The cloudy eyes momentarily cleared, and the stranger said yes, please, he was a Methodist. The doctor sent for Methodist minister Abe Mulkey, who in later years became a famous evangelist.

Mulkey arrived and asked the man his name but got no response. He began to pray quietly over the bedside. Before he could get far, however, the stranger awoke, caught the minister's gaze, and whispered that, forgive him, he was not, in fact, a Methodist. He was a Jew, and could he please talk to a rabbi?

Like many Texas towns, Corsicana had a Jewish population, as many as three hundred by some counts, but they had no synagogue and no rabbi. Mulkey sent instead for a prominent merchant, a leader of the Jewish community. When the merchant arrived, he took Mulkey's chair at the bedside. The stranger was now very near death, and the two had only a moment to pray together—long enough for the man's flawless Hebrew to convince the merchant that he was undoubtedly Jewish—before the stranger died, his name still unknown.

Though without a synagogue, the Jews of Corsicana had organized themselves into an informal congregation, and they had set aside a piece of ground nine years earlier for a Jewish cemetery with a low fence around it to separate it from the non-Jewish graves nearby. They resolved that this was the only fitting place to lay the stranger to rest. They took up a collection, purchased a plain headstone, and engraved it with the simple epitaph "Rope Walker." It is there to this day in the Hebrew Cemetery in Corsicana, a reminder that in life, and perhaps especially in Texas, there is no greater virtue than balance.

ACKNOWLEDGMENTS

I am indebted, first, to the hundreds of people—independent researchers, family archivists, genealogists, memoirists, and amateur enthusiasts—who supplied the primary documentation on which my work is based. Without their pioneering efforts, I could never have begun this book.

The suggestion that I write about Texas Jewry came from Robert Abzug, the director of the Schusterman Center for Jewish Studies at the University of Texas at Austin, and through many years of research and writing, he has been a source of solid advice, ideas, and professional mentorship. The other members of my dissertation committee—Seth Wolitz, Leonard Dinnerstein, Mark C. Smith, Steven Hoelscher, and the late Robert Crunden—each contributed in different ways at different stages of my research, and their influence is ingrained throughout this volume.

Three people offered critical help as the manuscript took shape. Hollace Ava Weiner's own publications on Texas-Jewish history, her deep knowledge of the people and documents that compose it, her friendship and support, and her generosity in sharing ideas and materials have contributed more to my work than I can possibly say. Mark K. Bauman has been a constant source of encouragement and advice, especially in his role as editor of *Southern Jewish History*. Through his meticulous and penetrating comments on my contributions, he has not only helped me produce better articles but also has made me a better writer and historian. Stuart Rockoff, a graduate school colleague, now the director of the History Department at the Goldring-Woldenberg Institute of Southern Jewish Life, has long shared my interest in Texas-Jewish history, and I relied on his familiarity with whatever issues I was trying to work out. Hollace, Mark, and Stuart all read the manuscript and offered substantial recommendations for improvement. Although I have not been able to make every change they suggested, I have made most. The book is infinitely better for their trouble.

Jim Burr of the University of Texas Press contacted me in 2003 about publishing my dissertation, and as I worked through the revisions, he has been a steady and patient guide through an unfamiliar process. Also at UT Press, Leslie Tingle and Sally Furgeson have provided invaluable guidance in bringing this book to publication. Much of my work has depended on the support and guidance of dozens of librarians. In Glendive, Montana, where I wrote my dissertation while teaching at Dawson Community College, I would have been lost without the help of Andrine Haas and MaryAnn Clingingsmith, who processed innumerable interlibrary loan applications and helped me locate materials that would otherwise have been unavailable. In Corpus Christi, the library staff at Del Mar College, especially Vivian Brown, has been excessively patient and responsive to my many requests. In addition, I especially thank Claudia Anderson of the Lyndon Baines Johnson Presidential Library; Beth Andresen at the Dallas Public Library; Ellen Brown of the Baylor University Library; Gerry Cristol, archivist of Temple Emanu El in Dallas; Joel Draut at the Houston Public Library; Julie Koven and Lyn Slome of the American Jewish Historical Society; Patrick Lemelle of UTSA's Institute of Texan Cultures; Kevin Proffitt, Camille Servizzi, and Elisa Ho at the American Jewish Archives; Leslie Wagner and Mandy Dossey at the Dallas Jewish Historical Society; Judy Weidman of the Temple Beth Israel Archives in Houston; and the staffs of the Austin History Center, Perry-Castañeda Library, Texas State Library, and Center for American History in Austin.

Many individuals have shared their expertise, insights, and materials with me and have offered encouragement, often at critical moments. I especially wish to thank Valery Bazarov, Rachel Heimovics Braun, Tobias Brinkmann, Suzanne Campbell, Maxine Cohen, Barbara Fagin, the late Edna Friedberg, Rabbi David Geffen, Kay Goldman, Martin Goldman, Eric L. Goldstein, Neil Gurwitz, Charles and Jan Siegel Hart, Ginger Jacobs, Harriet Denise Joseph, Cathy Kahn, the late Rabbi Robert I. Kahn, Sharon Kahn, Rabbi Jimmy Kessler, Rosanne Leeson, the late John Livingston, Lauraine Miller and Larry Rose, Abraham Peck, Renato Ramirez, Leonard Rogoff, Rabbi

Kenneth Roseman, Glen Rosenbaum, Barbara Rosenberg, Jeanne and Joe Samuels, Louis Schmier, the late Saul Viener, Deborah Weiner, Stephen Whitfield, Cornelia Wilhelm, and Helen and Larry Wilk.

I have been fortunate to receive financial support, which has helped greatly in completing this work. I am honored, in particular, to have received a Loewenstein-Wiener Fellowship Award from the Jacob Rader Marcus Center of the American Jewish Archives in 2000, which allowed me to make two invaluable visits to their collection. Many thanks to Gary Zola, Fred Krome, Kevin Proffitt, and the extraordinary staff at the Archives for their hospitality. A Project Completion Grant from the Southern Jewish Historical Society allowed me to collect and include a wide selection of illustrations. I am grateful for the Society's generosity, and I thank Phyllis Leffler, Bernie Wax, and Scott Langston for facilitating the grant.

Portions of this book have been previously published, and I thank the *Jewish Herald-Voice* of Houston for permission to reprint material from my article about Edgar Goldberg, my great-grandfather and that newspaper's founding editor, as well as *Southern Jewish History* for allowing me to republish portions of my articles about Kinky Friedman and Edgar Goldberg.

My parents, Barbara and Edward Stone, have provided love, support, and encouragement without which this book would not have been possible. My family is my most personal link to Texas-Jewish history, and so this work is dedicated to my grandparents: Arthur and Miriam "Billie" Stone and Albert and Dorothy Green.

My wife, Shannon, has been an advocate for this project, a helpful and insightful advisor in matters of expression, and a great friend to me throughout this long experience.

THE CHOSEN
FOLKS

✳

Introduction

Kinky Friedman, the country singer, crime novelist, and former Texas guber-
natorial candidate, once described himself as "the bastard child of twin
cultures." "Both cowboys and Jewboys," he explained, "wear their hats in
the house."[1] This is a typical Friedman throwaway line: clever, a bit crass,
played strictly for laughs. Like many of the jokes that pepper his songs and
novels, though, it hints at something deeper. By calling himself a "bastard
child," Friedman implies that his two heritages, Texan and Jewish, are incompatible in some way, that their marriage cannot produce a legitimate
child. At the same time, he calls them "twin" cultures, indicating that, however incompatible they appear, they still have much in common. The joke
unites the two groups, each with its distinctive headgear, while reminding
his listener that Stetsons and yarmulkes are really not the same at all.

The paradox in Friedman's joke lies at the heart of Jewish life in Texas:
Jews are both part of Texas history and not part of it, at home in the state
but distinct from most of its people. They have managed to walk a fine line,
accommodating the demands of secular life in Texas without sacrificing
their separate religious and ethnic heritage. And they have found ways to
contribute enormously to the state's economic, political, educational, and
artistic institutions while remaining loyal to a faith whose center of spiritual
and institutional energy has always been somewhere else.

This book examines the juncture of these two cultural traditions, Texan
and Jewish. Its method is primarily historical, and it explores in detail many

key developments in the growth of the Jewish community in Texas, numbering today some 130,000 people. Rather than make an attempt, however, to narrate the Texas-Jewish story comprehensively, I am interested in the evolution of an idea, that of the frontier, and its pivotal role in shaping Jewish identity and self-definition in Texas. Although I have not included every significant fact or every interesting person, or provided information about every one of the innumerable Texas cities and towns in which Jewish life occurred, I have selected for emphasis those events that best reveal the frontier idea in action. The frontier is so crucial a metaphorical force in Texas-Jewish history, however, as to be inseparable from it, and the events in which it most reveals itself are generally the same ones that would receive attention whatever means of selection an historian were to use. The following pages offer the first continuous narrative of Texas-Jewish life and are the first to tell the story of the Jews in Texas within a coherent interpretive framework. Gaps and absences in that story should prove only that much has yet to be learned and explained.

The Idea of Frontier

Texas is at the intersection of two distinct and sometimes competing narratives that established the symbolic context of Jewish life in the state: the American frontier and the Jewish Diaspora. Texas is both a quintessential frontier and, as Jewish historian and philanthropist Cyrus Adler wrote in the 1920s, "one of the last corners of the Dispersion," and Texas Jews are part of both the movement of Americans into the West and the scattering of Jews across the globe.[2] As frontierspeople entering a forbidding environment in search of economic opportunity, they often made poor Jews, removing themselves from population centers where the requirements of their faith would have been easier to maintain. As Jews, they often made poor frontierspeople, as they continued to look back to Jewish religious tradition and to Zion for the sources of their identity, rather than permitting the melting pot of the American frontier to absorb them. As frontierspeople, they saw their venture into the West as part of a necessary and admirable project to build a lasting community where none had existed before. But as Diaspora Jews they also knew that they were building a life in exile, far from the sources of Jewish meaning and identity and outside the consciousness of most Jews.

A frontier, in its widest sense, involves an interaction between different groups of people that requires them to define themselves in relation to one another. A frontier need not be a physical or geographical place but rather a set of ideas that gives meaning to physical reality. It has both literal and figurative significance. In the original French, *"frontière"* describes a national border, and frontiers are often political or cultural boundaries taking physical form on maps or marked on the ground itself. In American history, similarly, "frontier" is usually used in the context of westward expansion to describe new territory that was discovered, claimed, fought over, settled, and eventually annexed into the nation. It also describes a set of physical conditions created by the lack of civilized order and effective government: the American frontier was the "Wild West."

But these conditions, strictly speaking, are not what make a frontier. The external reality is only an outward expression of a conceptual divide, a perceived difference between the people or conditions that exist on either side of that divide. A frontier is fundamentally a line between "us" and "them" and marks differences of culture, personality, condition, and identity among groups of people. The meaning of frontier, then, lies not in physical space but in group identification. Frontiers often take material form, certainly, but reflect inward struggles over how to define one's own group among outsiders and how to maintain one's distinctive identity in the presence of others. Thus Jews, who have lived in nearly all of the world's places among nearly all of its peoples, are the quintessential frontierspeople.

Nineteenth-century Texas Jews encountered the frontier in its most literal, material sense—a sparsely populated region at the edge of Euro-American settlement that offered few of the inducements of "civilized" life. The American frontier lay between settled and unsettled portions of land, between areas that were under the control of the American government and American social institutions and those that fell under the dominion of non-Americans or of no one at all. For Jews, this frontier also distinguished places with Jewish people and institutions from those without. To cross that line, to enter the frontier, was to move away from established centers of Jewish life into a condition that made the practice of their faith and the preservation of their particular identity much more complicated. In such a place, Jews formed a small and marginal religious community, set apart from the mainstream of American Jewry and from Jewish events around the world. The awareness of being peripheral was a condition of Jewish life in early Texas, and the long-term effects of that original condition have been profound.

To offset their marginality and preserve a connection to their people's history, Jews on the Texas frontier often described their settlement in Texas

4

in prophetic terms, arguing that their sojourn into the American West made them more like their biblical ancestors than were their urban contemporaries. "Like the tent of our Patriarch Abraham in the desert," wrote a Houston rabbi's descendant, "[his] home radiated the warmth and splendor of Torah life."[3] In her history of the El Paso Jewish community, Fanny Sattinger Goodman elaborated the same analogy: "In this Desert Environment, similar to the one in which their forefathers travelled on the way towards the Promised Land, there came to the pioneers of the eighteen hundreds 'A Behest from the Prophet, to prepare the way in the wilderness.'"[4] The desert provided a common trope for Jews venturing into the American West. California Congressman Julius Kahn, to cite one of countless examples beyond Texas, declared in 1919 that "the United States is my Zion and San Francisco is my Jerusalem."[5] Nevertheless, Jews in the western states, especially in the earliest years of their settlement, faced hardships that belied their hopeful evocations of milk and honey. The struggles of the material frontier for Jews in Texas—the difficulty of maintaining Jewish identity where no Jewish community existed—are examined in the first two chapters of this study.

The material frontier was short-lived, however, and by the early twentieth century most Texas Jews lived in the state's largest cities, where Jewish facilities were available, if not plentiful, and the observance of Jewish rituals was as convenient as it was almost anywhere else in the country. If Texas lacked the profound, all-encompassing Jewish life available in New York, it could consistently provide the rudiments of Jewish community, ritual, and practice. Participation in nationwide organizations like B'nai B'rith, the Union of American Hebrew Congregations, the Central Conference of American Rabbis, and the National Council of Jewish Women drew Texas Jews into closer relationships with co-religionists in other parts of the country and mitigated the isolation that had characterized their community's earliest years. Nevertheless, the frontier idea remained crucial to Jewish identity in Texas. As the material frontier ceased to be a factor in their lives, Texas Jews internalized and transformed it into a changing set of symbolic boundaries that continued to define and distinguish them from both non-Jewish Texans and non-Texan Jews.

In defining their particular place in the world, Texas Jews enacted the observation of sociologist Fredrik Barth that groups living in pluralistic societies, where interactions with other groups occur continuously, must define more concretely the cultural boundaries that distinguish them from others. "The critical focus of investigation from this point of view," he writes, "becomes the ethnic boundary that defines the group, not the cultural stuff that it encloses."[6] Groups define themselves, that is, in contrast to others, across imaginary lines of difference, rather than by inherent qualities. Identity is not built on something essential and unchanging but is defined by borders that slip and shift through negotiation and conflict. Cultural identity is itself, then, a set of frontiers, and pluralistic Texas, where so many cultural groups collide, is a frontier society in more ways than one. The Jews in Texas, a minority deeply concerned with defining and maintaining their distinctive character, were always, and are still today, frontierspeople.

Jews and Other Texans—Texans and Other Jews

As a tiny ethnic and religious minority, rarely more than 0.6 percent of the state's population, Texas Jews continually managed cultural boundaries, drawing and maintaining lines of difference to define their place within and to distinguish themselves from the rest of the diverse Texas population. The first factor in play was racial: central and eastern European Jews felt included in the state's Anglo majority. Indeed, there was no real alternative in a state whose rich ethnic diversity had traditionally been simplified into stark racial categories—Anglo, Black, and Mexican. The term "Anglo," as Texas historian T. R. Fehrenbach once explained, essentially referred to people who fit into neither of the other two groups. "By this definition," he wrote, "ethnic groups as diverse as Irish Catholics, Jews, Lebanese, Norwegian, Chinese, Greek, German, Czech, and Polish Americans in Texas are all Anglos and consider themselves such."[7] In this sweeping usage, "Anglo" designated only vaguely what an individual was but more emphatically what he or she was not. Such labels left no room for subtleties. By identifying as Anglos in this racialized system, Jews could be part of the white majority and share in the state's commercial and political power structures. To be anything else was to face a life of diminished opportunity. As long as it would have them, and usually it would, Jews opted to join the majority.

In fact, Texas Jews were generally delighted to accept the state's Anglo history as their own, and they often displayed pride in identifying themselves with triumphalist, even racist, retellings of the state's past. Rabbi Henry Cohen of Galveston (a native Londoner and so an "Anglo" in even the strictest sense) was the first researcher to begin documenting the history of Jews in Texas, and he made special efforts to identify Jews among the state's pioneering Anglos. According to Cohen, for example, the Alsatian Henri Castro (Cohen anglicized him to Henry), who organized a colony in South Texas and founded the town of Castroville, had done nothing less than establish "a permanent home for civilized men between San Antonio and the Rio Grande," something "which both Spanish and Mexican power had failed to do." Despite Castro's French tongue and Spanish surname, not to mention his flimsy connection to Judaism, Cohen seized on him as a pioneering Texas Jew and emphasized his "heroic" exploits.[8]

Cohen described at length the various threats to the survival of the Castro colony, notably "the attacks of bandits and degenerate Mexicans," as well as gun-toting Indians he called "savages." For overcoming such obstacles, Castro deserved "to be enrolled among the most prominent pioneers of civilization in modern times."[9] Cohen included Castro in his canon of heroic Anglo Texans while carefully distinguishing him from the supposedly less advanced Spanish, Mexican, and Native American cultures excluded from his narrative. For Cohen, Jews were part of the conquering Anglo majority, not a subordinated minority, and they deserved to take their place among the state's elite. At the same time, however, Cohen's goal clearly was not to erase all difference between Jews and other whites: he published his remarks about Castro in a Jewish historical journal. Indeed, the efforts of Jewish Texans to preserve their separate ethnic and religious identity while still claiming the rewards of Anglo identity shaped much of their twentieth-century experience, as many of the chapters that follow explain.

As Texas Jews negotiated their differences from other Texans, they also defined themselves in contrast to other non-Texan Jews. Jewish Texans were keenly aware of the geographical and conceptual distances between themselves and the world's Jewish centers. "[I] want to tell you," wrote a nineteenth-century immigrant in El Paso to his family in Germany, "that this place is nearly the end of the world and the last of creation."[10] As the twentieth century progressed, however, Jews from eastern Europe and from New York arrived in Texas, bringing a more traditional religious style and a stronger devotion to Zionism, the movement dedicated to the establishment of a Jewish homeland in Palestine. Their presence changed the ways that Texas Jewry related to larger Jewish communities. Still, many Jewish Texans continued to view other Jews across a frontier of social and cultural difference and to consider themselves a separate, equally legitimate, Jewish community. Thus, to examine Texas Jewry only in the context of the Diaspora, as a story of isolated people far from the centers of their faith and culture, cannot adequately explain what has happened in Texas. Texas Jews must be viewed as people seeking to establish themselves in a new homeland as a group among other Texas cultural groups. They are people of the Diaspora, but, more importantly, they are people of the frontier.

Rabbi Henry Cohen in his Galveston study, ca. 1950.
Rosenberg Library, Galveston, Texas.

West of Center

Recent scholarship suggests that the Diaspora idea, with its implication that the Jewish universe has a center, is insufficient for explaining Jewish life throughout the world, and that the frontier provides a more useful interpretive framework. Sander L. Gilman and Martin Shain's *Jewries at the Frontier* explores Jewish communal and spiritual life in "frontier" communities like China, South Africa, Alaska, and, in an essay by Seth Wolitz, Texas. In his introduction, Gilman suggests that Jewish historians dispense with the idea of the Diaspora as "the overarching model for Jewish history":

> This model [has] been reinforced by the role that Israel and Zionist historians have had in reshaping the narrative of Jewish history. It was (and remains) the model of "you" and "us." It is the imagined center which defines me[, a Diaspora Jew,] as being on the periphery. "Israel," the lost Garden of Eden, the City on the Hill, is its center; all the rest of Jewish experience is on the periphery.[11]

In a diasporic "center/periphery model," American Jewry is peripheral to the Israeli center. The United States in turn has produced its own Jewish center, New York City, and so other American Jewish communities, including Texas, are peripheries of a periphery. They stand in relation to world Jewry as, perhaps, Ireland stands in relation to Europe—an island off the coast of an island off the coast.

Consequently, a belief has prevailed that American Jews are necessarily New Yorkers. In titling his 1976 classic history of the Lower East Side *World of Our Fathers*, for example, Irving Howe excluded the experience of thousands of American Jews whose fathers (or mothers, for that matter) were not from Howe's old neighborhood. A few years later, apparently hoping to correct the oversight, he coauthored a second volume looking at American Jews beyond New York but only piled insult on injury by calling it *We Lived There Too*.

Similarly, in her study of the postwar migration of New York Jews to the Sunbelt, Deborah Dash Moore smoothly omitted the existence of most of the nation's Jewish communities. "Nineteen forty-five marks a turning point for American Jews," she says. "That year they crossed a threshold to embrace the fulfillment promised by America. Behind them lay the immigrant working-class world—their parents' world of passionate politics and a vibrant Yiddish culture, their childhood world indelibly associated with New York City and the other large cities of the Northeast and Midwest." This description only pertains to some American Jews and not, as Moore implies, to all of them. She goes on to say that "[i]n the postwar era Jews discovered Houston and Dallas, Atlanta and Phoenix, and especially Miami and Los Angeles."[12] The suggestion that these communities were unknown until New York Jews "discovered" them, crossing the Hudson like Columbus over the Atlantic, is deceptive. They all had thriving Jewish communities long before World War II. Placed at the center of this model of American Jewry, New York stands as the only American Jewish experience, and all others vanish.

More troubling than this omission is the question of spiritual authenticity underlying such approaches: Jews on the periphery are somehow less Jewish, or are Jewish in some lesser way. "Center," after all, describes not only a geographic location (Israel, New York), but also a spiritual core of authentic Jewish practice and intuitive awareness of one's Jewish identity. In its religious form, this core is Orthodox ritual and belief; conceived linguistically, it is Yiddish and Hebrew; conceived culturally, it is the *Yiddishkeit* (Jewish culture and language) of eastern Europe; conceived socially, it is political Zionism and a wish for the ultimate ingathering of the Jewish people. If these characteristics mark the center, the only authentic Jewish "Us," then most of the world's Jews—those in the Americas (except, perhaps, in New York), those who are Reform, those who acculturate or intermarry, those who don't know a *schlemiel* from a *schlemazel*—are "Them," consigned to the margins and alien to their own cultural and religious heritage.

The question of authenticity is a recurring theme in depictions of Texas Jewry. In 1997, for example, a satirical article appeared in the humor magazine *The Onion*. Under the headline "Jewish Texans Commemorate Holocaust . . . Texas-Style!" the writer describes Holocaust Hoedown '97, a month-long program sponsored by the West Texas chapter of B'nai B'rith "commemorating the 20th century's darkest hour." Rabbi Leonard "Too Tall" Sussman of San Antonio opened the proceedings by laying a wreath at B'nai B'rith headquarters in Lubbock and reminding his listeners that "[i]f we do not remember the past, we are doomed to repeat it. . . . Never again, y'hear?" He closed with a "Yee-haw!" and lit the Eternal Flame, over which "a spit will be installed for Wednesday's kosher steer cookout." Additional highlights included "a Main Street parade featuring red, white and blue Texas blossoms spelling out 'Don't Mess With The Jews'; a special appearance by six-time Zionist calf-roping champion Barry Lowenstein; and daily double-bill showings of *Schindler's List* and John Wayne's *True Grit*." A photograph, captioned "Texas Jews rustle up some memorial grub," accompanies the article. The picture shows two men cooking steaks over a pit. One wears a black, broad-brimmed hat, thick gray beard, and dark coat; the other a short black beard with sidecurls and a casual burnt-orange shirt, leather vest, and a somewhat Stetsonish fedora. Both wear cooking aprons, one bearing an image of the Texas flag (with a six-pointed star) and the other the motto "Never Again, Pardner!" A group of Hasidim mosey around behind them against a background of blue sky and desert mountains.[13]

At first glance, the humor of this piece lies in the apparent incongruity of Jews in Texas and in the assumption that Texas Jews must be conspicuously different from normal ones. The article mixes, for comic effect, iconography familiar from both Jewish and Texan stereotype: barbecues, boisterousness, desert expanses, beards, Semitic names, and broad dark hats. Beneath the humor, though, is a commentary that gives the satire its edge. These characters are more than Jews out of place. They are acculturationists who fail to realize how far they have fallen, how far they have drifted from any genuine sense of Judaism. They are entirely unaware of their own vulgarity, of the cheapness with which they treat what should be a somber

"Texas Jews Rustle Up Some Memorial Grub." Illustration from article "Jewish Texans Commemorate Holocaust . . . Texas-Style!" February 12, 1997. Reprinted with permission of *The Onion.* © 2008, by Onion, Inc. www.theonion.com.

occasion. Nothing could be in poorer taste, after all, than a *barbecue* as a way of memorializing the ovens of the Holocaust. The article's author implies that the celebrants have so readily accepted the trappings of Texas identity that they have made their Jewishness less authentic, a meaningless and ill-fitting costume.

If actual Texas Jews feel uncomfortable in their "Texanness," however, they have rarely shown it, refusing to yield moral and spiritual authority to Jews anywhere else. Nineteenth-century Texas correspondents to national

Jewish newspapers signed letters with pseudonyms like "Lone Star" and "Alamo," and they reported proudly on their community activities "[a]way out here, on the rolling prairies of Texas."[14] More recently, individual Texas Jews have emphasized the presence of their families, or even of themselves, at the state's origin—even if they had to stretch the truth a bit. Bertha Bender, a longtime resident of Breckenridge, reminisced after her 101st birthday that "Texas had become a state in 1885, just three years before my birth, and it seemed we were destined to grow together."[15] But Texas actually became a state in 1846 and again, following the Civil War, in 1870, long before Bender was born. She also neglected to mention that she immigrated to the United States from Lithuania, but did not arrive in Texas until she was twenty-six years old. The force of Texas identification can be strong enough to subsume simple historical reality.

In fact, as Seth Wolitz writes in his contribution to *Jewries at the Frontier*, many Texas Jews are at peace with their peripheral status:

> [E]ven though New York functioned and functions today as the center of Jewish-American life, the Texas Jew, while accepting his peripheral condition from the New Yorker's perspective, does not feel decentered. The Texas Jew sees New York as the alternative vision and considers the Texas-Jewish experience no less valid and perhaps more desirable.[16]

Wolitz, however, argues that the Jewish identity claimed by "third generation" Texans is thoroughly compromised: "Traditional Ashkenazic ethnicity," he writes, "is surely gone, or at least distinctly transmogrified into a new Texas-Jewish expression." Today's Jewish Texans have "no consciousness that there is any significant difference between the present Jewish identity and that of the past." They wrongly believe, moreover, that their acculturated, "Texanized" sense of Jewish identity is authentic, that Jews have always believed what Texans believe today. Wolitz does not dispute that Texas Jews feel at home in Texas. They claim "originary rights," in fact, by pointing out the presence of Jews in the state's early history, and they produce historical and creative texts that "have reinscribed this Texas Jewishness back into the original Jewish culture of the first generation so that the ancestors are proto-Americans or proto-Texans." But such a reinterpretation of the past, he suggests, is ultimately self-deluding, and "the delightful aporia called the 'Texas Jew'" is a fallen creature.[17]

Wolitz's critique proceeds from his assumption (shared, it seems, with the editors of *The Onion*) that there is, in fact, an essential Judaism, a spiritual center, and that Texas Jewry is peripheral to it and thus inferior. In contrast, Sander Gilman proposes using the idea of the frontier as a means of describing peripheral communities without questioning their authenticity. Rather than presuming an essentialist standard of Judaism, next to which others are second-rate, Gilman argues for a new rendering of Jewish history "marked by the dynamics of change, confrontation, and accommodation; a history which focuses on the present and in which all participants are given voice." Gilman finds the source of such a narrative in the idea of the frontier, "a place not defined by a center and a periphery, but by a constant sense of confrontation at the margin." If Jewish history is, in fact, a story of confrontation at the margin, then Jews in peripheral places, where contact with non-Jews is commonplace and unavoidable, become central to the Jewish experience. By suggesting that Jewish history be retold "as the history of the Jews at the frontier, a history with no center," Gilman validates "marginal" Jewish experiences, like those which occurred in Texas, as genuinely, even profoundly, Jewish.[18]

Frontiers and Borderlands

"Frontier" is a complicated term with a controversial history, and it will be helpful to trace its meaning through many of its possible interpretations, as Gilman does. Any understanding of the significance of the frontier in American history begins with Frederick Jackson Turner and his conveniently titled 1893 address, "The Significance of the Frontier in American History." Turner offered a vision of an American nation defined by its frontier, by the restless urge of its people to move ever westward. "The peculiarity of American institutions," Turner wrote, "is the fact that they have been compelled to adapt themselves to the changes of an expanding people." That is, what made Americans American was the existence of a frontier and their urge to push into it. Turner understood that frontier to be an actual geographic location: the line marking the western extreme of Euro-American settlement, the "margin of that settlement which has a density of two or more [Americans] to the square mile." In less quantifiable terms, the frontier was also a place fraught with cultural significance, the point where the wilderness met western civilization and consumed it. As Americans advanced westward, Turner wrote, "the frontier [was] the outer edge of the wave—the meeting point between savagery and civilization."[19] Turner touched a resonant chord. More than just settlers or colonists, pioneers in American popular mythology are culture heroes who redeemed the wilderness from savagery.

Many later western historians, including Patricia Nelson Limerick and Richard White, rightfully criticized Turner's approach, going so far as to reject the frontier entirely as a useful means of understanding the history of the American West.[20] "When clearly and precisely defined," Limerick writes, "the term 'frontier' is nationalistic and often racist"; in essence, it is "the area where white people get scarce." Rather than viewing westward expansion as a civilizing process, "New Western Historians," in Limerick's summarization, prefer to use terms like "invasion, conquest, colonization, [and] exploitation." They recognize what Turner did not: westward expansion was no simple process of a monolithic civilization meeting and subduing its opposite. It was, rather, a "convergence of diverse people—women as well as men, Indians, Europeans, Latin Americans, Asians, Afro-Americans . . . and their encounters with each other and with the natural environment."[21]

Although he accepts the validity and necessity of the New Western Historians' critique, Sander Gilman looks past it for a definition of "frontier" that may describe Jews in any marginal community. The American frontier, after all, which can certainly be described as a place of racism, conquest and exploitation, is only one of the many frontiers Jews have inhabited around the world. To show that the frontier can be "a useful category for the writing of the new Jewish history,"[22] Gilman draws on the work of Stephen Aron, another historian of the American West:

> Rather than banishing the word for past offenses, western historians need to make the most of the frontier. Reconfigured as the lands where separate polities converged and competed, and where distinct cultures collided and occasionally coincided, the frontier unfolds the history of the Great West in ways that Turner never imagined.[23]

Kerwin Lee Klein has similarly redefined the frontier as "a zone of cultural interaction" rather than a fixed line or a boundless region.[24] Aron and Klein imagine the frontier in terms of cultural boundaries more than geographic place. Frontiers are the placeless imaginary spaces in which cultural interactions occur.

Gloria Anzaldúa, a Chicana poet who grew up along the U.S.-Mexico border in South Texas, has further refined the idea of the frontier as a "borderland," a permeable region of cultural interaction. Borderlands, she writes, may be physical and political, as the "Texas-U.S. Southwest/Mexican border," or they may be the "psychological borderlands, the sexual borderlands and the spiritual borderlands" which "are physically present wher-

THE CHOSEN FOLKS

14

ever two or more cultures edge each other, where people of different races occupy the same territory, where under, lower, middle and upper classes touch, where the space between two individuals shrinks with intimacy." While "borders" are established "to define the places that are safe and unsafe, to distinguish *us* from *them*," a "borderland" is "a vague and undetermined place . . . in a constant state of transition."[25] Anzaldúa's borderland is multinational, multiracial, and multilingual; it is gendered and sexualized; it is simultaneously intimately personal and dangerously public. It is a place where distinctions between Us and Them lose their meaning in the process of personal and cultural interaction. Anzaldúa's borderland, her frontier, is any material or psychological space in which intercultural collisions occur.

Frontierspeople, the inhabitants of any such borderland, are not those who conquer the West but those who, in any context, go out and encounter the "Other." They must be perpetually self-defining, drawing imaginary lines around themselves that separate them from others. They internalize the frontier, transforming what was a geographic, Turnerian dividing line between civilization and savagery into subtler conceptual and symbolic boundaries distinguishing them from all Others, or, as Anzaldúa suggests, dissolving those distinctions altogether. As the essays in *Jewries at the Frontier* demonstrate, Jews draw and redraw such lines on frontiers around the world and across history, balancing the urge to acculturate with the competing urge to remain different. "Jews confront and are confronted," Gilman writes, "by the inhabitants of each land, from medieval Britain to Poland to China to India to Palestine."[26] The result is a variety of possible "Jewries," all equally valid. Instead of writing off frontier Jews as tragic examples of declension, a Jewish history built on the frontier idea allows us to see "peripheral" communities like Texas as, in fact, central to Jewish history. They are part of a perpetual process of reimagining and revivifying the meaning of Judaism in the Diaspora.

Moreover, if the frontier experience can unite such disparate Jewish experiences as those of Poland and China, it is also a useful way to understand Jewish life throughout the United States. To be sure, the frontier experience of Texas Jews is frequently repeated in other American regions. Published studies of local Jewish communities, especially in the South and West, have emphasized their distance from the Jewish centers, as revealed in their titles: Eli Evans' classic work about southern Jewry, *The Provincials*; Carolyn Gray LeMaster's *A Corner of the Tapestry*, about the Jews of Arkansas; Sophie Trupin's recollections of her North Dakota upbringing, *Dakota Diaspora: Memoirs of a Jewish Homesteader*; Linda Mack Schloff's *And Prairie*

Dogs Weren't Kosher: Jewish Women in the Upper Midwest Since 1855; and *The Jews of Wyoming: Fringe of the Diaspora* by Penny Diane Wolin. "You feel a separateness from the community," says one of Wolin's Wyoming interviewees. "If you read Genesis, about Abraham and Isaac and all those stories, you get a sense of people who are just out there alone in the desert with nobody else. And that's what it's really like out here." "Out here in Laramie," says another, "we're as far removed as possible from a coherent, cohesive Jewish community. You make it yourself here. You can't rely on institutions that already exist."[27]

These and many similar examples suggest that the frontier model is useful not only in describing Jewish life in Texas, or even in other southern and western states, but also may in fact be an essential metaphor for understanding American Jewish life in general. American Jews are, and have always been, frontierspeople. Fredrik Barth's claim, furthermore, that boundaries are more important in shaping group identity than the "cultural stuff" they enclose, means that it is unnecessary to attempt specialized descriptions, as several generations of American Jewish historians have done, of "western," "southern," or "northern" Jews: all are frontier Jews. This insight is especially helpful in dealing with Texas, where regional boundaries are problematic. Texas is sometimes southern, western, or southwestern depending on context, who is doing the naming, and why. As will be seen in the following chapters, regional identification is as manipulable a concept as any other form of group identity. It is unnecessary, and even undesirable, to make a definitive decision about which American region Texas is part of, because it is part of several in varying ways at different times. Texas itself is a borderland, and regional lines, like religious and racial lines, are just another set of terms open to interpretation in the process of defining group identity.

"Ride 'em, Jewboy"

A number of examples attest to the potent intermingling of cultural experiences that occurs in Texas and to the symbolic possibilities that the Texas-Jewish experience can provide. In her contribution to a 1988 collection of essays about her Orthodox Jewish family, Judith Geller Marlow, who grew up in El Paso but later moved to New York, provides one such instance. She begins by describing the physical environment in West Texas as "a valley with bare mountains surrounding it. There is no green lushness there. There is no water nearby; it is isolated, the closest large city 250–350 miles away. It is arid, very hot. The summers are hot, over 100 degrees daily, no humidity. Winters are cold—there are no fall or spring seasons." Why so much climatic detail? "Because whenever I hear the stories of the Jews wandering in the desert, trying to come together as a people before entering the promised land, I *identify* with them." The Jews' time in the desert of Sinai, she says, "was a necessity in the formation of the Jewish nation" and, like them, "I was formed in the desert, as a person and as a Jew."[28] The desert was an exterior setting for Marlow but had deep inner significance for her as well.

In a city with a very small Jewish population, moreover, Marlow says that she "truly felt [herself] as a minority in Christian America," an experience that also "shaped my existence as a Jew." Jewish identity for Marlow came, in part, from contrasting herself with the Christian majority, but it also arose from the differences between Marlow, an Orthodox Jew, and other Jewish El Pasoans. Like Jews throughout the nation who had sought to Americanize, Marlow says, El Paso Jews "kept, at most, the outer structure of Jewish life" but were missing "the richness and quality of the essence of being Jewish." The "daily rituals are performed in the shul," she writes, "the form and structure are all there—but, for me, the soul was missing."[29] Marlow fixes her own Jewish identity by triangulating herself against ancient Jews, contemporary El Paso Jews, Christians, and a forbidding natural environment.

That sense of something missing drives Marlow deeper into herself and toward her own vision of Jewish meaning. "What growing up there did for me," she writes, "was make me want something *more* authentic. My experience gave me an appreciation of having a real Jewish experience and perhaps made it a need more acute than for those for whom it has always been available at their fingertips." In the language of centers and peripheries, Marlow describes El Paso as a peripheral and therefore less genuine Jewish experience than those available elsewhere. But she turns a "wasteland of a desert without water" into the wellspring of her Jewish identity, the "foundation for me . . . for desiring more." She later found, in New York, the kind of Jewish community she had sought. Marlow's narrative demonstrates both the opportunity and the risk that frontiers provide. As a Jew in an isolated place, she was unable to find the kind of rich communal experience she wanted, but the very conditions that caused her distress allowed her to transform her experience not only into a positive one but also a revelatory one. "I had to wander from the desert to New York to find that quality and essence," she says, "but I don't think I would have wanted it so much if I hadn't begun in the desert."[30]

In a brasher way, Kinky Friedman has built a career out of merging Texas and Jewish qualities into a unique and provocative persona.[31] With his band, the Texas Jewboys, Friedman released three albums between 1973 and 1976; broke a song, "Sold American," into the Country Top Ten; and appeared on the Grand Ole Opry. The Jewboys, though, were hardly a typical country-western band. Friedman described them as "avant-garde" and "a cult band," and one early reviewer proclaimed them "the world's first Jewish-longhaired country band."[32] Lester Bangs, a *Rolling Stone* music critic, praised the group's first record and hailed Kinky as "a stocky cigar-chomping Jew from Texas," who was "a true original, blessed with a distinctive wit and a manner of carrying himself both musically and personally that begins to resemble the mantle of a star."[33] Friedman's "macho, cigar-chewing posturing is classic," according to London's *Melody Maker* magazine in 1973. "Wearing . . . a 10-gallon hat, a pearl-buttoned velvet shirt with tinted glasses, and cowboy boots with . . . gold Stars of David embroidered; there's no sight quite like it."[34] Friedman's style, which he called "Texas-Jewish flamboyance," accented Texan fashion accessories like hats, boots, and belt buckles with recognizably Jewish symbols, displaying his wish to be conspicuously Texan and Jewish at the same time.[35]

Not everyone was as impressed as Bangs and other music critics with Friedman's persona. When the Texas Jewboys first came to national attention, Friedman received complaints about his unabashed use of the word "Jewboy," a term that in almost any context is disparaging. A term of belittlement that charges Jewish men with childishness, dependency, and weakness, it evokes Jews' long history of persecution and, in some measure, blames them for their own victimization: had they been more mature, more manly, perhaps they could have defended themselves more successfully. In the contexts in which Friedman used the term, however, particularly when he so frequently turned it on himself, it became less an insult than a deeply evocative and even empowering expression. In calling his band "Kinky Friedman and the Texas Jewboys," Friedman punned closely on the name of the western swing band "Bob Wills and the Texas Playboys," a group that revolutionized Texas popular music in the late 1930s and early 1940s. Friedman's usage of the anti-Semitic slur "Jewboy" recalled the word "playboy" and borrowed some of its meaning, suggesting something more masculine, adult, and aggressive than the term standing alone could do. These were not, after all, simply "Jewboys," whose whole sad history was too familiar, but they were *Texas* Jewboys, a new breed, rougher and tougher than before. The term of belittlement was still there, of course, and it still shocked, but through a deft pun, Friedman turned it into its opposite: an expression, at least in a 1970s context, of masculine strength and sexual prowess. The pun suggested that acculturation into Texas culture had made the Jew manlier than ever before.

Friedman put the same pun to a more profound use in one of his most popular songs, "Ride 'em, Jewboy," a piece that served as the band's theme song and that Lester Bangs praised as "both an anthem of ethnic pride and a hauntingly evocative slice of classic American folksong."[36] Released on Friedman's first album in 1973, it is a somber ballad to the victims of the Holocaust. The slow song's simple rhythm is carried on an acoustic guitar, in the style of cowboy campfire songs. Its mood and sound resemble "Home on the Range" as much as anything more recent. The lyric draws a comparison between the persecuted Jew and the mythic cowboy of the prairie as Friedman fuses the cowboy's unrooted, solitary life into the Jews' history of oppression and forced migration:

> Ride, ride 'em Jewboy,
> Ride 'em all around the old corral.
> I'm, I'm with you boy
> If I've got to ride six million miles.[37]

On the surface, this could be any one of a hundred western folk ballads in the "git along little dogie" tradition, songs sung by cowboys on the cattle drive or, more likely, by Gene Autry in the movies. But Friedman again adapts the word "Jewboy" to his own purposes, this time playing with the cliché "ride 'em, cowboy." The pun tells the listener that this is a song with two contexts, Texan and Jewish, and allows double meanings to emerge from the lyric's imagery. Later in the song, a description of candles glowing in a window evokes both the prairie tradition of lighting a candle to help the wanderer find his way home and the lights of Sabbath or Chanukah; the "Jewboy" is reminded of a time "[w]hen on your sleeve you wore the yeller star," recalling both the badge of a western lawman and the identification tag of Jews in Nazi Europe; the singer's willingness to "ride six million miles" recalls the six million Jewish Holocaust victims; and, most ominously, "the smoke from camps a'risin'" is both the comforting image of a campfire in the wilderness and the horrific one of Nazi smokestacks. The pun in the title permits us to see these double images and defines the piece as a Holocaust memorial set in the tradition of American western music.

The juxtaposition of these two traditions, western campfire song and Holocaust commemoration, is a peculiar one, but it works. Borrowing the traditional scene of the cattle drive, Friedman casts Jews as the cattle, "helpless creatures on their way," who are "driven relentless 'round the world" and ultimately to the slaughter. Later they are "wild ponies" whose "dreams were broken, / Rounded up and made to move along." Friedman's allusion to the Jewish history of abandonment and persecution, culminating in the Holocaust, and his use of the word "Jewboy," a familiar expression of weakness, underscore the theme of Jewish victimization.

However, as the word "Jewboy" reminds the listener of Jewish helplessness in the face of the Nazi threat, it also puns on "cowboy," a word with very different meanings. When we see the figure the narrator addresses not as the cattle but as a fellow rider, the phrase "ride 'em, Jewboy" suggests a position of strength and power atop a horse in charge of the drive. The word is recast, giving the impression not of a Jewish victim but of a Jewish cowboy, a product of the Jewish past but with a cowboy's toughness and control. Drawing on the mythic history of the American West as a place of boundless opportunity and limitless futures, the narrator tells the Jewish cowboy that he will always remember his tragic past ("old memories still live behind ya"), but that he should not "let the morning [with a pun on 'mourning'] blind ya." With stereotypically Texan optimism, the singer insists that "the road ahead [is] forever rolling" and that "anything worth cryin' can be smiled."

Friedman's creative use of the familiar icons of both traditions and his clever manipulation of their imagery draw the two together in an unexpected and meaningful way. Both the Jewish and the cowboy traditions, as presented here, involve wandering, restlessness, loneliness, regret, and loss. The cowboy and the Jewboy are both melancholy figures, haunted by the past, isolated from society, and cut adrift from community. In the Jewish tradition this is, of course, a tragic experience, a reminder of ancient persecution. But by blending that interpretation with Texas frontier imagery, Friedman presents a distinctively Texan Jew with a distinctively Texan Jewish memory. The tragic past is part of who he is, but as a Jewish cowboy rather than simply a "Jewboy," he need not be diminished by it.

Not many Texas Jews are as explicit as Kinky Friedman and Judith Geller Marlow in describing themselves as distinctively Texan or in seeking the common ground between Texas and Jewish history. The symbolic boundaries by which Marlow and Friedman define their Jewish identities, however, have subtler correlates in virtually everything that Jewish Texans have done throughout their history. Establishing and maintaining imaginary frontiers that define them in contrast to other Jews and to other Texans is characteristic of the Texas-Jewish experience. Like the residents of Gloria Anzaldúa's borderland, the ethnic, religious, and linguistic identities of Texas Jews shade off at the edges into qualities acquired from other groups. In turn, Jewish Texans have contributed their particular historical perspective to the development of Texas society.

The following narrative traces not only the historical experience of Jewish Texans but also the evolution of their sense of themselves as particular kinds of Jews and particular kinds of Texans. The nuanced and malleable concept of the frontier is the shaping force behind that evolution. The first two chapters examine the frontier experience when it was still a material reality, though one abounding in symbolic meanings. The first Jews to enter Texas ventured into a place with little organized social life, let alone of a specifically Jewish sort, and their efforts to preserve a sense of Jewish identity, outlined in Chapter 1, were minimal. As Chapter 2 explains, Jewish institutions in Texas began to take shape in the mid-nineteenth century, and Texas Jews became part of national and regional social and commercial networks that loosely connected them to more populated Jewish communities. Despite these connections, Jewish Texans continued to emphasize their isolation and solitude, defining their Texas home as a wilderness.

The third chapter moves into the early twentieth century, when Texas could not accurately be described as a wilderness, nor its Jewish population as isolated, but the frontier myth remained critical. Indeed, it was evolving into an idea that could be marketed to potential Texans, and Jews inside and outside Texas emphasized the state's underdeveloped aspect as an inducement to immigrants. Similarly, Chapter 4 examines another way in which lines of group difference could be manipulated—in this case, by the editor of the state's first Jewish newspaper, who deliberately described his readership as proud, even unreconstructed, Southerners. His bold regionalist appeal was at odds with the emerging reality, but it was effective in selling papers and establishing an enduring Texas-Jewish institution. The fifth chapter, treating the rise of the Ku Klux Klan in the 1920s, shows that Jews alone did not hold the power to shape their own group identity. The Klan, which achieved astonishing credibility following the First World War, was built on a self-conscious appeal to white supremacy and nativism, and Texas Jews were surprised to find themselves placed outside those categories. The resurgence of the Klan forced Jewish Texans to redraw social and ethnic lines in new and complicated ways and to choose among competing aspects of their own identities.

The sixth and seventh chapters deal with the effects of watershed events of World War II on Jewish Texans. While the war raged in Europe, Houston Jews divided over Zionism, a conflict that tore apart the state's largest and oldest Jewish congregation. More was at stake than the establishment of a Jewish state, at that time still an idea rather than a reality. Houston's Jews fought about the meaning of American citizenship and whether American Jews were Jews first or Americans. The frontier had become fully internalized, now taking the shape of an inward conflict between the most profound elements of personal identity. By the 1940s, as the dividing lines between and among Jews became more complex, the frontier emerged as a threat to the internal cohesion of the Jewish community. At the same time, though, the epochal events of the decade, as Chapter 7 explains, gave Jews much to hold them together. The demands of the war itself, the discovery of Hitler's gruesome intentions for the Jews of Europe, and the establishment of the nation of Israel made ideological distinctions among Texas Jews, as elsewhere, less important. These were binding forces that established a foundation on which to build all subsequent Jewish history.

The final two chapters examine ways that the frontiers of Jewish identity in Texas were reformulated and reimagined in the latter half of the twentieth century. During the civil rights movement of the 1950s and 1960s, Jews played a pivotal if often overlooked role throughout the South, and Jewish participation in civil rights in Texas has been almost entirely ignored. Chapter 8 deals with it in detail, considering especially how Jews consciously used their unique situation—inside the social mainstream yet apart from it—to push civil rights programs forward. This chapter follows the evolution of the frontier into an idea with new power: by negotiating lines of ethnic and social difference, and by looking at Texas society from a uniquely Jewish perspective, Jews were able to help motivate meaningful and lasting change. Finally, Chapter 9 considers the current situation of Jewish Texans as their community grows larger, more diverse, and more integrated with national and international Jewish institutions. In this setting, the frontier remains a useful metaphor for determining what is still distinctive about Texas Jewry. Jewish writers (including, it must be said, me) continually invoke it to explain their lives in Texas.

ONE

Los Judíos en la Frontera

By some accounts, the history of Judaism in the United States began in Texas.
In 1579, nearly seventy-five years before the first Jews arrived in New York,
the Spanish crown granted an enormous land charter in New Spain, including much of what is now northern Mexico and South Texas, to a Christian
descendant of Portuguese Jews. Luis de Carvajal y de la Cueva was born in
Portugal to New Christian parents, Jews who had converted to Catholicism
under threat of punishment by the Spanish Inquisition. In his youth, Don
Luis traveled and worked throughout Portugal and Spain, but after a series
of business setbacks he decided to sail for Mexico with a cargo of Spanish
wine to sell there. With the proceeds, he purchased a cattle ranch near Panú-
co and soon entered naval service under the viceroy. In this capacity, Carvajal led an expedition against British pirates who had washed ashore after
suffering defeat at sea against Spanish vessels. Outnumbered, he captured
eighty-eight prisoners, whom he turned over to the Mexico City authorities.
Soon after, Carvajal led attacks against the Chichimecan Indians of northern
Mexico and quelled a native insurrection that threatened colonial settlement in the farthest reaches of the Spanish frontier. As a reward for these
exploits, King Philip II made Carvajal governor of forty thousand square
leagues of territory to subjugate and colonize with Spanish and Portuguese
settlers.[1] The New Kingdom of Leon (or *Nuevo Reyno de Leon*), as Carvajal
titled his grant, was the first European polity to include portions of Texas,
and its conqueror and governor came from a formerly Jewish family.

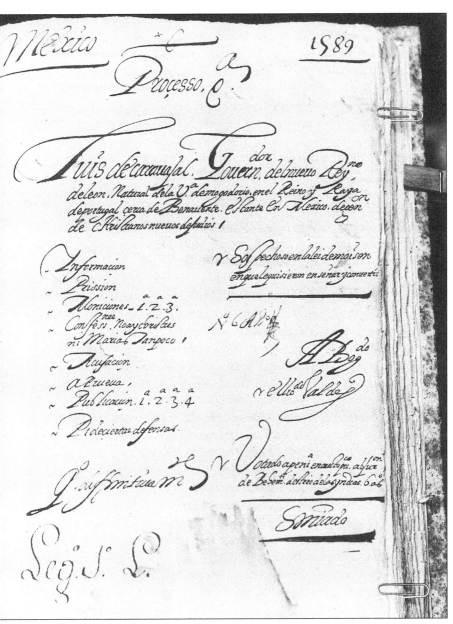

The 1589 document, called a *processo*, with which the Mexican Inquisition brought charges against Luis de Carvajal, identified here as the governor of the New Kingdom of Leon ("*nuevo Reyno de Leon*") in Mexico. He is described as descended from New Christians ("*christianos nuevos de Judíos*") and is suspected of following Mosaic law and of seeking to teach and convert others ("*Sospechoso en la lei de moison en que le quisieron enseñar y convertir*"). The left side of the document lists the legal procedure he was to undergo. American Jewish Historical Society.

Don Luis' rising fortunes would have been impossible had his New Christian status been known, and he was careful throughout his life to keep it secret. For many in his extended family, however, Judaism was more than a secret inheritance. The governor's sister, Francisca; her husband Francisco Rodríguez de Matos; eight of their children, including Luis de Carvajal the Younger, the governor's namesake and heir apparent; and even the governor's wife Guiomar were crypto-Jews, official converts to Catholicism who covertly maintained Jewish ritual practices. Many of these joined the governor in settling his colony, which, far from the center of Inquisitional power in Mexico City and even farther from the Spanish crown in Madrid, briefly provided refuge for as many as several hundred crypto-Jews.

Ordinarily, Spanish land grants in the New World required that potential colonists certify to the government that they were descended from Old Christians rather than from converts to the Holy Faith. For reasons that remain unclear, Carvajal's charter did not contain this provision, requiring only that Carvajal himself certify their Christian ancestry. This, significantly, he neglected to do. It may be that he leveraged his military successes to open a loophole through which his family could pass into the relative safety of the Mexican frontier; it is also possible, as Carvajal attested, that he knew nothing of his relatives' reversion to the Jewish faith. In any case, there were probably crypto-Jews among Carvajal's colonists, some of whom may have been not only the first Jews in Texas, but also the first to enter lands that would become the United States.

Granting Carvajal's colonists this important distinction raises great problems, however. The Mexican Inquisition investigated and punished many of Carvajal's family members and other colonists, burning three of his near relatives at the stake, and Don Luis himself died a prisoner, in part because of his role in harboring them. But because of the secret nature of their religious devotion, and because the only evidence of it that exists today comes from documents prepared by the Inquisition in prosecuting them, it is impossible to verify with certainty that the Carvajals were, in fact, guilty of the crime the Spanish called "Judaizing."

Scholars have drawn a tremendous amount of documentation from Inquisitional records, but irregularities in the legal process make the documents' reliability doubtful. The original charges against the governor, for example, were initiated by the Spanish viceroy in Mexico, a political rival who resented the appropriation of so much land to the Carvajal family— land that would be forfeited if the Carvajals were found guilty of the charges.[2] The Inquisition, in pursuing its investigations, regularly tortured defendants until they confessed, and common knowledge of this procedure led many to confess immediately upon being charged rather than wait to be tortured. The Inquisition provided defense counsel, whose primary role was to encourage clients to confess; counsel who argued for their clients' innocence could themselves be charged with defending a heretic.[3] Finally, on one occasion the governor's nephew was visited in his cell by a "well-coached spy" who emerged the next day prepared to testify in detail about the defendant's heresy, supposedly revealed during the single night he spent with him.[4] With so much of the Inquisition's evidence tainted and even manufactured, it is impossible to reach a fair conclusion on the Carvajals' guilt. The colony may have harbored large numbers of secret Jews, but it is equally possible that the trials were a sham. The best we can say is that if the Carvajals were not actually crypto-Jews, then the sheer number of documents in the Inquisitional records, and their detail, make the magnitude of the Inquisition's fraud hard to fathom.

In addition to the uncertain documentation of their Jewishness, there are further problems in identifying the Carvajals as the precursors of Jewish life in Texas. Even though the Carvajal grant included the area that is now South Texas, Carvajal established no Spanish settlements north of the Río Grande in present-day Texas, nor is there any indication that he or any of his crypto-Jewish colonists ever crossed the river into what is now Texas. After the governor's death in 1590, one of his subordinates, Gaspar Castaño de Sosa, led an expedition across the Río Grande and along the Pecos through modern-day West Texas toward the Spanish colonies in New Mexico. Modern researchers have identified Castaño de Sosa and many of his followers as crypto-Jews. In the wake of the arrests of Carvajal and his kinsmen, as Inquisitional power took hold in Mexico, it is plausible that Castaño de Sosa and his followers may have sought refuge in New Mexico, where modern evidence suggests a stronger and more lasting crypto-Jewish presence. In any case, the refugees were captured and returned to Mexico City.[5] The Castaño de Sosa expedition, which was only in Texas long enough to cross it, left no record of its passage and certainly no settlements or institutions. If these were the first Jews to set foot in Texas, they left a light footprint; if Texas-Jewish history begins here, it is a faint and enigmatic beginning.

No connection exists between Spanish crypto-Jews, who may or may not have entered the state, and the Ashkenazic (non-Spanish) Jewry that predominates in Texas today. The Sephardim, if that is what they were, left no records, no institutions, and no descendants in Texas. Still, they have figured prominently in every recent history of Texas Jewry. Most dramatically, as in New Mexico and throughout the Southwest, Hispanic Texans have come forward with claims of Sephardic ancestry based on family legend or on family customs whose origins are long forgotten but that superficially resemble common Jewish practices.[6] They are, they say, descended from Carvajal colonists, though there is no reason to think that their ancestors were in Texas at the time of the Carvajals.

Despite, or because of, the difficulty of verifying the tantalizing possibility of a Jewish presence in Spanish Texas, the Carvajal colony has become a kind of origin myth for today's Texas-Jewish community. As an origin myth, the story of the crypto-Jews foreshadows and illuminates the directions Jewish life in Texas took as it developed over later centuries. Like these supposed first Texas Jews, Jewish Texans preserved ritual and communal traditions that were out of place, even discouraged, in Texas. They faced not only the threat of overt hostility from non-Jews, but also the more insidious risk of assimilating out of existence, of blending so thoroughly into the Christian mainstream that they would cease to exist as a separate people. The crypto-Jews offer an ancient survivor's tale of maintaining Jewish distinctiveness in the face of enormous pressure to conform. Whether true or not, this myth has resonated deeply with later generations and provides a conceptual link, though not a cultural one, between today's Jewish Texans and their Spanish antecedents.

Settling the Texas Frontier

Texas has been a frontier since first entering European consciousness in the sixteenth century. Originally the distant northern edge of Spanish holdings in the New World, it was sparsely populated by Spanish settlers and was often considered as much a burden to provincial administrators in Mexico City as an asset. The only major Spanish settlement in Texas was the mission outpost of San Antonio de Bexar, established around 1690 in order to Catholicize native peoples in the area and to serve as a de facto capital of the region. As the French population to the east in Louisiana grew, Spain became increasingly concerned about French encroachments into Spanish Texas. To defend against the threat, Spain established military outposts near the Spanish-French border—actually a sizable disputed territory rather than a boundary line—at La Bahía (later Goliad) and Nacogdoches. With the exception of these small and distant outposts, the fringe of its New World empire, Spain had little interest in colonizing the region. It was difficult to find soldiers, let alone colonists, interested in settling in such a forbidding place, far from the communities to the south and threatened on one side by increasingly territorial native tribes and on the other by occasionally violent French colonists. For the time being, the region remained a massive buffer zone, virtually unpopulated by Europeans. When, at the end of the French and Indian War, Spain acquired the Louisiana Territory from France, removing the eastern threat, Spanish interest in Texas languished even further. At the dawn of the nineteenth century, the region was home to fewer than five thousand European inhabitants.

The situation changed, though, when France reclaimed the Louisiana Territory in 1801 and sold it two years later to the United States, which immediately began to explore and settle it. Texas suddenly lay along the international boundary between New Spain and the United States, a young nation that made no secret of its wish to expand westward. The Spanish crown began to fortify Texas against the perceived American threat. Texas was rapidly developing its character as a cultural crossroads, a borderland region in which Spanish, French, native, and U.S. interests collided and interacted.

When Mexico, including its Texas province, declared independence from Spain in 1821, the new government sought ways to subdue and cultivate the wilderness on its northern frontier between San Antonio and Nacogdoches. To accomplish this, Mexican authorities promoted immigration into the region by anyone, including Americans and Europeans, willing to live there, to establish permanent residence, and to become a Mexican citizen and a Roman Catholic. To this end, Mexico granted large tracts of land to *empresarios*, independent agents who in turn were responsible for recruiting potential colonists, moving them to the grant, parceling out individual tracts, providing whatever supplies and building materials were needed, and overseeing the development of the colony. The religious and citizenship requirements were strict on paper but laxly enforced, and many of the colonists involved in these schemes never made the required declarations. This loophole opened the door of Mexican Texas not only to Anglo-American Protestants but also to a handful of Ashkenazic Jews.

The first of the *empresario* grants, made in 1821, established a colony in Southeast Texas chartered to and managed by Stephen F. Austin. The families that Austin recruited to settle there became the quasi-mythic "Old 300" that represents the beginning of official Anglo-American habitation in Texas. Among these original three hundred families was one that historians have identified as Jewish, although it is unlikely that they were Jews or even descended from Jews.[7] The Isaacks, a large family including the father, Elijah, his wife Esther Donaho Isaacks, and at least eight of their ten children, ventured to Texas in 1822 from Pike County, Mississippi. Elijah settled on Walnut Creek near the present-day site of Jasper. One of his sons, Samuel, arrived slightly ahead of the family, leading later researchers to identify him as Texas' first Jewish resident. Samuel Isaacks later joined the Austin Colony (perhaps as a squatter, according to family legend, before Stephen Austin himself came to stake out the colony) and received a grant from Austin in what is today Fort Bend County. He served in the war for Texas independence, received some land in Polk or Angelina County, and eventually lived and worked in the tiny village of Houston.[8]

An Isaacks descendant and family genealogist took up the question of the Isaacks' Jewishness in 1935 after conducting extensive archival and oral history research. "There is . . . a tradition in my immediate family, but with no other so far as known, that some three centuries ago a family of Jews, one of whom was our ancestor, lived in Wales and [he] married a Christian woman, on account of which his family disowned him." In retaliation, this ancestor "renounced Judaism and added the 'k' to his name to distinguish him from the Jews." The writer claimed to have believed this story "until . . . I began delving into the history of the family" and concluded that the family's original immigrant to the United States in 1725 "was either Scotch or Welsh" but not Jewish. He states that the spelling of the family name, with its distinctive "k," is uncommon but recognizable as Scottish.[9] Whether the tradition of Jewish origin is true or not, it is evident that by the time Samuel Isaacks arrived in Texas his family was no longer Jewish, if it had ever been.

Although *empresario* arrangements were responsible for most Anglo immigration to Mexican Texas, Jews were not involved in them. Those Jews who had settled in other parts of the United States, especially in the South, were urban merchants and businesspeople, rarely skilled or experienced as farmers or builders, the occupations the *empresarios* considered most valuable. In addition, the Mexican requirement that colonists convert to the Roman Catholic faith likely deterred many potential Jewish immigrants. Although Mexican authorities generally neglected to enforce this requirement—most settlers in the Austin Colony either never converted or did so in name only—it is hard to imagine that practicing Jews would be eager to enter a nation whose 1824 constitution declared emphatically that "[t]he religion of the Mexican nation is, and will be perpetually, the Roman Catholic Apostolic" and that "[t]he Nation will protect [that religion] by wise and just laws, and prohibit the exercise of any other whatever."[10] These requirements probably explain the absence of Jews from *empresario* colonies.

Jews were, however, among the individual settlers who arrived in Mexican Texas outside the official colonization schemes. Thousands of Americans and Europeans were lured into Texas by rumors and letters generated by earlier colonists and by a steadily developing folklore describing Texas as a near-paradise. Many were fugitives from American justice seeking refuge and a new start in the relatively unpatrolled frontier. Of the newcomers, legal and illegal, most were Americans, and of these most came from the southern United States, particularly from the neighboring states of Arkansas and Louisiana, as well as from Tennessee. New Orleans, the cultural capital of the South, was an important way station, attracting migrants from all parts of the United States, holding them sometimes for months or years, then sending them on their way to the Texas ports of Galveston and Indianola. With a population either native to or arriving from the southern states, Texas took on the unmistakable imprint of the American South, including cotton agriculture and slavery. By 1830, there were about ten thousand Anglo Americans in the province, who brought with them more than one thousand African-American slaves. Together, these composed a non-Mexican population nearly three times the size of the province's Spanish-speaking population.[11]

Among this growing number of independent settlers were Jews in the merchant trades who appear to have blended into the mainstream of American and European immigration to Mexico. The first clear report of open and self-conscious Jewish life in Texas comes from Abraham C. Labatt, a Jewish activist who helped establish synagogues in South Carolina, New Orleans, and San Francisco and was a leading member of those Jewish communities. Labatt's work in a New Orleans trading business in the early 1830s took him briefly to the Texas Gulf Coast town of Velasco, at the mouth of the Brazos River near modern Freeport. In Velasco, Labatt met two merchants whom he knew as Jews: Jacob Henry, an English immigrant, and South Carolinian Jacob Lyons, whom Labatt had probably known in Charleston. Evidence that Labatt may have returned later to Velasco to live indicates that there was enough Jewish activity in the town to satisfy a man who had participated in some of the most prominent Jewish communities in the South and West.[12] This tiny Mexican coastal settlement, then, was the site of the first true Jewish community in Texas. The Jews there were soon joined by a handful of Jewish merchants scattered throughout the small settlements of East Texas.

Texas Jews under Mexican rule lived not only along a national boundary and in the permeable geographic zone between Anglo and Mexican control, but also in an internalized borderland between ways of life and between personal identifications. They were members of a white minority among Mexicans but also members of a Jewish minority among whites. They were Catholics who had once been Jews—or perhaps remained Jews but called themselves Catholics—and if they remained Jews, they lived in violation of the laws of the nation that had welcomed them. As they negotiated these interactions, few if any Texas Jews managed to live a traditional or even recognizably Jewish life, and no documentation exists of anyone openly practicing Judaism in Texas in the periods of Spanish or Mexican rule. This is undoubtedly one of the reasons that so few Jews joined the thousands of Anglo Americans venturing to Texas.

When the Republic of Texas won its independence in 1836, however, a more familiar, American-style democratic government came to oversee the process of colonization. The Texas Declaration of Independence explicitly condemned Mexico's official protection of a single faith, complaining that Santa Ana's tyrannical government had prohibited "the right of worshipping the Almighty according to the dictates of our own consciences."[13] The Texas Constitution subsequently established religious freedom, requiring that "[n]o preference shall be given by law to any religious denomination or mode of worship over another."[14] To be sure, the framers of the Texas Constitution intended to preserve a Protestant right of worship among the Republic's largely Catholic population, but the new nation's promise of religious freedom would extend to Jews as well. News of the Republic's religious tolerance was reported in the European Jewish press, and American promoters of Jewish immigration recognized Texas as a suitable destination for Jewish migrants.[15]

Still, the number of Jewish immigrants to Texas in the years of the Republic remained low, and Jews continued to avoid the organized colonization schemes proliferating under the new government. Following Mexican officials' example, Texas leaders seeking to increase the population of their vast territory granted charters to organizations of all kinds, providing land for settlement at very low cost. In addition to promoting immigration among Americans, the Texas Republic opened its doors to Europeans as well. In particular, large numbers of Germans arrived, usually as part of schemes arranged in Germany to promote migration and agricultural settlement in America. Agencies like the Society for the Protection of German Immigrants in Texas (*Adelsverein*) established many German towns on the Texas frontier in the 1830s and 1840s, most notably Fredericksburg and New Braunfels. These settlements tended to be exclusive and homogeneous, often including entire families or consisting of settlers from the same European towns, and they were overwhelmingly Protestant. It is a curiosity of the land grant system that Germans were so plentiful among new Texans but that German Jews were not among them.

The handful of Jews who made their way to Texas before and during the years of the Republic went as independent adventurers seeking whatever opportunities were available to them. Most were originally from central Europe but had spent at least some time in American cities, often Baltimore, Charleston, or New Orleans, before traveling on to Texas. These cities served as commercial and social "hubs" sustaining a network of Jewish settlement throughout the South, just as San Francisco would later do for the West. Thus, Texas was part of a larger regional and national structure that directed immigrants seeking commercial opportunities into the emerging frontier.[16] This pattern remained in effect long after independence and statehood, and Texas cities in turn became centers of local networks connecting rural towns throughout Texas and neighboring states. Galveston and Houston grew together by linking smaller hinterland communities to New Orleans and the rest of the cotton South, while Jews throughout South and West Texas and along the Mexican border joined congregations in San Antonio. Well into the twentieth century, El Paso rabbis were providing support to communities not only in West Texas but also in New Mexico and Arizona.

Despite these networks, the Republic of Texas saw little active Jewish life. Indeed, early Texas Jews' willingness to seek commercial opportunities in a place without active Jewish communities, even to abandon cities in which Jewish life was more abundant, indicates that religious devotion and strong Jewish identification were relatively unimportant to them. This fact is not surprising, considering the central European Jewish world from which most of them came. Western and central European Jewry in the nineteenth century, the period of political emancipation and of the development of Reform Judaism, was undergoing a decisive change. Increasingly liberal legal conditions emboldened European Jews, opening to them a greater participation in public affairs, education, and economic activities, and they sought to enjoy more fully the benefits of European citizenship. To do so, many of them willingly disregarded or concealed their Jewish origins. At issue was nothing less than the question of whether Jews would continue to exist as a distinct people, would integrate entirely into European culture, or would find some negotiated middle ground between these extremes. Most sought the middle, and thus Judaism became not so much an immutable quality of personal history and identity as a character trait, a quirk of family descent that one could emphasize or deny in making a place in a pluralistic gentile society. In the name of social integration and economic opportunity, many were prepared to barter it away entirely.

Fluid Identity: The Case of Adolphus Sterne

Most central European Jews who migrated to the United States in the early nineteenth century had accepted this bargain, venturing far from European centers of Jewish religion and intellectual activity to seek their fortunes in a frontier nation. Those who passed through American cities into the West entered a true frontier, a dynamic and heterogeneous society in which a person's origins were only what he or she claimed. The first European Jews to arrive in the Republic of Texas shared with their emancipated European families an ambivalence toward Jewish identification and religious practice that made them difficult to identify later as Jews but which suited the frontier environment they found.

Galveston rabbi Henry Cohen, the first researcher to write about Jewry in Texas and still the one who gave the most attention to this early period, found only a few Jews in the Texas Republic. Simon M. Schloss, for example, was born in Frankfurt-am-Main, moved to Texas in 1836, and pursued "the real estate business." Albert Emanuel, born in Germany, traveled to New Orleans and then in 1834 to Texas, where he supported himself through "mercantile pursuits." Samuel Maas, also originally of Germany, passed through New Orleans in January 1836 on his way to Nacogdoches, where he was a "merchant" and later "entered the real estate business." Jacob Mussina "engaged in mercantile pursuits" in Galveston and later in Austin. His brother Simon "engaged in various callings," including law and "a real estate business" in Galveston. Isadore Dyer, born in Dessau, Germany, moved to Galveston in 1840 and "engaged in mercantile pursuits."[17]

From the few individuals Cohen identified, a number of commonalities present themselves about the Jews of the Republic of Texas. First, most were central European by birth, arriving in Texas only after settling first in other American communities. Secondly, they were clearly drawn to what Cohen repeatedly described as "mercantile pursuits." Unlike most immigrants to Texas at the time, none were farmers or laborers. Finally, and most importantly, these Jews appear to have had a very loose attachment to the practices and traditions of Judaism or to have ignored them altogether. Cohen noted without comment, for example, that the sister of Jacob and Simon Mussina "married the Rev. Mr. Henderson, the first Presbyterian minister at Galveston."[18] He said that Isadore Dyer hosted the first Jewish religious services in Galveston at his home, but not until 1856, years after arriving in Texas. Cohen had nothing to say about the religious activities of Schloss, Emanuel, Maas, or the Mussina brothers. Modernity had worked its magic on these European Jews, who had sought out the American frontier for the economic advantages it offered, even if it made the meaningful practice of Judaism impossible.

Building on Cohen's identifications, later historians have elaborated on the biographies of a few Jews in Mexican and Republican Texas, though they, too, exhibited few clear outward signs of their Jewishness. Albert Moses Levy was one of the most conspicuous of these Jewish pioneers, arriving during the war for Texas independence and serving as a surgeon in General Sam Houston's army. Levy's parents and siblings were active in the Sephardic synagogue in Richmond, Virginia, but Albert revealed no signs of Jewish faith or practice during his years in Texas. His marriage to an Episcopalian woman in Matagorda and the baptisms of his children suggest that he made little or no effort to sustain a Jewish life.[19] Other early Texans whom historians have identified as Jews include the *empresario* Henri Castro, an Alsatian descendant of Jewish converts to Catholicism who established a settler colony and the town of Castroville near San Antonio; Herman Ehrenberg and Avram Wolf, who were enlisted in the Texas army and were involved in engagements before and during the Mexican siege of the Alamo; Eugene Chimene, who fought in the Battle of San Jacinto; and Dutch immigrant David Kokernot, trained as a riverboat pilot on the Mississippi, who briefly commanded a schooner in the Texas navy and participated in several land battles, including the Grass Fight in 1835. These men's participation in signal events in Texas history is recorded clearly, but their identification with Judaism is much less certain. In several cases, Cohen's inclusion of them in his early historical essays stands as the only extant evidence of their Jewishness.

Ambiguities plague any effort to verify the Jewish background of early Texans because their lives were so disconnected from the communal institutions that kept records. Although there were men (and a few women) of refinement and gentility among them, and many preserved commercial and social ties to larger cities, they were nevertheless people who chose a life of relative remoteness, discomfort, and potential danger. They may have been the first de facto Texas Jews, but until there were enough Jewish settlers to establish permanent and active religious communities in Texas cities, Jewish religious identity had little real meaning. In the meantime,

Jews in Texas lived on an internalized frontier—an interior version of the borderland between wilderness and civilization, between Texas and the United States, between Anglo and Mexican. In this borderland of identity, they could choose to acknowledge their Jewishness in public or in private or not at all. They could be both Jew and non-Jew simultaneously or alternately as circumstances required.

The best example of the fluidity of Jewish identity on the Texas frontier is Nicholas Adolphus Sterne, a German immigrant who arrived in Texas in the early 1820s and spent most of his adult life in Nacogdoches, then the dominant city of eastern Texas. A participant in the Texas Revolution, Sterne was one of the heroes of Cohen's early histories of Jewish Texans, and Cohen rapturously quoted long passages detailing Sterne's activities on behalf of Texas independence. Cohen never, however, made Sterne's Jewishness explicit. Sterne was in fact a man of true religious conviction, though of no particular denomination. His exact religious affiliation has eluded historians of early Texas who have relied precariously upon each other's assumptions and misattributions.

A single example exemplifies not only the difficulties in pinning down Sterne's religious identification but also, and more importantly, historians' tendency to disregard facts in order to claim prominent early Texans as Jews. Possibly on Cohen's authority, Marquis James, a biographer of Sterne's friend and compatriot Sam Houston, identified Sterne as "a rosy little Rhineland Jew."[20] This was apparently a description of James' own creation, as he neither placed it in quotes nor provided a citation. Years later, M. K. Wisehart, another Houston biographer, called Sterne "a little rosy-cheeked Jew," clearly paraphrasing James.[21] Archie McDonald, in his introduction to Sterne's diary, remarks that Sterne was "much more than the 'rosy little Jew' that he is so often called by Houston biographers," probably meaning James and Wisehart.[22] Finally, in an error of astonishing significance, Ruthe Winegarten and Cathy Schechter claim that *Sam Houston himself* had referred to Sterne as "the rosy little Jew."[23] If Houston, who knew Sterne intimately, had made such a statement, it would have put to rest any question of Sterne's religious affiliation, but he did not. In spite of an apparent wish among historians to claim Sterne unequivocally as a Jew, the facts and his descriptions of himself reveal a far more complex and amorphous identity. As a man of the frontier, Sterne drew on many religious traditions to find his place, crossing easily over the boundaries that separated one religious group from another.

Harriet Smither, the first editor of Sterne's diary, claimed that Sterne was born in Cologne in 1801 to a Lutheran mother and an Orthodox Jewish father, Emmanuel Sterne (or Stern), though such a union suggests that his father was probably not truly Orthodox. It is evident from the diary that Adolphus received a Jewish upbringing.[24] His mother soon died, and his father remarried. Sometime before 1824, the Sternes immigrated to New Orleans, where Emmanuel was unsuccessful in business and a founding member of the Israelite Congregation of Shanarai-Chasset. Adolphus may have preceded his parents to New Orleans, as records indicate that he was in the city from 1817 through 1826, when he was active in the Masonic Order. He left no record of himself as a participant in the city's growing Jewish community.[25] Sterne ventured briefly to Tennessee, where he be-friended Sam Houston, and then in the late 1820s moved to Nacogdoches, Texas, to open a trading business. Nacogdoches was still an outpost on the Mexican frontier and a popular stopping point on the overland route be-tween Mexican Texas and the United States.

There was virtually no Jewish population in Texas at the time, so in moving there from New Orleans Sterne left a place with an increasingly active community for one with almost none, clearly not the action of some-one committed to Judaism in any traditional way. In 1828, Sterne married Eva Catherine Rosine Ruff, a devout German-born Catholic who had come to America as a child and had grown up among Louisiana's planter class. The couple were among the leading citizens of Nacogdoches, and Eva was a famously gracious hostess. They maintained friendships with many of the most prominent figures in early Texas, including David S. Kaufman, Thom-as Rusk, and Davy Crockett. Adolphus rekindled his friendship with Sam Houston, who became a frequent overnight guest at the Sternes' home.[26] Between 1833 and 1835, for personal or political reasons, Sam Houston chose to join the Catholic Church. Eva Sterne stood next to Houston as his sponsor and godmother throughout the baptism ceremony, which occurred either at the mission in Nacogdoches or, according to some ac-counts, in the Sternes' own parlor. Eva also engaged her own confessor, Père Chambondeau of Louisiana, to perform the rite.[27] Adolphus Sterne, plainly, had not only married a Catholic woman, but an especially sincere and active one.

Sterne himself officially converted to Roman Catholicism around the time he and Eva married. Archie McDonald explains how Mexican Texas' legal requirements forced Sterne to consider Catholicism, while Eva "suc-

Eva Catherine Rosine Ruff Sterne. East Texas Research Center, R. W. Steen Library, Stephen F. Austin State University, Nacogodoches, Texas.

Nicholas Adolphus Sterne. Center for American History, University of Texas at Austin, CN 04606.

ceeded in assisting Mexican law in converting him to that faith."[28] McDonald also claims, however, that Sterne remained conscious of Jewish religious obligations. On the unnamed authority of "one Jewish historian," McDonald states that Sterne opted out of Houston's baptism ceremony "because the baptism occurred on *Erev Yom Kippur*" (the evening preceding the Jewish Day of Atonement).[29] This explanation conflicts with Houston biographer Marquis James' report that afterward Sterne "gave a party on the porch of his home and opened considerable wine." If Sterne was observing the Jewish holiday, he seems not to have been fasting.[30] More importantly, McDonald's statement is undermined by the fact that no official records of the baptism exist, and historians do not agree on the *year* in which Sam Houston converted, let alone the season or exact date. The assertion that it occurred on Yom Kippur is an attempt to strengthen Sterne's Jewish credentials, as is McDonald's equally unsubstantiated claim that Sterne spoke Yiddish.[31] In their zeal to assign a Jewish identity to Sterne, a prominent figure in early Texas history, modern researchers have reached far beyond what the evidence actually supports.

Yet Sterne's Jewishness is much more than historians' fantasies. Sterne's own diary, in which he kept a meticulous accounting of his daily business activities, community contacts, and personal observations from 1840 to 1844 and again briefly in 1851, is a singular resource. It provides ample evidence that Sterne was aware of Jewish holidays, had an interest in Jewish religious practice, and maintained close friendships with clearly Jewish fellow-citizens. He noted the occurrence of Yom Kippur, for example, in 1840 and 1843 (writing the holiday's name in Hebrew script), though he made no mention of any further observance.[32] The diary reveals a deeper interest in Jewish ritual when, on July 15, 1841, Sterne reported having read "a Book . . . containing the Service of *Yom Kippur* in the Portuguese ritual" that had been given to him by a Mr. DeYoung of San Augustine, a neighboring town.[33] Elsewhere in the diary, Sterne described DeYoung as "a German Jew of the *old reverend class*," and his wife as a "very much accomplished" woman who "deserves a better looking Husband."[34] In spite of the dig at DeYoung, it was apparently a close friendship. Sterne frequently stayed with the DeYoungs when in San Augustine on business, and he and his wife hosted them in Nacogdoches on many occasions.

These examples suggest that Sterne, though not a practicing Jew, was familiar with Jewish tradition and expressed an abiding interest in it. In 1843, he took the additional step of criticizing DeYoung's Jewish business partner, Mr. Flatau, for inadequate attention to his faith. "[T]o day is Yom Kippur," Sterne noted. "Mr Flatau is doing Penance, nonsense, to keep up a Religion only one day in the year."[35] The comment is deeply informative. The use of the distinctively Catholic term "Penance" suggests that Sterne was a Christian viewing Jewish behavior from the outside, but the remark also reveals that Sterne was conscious of the Jewish holiday and expected those of the Jewish faith to respect it appropriately. While remaining an outsider, Sterne was enough a part of Judaism to take its practice personally and to note, even to condemn, the practices of others. Sterne took a similar jab at Flatau in December 1843, when he learned of plans to publish the San Augustine *Literary Intelligencer*: "Edited or *Fathered* by L.A.L Laird and *T.M. Flatau*, the Paper is to be a *Methodist* Paper—(oh! dear)—& to be under the management of a *Son of Abraham* verily I am tempted to belive in Parson Miller's Doctrine [that the end of the world is imminent]."[36]

Sterne's deep personal interest in Judaism camouflages the fact that he was a practicing Christian, though of no particular denomination, and his diary records his activities with several Christian groups. In February 1841, he described dining with a pair of priests with whom "an arrangement was made to build a Roman Catholic Church" in Nacogdoches, with Sterne and two other residents "appointed the Principal Committee."[37] On one Sunday in 1851, he recorded that he "went to church (catholic)," but that he found "nothing very new Stirring." Several months later, he "went to the Methodist Church where Mr Becton formerly of Nacogdochez County preached."[38] This pattern of events suggests that it was important to Sterne to attend religious worship but that he comfortably rotated among churches.

Sterne also frequently attended camp meetings held in the area, a clear sign that he was part of the frontier religious fluidity that camp meetings embodied. Significantly, Sterne was critical of fellow citizens who treated the meetings as more social than religious events, and he condemned their lack of genuine faith and respect for religious tradition. In July 1842, for example, he reported that "all hands in Town [had] gone out to Preaching" and hoped that "they all got Religion for God Knows they have none." The next year he attended another meeting where "Mr Becton preached, Mr Cawley exhorted, and a great many prayed." Sterne expressed confidence that their prayer would be heard, "provided it is sincere" but, he noted, "there is the rub." An exception to the many believers whom he felt could "be put down upon the *doubtfull* list" was Captain Vail, a participant praised as "not alone a very zealous Christian but a most Complete believer in Miller's Doctrine," a millennialist faith at that time.[39]

It is meaningful that Sterne reserved his praise for someone of clear, if unpopular, religious devotion. Sincerity apparently mattered more to Sterne than the particular tenets of any one group. Thus, he offered judgment in his diary of clergymen who spoke at these events, admiring, for example, "a Mr Porter from Mississippi" who "is realy a Preacher of the Gospel of the very first Class." After Porter's sermon, Sterne noted that a listener "said a few foolish things about the Citizens of Nacogdochez not hearing or going to hear Preachers of the Gospel." Rising to his townspeople's defense, Sterne blamed the clergy's lack of spiritual fervor. "[W]ell he may say Brayers of the Gospel," Sterne wrote. "[L]et the Presbitery send men like Porter, who can *teach* us, and *explain* to us about matters of *Christianity* we do not understand, and all will gladly embrace the opportunity to go and hear, and perhaps to be convinced—but if *ignoramuses* are sent amongst us they will meet with the encouragement they deserve."[40]

In these passages, Adolphus Sterne made it clear that he was not traditionally Jewish, but it is also too easy to regard him simply as a Christian and therefore beyond the pale of Texas Judaism. Judaism was obviously close to his heart and often in his mind—much more so, one must think, than it was for the average Anglo settler in Texas. Sterne was a man living at the confluence of several religious traditions, heir to a dual heritage by birth, living under conflicting political and religious requirements, and greatly inspired by secular rationalist thought. He was representative of the fluidity that personal identity assumes in frontier environments. Mexican and Republican Texas did not offer Sterne, or anyone else, the freedom to be actively Jewish. No Jewish institutions existed, no Jewish clergy visited their communities, and no significant Jewish population was present to support religious activities. Texas was still a frontier, not a place for religious absolutism, and Adolphus Sterne's identity was suitably ambiguous.

In the model of the crypto-Jews, and like other early Texans, the state's first Jewish settlers lived in a region that was not only a frontier in terms of the material conditions of their lives, but also in terms of their ethnic and spiritual identities. Unable and probably unwilling to live traditional Jewish lives, they identified loosely with Jewish tradition while conforming to the outward appearance of other white Texans. They simultaneously were and were not Jews, just as Stephen F. Austin's Old 300 were and were not Catholics, as Anglo Texans were and were not Mexicans. In a province of rapidly changing national control and of criss-crossing personal identifications, Texas Jews embodied the permeable ethnic boundaries that characterized the Texas frontier. In later years, as their numbers increased, as they made homes in the growing urban centers, and especially as the original population of male adventurers was supplemented by the arrival of the women and children necessary to begin forming real community life, Jews would begin to set themselves off as a group by distinguishing themselves from other Texans.

TWO

A "Wild Indian Region"

AT HOME ON THE FRONTIER

Isaac Leeser, the Philadelphia editor and one of the most vocal and influential rabbis of the antebellum era, saw world Jewry's future on the expanding American frontier, "where the climate is mild, and the soil new and fruitful, capable of making ample returns for the labours of the husbandman."[1] He was pleased that his monthly newspaper, the *Occident*, reached subscribers throughout the nation's hinterland who found in the paper a connection to a vast national network of Jewish communities. "Our work goes to fully an hundred small places, where we have a single subscriber in each," he marveled. "It may be that each of these readers is the only Israelite in the place, or that there are one or two others near him." Leeser worried that the isolation of these "solitary sojourners" and the lack of Jewish religious institutions would drive them toward other faiths. As an example of a state with a low Jewish population, he offered "the immense State of Texas," where "although many Jews live scattered here and there, there is but one incipient congregation." As in other such states, Texas Jews "are often lost among the masses, because they are without religious instruction."[2] Leeser shared an ambivalence common to many American Jews: frontier regions like Texas offered both opportunity and risk, both the chance to advance economically and the potential to be lost to Judaism forever.

Leeser had previously printed letters from Texas subscribers that may have put him in mind of the situation there. In 1850, E. Wolff of Eagle Pass on the Mexican border had written to Leeser. Wolff described himself as "a constant reader" of the *Occident* who would be at a loss without it "in this Wild Indian region." Wolff arranged through a complicated chain of agents to have ten dollars sent to Leeser, in exchange for which he wanted a subscription along with back issues and "any Jewish tracts that may have appeared."[3] Leeser had received a similar letter from Isaac Jalonick of Belton, in Central Texas. "It will surprise you Sir to hear from such remoot part on the frontier of Texas," Jalonick wrote. Jalonick asked for a subscription and some bibles and prayer books, promising to remit payment as soon as practicable, but "hear we cane not obtain payper muny when we Please, & I Live a long wais from the [coast]." Signing himself "a True Jew & a frend to our [cause]," Jalonick presented himself as a man dedicated to his faith, whose wanderings had taken him to a place where its practice was exceedingly complicated.[4]

Neither Wolff nor Jalonick expressed regret at their isolation. On the contrary, by reaching out to Leeser for Jewish newspapers, bibles, and other publications, they were attempting to reconcile their faith with the realities of the "Wild Indian region" they inhabited. Indeed, the fact that they corresponded with Leeser suggests that they were not as isolated as they (or he) claimed but maintained ties in the Jewish world they had left behind. Texas Jews have frequently described themselves as remote and isolated from Jewish life, even as they preserved deep social, religious, economic, and institutional contacts with other communities. By emphasizing their remoteness and the backwardness of their surroundings, in fact, frontier Jews distanced themselves from gentile Texans and identified more strongly with a universal Jewish community: as long as they remained conscious of Texas as a wilderness, they could never fully be absorbed into it, remaining instead part of the more cosmopolitan Jewish world outside it.

Thus, Isaac Jalonick described his sojourn to Texas in prophetic terms, as part of the divinely sanctioned dispersal of the Jewish people around the globe. "[I]t is as it shuld be," he wrote. "[T]he prophicing [must] be full fild."[5] Twenty years later a correspondent in Denison, north of Dallas, wrote to the *American Israelite* to express a similar view. "'A voice crieth in the wilderness, Prepare ye the way,'" the writer quoted. "Yes, indeed, in the wilderness, in the full sense of the word, are we preparing the way of Judaism, and through it, to civilization and universal brotherhood." Aware of their isolation, these writers chose to see themselves as bearers of Jewish civilization into a new world rather than worry about the risk of assimilation. "[A]t the very borders of civilization, on the frontier of Texas," wrote the Denison correspondent, "we celebrated [Yom Kippur], and verily, you with your temples and organs and preacher could not have been more devout and sincere than we were, in our little frame-house, destitute of all furniture and ornaments save a few dozen chairs and a dry-good box improvised as a desk."[6] Their frontier condition did not endanger Judaism, they claimed, but revivified it and enhanced its authenticity.

The geographic frontier, the sheer physical distance between Texas and older American settlements, separated Texas Jews in a very real way from other Jews, fostering a sense of isolation that provided both danger and opportunity. At the same time, an imaginary version of such a divide, an internal frontier, distinguished Texas Jews from the other Texans who shared the state with them. Jews wanted to make a place for themselves in Texas society, but theirs was a distinctive condition. They were part of Texas and yet not part of it, at home there but connected by faith and history to communities elsewhere. Like the geographic frontier, this internal frontier was always moving, as Texas Jews continually defined themselves in contrast to other cultural groups, which were themselves only then taking shape in Texas. On one hand, their European ancestry ensured that Jews would take their place within the state's Anglo majority, and nineteenth-century Jews readily adopted white prejudices toward black, Hispanic, and native minorities. At the same time, as if mindful of Isaac Leeser's warning about utter absorption into the gentile mainstream, they looked for ways to distinguish themselves from other whites by reconnecting themselves with Jewish tradition and establishing separate Jewish religious institutions.

Ashkenazic or Anglo?

Isaac Leeser had anticipated that agriculture would draw Jews into the West, but the region's emerging cities and the promise of commercial success provided a far greater lure. With the annexation of Texas into the United States in 1846, travel there became easier than ever, and the state's rapidly growing population created openings for peddlers and retail merchants that an influx of Jewish entrepreneurs quickly filled. Galveston and Houston, the state's largest cities, became its earliest centers of organized Jewish life. Separated by about fifty miles and a longstanding rivalry, the pair nonetheless formed a commercial unit, a port and a distribution point, linked by rail and by the Gulf of Mexico to state, regional, and global commercial centers. While Galveston developed into a miniature New Orleans, a port city of mingling cultures and international influence, Houston took over the business end of the partnership, providing the trading center and rail junction for goods arriving at its island-bound sister city, which were then distributed throughout the hinterland. While Houston looked toward the Texas interior, to the rural expanses of a growing state, Galveston cultivated a more sophisticated international flavor, by 1848 drawing regular trade and steamer service from London and from Bremen, Germany, as well as from New Orleans and New York. Galveston's Jews, leaders of the city's merchant class, were at the forefront of making and preserving commercial contacts with the outside world. Other Texas towns, especially in the cotton regions of North and East Texas, were also growing into major commercial centers, and Jews both contributed to and benefited from the trading networks they joined.

Although the Jewish population increased, Jews still remained a tiny minority in each Texas city and in the state as a whole. By 1900, when Jews represented more than 1.25 percent of the American population, they numbered only 0.5 percent of the population of Texas. In larger cities like Houston, Galveston, and San Antonio, where Jews were most likely to live, they rarely constituted more than 3 percent of the total.[7] As an extreme minority, Texas Jews, as in most American communities, were obliged to intermingle with gentiles, to share their cultural and social life, and to rely on them as neighbors, customers, and friends. Their close social and business connections with gentiles often overshadowed the more attenuated connections they maintained with Jews in other regions and undoubtedly contributed to their sense of isolation.

Although Protestant Anglo-Saxons were the dominant group in the emerging Texas society in which this tiny Jewish minority found itself, Texas cities and towns, especially after statehood, were mélanges of ethnic, religious, and cultural groups. Cultural geographer D. W. Meinig reports, for example, that in the 1880s the town of Victoria had a population of fewer than four thousand, "composed of Anglos, Germans, Negroes, Poles, French, and Mexicans (ranked by numbers); and in church populations of Roman Catholic, Lutheran, Presbyterian, Episcopalian, Jewish, Baptist, Methodist, and Christian [Disciples of Christ]."[8] Larger cities, particularly the commercial centers, offered still more complex mixtures in which Jews established their religious, communal, and social lives.

It is easy to assume that because of their European background Jews naturally became part of the state's Anglo majority—that convenient, if imprecise, catch-all term that covers everyone who is not black, Hispanic, or American Indian. In fact, the acceptance of Jews into Anglo society in

Texas was neither unconditional nor inevitable. Jewish Texans achieved it only by consciously aligning themselves with white society while just as consciously contrasting themselves to nonwhites. Creating a Jewish place in this emerging society meant determining both what Jews were and what they were not, marking off the internal frontiers that lay between them and everybody else. And because definitions constructed in this way are constantly susceptible to reinterpretation, Jews could never be entirely sure that their privileged status as whites was secure. As Eric L. Goldstein insightfully demonstrates, integration into the white mainstream was never inevitable for American Jews, nor altogether desirable. Jews "presented a mix of qualities that was unusual among American 'racial' groups and proved particularly resistant to categorization within the black-white system." At the same time, Jews understood that conforming to the standards of conventional "whiteness" would deprive them of valuable Jewish qualities, that "whiteness sat uneasily with many central aspects of Jewish identity." For many American Jews, and certainly those in Texas, achieving whiteness presented both opportunities and costs and, as Goldstein writes, was always "slow and freighted with difficulty."[9]

As they did elsewhere in the South and West, Jews in Texas cities earned their way into white society primarily through commercial enterprise. Economic development was prized in urban areas, and Jews could position themselves at the center of what mattered most. Houston, for example, was a new city at the birth of the Texas Republic and a popular destination for immigrants with mercantile hopes. At least one Jewish merchant, Eugene Chimene, who had fought at the Battle of San Jacinto, was in Houston at the city's founding in 1836, and another, Henry Wiener, arrived soon afterward. Michael Seeligson opened a store in about 1839 near the steamboat landing and operated it for about a year before moving to Galveston. Isaac Coleman settled in Houston in the early 1840s after peddling goods around the countryside. Jacob de Cordova, born into a Sephardic family in Jamaica although never an observant Jew, lived in Houston from 1839 to 1842, soon becoming one of the state's most successful real estate promoters. By 1850, a mere seventeen Jewish adults (eleven men and six women) were included in Houston's total white population of 1,863 but were prominent among the city's merchant class.[10] In 1855, when Houston's Jews formed the state's first Hebrew Benevolent Society, the *Houston Telegraph* reported enthusiastically that citizens "professing the faith of Abraham, Isaac, and Jacob" had formed the organization to benefit members of their "church" who were suffering "pecuniary or physical distress." The editor claimed personal acquaintance with several of the organization's officers and knew them to be "among the most kind-hearted, humane, and high-minded business men of our city."[11] The comment suggests the depth of the business and social connections between Jews and non-Jews in Houston, as well as the degree to which white gentiles in the city accepted Jews as fellow citizens.

After statehood, Jews played leading roles in the business communities of other Texas cities. During the years following the Civil War, the Galveston firm of Leon and H. Blum, established in 1858 as the first major wholesale dry goods business in Texas, grew into an operation with offices in New York, Boston, and Paris.[12] Samuel Schutz arrived in El Paso in 1854 when the city was little more than a cluster of adobe buildings, and his store became one of the city's leading businesses. In East Texas, Jews were especially visible in the river trading city of Jefferson, representing as much as 8 percent of the 1850 population. One of them, Israel Leavitt, operated a tavern that appears to have been the first Jewish-owned business in town. For a brief time in 1847, it served the community as a temporary courthouse, a sign that Leavitt enjoyed the trust and respect of the people of Jefferson.[13]

Jewish businessmen, in fact, were early residents of frontier communities across the nation. Jewish peddlers, most prominently Levi Strauss, were among the first to recognize the mercantile potential of the California Gold Rush, and booming San Francisco quickly became the largest Jewish community in the West, far surpassing older settlements in Texas. From there, Jewish peddlers fanned out throughout Northern California and the Pacific West, establishing communities and commercial businesses in Portland and Seattle that retained close ties to San Francisco.[14] Decades later in the Appalachian coal country, sometimes described as "one of America's last frontiers" because it was barely settled until the 1890s, Jews followed opportunities to new hill towns like Keystone, West Virginia, which one resident described as "a frontier town with fourteen saloons and about fifteen Jewish families."[15] In all of these growing areas, as in Texas cities, Jews became part of the white power structure by meeting the need for shops, trading firms, and other businesses.

In 1853, in a telling example of Jewish acceptability to other whites, Galveston citizens elected Michael Seeligson, a merchant who had moved there from Houston in about 1840, as their mayor. The Dutch-born Seeligson frequently corresponded with Isaac Leeser, the Philadelphia editor of the *Occident*, often including bits of Hebrew script in his letters, and there is no doubt that Galvestonians knew him as a Jew. In a published letter to Leeser, in fact, he declared that his primary intention in running for mayor

Michael Seeligson. Rosenberg
Library, Galveston, Texas.

was to show that a Jew could achieve such an office. "This is certainly an
Evidence," he wrote, "[that] if our people would only sustain their rights
and privileges in this republican country, and Demean themselves accordingly, they can be elevated to any office they aspire." However, Seeligson
tempered his optimism with the acknowledgment that a certain amount of
latent anti-Semitism existed in his city. "I accepted the office," he explained,
"to thwart the Designs of a certain Clique who by the by were preaching
publicly the Crusades against our Nation."[16] Acceptance in white society remained conditional upon Jews' own behavior and their ability to contribute
commercially to the general community.

Race, Class, and Slavery

The presence in Texas of African-American slaves tended to make Jews
more acceptable as whites. Anti-Semitism was a less salient reality than that
Jews were not subject to enslavement, and Jews appear to have willingly
and actively joined other whites in exploiting the labor of black Texans.
Although it was rare for Texas Jews to own slaves, their involvement in
the commercial economy of the state and region meant dependence upon
slavery for their livelihoods. Without slave labor, Jewish merchants would
have had fewer goods to trade and fewer customers with the cash to buy

them. Slavery, moreover, made race the only social marker that really mattered and thus sped Jews' integration into the white mainstream, a fact they readily used to their advantage.[17]

Few Texas Jews questioned slavery's efficacy as an institution or the moral ground upon which it rested, and none did so in public. In this they joined the vast majority of southern and American Jews, most of whom benefited directly or indirectly from slavery's existence. Among Texans, Jacob de Cordova, a Sephardic land agent on tour in the Northeast promoting Texas land sales, laid out a position that may have resonated with many Jewish Texans. "By a wise provision of our State Constitution," de Cordova explained, "the institution of slavery has been guaranteed to Texas." Texans were, he said, "jealous of this right and will not allow any intermeddling with the subject." It was fine to hold contrary views, he informed his audience, and any non-slaveholder would be welcome in Texas provided that "he shall pursue the even tenor of his way, mind his own business, and leave his neighbors to attend to theirs." Personally, de Cordova wanted it "distinctly understood that [my] feelings and education have always been pro-slavery."[18] De Cordova, born and raised in Jamaica amid some of the worst conditions for slaves in the Americas, cared most about the commercial development of his state. If slavery provided a means to that end, so be it.

In addition to such rhetorical support for slavery, some Texas Jews participated directly in the system as slave owners. The ownership of slaves was common among Jews throughout the states in which slavery was practiced, a marker of Jewish integration into the white mainstream. One scholar found that nearly 80 percent of southern Jewish households in 1820 included at least one slave.[19] Statistical data on Jewish slave ownership in Texas is hard to come by, but anecdotal evidence suggests that it was much less common than elsewhere in the South and reserved for the wealthiest Jews. Few Jewish Texans were planters, so they did not need field hands or laborers, but as rising members of the state's commercial class, they were drawn to the symbolic power of slave ownership and to its usefulness as a marker of success and status. Thus, Galveston, the state's cosmopolitan commercial center, was also the center of Jewish slave ownership. There is little sign of its existence anywhere else.

Galveston was a major slave-trading center, and it was easy for wealthy residents to acquire slaves to work as household servants or for light work in the city. Joseph Osterman was a typical Texas-Jewish slave owner. The 1860 U.S. Census estimated Osterman's worth at $191,000, making him one of Galveston's wealthiest citizens.[20] His wife Rosanna was responsible for bringing the first piano to Texas, and she built the state's first hothouse, part of a garden "noted for its almond and olive trees, and tea and coffee plants."[21] As part of the genteel, leisured lifestyle they enjoyed, the Ostermans owned eight slaves, including children.[22] Other Jewish slave owners in Galveston included Isadore Dyer, who owned a fifty-year-old couple, and Samuel Maas, who owned an older couple and a teenage girl. Mollie Levy, wife of Galveston's rabbi, Henry Cohen, came from a family that owned at least one slave, and Mollie kept in the home she shared with the rabbi a "low rocker . . . which had been given to Mrs. Cohen by her family's former slave, who used to rock her to sleep in it."[23]

Although slave ownership was only for the privileged, those who held anti-slavery views kept their opinions to themselves until after the Civil War. Julius Henry, the first Jew to settle in Corpus Christi, recalled being harangued by a white woman as "a black Abolitionist" for giving a coin to a slave child who had brought him water. Henry, newly arrived from Europe, was troubled by the exchange and claimed to have become a Republican on the spot.[24] The Civil War provided an opportunity for other Texas Jews to act on their anti-slavery views. When word of the Emancipation Proclamation arrived in 1863, Joseph Landa of New Braunfels immediately freed his five slaves, an act that his Confederate neighbors considered treasonous. Landa fled to Matamoros, where he remained until the end of the war, leaving his wife and children behind to tend the flour mill and other family businesses. According to his son, Landa's "sympathies were with the South," but he nevertheless felt compelled to offer freedom to his slaves at a time when it was socially inexpedient to do so.[25]

In spite of his apparent anti-slavery sentiment, Landa had offered his service to the Confederate army and only avoided enlistment because of a physical disability. Many Jewish Texans supported the Confederate cause and served in the southern army, but this was often an accommodation to the will of the majority, not an expression of their own views on slavery. Harris Kempner, for instance, who after the war founded a Galveston dynasty of cotton and sugar magnates, "had taken on the ways of the white South in all appropriate respects," according to biographer Harold Hyman, "and accommodation specifically to human slavery and to white supremacy generally was one of them."[26] When Kempner was asked later in life why he, once a victim of European anti-Semitism, had supported the Confederacy in its effort to secure slavery, he replied, "I came to America to be an American, and I tried to adapt my ways to American ways." His neighbors, he noted, "were all for the South," and "I was one of them." The issue of slavery "did not mean so much to me" as "the right of a people to govern themselves as they thought best. I knew what it meant not to have that right."[27] Kempner's explanation is striking and deeply significant. This Jewish immigrant who had felt persecution in Europe identified not with the suffering of another oppressed minority group but with the southern states that were oppressing them. Kempner never owned slaves himself—perhaps a sign of latent moral qualms—but his identification with the white South was otherwise complete.

By the end of the Civil War, the mainstream press began to report admiringly on some of the Jews in Texas communities. When Rabbi L. Steiner of Houston's Congregation Beth Israel died in 1867, the *Houston Transcript* reported (and the *American Israelite* reprinted) that Steiner was "learned, profound and accomplished," depicting him as "a man of great profundity as a historian and a linguist, besides being an accomplished musician and painter." The *Transcript* went on to describe Steiner as a "firm and able advocate of the Jewish faith [who] has been gathered to his fathers," and "though he disavowed the divinity of Jesus, there are few Christians . . . who will lack the charity to believe that his immortal soul is registered upon the Book of Life in the New Jerusalem prepared for God's chosen people."[28] To be sure, this is muted praise—the writer seemed to say that Steiner was pretty admirable for a heathen—but the *Transcript* could have remained silent, and the praise seems sincere.

Other newspapers also reflected a greater acceptance of Jews. The *Dallas Herald* urged its gentile readers to attend an event sponsored by the Ladies' Hebrew Benevolent Association to raise money for a new synagogue. Dallas Jews had been quick to answer community needs, wrote the editor, and the city owed them gratitude.[29] Jewish women in Galveston led civic activities, working to improve their city, most often alongside Episcopalian and Presbyterian women representing the most elite Christian groups. Rarely did they work with Baptist, Catholic, and African-American groups, those at the lower end of the social spectrum.[30] National Jewish newspapers also reported on gentile acceptance of Texas Jews. In 1879, the *Jewish South* affirmed that Austin's roughly 250 Jews all seemed to be in "good circumstances, doing well and . . . very much respected among the Gentiles." Many, in fact, were "old citizens of Austin, having resided there for the past twenty-six years [who] in particular are enjoying the respect and goodwill of all."[31]

In aligning themselves with the white "Us" of Anglo society, Jews also insisted that they were different from the non-white "Them." They sought out blacks and Hispanics as customers, but did not blur the racial lines marking them as separate peoples. Texas Jews participated actively, even enthusiastically, in the racism of their time, and there is no reason to doubt that they were sincere in their bigotry. An 1882 letter from Houston rabbi Jacob Voorsanger, who later gained greater fame as a religious leader in San Francisco, is a case in point. Voorsanger wrote to the *American Israelite* to condemn African Americans' celebration of Juneteenth, an annual holiday honoring the abolition of slavery. Juneteenth commemorates the June 19, 1865, arrival in Texas of a Union general bearing official word of the Emancipation Proclamation and declaring free more than 250,000 Texas slaves. "The negroes had a procession," Voorsanger reported, "[and] scowled at the white folks, upon whom they are absolutely depending for bread and meat." He blamed the celebrants and their supporters for the death of a white citizen and the assault of a police officer. At times like this, Voorsanger continued, "one feels that the colored gentlemen are being very far from the level where a white man cares to meet with them." They are acceptable, he said, "if pursuing their ordinary avocations as the hewers of wood and water carriers of society," but when Republicans stir up their "sluggish blood" they become "intolerable, if not absolutely dangerous."[32] Voorsanger's language, as well as his lack of sympathy for the black celebrants and his antipathy toward the Republican Party, repeat the conventional wisdom of the white mainstream in post-Reconstruction Texas. Instead of joining African Americans in celebrating their escape from bondage (as Jews commemorate their own liberation from slavery every Passover), Voorsanger modeled common prejudices and condemned Yankee agitators. His comments are those of a man who saw himself as a leading white citizen, not a member of a persecuted minority.

Another prominent Jewish Texan of the post-Reconstruction period revealed a more sympathetic attitude toward African Americans, but one still tinged with prejudice and paternalism. When William Levy, the Jewish mayor of the North Texas town of Sherman, addressed an integrated crowd at the opening of a technical school for black students in 1890, he spoke glowingly of African-American achievement—especially the example of "Fred Douglass," an alarmingly patronizing reference to the formidable civil rights leader. Levy reserved his highest praise, however, for the Jewish people whose experience he felt should serve as a model for the school's disadvantaged students. Holding himself up as the image of success, he asked them to "look me right in the face" to behold "a man whose ancestors were also slaves . . . and they were longer in slavery and worked harder and suffered more under the rod of the overseer and the lash of the tyrant than you and your fathers and mothers." All the nations that had persecuted Jews, he said, had crumbled into dust, while "Israel has remained, has outlived them all." His black listeners could hope for similar success, he said, if they would follow the Jewish example and "work intelligently, patiently and tirelessly." [33]

Levy's real message, however, came through later in his speech when he said that in addition to working hard, black Texans should also learn to keep their place if they hoped to succeed. They must, he said, behave appropriately, recognizing "that it is wrong to lie, to slander, to insult . . . that it is wrong to cheat, defraud, deceive, to be dishonest, steal or kill; that it is wrong to disturb the peace, to quarrel and fight, to get drunk, play cards for money, or 'shoot craps,' as you call it." Moreover, he advised that "the farther they keep away from politics and politicians, and attend rather to their families and their bread and meat, the more blessing they will deserve."[34] Levy's self-serving address emphasized the importance of keeping the peace and discouraging black political activity, even as it held out to his black listeners the promise of equality if they remained patient and played by the rules the majority set for them. As mayor, Levy had reason to encourage peacefulness and order; as a Jew, he had the example of Jewish achievement to allude to; as a liberal, he claimed to have the best interests of his listeners at heart. His speech, however, was a thinly veiled attempt to keep his audience in line and to delay blacks' advancement. Although willing to use his Jewishness as part of his appeal, Levy identified primarily with his position as a white citizen and a civic official rather than with his listeners' experience.

"The Last of Creation"

In communities like Houston and Sherman, where Voorsanger and Levy lived, African Americans were the largest minority group against which Jews could define themselves. In other parts of the state, however, other groups predominated, and Jews confronted these as well in their effort to distinguish themselves within the state's complex racial mixture. In El Paso, Laredo, Brownsville, and smaller communities on both sides of the national border, Jews worked closely with Mexicans and with Mexican Texans, or Tejanos, as neighbors, employees, and customers. Whereas in East Texas, African Americans were a minority whose friendship Jews sometimes sought but did not find necessary, Tejanos were the majority in most border communities. Jews, who were typically retailers and depended upon the good will of their customers, could not afford to be patronizing or neglectful toward them. As a result, they related to Mexican-American people in complex ways. They absorbed prejudices common among whites but, unable to escape the pervasive influence of Mexican culture, they often came to admire its color and vibrancy.

The letters of Ernst Kohlberg to his family in Germany magnificently illustrate the complexity of Jewish feeling toward Mexicans and Tejanos. Kohlberg arrived in El Paso in 1875 as the protégé of Samuel Schutz, a fellow Westphalian who had set up shop in the town in 1854 and had become one of the city's leading retailers. Schutz hired Kohlberg as a store assistant in his establishments on both sides of the Río Grande. Under their agreement, Kohlberg worked without pay for several months to repay Schutz for the cost of his travel from Europe. Despite initial homesickness—"I want to tell you," he wrote his family in Germany, "that this place is nearly the end of the world and the last of creation"—and his unhappiness with his contract, Kohlberg soon warmed to El Paso. He began simultaneously studying both English and Spanish and described for his family the distinctive foods he was enjoying. Principal among these was "chile or Spanish pepper." Chile, he wrote, "is eaten green when roasted, tho the Mexicans even eat it raw, or it is eaten cooked with cheese when it is ripe." At first, he wrote, "chile and everything connected with it was a hellish kind of food for me," but after nearly a year in Texas, "I almost can swallow it like a Mexican and I miss it if it is not served." A photograph Kohlberg sent after six years in El Paso showed him armed with a long six-shooter and wearing a broad sombrero and Mexican shawl.[35] Whether this was a costume or not, Kohlberg was clearly reveling in his new frontier identity, including the Mexican influence El Paso offered him.

Kohlberg also encountered various groups of Native Americans in West Texas. As was common among whites on the American frontier, Kohlberg expressed respect for those tribal groups whose weakened condition rendered them no longer a threat to whites' lives and commerce, while condemning those who remained resistant. Thus, with notably faint praise, he described the domesticated Pueblo of nearby New Mexico as "not savages" and contrasted them to nomadic Texas Comanches and Apaches, the "wild Indians." Kohlberg attended a Pueblo dance festival and described it in detail, though he was aesthetically unimpressed with what he saw. "The noise of their musical instruments and their singing," he wrote, "gave me a headache from which I did not recover for two days." He found no "grace

Ernst Kohlberg. University of Texas at El Paso Library, Special Collections Department.

or beauty" in their dances, observing that the "continuous hopping up and down is very hard work and the sweat trickles from the heads of the dancing men and women." Nevertheless, Kohlberg revealed a genuine interest in Pueblo culture and offered to write more about "these red men when I know them better."[36] He collected a pair of moccasins to send back to Germany as a curiosity.

Kohlberg showed no interest, however, in learning more about the Apache, who were then, as he said, "on the war-path." He told his family about a raid in which Apaches robbed a shipment of Mexican merchandise on the road to Santa Fe and wounded the driver. After American soldiers took the lives of fifteen Apaches in response to another raid, Kohlberg reassured his family that he was safe. "Do not for a moment think that we are in any danger from this band," he wrote. The Apaches' "chief characteristics are their cowardice, their love of thievery, and their hatred of any kind of work," which, he seemed to feel, made them ultimately harmless. Many Germans, he observed, were inclined to pity the Indians, but Kohlberg warned his family against that view. To Kohlberg, as to most whites on the American frontier, natives represented the opposite of civilization and deserved only scorn and abuse, and he advised his family not to sympathize with "the redskin dogs."[37] No longer a German, Kohlberg expressed his new American identity through his loathing of the frontiersman's traditional enemy.

Through such rhetorical boundary-drawing, Texas Jews created a distinctive group identity by defining precisely what they were (Anglo) and what they were not (black, Mexican, or Indian). By adopting the conventional white prejudices and expressing them openly, Texas Jews made themselves acceptable as members of the white majority. It remained, however, to guard against what Isaac Leeser had originally feared, that assimilation into the mainstream was a greater threat to Judaism than anti-Semitism. Texas Jews became Anglos by refusing to be anything else, but for their distinctive religious identity to survive they would have to build Jewish institutions to rival Christian ones.

Raising the Standard of Judaism

Jewish settlers had lived in Texas cities for several decades before achieving the population necessary in any one place to support lasting institutions. Always small in number, they tended also to be a mobile group. Like Michael Seeligson and Jacob de Cordova, many worked for a while in one city and then moved on to others in the region. For institutions to survive, the population had to be both large and stable.

That finally happened in Galveston by the early 1850s, some twenty years after the first Jewish merchants had begun to arrive. In 1850, there were twelve Jewish adults and fourteen children in Galveston, comprising four families.[38] One extended family in particular, the Dyers, had the greatest influence on the city's incipient Jewish community. Leon, Rosanna, and Isadore Dyer were siblings born in Dessau, Germany, between 1807 and 1815, who immigrated to Baltimore with their parents in the late 1810s. The family soon split up, following business opportunities in other parts of the country. Leon, the oldest, was the first to arrive in Texas, leaving his branch of the family business in New Orleans in order to participate in the Texas Revolution. Rosanna married a Dutch-born merchant and jeweler, Joseph Osterman, who was a charter member of the Baltimore Hebrew Congregation. When Osterman suffered business setbacks, Leon, who was impressed with Texas' commercial potential, sent word to his brother-in-law to try his luck in Galveston. Leon provided some capital and collected a stock of goods for Osterman to sell after he arrived, described as "general merchandise, which included everything: from horseshoes, to a coffin, to a bag of coffee."[39] Osterman moved to Galveston in 1837 to open a shop in a tent he set up in a vacant lot not far from the port, and Rosanna joined him the following year. The third Dyer sibling, Isadore, joined the family in Galveston in 1840 and started an insurance business.[40]

The system of chain migration that the Dyers and Ostermans exhibited—sending a first family member who, once established, brought the others behind him—was not just a common pattern in Texas. It was the way many Jews, and immigrants of every national origin, arrived in the United States. It also indicates that, despite their physical distance from older communities, the Dyers and Ostermans were well connected to other parts of the country and maintained contacts there. In a telling example, after Rosanna Dyer Osterman died in 1866 in a steamship explosion in Vicksburg, Mississippi, her will revealed that she had left much of her family fortune to both Jewish and non-Jewish charitable causes in several states. In the will, she requested burial in New Orleans beside her husband, but she left a large amount of money to charities in Galveston. These included a nondenominational Widows' and Orphans' Home; $5,000 for the construction of the city's first synagogue (the largest single bequest); and a fund for the support of indigent Jews "if any there be." She also gave smaller amounts to support a wide array of Jewish charities in Philadelphia, New York, New Orleans, and Cincinnati.[41] Her will is not only an example of remarkable generosity, but also the legacy of a woman mostly unimpeded by her distance from Jewish centers larger than Galveston. While living in a place where Jewish facilities needed building from the ground up, Rosanna Osterman remained cosmopolitan and well connected to the outside world.

The Dyers and Ostermans were primarily responsible for the first permanent Jewish institution in Texas, the cemetery in Galveston. When Isadore Dyer's six-year-old son died in 1852, Joseph Osterman purchased a plot of land and donated it to the Jewish community, while his wife, Rosanna, arranged for Rabbi M. N. Nathan of New Orleans to travel to Galveston to conduct the ceremony. The *Galveston Daily News* described the consecration and funeral as "the first [worship service] ever performed publicly by a Hebrew minister in Texas," and Isaac Leeser reported the event in the *Occident*, noting that Nathan's service "was listened to with great attention by the few of our faith in the city," as well as "a large number of Christian friends."[42]

Nathan also recognized the small gathering as a milestone. It was "the first public assemblage in a quarter so remote from the birth-place and cradle of our religion," where Jews were meeting "to lay the foundation-stone, as it may be termed, of the edifice of Judaism." Nathan emphasized the community's isolation but asked his listeners to look forward to a day when "large congregations of our brethren will abound in this gigantic State of the Union" and when future generations would "naturally be excited to ascertain who first unfurled and raised the standard of Judaism in this section of the West." To those who might doubt such a future, Nathan addressed a question: "Who, half a century ago, would have ventured to say, that on this verdant prairie, which once resounded with the war-whoop of the Indian,—which echoed back the footfall of the Mexican hunter's steed,—which rang with the boisterous mirth, the profane words of the ferocious and unprincipled buccaneers, the name of the Eternal God of Hosts would be invoked by Israelites, in the primitive tongue?"[43] Nathan described his congregants to themselves and to their Christian neighbors not as lost and isolated souls on a lonely frontier, but as the vanguard of Jewish advancement, even of civilization itself, and he urged them to push fervently into that future.

Nathan was not blind, however, to the difficulties his listeners would face. They lacked spiritual leadership, he knew, and he noted that "[i]t may be long ere another Jewish minister may address you." He acknowledged their small number, "too few," he said, "to build a Synagogue, to form a

Although the identity of this portrait is in doubt, it has traditionally been identified as Rosanna Dyer Osterman. UTSA's Institute of Texan Cultures, No. 068–2488.

congregation for public worship." Isadore, who had married a Christian woman, was surely unhappy to hear Nathan tell them that they had been lax in seeking Jewish marriage partners and in "[stamping] your offspring with the seal of the covenant of circumcision," and the rabbi further chastised them for attending Christian worship services "to pray to a mediator, whom no instructed Israelite believes in, and listen to dogmas and doctrine to which you cannot subscribe." He reminded them of the religious options that were available to them even in their remoteness. They could pray at home, they could circumcise their sons, and, with "respectable and populous congregations . . . in your immediate neighborhood," presumably Nathan's own congregation in New Orleans, they could seek "suitable alliances with Hebrew blood" for their children. These were things that they were "bound to do as Hebrews, Israelites, [and] Jews." Notably, Nathan did not condemn his small group of congregants for their decision to remove themselves from larger and better organized Jewish communities. Rather, he challenged them to rise to the occasion and promote a Jewish life and outlook. "In almost the same position as our progenitor Abraham occupied nearly 4,000 years ago," he said, "do we, at this moment stand."[44] His listeners had an opportunity, he claimed, to be the agents not only of Jewish survival but also of the growth and development of Judaism itself.

It is possible to interpret Nathan's statement in two ways, each of which can tell us a great deal about how these early Texas Jews understood their frontier condition. On the one hand, we can take him at his word, reading into his comments only the meanings he clearly stated. In this sense, the Galveston Jews who gathered to consecrate their cemetery were pioneers pushing against the limits of civilization in order to advance not only their own fortunes but also the future of Jewry. By building Jewish institutions and following Jewish practices in "a quarter so remote from the birth-place and cradle of our religion," they were *serving* their faith, not carrying it heedlessly into the wilderness to be destroyed. In Nathan's view, their movement west had purposefulness and a kind of religiously sanctioned missionary zeal. If Galveston's Jews were not seeking to convert their Christian brothers, they were at least preparing the way for future generations of Jews.

On the other hand, it is also possible to hear more than a hint of rationalization in Nathan's comments. Galveston's Jews were not missionaries, nor had they ventured to Texas for the cause of religious freedom. Texas simply did not represent to them what, for instance, Utah represented to the Mormons. If anything, conditions in Texas ran directly counter to the purposes of religious survival and continuity that Nathan extolled. If it had been really important to the Ostermans and Dyers to remain traditionally observant, they would never have left Germany or at least would have remained in well-established American cities. Texas' economic opportunities were available only at some cost to their religious devotion and, one assumes, with a certain amount of guilt. Nathan's message may have eased the consciences of Texas Jews who, isolated among gentiles yet steadily pursuing financial prosperity, could not help but feel that they had sold their birthright. Nathan's words reshaped the Jewish presence in Texas into an expression of Jewish identity, not a denial of it, and thus relieved their guilt even while exhorting them to greater devotion.

In whatever ways they could, many of the Texas Jews present, and possibly many others who read Nathan's address in the *Occident*, took his message to heart, perhaps hoping that by maintaining whatever forms of traditional Judaism were possible they could justify their presence in Texas as something more than commercial opportunism. Instances abound of Texas Jews making efforts under trying circumstances to preserve religious traditions. A few months after the cemetery dedication at which Nathan had compared Galveston's Jews to "our progenitor Abraham," for example, Michael Seeligson wrote to the *Occident* about a member of the community who, in the absence of a professional circumciser, determined to perform his infant son's circumcision himself. "People endeavored to persuade him to wait till the child could be taken thither, or a Mohel be sent for," he wrote. "But he replied, that our Father Abraham performed this duty on the eighth day, why should he not do it also?"[45] The *Occident* later reported on a Houston couple who, when they could not afford to bring a *mohel* to town, resolved to wait to circumcise their son until one was available. The ceremony was finally performed *eight years* later, with "such solemnity and with such composure on the part of the boy," the *Occident* reported, "that it made a deep impression on all the by-standers"—though, one imagines, not nearly the impression it made on the boy himself.[46] Not all efforts to follow Nathan's recommendations took such extreme form. By 1856, the Galveston community was meeting regularly at the home of Isadore Dyer for prayer services in what Henry Cohen later identified as "a special room dedicated to that purpose."[47] The *Galveston News* reported on Yom Kippur 1859 that "our Jewish fellow citizens have closed their places of business to celebrate it as a day of fast and prayer."[48]

A similar pattern prevailed in neighboring Houston. As the Dyers and Ostermans had directed the establishment of early institutions in Galveston, Lewis A. Levy, probably the first permanent Jewish settler in Houston, took the lead in that city. Born in Amsterdam in 1799 to a family with Portuguese origins, Levy moved with his family to London where he married a cousin, Mary A. Levy, in 1817. In 1818, their growing family left for the United States, settling in Richmond, Virginia, where they were members of a Sephardic congregation, Beth Shalome. The couple moved, with a new daughter, to New Orleans in 1831 and then, after neighboring Texas had achieved its independence, to Galveston in 1838 and to Houston in 1840. Levy purchased about fifteen acres of land from Sam Houston and opened shop as a merchant and dealer in land certificates. He and Mary ultimately had twenty children, including their daughter Hannah, whose 1847 marriage to Henry Wiener was probably the first Jewish wedding performed in Texas and one of the first marriages between permanent residents of Houston.[49] When he died in 1861, Levy was "acknowledged as the leader of the young Houston Jewish community."[50]

In 1854 Levy organized a collection for New Orleans yellow fever victims, a sign that he shared a sense of community with Jews across the country contributing to that cause. His efforts led to the formal establishment of the Hebrew Benevolent Society in 1855, with Levy as its first chairman.[51] According to Jacob de Cordova, the group had "also under its control a burial-ground," confirming the establishment of the Houston Jewish cem-

Lewis A. Levy. Courtesy of
Rosanne D. Leeson.

———

Mary A. Levy. Courtesy of
Rosanne D. Leeson.

etery in 1854.[52] Levy was also instrumental in the 1859 formation of the
state's first Jewish congregation, Congregation Beth Israel of Houston, and
was one of its first members.[53] Beth Israel was chartered by the state that
year and also placed an advertisement for a religious leader in the *American
Israelite*. "The Hebrew Congregation Beth Israel, (House of Israel) is desirous of engaging a gentleman who is capable to act as Chazan, Schocket,
Mohel and Bangal Koray," the ad stated. The salary was a fixed $1,000 a
year, "besides perquisites, which, if he be a Mohel, will reach a considerable
amount, as there is no Mohel in the country."[54]

Houston Jews had organized their congregation under Orthodox precepts, and this advertisement illustrated their desire to worship in traditional
ways. Their request for a *chazan* (cantor and prayer leader), *schochet* (kosher
slaughterer), *mohel* (circumciser), and "bangal koray" (*ba'al korey*, Torah
reader) was an effort to furnish themselves with the basic services necessary
for traditional Jewish life. The request for a *mohel* demonstrated that their

community was growing, or had plans to grow, and needed to be prepared to welcome new members into Judaism in the appropriate way. Within a year of the advertisement, Beth Israel employed the state's first full-time Jewish religious leader, Zacharias Emmich, who presided at regular Orthodox worship services although he was not officially ordained as a rabbi. In March 1860, the *Occident* reported that Houston Jews had erected a "handsomely fit up" wooden house of worship in the downtown area, "the front of which is used as a Synagogue, the back portion as a meeting room."[55] The Houston Jewish community, even at this early stage, was clearly dedicated to living as full a Jewish life as it could in its remote location.

The pattern of community development exhibited in Houston and Galveston was typical of nationwide patterns. Generally, the initial Jewish community would form a Hebrew Benevolent Association to care for the indigent poor and to establish a cemetery. When their numbers grew large enough, they formed a congregation, usually borrowing space in a storefront or church to hold services until, often many years later, they could raise the funds for a synagogue and a professional rabbi. Jewish schools often followed, along with the hiring of professional Hebrew teachers. Texas communities, like those throughout the country, reported their progress to national Jewish newspapers like the *Occident* and the *American Israelite*, which recorded their growth like parents notching a doorframe. The columns of these papers are filled with breathless reports of community development from towns of every size and region. The Texas frontier, then, was but one of numberless places adhering to a common pattern and, despite frequent claims to the contrary, was never as isolated as Texas Jews might profess.

Small Towns and Divided Cities

As Jews in Galveston and Houston built religious institutions, smaller Jewish communities began to appear throughout the state. In 1851, Michael Seeligson reported to the *Occident* that "[t]here are not many Jews in the state," but "you will find a sprinkling of them in every village."[56] Joseph and Helena Landa and their children were the only Jewish family in the German Hill Country town of New Braunfels, but they maintained Jewish customs with a frontier family's tenacity. Helena prepared her own matzoh every year for Passover, to the delight of her neighbors and the family's African-American servants, by mixing flour and water, rolling it flat, cutting out the squares with a tin form, then rolling spurs with large rowels across the dough to make air holes.[57] San Antonio Jews consecrated a cemetery in 1854 and began holding services under the auspices of a Hebrew Benevolent Society in 1856. The *American Israelite* reported in May of that year that the city held about fifty Jews, "most of them flourishing merchants." They had "organized themselves into a congregation, purchased a lot of ground for a burial place, and will at an early date furnish a room for a temporary Synagogue."[58] In the 1850s, the Doppelmayer, Wolf, Exstein, Grossman, Bernstein, and Weisman families, in a classic example of chain migration, followed a pioneering relative from Syracuse, New York, to the East Texas town of Marshall. By 1860 the South Texas community of Victoria had enough Jewish residents to hold *minyan* (prayer group of ten members minimum) services in honor of the High Holidays.[59] Even before the Civil War, Texas Jews had established a lasting pattern of dispersed settlement to countless small towns.

The Civil War briefly halted immigration into Texas, but it continued faster than ever in the decades after the war. Between 1860 and 1900, the state's population increased fivefold, from about 604,000 to a little more than 3 million.[60] A spate of postwar rail construction made Texas the crossroads of several transcontinental lines and connected the cities of Dallas, Fort Worth, Waco, San Antonio, and Houston to traffic throughout the nation. Other lines traversed West Texas, linking the United States and Mexico through El Paso, Laredo, and Eagle Pass. Dallas boomed as the rail juncture of northern Texas, growing from 3,000 inhabitants in 1870 to 10,000 in 1880 and more than 40,000 by 1900.[61] Throughout Texas, towns grew into cities because of the commerce and immigration provided by the railroads. The influx of new settlers brought many more Jews, and the relative ease of travel through the state dispersed them well beyond the coastal centers and large cities. Most of the Jewish newcomers were merchants following rail lines to the state's newest centers of commercial activity—or occasionally making centers of commercial activity where none had existed. Isaac and Lehman Sanger, for example, arrived in Texas in the late 1850s and opened a series of retail and clothing stores throughout the state. After the success of their first stores in the railroad towns of McKinney, Decatur, and Weatherford, they were joined in Texas after the Civil War by several additional brothers. As the Houston and Texas Central Railroad expanded between 1865 and 1872, they followed its lines establishing stores in Millican, Bryan, Calvert, Kosse, Groesbeck, Corsicana, and Dallas, where Sanger Brothers became the premier retailing establishment in a famously retailing city.[62]

As Jews arrived in greater numbers, they supported the development of new Jewish associations, congregations, and schools. Chapters of the Inter-

The storefront operated by brothers Lehman and Philip Sanger in Bryan, Texas, opened in 1867 after the Houston and Texas Central Railroad reached the town. Note the presence, even in this frontier town, of several Jewish-owned shops. From the collections of the Texas/Dallas History and Archives Division, Dallas Public Library, MA83.18/61.

national Order of B'nai B'rith, the Jewish fraternal society, sprouted in large and small communities throughout the state, providing guidance and financial support to other communal projects. Galveston established the B'nai Israel congregation in 1868, while the Central Texas town of Hempstead, with a fraction of Galveston's population, formed a Jewish prayer group in the mid-1870s under the leadership of the eastern European scholar Heinrich Schwarz. Upon his arrival from Prussia in 1873, Schwarz became the state's first ordained rabbi. New congregations soon joined the list: B'nai Israel of Victoria in 1872, the Hebrew Sinai Congregation of Jefferson in 1873, San Antonio's Beth-El in 1874, Emanu-El of Dallas in 1875, Austin's Beth Israel in 1876, and Waco's Rodef Sholom in 1879. By 1880, the state's Jewish population had climbed to about 3,300, enough to sustain thriving Jewish communities and facilities in a number of towns. One survey that year counted seven active congregations in the state, thirteen benevolent societies or cemetery organizations, and measurable Jewish populations in thirty-three cities and towns across the state.[63] By 1900, congregations had also been formed in Brenham (1885), Tyler (1887), Marshall (1887), Fort Worth (1892), Corsicana (1898), and El Paso (1900).[64] With few exceptions, these new congregations embraced Reform Judaism's liberalization of Jewish practice and emphasis on American rather than universal Jewish identity. Reform was then the choice of the vast majority of American congregations, it was especially dominant in the South and West, and Texas communities fit that pattern.

As congregations grew in Texas cities, they attracted the state's first full-time pulpit rabbis, although these appear not to have had much rabbinical training or genuine credentials. They also tended to serve short terms before moving on to more prestigious posts. Zacharias Emmich served less than a year at Beth Israel and was followed by a string of others before Jacob Voorsanger arrived in 1878 and stayed for eight years. Galveston's first rabbi with formal credentials was Abraham Blum, who took the post at B'nai Israel in 1871. In 1875, Temple Emanu-El in Dallas hired Rabbi Aron Suhler, who held the post for four years before moving to lead the Jefferson congregation and was succeeded in Dallas by H. M. Bien.

In addition to serving their own congregations, the first rabbis traveled throughout the state providing religious leadership to more remote Jewish communities that could not afford full-time rabbis. Rabbinical "circuit preaching" had long been discussed in national Jewish circles and in the Jewish press, and it was a topic of much concern and debate among national Reform leaders, including Rabbi Isaac Mayer Wise, founder of both the Union of American Hebrew Congregations (UAHC) and the Hebrew Union College. However, the especially great distances between Texas towns, which prevented rural Jews from traveling into the cities for religious activities, caused Texas rabbis to be the first to take action on the matter of circuit preaching. Jacob Voorsanger wrote in the *Jewish South* that many Jews in Texas and throughout the South "would engage in the holy cause [of Judaism] if they would receive the proper encouragement." The Houston rabbi complained that "the U.A.H.C. is very slow in instituting circuit preaching, hence the friends of Israel must strike out unaided."[65] In 1879, Voorsanger, Blum, and Bien designed their own circuit-riding scheme, which they offered to Isaac Wise as a model for other parts of the country.[66] "After this," Voorsanger promised, "small communities who desire Sunday Schools or lectures can have no excuse."[67] Wise noted the achievement in the *Israelite* and delighted in reporting "one of the first instances of the rite of circumcision having been performed in Mexico," which occurred when Blum "was summoned to undertake a journey of 500 miles—almost entirely in a traveling carriage—to circumcise a Jewish child at New Laredo."[68] The Texas plan was successful and admirable, but it took the UAHC more than fifteen years to adopt a similar national circuit-riding program.

The Jews living in the young communities served by these rabbis held a striking diversity of religious views. Neither their national origin—they came from both eastern and central Europe—nor the denominational character of their communities showed a discernible pattern. Traditional Judaism was well represented throughout the state, and a few communities managed to put together the necessary facilities to preserve Orthodox practice. When Houston's Congregation Beth Israel was chartered in 1859, according to a report in the *Occident*, it followed "the Polish Minhag [prayer service], with some changes, which will not conflict with strict *orthodox principles*."[69] Significantly, traditional Judaism also thrived in smaller communities. Rabbi Heinrich Schwarz, the only trained Talmudist in Hempstead, Texas, continued his scholarly work, even taking on a few students, including Jacob Voorsanger, and he and his family built a small *shul* (house of prayer, synagogue) behind one of their homes. Although making some concessions to American life—he eventually removed his yarmulke for all but religious occasions—Schwarz and his family maintained traditional practice.[70] In Brenham, Orthodox Jews established Congregation B'nai Abraham and built a synagogue. When it burned in 1893, they replaced it with a small, white building with a peaked roof, which from the outside looked like a Baptist church. Inside, however, was a European-style synagogue with an octagonal *bimah* (an elevated platform on which the Torah is read) and a women's gallery upstairs for traditional worship.

In many Texas communities, conflicts arose between Orthodox and Reform Jews. Whereas in large American and European cities subgroups with different ritualistic preferences could worship separately, Jews in Texas frontier communities, as in other young communities across the nation, could not afford separate facilities. Different denominations were forced together into shared institutions.[71] A community was fortunate to be able to raise the means to sustain a single congregation. Only the largest could support separate facilities for traditional and Reform practice, and conflicts regularly arose as congregants tried to strike a balance. The Hebrew Benevolent Society in the Central Texas town of Rockdale, for example, began as a cooperative effort between traditional and Reform groups but later split over the question of whether or not to wrap a corpse in a white shroud before burying it in the town's Jewish cemetery.[72] In 1893, David Frosch moved his family from Galveston to Houston, in part to escape the con-

Temple B'nai Abraham, Brenham, Texas. Photo by Larry L. Rose © 2005.

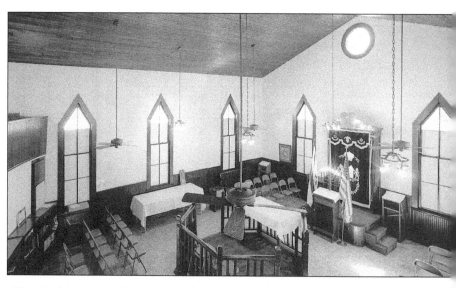

B'nai Abraham's exterior blends into the Hill Country landscape, but its interior reveals the building's function as a traditional Jewish place of worship. This photo, taken from the upstairs women's gallery, shows the octagonal *bimah*, on which the Torah was opened and read. These features are typical of eastern European synagogues. Photo by Larry L. Rose © 2005.

stant antagonism between Galician and Lithuanian Jews in a city "where these geographic differences became almost a matter of life or death."[73] If Frosch was able to find peace in Houston, it was only because adherents of traditional and Reform practice had resolved their most contentious disputes, resulting in the rededication of the synagogue along Reform lines.

Similar controversies and negotiations, with mixed results, arose in communities throughout the state. In Calvert, for example, a plan to sponsor community-wide High Holiday services in the Central Texas town fell apart in 1879 when members failed to agree on which Yom Kippur prayer book (*machzor*) to use. "Some of the members insisted upon having the old orthodox Machsar-service," a correspondent told the *Jewish South*, "and the balance, not to mar the harmony, acquiesced in that very unreasonable demand." The result, he said, was a disaster. No local leader was willing to officiate at "a mere farce," so the community paid an outsider, a "tramp, vulgo travelling Chasan" who "by his style and general conduct fully succeeded in disgusting everybody and in degrading and disgracing Judaism."[74] Other efforts to avoid this sort of acrimony were more successful. Worship services in Dallas had been conducted along Reform lines, alienating the city's Orthodox inhabitants, who therefore, according to a correspondent in the *Jewish South*, "kept away from us, and on holidays had services of their own." Community leaders sought to reunify the two groups by drafting their own *minhag* (prayer service), the *"Minhag Dallas,"* which blended the two forms of worship.[75] Although few congregations were as bold, compromises like this characterized the state's earliest Jewish communities and their efforts to balance the views of their diverse participants.

While making efforts to merge into the white Texas mainstream, to set themselves apart from the state's racial minorities, and to establish their own distinctive religious and communal structures, many Texas Jews continued to feel the lack of strong Jewish institutions and facilities. In 1873, David Hirsch of Corpus Christi was obliged, in an almost Faulkneresque event, to carry his wife's body 130 miles on a horse cart to bury her in a Jewish cemetery. The incident so affected a gentile citizen of Corpus Christi that he donated a plot of land in town to establish the Hebrew Rest Cemetery.[76] Jewish Texans also remained self-conscious about their distance from other, larger Jewish communities. Ernst Kohlberg wrote repeatedly that he might have done better to have remained in New York, where he first arrived in America, rather than to have gone to El Paso, a place that, he told his family, even New Yorkers spoke of as "so far away, about the same as you do."[77]

The frontier, then, was both a reality and a state of mind. The physical distance between Jews within Texas, not to mention between them and Jews in other states and other nations, was indeed great, and it often presented real obstacles to the fulfillment of basic Jewish religious obligations. In the late nineteenth century, Texas Jews were building institutions, recruiting religious leaders, and expanding their numbers in cities and towns across the state, all of which eased these limitations and made Jewish life possible. As the activities of the Dyers and Ostermans clearly reveal, living in the "wilderness" offered genuine hardships but also great opportunities to build and develop rich and meaningful Jewish lives. However, the establishment of Jewish facilities in isolated towns did not make Texas a Jewish center, and the connections migrants maintained to larger communities back East sometimes emphasized the distances they had to travel to return. At best, Texas remained an outpost of Judaism where communal religious life was no longer beleaguered but hardly convenient or comprehensive. Even as the wilderness receded before the railroad, the synagogue, and the department store, Texas Jews remained peripheral.

THREE

The Possum and the Zionist

*In the winter of 1904, Jacob de Haas, the British-born secretary of the Federa-*tion of American Zionists, set out on a two-month tour of the American South to promote Zionist organization in the region. Editor of the Federation's New York journal, *The Maccabaean,* and formerly the personal secretary to Theodor Herzl, the founder of modern Zionism, de Haas was an accomplished organizer and activist, but he had his work cut out for him in the South. Before his trip, there were only eight chartered Zionist groups, numbering about 150 members, in the entire region.[1] The vast majority of southern Jews were followers of American Reform Judaism, which had officially renounced Jewish nationalism in its effort to make religious practice more consonant with American life. Reform prayer books eliminated references to the restoration of Jerusalem, and in 1885 a Pittsburgh convention of Reform leaders adopted a platform that explicitly rejected the effort to establish a political home for the Jewish people, asserting that only America offered genuine security and opportunity for Jews.

Reform leaders, especially the formidable Rabbi Isaac Mayer Wise of Cincinnati, virulently opposed Zionism on the grounds that it emphasized Jews' ethnic distinctiveness rather than their Americanism. Wise had trained nearly all the Reform rabbis in the South, who in turn passed their misgivings on to their congregations, often with heavy doses of misinformation. De Haas observed that "the Reform Jew is [not] per se an Anti-

Zionist," but "in most cases he is so out of respect for his Rabbi, mostly because he has not the faintest notion as to its objects." He met a Jewish man in Montgomery, for instance, "who seemed to think that somehow Zionism and Christian Science must be related. Verily the Southern Rabbis have promulgated strange ideas amongst the people." An Alabama woman expressed interest in the movement but wanted to know, "[M]ust we all go back to Palestine[?]" De Haas optimistically maintained that Zionism had made "rapid strides" in the South, but it was clear that a major educational campaign was necessary to bring most southern Jews around to the Zionist cause.[2]

For de Haas, Zionism was the best hope of counteracting the damage that the Diaspora had done to Jewish consciousness. He saw southern communities as "naturally estranging places," where Jews lived "peculiar lives" and where Jewish tradition was visibly deteriorating. Zionism was the cure for the disease of dispersion. "The orthodox Jew," he wrote while in Texas, "is allowed to shift for himself, there is no organization to strengthen his consciousness, and in the long run orthodoxy in the South is more a matter of opinion than a matter of practice." To de Haas, it was essential that the scattered supporters of traditional Judaism understand that "they are not an isolated handful struggling against the odds, but part and parcel of Jewry in a real and actual sense." Thus, he described for southern audiences "the Jewish brotherhood which Zionism is creating, the measure of love and sacrifice it is calling forth," and he "pleaded for support on the basis of Jewish pride and dignity." What was at stake was not only the success of the Zionist movement, but also the survival of Judaism itself. "[W]e have not only to make Zionists of hundreds of Jews," he wrote, "but . . . there are thousands of Jews whom we must endeavor somehow to save as Jews for their own sakes, and the sake of the house of Israel."[3] He was a messenger, that is, for the idea that Judaism has an authentic spiritual core of faith, tradition, and practice. The Zionist movement he represented sought to restore the spiritual center by securing the Jews' geographic center and ending the Diaspora. Those on the periphery, geographically *and* spiritually, would ultimately be gathered back into the center.

By the time de Haas arrived in Texas, the most westerly segment of his journey, he had spent more than three weeks in constant travel and activity, and he was tiring. After long visits to Houston and Galveston, he arrived in Waco on the morning of Christmas Eve, a Saturday, hoping to spend the Sabbath recuperating. "I snugged away," he wrote, "into a little Texan town." But the Jewish names over many downtown stores, even in

Jacob de Haas. Jacob
Rader Marcus Center
of the American Jewish
Archives, PC-924.

this Baptist stronghold, intrigued him, and as he made inquiries he learned "that almost every town on the route between Houston and Waco had its little collection of Jews, from a single family to twenty or twenty-five."[4] De Haas had, in fact, recognized evidence of a Jewish presence as he passed through some of these towns on his way to Waco. "I thought I was the only Jew here," he wrote his wife from Marlin, where he had stopped for the night, "but I had not stepped out before I saw the name of Levy, then two ending in 'ski,' watch-makers & jewellers & a Jewish money-lender—verily we are scattered."[5]

De Haas found more tales of local Jews in a copy of the *Waco Times-Herald*. In particular, he delighted in a story about the city's rabbi, Dr. Berenhard Wohlberg, making "a brilliant, and witty speech at a 'possum and 'tater supper.'"[6] The paper described the event as "a large party of business, professional, traveling and other men" who gathered annually to listen to one another give witty toasts and "to feast upon the old southern dish, 'possum and taters.'" Before a group of some two hundred of the town's prominent citizens, including future governor Pat Neff, Rabbi Wohlberg had addressed "The Moral Effect of the Possum" and had received enthusiastic applause for his discussion of that rodent's progressive social virtues: "P" was for philanthropy, "O" for obedience, "SS" for scientific sanitation, and so on.[7] De Haas noted in his journal that such a thing "seemed so unique, so bizarre from what we consider ordinarily to be Jewish life, and yet," he acknowledged, "I felt that it was all so natural here." De Haas was pleased the next morning to meet Dr. Wohlberg and to learn that he was a Zionist.[8]

That de Haas could describe Wohlberg's participation in the event as both "bizarre" and "natural" illustrates how Texas Jewry somehow lay both at the periphery of Jewish life and also at its center. De Haas perceived that Texas Jews were creating something alien to his traditionalist perspective, and yet its suitability in its own surroundings enchanted him. "How can I help remarking on the adaptability of our people," he wrote in Houston. "A grocer riding on horseback in perfect Texan style and a few years ago he was in a Russian slum."[9] Leaving New York behind, Jacob de Haas had ventured into the frontier, where Jewish identity was still fluid, uncertain, and less clearly defined than it was in the East. The Jewish Texans he met were at home on their frontier, and a paradoxical image of the Texas Jew was taking shape before de Haas' eyes: peripheral yet centered, self-confident and self-conscious, exiled but into an unexpected Promised Land. Texas was a frontier where Jews had made their homes and founded a homeland, even as they remained aware of themselves as a people in exile.

The story of the Possum and the Zionist also reveals how much meaning the idea of the frontier continued to hold in Texas long after the actual frontier had vanished. No longer a geographic, social, or economic reality, the frontier remained what essentially it had always been: a set of imaginary lines defining group identity, symbolic markers setting off "us" from "not us." By 1904, the material frontier, which had dictated the conditions of life for the previous generation, had closed. Railroads, telegraphs, telephones, national banking and retail distribution systems, rural mail delivery, and newspapers with national circulation had integrated Texas fully into national social, economic, and political networks. Moreover, no one could credibly describe Waco, a city with more than twenty thousand residents and an electric trolley system, as wild or unsettled. The city, in fact, had long been a prosperous railroad and shipping hub, a center for cattle and cotton trading as well as cloth manufacture, and a debarkation point for settlers heading farther west into the real frontier.[10]

For the Waco elite, the Possum and Tater Supper was clearly not just another professional banquet, but an elaborate ritual of identifying with a lost past and a disappearing way of life. The Waco diners, most of them engaged in commercial pursuits, sat down in an elegant hotel dining room to share a meal they would surely never eat under any other circumstances. The peculiar menu, "the old southern dish, 'possum and taters'" (and ap-

"Eat, drink and be merry for to-morrow you will nearly die"—*John Fall*

Menu

Oh, wonder! how many goodly creatures are there here—*The Tempest*

Clam Bouillon

Sliced Tomatoes   Cabbage Slaw   **BUDWEISER**

"Why then, the world's mine Oyster, which I with sword will open"
—*Merry Wives*

                                 SCHLITZ

Roasted Oysters in Shell

Potatoes French Fried   Grated Horseradish
     Shrimp Salad   Celery

    "Every why hath a wherefore"—*Comedy of Errors*

                               CLARET

Possum and Taters

Olives   Radishes   Potato Salad
        Brown and White Bread
Pickles   Sliced Beets   Corn Bread

"Now good digestion, wait on appetite and health on both"—*Macbeth*

                          RHINE WINE

Assorted Cakes   Jumbles
    Cheese Fingers   Assorted Crackers
          Coffee   **McK'S BIRD CIGARS**

"Now, good Angels, shade their persons under your blessed wings"
—*Henry VIII*

Menu from the Possum and Tater Club program, 1904. The Texas Collection, Baylor University, Waco, Texas.

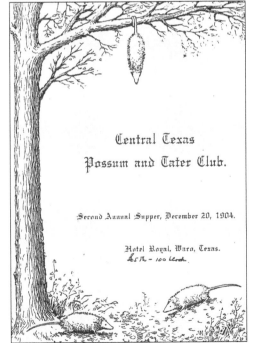

Central Texas Possum and Tater Club.

Second Annual Supper, December 20, 1904.

Hotel Royal, Waco, Texas.

Possum and Tater Club program cover, 1904. The Texas Collection, Baylor University, Waco, Texas.

Austin Avenue, Waco, Texas, taken in the 1890s a few years prior to Jacob de Haas' visit to the city. Notice the prominence of the Sanger Bros. store on the right, as well as the streetcars and tracks visible in the road. The Texas Collection, Baylor University, Waco, Texas.

parently it *was* opossum), was selected and prepared especially for its symbolic value, for its power to evoke an impoverished rural existence that was no longer the experience of the men in attendance, if it had ever been. The Possum and Tater Supper was a kind of hazing ritual for wealthy townspeople who secured their membership in Waco's business and professional fraternity by pretending to eat as if they were poor rural folk rather than the eastern elite they had come to resemble. Suitably, the evening's program also included an oyster-eating contest and a selection of imported wines.

By joining in the dinner and partaking of its spectacularly non-kosher menu, Rabbi Wohlberg proved himself a member of that fraternity. Born in Breslau and educated in the *yeshivas* (Torah schools) of Europe, Wohlberg was hardly a born frontiersman, but he had served congregations in Canada and in other southern states, indicating a willingness to venture away from the centers of Judaism to serve more remote communities. In his two years as religious leader of Waco's Temple Rodef Sholom, he had won the respect of the city's professional class, which included many members of his congregation. Wohlberg cultivated a sense of partnership between Waco Jews and gentiles—his Supper address included a plea for funds to build a

YMCA building—and his participation in the event reveals the degree of his neighbors' acceptance. Their approval, however, depended upon his willingness to internalize (literally, in this case) an imaginary frontier heritage that was not his own. He accepted their hospitality, and so they accepted him as a real Texan.

Many other Texas Jews had made a similar bargain, suiting their religious practice to norms established by gentile Texans and borrowing from Texas myth to define their own experience. Thus, when Jacob de Haas arrived and urged Jewish Texans to look to Palestine to do the hard work of irrigating fields, erecting buildings, and organizing communities, it was easy for Jews so enmeshed in Texas life to respond that they had already done it. Their homes and futures were in Texas, and they knew that the contortions they had performed to become Jewish Texans had shaped them in permanent and probably beneficial ways. Wohlberg, for instance, possessed a religious faith, European education, and Zionist outlook that all linked him to a global Jewish community, and he welcomed de Haas warmly as a fellow Zionist. Still, his first loyalty was local, and his activity on behalf of the Zionist cause was directed toward building Jewish institutions in Waco rather than toward any real hope of ideological or political Zionist success. At de Haas' urging, Wohlberg worked to strengthen the local Zionist chapter, but their goals in doing so differed. De Haas sought the rededication of a Jewish religious and cultural center in Palestine to be a home for Jews at the peripheries. Wohlberg, another kind of Zionist, was working to develop a Jewish homeland at those peripheries.

Promised Land

The idea of "promised land," so central to Zionist ideology, found a different purpose on the Texas frontier. As their communities developed, Texas Jews made many self-conscious efforts to present the state as a place of promise and opportunity for Jewish immigrants equal to any offered in scripture. To be sure, many American Jews held this vision of the United States as a golden land that, if not exactly what Abraham had in mind, was more than adequate to assure the security and prosperity of the Jewish people. Possibly every city in the nation provides examples of Jewish boosters drawing on biblical imagery to attract migrants to their communities and to express their satisfaction in being Americans. That such descriptions were more common in the West may have been related to its open spaces, economic booms, and egalitarian frontier society. Many parts of the West, moreover, including parts of Texas, resemble biblical landscapes, and their open spaces must have seemed more likely to supply the promised milk and honey than the brownstone canyons of New York or Baltimore.

Eastern cities had been places of hope and opportunity, but by the early twentieth century, when eastern European Jews rushed to the New World and Jewish neighborhoods became overcrowded and impoverished, the West provided new promises and new landscapes. "Early in February in 1907 we took the train to the Promised Land," wrote Minnie Landman of her family's arrival in Wyoming.[11] Sophie Trupin, raised on a North Dakota ranch, wrote of Jewish settlers on the Great Plains that "[e]ach was a Moses in his own right, leading his people out of the land of bondage—out of czarist Russia, out of anti-Semitic Poland, out of Roumania and Galicia." For Trupin's father, North Dakota was "a promised land free from anti-Semitism and degradation. This piece of land, rock-strewn and stubborn, was his and would be a legacy to his children."[12] In the West, the American idea of frontier met the Jewish idea of a desert promised land, and the combination was a powerful inducement to further Jewish migration.

The expectation that Texas could provide a secure and meaningful homeland ran throughout the history of Jewish settlement there. As early as 1850, Lewis A. Levy, the unofficial leader of Houston's tiny Jewish community, used Texas' growing reputation as an agricultural paradise to encourage his fellow Jews to join him. In a letter to the *Asmonean*, a Jewish paper published in New York, he argued that European Jews, suffering at the hands of despots and dictators, would have much better opportunities in America. "The amount of one year's tax where they now are," Levy claimed, "would pay for their transmigration, and then a whole continent would be open for them to settle in where they choose." Suggesting, as did others of his time, that the Jews' future lay in a return to agrarian life, Levy recommended Texas as particularly suitable for agricultural colonization. "In our own State," he wrote, "thousands of acres of land can be bought, within the settled portions of the State for the small sum of from 25 cents to $1 per acre; good arable, fertile land, where a man can make his living to his liking."[13] Levy made the availability of inexpensive land, a hallmark of frontier settlement, a selling point, but he gave his appeal a decidedly Jewish spin by then suggesting that Texas land ownership would make Jews "more independent than the Autocrat of Russia or the Emperor of Austria," both notorious anti-Semites. "Indeed," he continued, "I would not exchange my fifteen acre lot, with the house on it, and the garden around it, which I possess near the city of Houston for all thrones and hereditary dominions of both those noted persons." The future would reveal, he said, "who will have a shelter of their own 15 years from now."[14]

National Jewish spokesmen shared Levy's enthusiasm for marrying Jewish national hopes to Texas real estate. In the late 1870s, Charles Wessolowsky was an editor of the *Jewish South* who reported often on Jewish agricultural successes in the southern states, particularly in Texas, and tried to encourage support for the idea on a national level. The newspaper occasionally printed offers from Texas Jews to donate land at little or no charge to Jewish organizations seeking to colonize it.[15] During a visit to Hempstead, Texas, Wessolowsky remarked on the achievement of a handful of independent Jewish farmers there and suggested "how well it would be for some of our Jewish brethren living in those barbarous countries of Russia and Rumania to immigrate here to Texas, form Jewish colonies, [and] on this fertile soil pursue the avocation of our forefathers, [becoming] shepherds like Moses and David." Wessolowsky argued that in Texas, "where millions of uncultivated acres cry out for immigration, civilization and progress," Jews could "throw off their Russian shackles and Rumanian fetters and come here to this land of liberty and be a blessing to themselves and to this country."[16] Texas lands offered, that is, a chance for the Jewish people to re-center themselves, not through the distant promises of Zionism and eventual sovereignty, but immediately.[17]

Other early Texas Jews besides Levy took advantage of the opportunity to purchase relatively inexpensive land. For those who had lived under property restrictions in Europe, the symbolic value of land ownership was hard to resist. Texas offered in abundance precisely what Europe had denied them. Harris Kempner, for example, the patriarch of one of Galveston's most successful business families, "had great faith in Texas and in Texas lands," his son Isaac recalled. Kempner, who arrived in 1854, "came from the agricultural section of Poland and knew land was treasured there, but those in his religious and social status could not—were not permitted to—acquire it. He had great esteem for his right in this country to acquire land."[18] Holding extensive personal property in Galveston, Kempner also invested heavily in inland rural areas, a choice that paid off handsomely in the next generation as tracts in Sugar Land, near Houston, permitted the family's enormously profitable diversification into the sugar industry.[19] Other prominent Jewish landowners included Mitchell Westheimer, also the leader of a powerful business clan, who came to Texas in 1858 and purchased a 640-acre tract in what is now downtown Houston.[20] Finally, in perhaps the most impressive example, the Halff family of San Antonio came to control nearly a million acres of West Texas ranch land as well as large holdings in several other western states.[21]

Such cases of large-scale property ownership were not, however, the norm. Like Lewis Levy, most Texas Jews were merchants in urban centers. Even the Halffs kept their homes and a substantial retail business in San Antonio, traveling to their distant property only when absolutely necessary. Indeed, experience stripped of the sheen of promotion and ideology revealed that Jews were largely unprepared for the demands of Texas agrarian life. Rabbi Jacob Voorsanger of Houston, writing in the *American Israelite*, responded to Jewish press accounts of frontier life by condemning the "touching up of realities with the glow of poetry." He described the experience of three idealistic Russian immigrants he knew who had arrived in Texas hoping to make a living in farming. "[U]nder the hot sun of Texas their fortitude has given way," he wrote, "and . . . the mosquitoes have stung all their agricultural fancies out of them." The immigrants decamped to Houston to look for lighter work indoors. "It seems to me," Voorsanger mused, "that young men of sturdy frame who can not stand the midsummer sun will hardly become good farmers." Despite their sincere hopes of making a return to the land—and their impressive if impractical university educations—"these three refugees are out of work, hard-up, foot-sore and entirely undeceived as to the romance of farming." None of this was to say that Texas was not suitable territory for agricultural Judaism, Voorsanger emphasized, but only in the form of organized, well-populated colonies.[22]

Such organized efforts, however, had little more success. Attempts to promote a Jewish "return" to agriculture required that potential farmers acquire skills that had been lost to their ancestors for millennia. Eastern European Jews lived under laws that deprived them of property rights and permitted few to become farmers. In addition, the constant threat of legal persecution or physical attack strengthened feelings of kinship and community and encouraged European Jews to live near one another, in cities and towns, where they became predominantly merchants, artisans, and tradespeople. The great majority of Jews arriving in the United States with these skills remained in the large eastern cities, and even those who made their way inland tended to cluster in towns where they could practice the trades familiar to them or, as in countless cases, survive by peddling merchandise over a wide area. Generations of experience had conditioned them to urban life, and it did not occur to most that they could become farmers or should want to.

Despite these obstacles, ideologically driven Jewish leaders saw security and prosperity in a return to the land. Organizations like the Baron de Hirsch Fund, which sponsored the Jewish Agricultural and Industrial Aid Society (JAIAS), expended great energy and financial resources to make Jewish farming feasible. Between 1900 and 1933, the JAIAS provided more than $6 million in loans to Jewish farmers, which went to support more than nine thousand individual family farms.[23] The de Hirsch Fund's success at relocating immigrant Jews to the agricultural frontier was limited, however, by its administrators' desire to keep the colonists close to established centers of Jewish population. The Fund's leaders felt strongly that, although farming could be beneficial to Jewish character and self-sufficiency, agricultural efforts would fail if colonists could not also enjoy a traditional religious life, one which necessitated a close relationship with major communities. In addition to such religious concerns, many of the Fund's benefactors lived in New York and Philadelphia and wished to be able to travel conveniently to the farms and communities where their money was being spent. The Fund provided assistance to Jewish farmers in forty states and in Canada, but most went to communities in the Northeast. About 70 percent of the Fund's expenditures were made in New York State, New Jersey, and Connecticut, while just 16 percent made it across the Mississippi River.[24] Agriculture could only provide a secure Jewish future, it seemed, if it did not stray too far from established urban communities.

Texas, out on the periphery of urban Jewish consciousness, received modest support from the JAIAS, about $9,000 to support thirteen farms.[25] In addition to making payments to individual farmers, the Society briefly considered Texas as a possible site for organized colonies and sponsored a scouting expedition to report on conditions there. Researchers worked for three months on Texas farms, only to find the heat oppressive and the land dry. They recommended against any attempt to establish Jewish colonies there.[26] On one occasion, though, prompted by local leaders' willingness to oversee a colony, the Society funded a small and ultimately abortive project near Tyler, in East Texas. The Tyler Committee, a local group led by Rabbi Maurice Faber, proposed a novel way of managing distant colonies. The JAIAS was to provide the funding, while the colonists and the Tyler Committee would oversee the project and make regular reports back to the Society in New York. Leaders in both New York and Tyler saw the plan as a possible model for future colonies in more distant parts of the West, perhaps laying the foundation for a network of local committees to operate colonies in their own areas. The Society put up the money for the purchase of land and equipment, and in 1904, five Russian-Jewish families were relocated and put to work. Within the year, however, an outbreak of malaria forced them to abandon the project and to relocate to older colonies in the

East. With the collapse of its vanguard effort, the Society's plan for such agrarian networks never materialized.[27]

Anecdotal evidence shows that another colony of Russian-Jewish farmers was established in 1912 near Midline, northeast of Houston. Apparently a private effort independent of the JAIAS, a group of eastern European Jews from St. Louis bought 4,300 acres and named it the Ida Straus Subdivision in honor of the New York philanthropist who had recently perished on the *Titanic*. The leader of the project was Jacob Goodman, an Orthodox Jew who oversaw Friday deliveries of kosher food from Houston and the construction of a *shul* in which the colonists held regular services. "The San Jacinto River," a later observer reported, "was their *Mikveh*," their ritual bath. Threatened constantly by the same malaria-carrying mosquitoes that had ruined the Tyler colony, the Midline effort lasted perhaps four years until its discouraged members dispersed to various Texas cities.[28] In addition to insect plagues, the problems of organizing, funding, and maintaining a colony so far from the centers of Jewish finance and leadership remained overwhelming.

While Texas' physical distance was an obstacle to successful agricultural colonization, some planners nevertheless used its remoteness as a selling point. Whatever the hardships, the wide-open spaces of the Texas frontier were a major inducement, and the mythic scale of the Texas landscape seems to have encouraged big thinking. A 1913 report in Houston's *Jewish Herald* described a plan to do nothing less than to "acquire an expansive acreage of untilled soil and transport the entire Jewish population of Roumania—250,000 Roumanians—from their native country into the heart of Texas, the largest State in the American Union." As Herman Loeb, director of the Philadelphia Department of Supplies and the plan's instigator, described it, such an arrangement would not only save the lives of Roumania's Jews but also would provide needed workers to bring the remaining American frontier under the plow. "Our country is in dire need of development," he claimed, and food prices remained high "due in large measure to the fact that thousands of acres of land are allowed to remain idle and do not produce anything." The arrival of a quarter of a million hard-working immigrants to till unused land would be a "blessing for Texas, whose surface has scarcely been scratched by the plow of the husbandman."[29]

Texas Jews confirmed the availability of uncultivated land and the opportunities it could provide. A supporter from San Antonio told Loeb of "the notable success of the people who have settled in Texas" and of "the acres of workable land waiting to be developed . . . the vastness of the State and the opportunity almost at hand." A recent sale of Texas lands for as little as $15 an acre proved to Loeb "that there must be plenty of vacant acreage in that State."[30] The Roumanian plan, like the agrarian colonies that preceded it, never came to fruition, although it is fascinating to consider the implications if it had. It would have brought an influx of immigrants to Texas equivalent to 6 percent of the state's total population at that time, increased the number of Texas Jews more than fifteen-fold, and radically altered the history of the state and, indeed, of the Jewish world. Despite its failure, the plan's ambitiousness highlighted the prevailing belief that Texas could become a kind of promised land for the Jewish people and that they, in return, would indeed be a blessing to Texas, where there was land "waiting to be developed." The two were seen as a perfect fit: Texas was good for the Jews, and the Jews were good for Texas.

Center and Periphery: The Galveston Movement

Such optimism about faraway Texas was hardly universal, and proposals like the Roumanian plan ran counter to the Zionist argument that the only long-term solution to Europe's "Jewish question" was a sovereign Jewish state. In the latter view, American communities like Texas were inferior, marginal, and temporary, and thus it is no surprise that few native Texas Jews considered themselves Zionists. Eastern European immigrants, who were much more likely to be Zionists, began arriving in their greatest numbers in New York and other northeastern cities around 1880, but they took a generation to filter into outlying areas dominated by Reform Jews of German background until well into the twentieth century. However, when eastern European immigrants steeped in Orthodox Judaism, Zionism, and the Yiddish language arrived in great enough numbers to have an impact, they brought a radically different religious and social vision to communities in Texas and throughout the South and West. Zionism challenged its American adherents to identify themselves with a nation yet undeclared rather than with the nation that had already welcomed them, emphasizing Jewish distinctiveness and nationalism rather than acculturation into American communities. This view was greeted coldly in most parts of the country, especially where the work of community-building was recent and where Reform Judaism was strongest.

The ideologies of Zionism and non-Zionism dramatically collided in Texas in an early twentieth-century effort to divert the flow of European Jewish immigration from New York to Galveston. Between 1907 and 1914, the coastal Texas city served as the portal through which some ten thousand hand-selected eastern European Jews entered the United States and dispersed throughout the Midwest and West. More than simply a port of entry, the city provided a name for the entire program, which organizers variously described as the Galveston Plan, the Galveston Project, and the Galveston Immigration Movement. New Yorker Jacob Schiff, the project's founder and financier, as well as one of the nation's wealthiest and most influential Jews, went so far as to describe the entire Trans-Mississippi West as "the Galveston Territory."[31]

The Galveston Movement presented a new strategy for relocating immigrants to the American hinterland. Schiff established a network of European offices, headquartered in Kiev, to recruit likely immigrants and promote the idea of entering the United States farther west than New York. Eventually working with local communal organizations, his staff tried to match individual immigrants to destination communities in need of their particular skills. Organizers could then facilitate immigrants' travel from their hometowns to Bremen, Germany, by sea to Galveston, and on by rail to their selected destinations. Although American law prohibited paying the immigrants' expenses or encouraging them to make the initial decision to immigrate, Schiff spent hundreds of thousands of his own dollars easing their passage into middle America.

Schiff's main purpose was to rescue the persecuted Jews of Russia, where pogroms and legal restrictions on residence and work were making life miserable and dangerous. According to his biographer, Cyrus Adler, Schiff worried that conditions in Russia "denied to Jews . . . the opportunity to settle upon the soil [and] crowded them into a small section of that vast Empire where they were almost obliged to live upon one another."[32] The United States offered equally vast and open spaces in which Russian Jews could live with greater freedom, mobility, and economic opportunity, but the doors of immigration had to remain open to them. Schiff and his associates feared that the visible crowding of immigrants into urban ghettos would lead American officials to close those doors. Clusters of poor, unacculturated, and often politically radical immigrants in American cities could foster anti-Semitism and lead to restrictions on Jewish immigration.[33]

On the whole, Americans had accepted the great waves of eastern European immigrants that began arriving after 1880, and Schiff himself wrote that "[w]e certainly cannot complain that our Gentile neighbors and fellow-citizens in New York or the other large seaport towns have been intolerant." Still, he worried that ever-greater numbers of immigrants arriving in northeastern cities would eventually lead to greater hostility toward all

Jacob Schiff. Jacob Rader Marcus Center of the American Jewish Archives, PC-3993.

Jews. "[C]onditions in New York and, no doubt, elsewhere," he wrote, "are gradually working up to a point where the Gentile population may begin to feel that it should agitate against [continued Jewish immigration], and I am impressed that we must not permit conditions to reach such a point."[34] In Schiff's view, anti-Semitism and immigration restriction would inevitably result from concentrated Jewish populations. Therefore, rescuing Russian Jewry required distributing immigrants throughout the United States so that they could blend into the population and contribute to as many of the nation's developing cities as possible. Schiff expected that immigrants would help build communities in the American hinterland because they would have "the pioneer spirit."[35] Finally, Schiff was concerned about the personal cost to himself and other New York Jews who, because of their city's popularity as an immigrant destination, found that they had to "care for almost 75% of all the immigrants who come to the United States."[36] Schiff wished to distribute the financial burden more equitably among America's Jews by distributing the immigrants themselves.

Still more important to Schiff, the dispersion of immigrants would challenge radical movements of the day that sought to strengthen the centers of Jewish identity. These centers could be geographical, as in the case of Zionism and Territorialism, which both sought to secure a Jewish homeland; ideological, as in the socialist labor movement called Bundism; or cultural, as in the Yiddishist Movement, which pursued the restoration of eastern European Jewish language and culture in the Diaspora.[37] By distributing the immigrants as widely as possible, to as many destinations as possible, Schiff planned to discourage the growth of Jewish ghettos, to prevent the creation of new ones, and thus to deprive these movements of the populations of poor and easily radicalized immigrants on which they thrived. Schiff was explicit in his opposition to Jewish radicalism, especially political Zionism, and wished to encourage accommodation to American practices. "[T]he Jew must maintain his own identity," he wrote, "not *apart* in any autonomous body but *among* the nations."[38]

Schiff favored an approach that would deliberately put immigrants out of reach of Jewish facilities and so discourage traditional religious practice, and he directed his agents in Europe to recruit immigrants who were willing to forgo the daily practices of traditional Judaism, who expressed a willingness to work on Saturdays, and who committed themselves to complete Americanization.[39] Israel Zangwill, a prominent Anglo-Jewish playwright and one of Schiff's most important colleagues in the Galveston Movement, objected that such requirements would lead to "euthanasia of the race and religion." Schiff agreed to relax them, but his goal remained to decentralize Judaism geographically and spiritually, to separate the immigrants not only from Jewish population centers but also from traditional Jewish self-identification.[40] Zionism and the other radical proposals of the time, he believed, offered little but the opportunity to manufacture new material and spiritual ghettos.

While it suited his ideological ends perfectly, Schiff was not the first to work on dispersing Jewish immigrants throughout the American West. In 1901, the Industrial Removal Office (IRO) had initiated a program to relocate Jews from New York to smaller communities across the country. With help from B'nai B'rith, then under the national leadership of former Galvestonian Leo N. Levi, the IRO recruited a network of agents in western towns to supply the organization with information about local job openings. IRO staff located Jewish workers in eastern cities who possessed the needed skills and gave them and their families financial assistance to move to the new town. The IRO hoped to create Jewish populations in the nation's interior that would be substantial enough to draw subsequent immigrants away from the eastern centers and into the underdeveloped heartland.[41]

Jacob Schiff had long supported the IRO in its effort to move Jews out of New York, but he saw a difficulty in convincing people who were already settled in Jewish neighborhoods to uproot themselves and relocate to the West. "After immigrants have once been landed at New York, Boston, Philadelphia, or Baltimore," he explained, "they generally prefer to remain there, and notwithstanding all the efforts of the established removal offices, only a comparatively small number leave these centers." Schiff proposed to divert the flow of immigration so that immigrants would never discover the temptations of New York. Instead, they would arrive farther west, in "the great American 'Hinterland,' where a constant demand for labor of all kind exists." The outlines of the plan were relatively simple. "What I have in mind," Schiff wrote, is "a project through which it shall become possible to direct the flow of emigration from Russia to the Gulf ports of the United States . . . from where immigrants can readily be distributed over the interior of the country, I am quite certain, in very large numbers." From the Gulf, "railroad lines diverge to the Pacific Coast, to the North and Northwest, as well as to the South and Southwest, which provide easy and cheap transportation to these sections."[42] Through existing IRO channels, organizers could match immigrants with destinations on the basis of needed skills or occupations. Schiff pledged half a million dollars of his own funds to the plan, which would, he hoped, "suffice to place from 20,000 to 25,000 people in the American 'Hinterland.'" With these settlers in place, chain migration would follow, and "a steady stream of immigration will flow through New Orleans and Galveston into the [western] territory."[43]

Whereas agricultural colonization schemes had sought rural locales for the immigrants they sponsored, Schiff's design placed immigrants in urban settings where jobs and Jewish neighbors awaited them, thus creating a core Jewish presence to enhance far-flung communities. Texas' distance from the Jewish communities of the eastern seaboard had made it unappealing to agricultural colonizers. Schiff, however, wanted to spread eastern European Jews over as broad a territory as possible, and so Texas' peripherality made it essential to his plans.

Schiff chose Galveston as the port of entry for a number of practical reasons. As the goal was to move immigrants into the Trans-Mississippi West, it made little sense to direct them to an East Coast port. Schiff assigned Morris Waldman, a rabbi and manager at the IRO in New York, to scout out a suitable entry point, and as he observed pointedly, "New Orleans or Galveston is nearer Nevada."[44] Eastern cities, including Baltimore and Philadelphia, already had crowded Jewish neighborhoods where immigrants might be inclined to stay, and Schiff and Waldman were both concerned about the prohibitive cost of cross-country transport from southeastern ports like Charleston.[45] To bring immigrants into the country at a point as far west as possible plainly seemed the wisest course.

West Coast ports were impracticable because the Panama Canal was underway but incomplete, so Schiff looked to the Gulf of Mexico. Initially considering New Orleans, he soon concluded that Galveston, which offered similar rail connections to all parts of the country, would be a better choice as it also received regular passenger service from Bremen, Germany, on the North German Lloyd Line. Finally, Galveston's decisive advantage over New Orleans was that, being smaller and less appealing, immigrants would prefer to take their chances in the cities pre-selected for them. Galveston was connected enough to meet the plan's practical needs, yet too peripheral to become another Jewish ghetto.

As his plan took shape, Schiff was busy locating assistance and resources. To run the European end of the project, he enlisted Israel Zangwill of the Jewish Territorial Organization (ITO). The ITO had offices in London and Kiev dedicated to securing an autonomous Jewish state somewhere in the world exclusive of Palestine, which Zangwill believed was too firmly in Arab hands to be viable. Although Schiff's plan to disperse Russia's Jews throughout the United States clearly ran counter to the ITO's mission, he nevertheless convinced Zangwill to join his Galveston effort, pointing out that unlike Zangwill's abstract long-term hopes, Schiff's project was an "immediately practicable" response to the "existing emergency" in Russia.[46] The ITO was to work with the German *Hilfsverein der deutschen Juden* (Aid Society for German Jews), which facilitated the emigration of German Jews, "to father the movement in Russia, to gather the proposed emigrants [in Germany], to arrange steamship routes, etc." Schiff assured Zangwill that his American colleagues would see to the immigrants' needs once they arrived in Galveston.[47]

To that end, Schiff directed the establishment in Galveston of the Jewish Immigrants' Information Bureau (JIIB) and assigned Morris Waldman, the New York IRO manager, to run it. Waldman arrived in Texas in the fall of 1906 with a letter of introduction from Schiff to Rabbi Henry Cohen, a childhood friend of Israel Zangwill. Cohen eagerly agreed to work closely with the JIIB, serve as its liaison to Galveston Jewry, meet the arriving immigrants, and see personally to their welfare while in his city.[48] A lifelong opponent of Zionism, Cohen shared Schiff's commitment to dispersing immigrants broadly over the nation's interior. "[T]his country could," he wrote, "without the least violence to itself, assimilate the world's Jewish

Henry Cohen with immigrants from the *SS Cassel*, July 1, 1907. UTSA's Institute of Texan Cultures, No. 073–0939. Courtesy of Mrs. Joseph Levy.

population and then have room for three times that number, exclusive of the regular quota of other foreign settlers."[49]

Henry Cohen met the first boat, the SS *Cassel*, at the Galveston pier on July 1, 1907. The ship delivered sixty Jewish immigrants for the Bureau to guide through the entry process and send on their way to inland cities. That was to be a complex task, as Cohen later described. After passing the government's medical and customs inspections, immigrants and their baggage were transported in wagons to the JIIB office half a mile away. There they were treated to a flurry of activity:

Then the distribution of mail long looked for by the aliens, the refreshing bath and the wholesome and generous meal; the facilities for writing home and for reading Yiddish papers published since the passengers' embarkation; the questioning of the individuals and the inspection of the consignee's record by the office management; the selection of localities according to the requisitions of the interior agents, and the purchasing of railroad tickets; and then, supper; the apportionment of food sufficient to last each immigrant for the whole up-country journey and a little longer; then the baggage wagons for the neighboring depot, and the departure from the bureau of those who are to leave on the night trains, the checking of baggage to destinations, and the leave-taking from one another after a month's constant companionship often pathetic; the comfortable placing of the travelers in the railroad coaches by the bureau's employees, then telegrams to the interior committees notifying them of the departure of their allotment, so that the latter should be met at the station; the retiring of the remainder to bed (what a change from the steerage bunks!) to leave on the morrow or thereafter, according to circumstances—all this and more must be seen to be realised.[50]

Throughout this cumbersome process, repeated dozens of times, Cohen served as interpreter, facilitator, and chief comforter to the immigrants, many of whom were disoriented and frightened. Alexander Gurwitz, who arrived from Russia in 1910 on his way to San Antonio, remembered Cohen as one of the few high points of an otherwise grueling voyage. Gurwitz observed "that he was equally considerate of all the immigrants, with gently reassuring words," and Cohen's offer of the opportunity to eat in a kosher restaurant made the devoutly Orthodox immigrant deeply grateful. Ensuring that they were comfortably fed and lodged, Cohen "was as a compassionate father to all of the poor, lonely immigrants."[51] Cohen's colleague, Rabbi Henry Barnstein (later Barnston) of Houston, noted that Cohen was largely responsible for the success of the Galveston Movement at the Texas end. "He was always at the beck and call of the immigrant," Barnstein told the American Israelite, "ever ready to plead his cause and fight his battles, always on hand to soothe, advise, encourage and welcome."[52] Years after their departure from Galveston, many immigrants wrote to Cohen to thank him for his help during their first days in America.

As Jewish immigrants began arriving in their city, gentile Galvestonians reacted with warmth and hospitality. Mayor H. A. Landes was on the dock to greet the Cassel and the first group of Schiff's immigrants, asking Henry Cohen to translate into Yiddish his personal welcome to Galveston and to America. One immigrant, in a response frequently recounted in support of the Galveston Movement, stepped forward and thanked the mayor in Yiddish, which Cohen translated. "We are overwhelmed," he said, "that the ruler of the city should greet us. We have never been spoken to by the

Rabbi Henry Cohen at the Galveston docks with a group of newly arrived immigrants, 1907. Jacob Rader Marcus Center of the American Jewish Archives, MS-263 2/2.

officials of our country except in terms of harshness, and although we have heard of the great land of freedom, it is very hard to realize that we are permitted to grasp the hand of the great man." He then promised, on behalf of the entire group, that they would try to be good citizens.[53]

The immigrants' apparent willingness to enter fully into American life, to claim the United States as their home, almost certainly helped win the support of gentile newspaper editors, who were, Cohen said, "vying with one another in their enthusiasm" for the Movement.[54] Texas newspaper editors saw direct European immigration as a boon to the state, and they found the immigrants acceptable, even desirable, new Texans. In its report on the *Cassel's* arrival, the *Galveston Times* noted that the immigrants were "an intelligent, hard working class of people, who hope by hard work and a law abiding life to found homes in our country where they can live happily."[55] A year later, the *Houston Post* offered its support, observing that Jews were an "industrious and law-abiding population" who were welcome in a growing state. At the same time, the *Post* claimed that Texas had much to offer the immigrants: "Texas has room within her borders for all the Israelites in the world, and then some," the editor wrote.[56]

Many Jewish Texans also recognized the potential economic benefits of the influx and offered their support to the Movement. While directing his family's interests in cotton and other investments, for example, Isaac Kempner also served as Galveston city treasurer, helping to rebuild the island after the 1900 hurricane that nearly destroyed it, and was later elected mayor. Like his father, Harris, he knew that private business success depended upon the city's general prosperity, and he worked throughout his life on behalf of both. Kempner understood that increased traffic through the Port of Galveston would not only generate more customers for the city's businesses but would also promote permanent population growth. His extensive involvement in Galveston's network of civic and social organizations made Kempner a powerful ally and an effective fundraiser for the Movement's local operation.

Other Texas Jews supported the Movement for the same ideological reasons that motivated Jacob Schiff, as a way of challenging the Zionist impulse. They feared that Zionism threatened the progress Jews had made in the United States and the opportunities for growth that still existed in smaller American communities. In a typical statement titled "Come to Texas," *Jewish Herald* editorialist Oscar Leonard outlined the argument in favor of the Galveston Movement. Leonard, the superintendent of the Jewish Educational and Charitable Association in St. Louis, recommended Texas as a more suitable site for Jewish development than Palestine. "The crowding of many Jewish families in one small space like the New York East Side," Leonard wrote, "brings a problem with it. What then is the remedy?" Zionists, Leonard explained, recommended colonization in Palestine, but "why not in the large state of Texas where the soil goes a begging for cultivators?" He acknowledged that many Jews would prefer not to be farmers, but "this is not a sufficient reason why they should be crowded into ugly, unwholesome tenements in large cities" when a state like Texas, with a wealth of smaller towns, waited "for willing hands and alert minds to help it devel-op."[57] Similarly, a 1912 *Herald* editorial argued that the Galveston Move-ment "points the way to a sane and just settlement of the vexed question of Jewish immigration" by sending immigrants into "the great regions of the South and West [where there] are many communities, and more will spring up, that need the pushful energy of the Jew."[58] Once again, non-Zionists marshaled rhetoric about Texas' benefits to demonstrate that continued dispersion, rather than the collection of population in Jewish centers, was the answer to Jewish hopes.

Despite its advocates, the Galveston Movement was not universally sup-ported by Texas Jews, though few quibbled with its ideology or goals. Isaac Kempner observed that Texas Jews in general expressed a "lack of deep interest in . . . national Jewish charities," an insularity and parochialism that made it hard for him to obtain their support for the Movement or for other national and international Jewish causes.[59] Many Texas Jews feared that they might become responsible for the support of immigrants who could not or would not find work. Schiff had promised Henry Cohen that the JIIB would do its best to limit the Galveston program only to those "sturdy" im-migrants who were "capable of becoming promptly self-supporting," but as the boats continued arriving and rumors spread of immigrants reaching their destinations without the promised skills, questions began to arise.[60] If immigrants were unemployable, a Waco merchant warned Cohen, "the hardship will fall on Galveston and on all Jewish Texans."[61]

Galveston Jews, who would carry the heaviest burden if the JIIB depos-ited unemployable immigrants on their doorsteps, were especially suspi-cious of Schiff's plans and insisted on assurances that Galveston would not become another Jewish ghetto. Needing their support, Schiff stressed that the JIIB's primary goal was to pass the immigrants through the port, onto the railroads, and to their designated out-of-state destinations as swiftly as possible. Indeed, when enlisting Cohen's help, Schiff was careful to explain that "it is not intended to permit arriving immigrants to remain in the sea-port towns, but to promptly send them on to their destination to the North and West of the Gulf ports."[62] Galveston was to remain a port of entry only, not a destination.

To this end, Morris Waldman of the JIIB in Galveston and his colleague David Bressler, a longtime civic activist who headed the Movement's office in New York, urged ITO recruiters in Russia to downplay Galveston and even Texas as desirable destinations. In the first months of the program, Bressler asked Zangwill "not to emphasize Texas and especially Galveston, in fact to say that Galveston offers no opportunity for the immigrant."[63] Morris Waldman also wrote to Zangwill to explain that "[Texas] cities and the whole state of Texas offer only limited opportunities for a small minority of our people." Because opportunities were greater in other states, Zangwill's groups should "say that Galveston is being used by us *only as a port of entry*, that none of the immigrants will remain here."[64] Indeed, all of the immigrants from the first two boats to arrive in Galveston went directly through Texas to other states, and in the course of the program fewer than three hundred of the ten thousand immigrants remained in Galveston. Most of those were either reuniting with family who already lived there or had sought the JIIB's help after traveling to Galveston on their own.[65]

Notwithstanding the concerns of their Galveston brethren, Jews in other Texas cities recognized the Galveston Movement as an opportunity to augment their numbers and to bring a needed infusion of new blood into their communities, and they did not wish to be left out. Civic leaders in Texas pressed the JIIB to send them their fair share of the immigrants, and the Bureau relented. Only a month after telling Zangwill "not to emphasize Texas and especially Galveston," David Bressler wrote again to say that the office had "added several cities in the State of Texas" to its list of available destinations and that "while we wish special stress laid on the fact that Galveston itself offers no opportunity for the immigrant, the State of Texas is otherwise not barren of opportunities for the newcomer."[66]

Once admitted to the plan, Texas became a popular destination, retaining more of the Galveston immigrants than any other state. According to a 1913 report (produced before statistics were available for 1914, the Movement's final year), organizers had overseen the relocation of 2,144 people in Texas—fully 25 percent of the program's total.[67] Most of these were direct placements to 56 communities, which received anywhere from 1 to 182 immigrants each. Houston, Dallas, and Fort Worth received the greatest number. In addition, the JIIB provided support for hundreds of "courtesy" and "reunion" cases, individuals traveling to Texas either on their own, outside the ITO's recruitment efforts, or to reunite with family members already in Texas. These additions not only swelled the numbers of the largest communities but also took Jews to tiny towns that organizers had not originally contemplated. These included Eagle Lake, a southeast Texas rice-growing center; Humble, a boomtown after the 1904 discovery of one of the state's largest oil fields; and Pecos, a far West Texas desert community of fewer than two thousand residents.[68]

In 1914 Jacob Schiff called a sudden halt to the Galveston Movement's operations and discontinued its funding. Logistical and political problems within and outside the organization had plagued it from the beginning, and Schiff finally wearied of the effort. His colleagues in Europe and the United States had struggled throughout the Movement's existence to quash rumors, spread in part by Zionists and Jewish socialists in Russia and New York, that the Galveston immigrants were to be put to work as forced laborers or prostitutes, charges that visibly dampened potential immigrants' enthusiasm.[69] U.S. law, which prohibited encouragement of immigration, also presented an intractable challenge. Schiff and his colleagues had scrupulously assisted only those immigrants who traveled of their own volition, offering Galveston only as an alternate destination for those who were already planning to emigrate. Federal customs officials, however, presumed that the JIIB provided critical inducements to European immigrants who might have stayed home otherwise, leading those at the Galveston entry point to apply the strictest possible standards to the incoming immigrants and to send an unusually high number of them back to Europe.[70] Between 1907 and 1913, for example, Galveston customs officials deported more than four times the number of female Jewish immigrants than did their colleagues in New York, claiming that the women were "morally defective."[71] In the end, the advent of World War I, which resulted in harsh federal restrictions on passenger travel and limited all transatlantic shipping, dealt a final blow to the Galveston Movement.

Zionism in God's Other Country

In its seven years of operation, the Galveston Movement placed some ten thousand Russian Jews into more than two hundred communities across the nation, primarily in the West and Midwest. As Schiff had hoped, their presence attracted other Jewish immigrants to those regions. On the whole, however, the results were disappointing to Schiff and his planners. The number of immigrants arriving through Texas never constituted even 4 percent of the total Jewish immigration to the United States in the years of the Galveston operation, utterly failing to meet Schiff's goal of redirecting the entire stream of Jewish immigration into the West.[72] Schiff offered several explanations for the failure, focusing especially on the length and hardship of the Galveston voyage and the stringent and inconsistent enforcement of U.S. immigration laws. But Bernard Marinbach, author of the definitive history of the Galveston Movement, suggests a deeper problem "of which Schiff was, perhaps, unaware." Despite the philanthropist's best efforts to promote the American hinterland as a suitable place for Jewish settlement, his own recruiting reminded potential immigrants of the hardships they would face there. By ordering his staff to give preference to "young, skilled, able-bodied men who were willing to work at anything, and even on the Sabbath," Schiff helped "to foster the popular impression that the 'Galveston Territory' was a spiritual wasteland which promised little but a hard life." Marinbach argues that the Galveston Movement proved that "the masses would always be attracted to New York and other well-established centers of Jewish life in the United States."[73] The relatively small number of Jewish immigrants who found the kind of opportunities that the Movement's advocates offered bears out this interpretation. Whatever golden promises the Movement made, the impression remained strong that a hinterland, however free, secure, and lucrative, was no place for a dedicated Jew to live.

The irony is that Texas supporters of the Galveston Movement, hoping to enhance the state's appeal, emphasized the very frontier qualities that, in hindsight, were detrimental to the plan's success. Texas offered distance from urban centers and the relative freedom that came with it. Texas also offered economic opportunity in a smaller, less competitive setting than New York or other eastern cities. In Texas, one had a chance to distinguish oneself from Jews at the center, to adapt to a different environment, or to become a different kind of Jewish American than those in larger communities. Not all the immigrants wanted these things, however. For those seeking a rich Jewish life, facilities in the West remained woefully inadequate. For them, Texas could never be a true Jewish homeland.

Traditional Jews who settled in Texas through the Galveston Movement often felt embattled in their religious practice, and most never lost their passion for Zionism despite all that Schiff had done to bring them to America. Alexander Gurwitz, a 1910 Galveston immigrant, commented in his memoir on Texas' advantages and disadvantages for the religious immigrant. "The lot of our people brings us far more changes in our state of being than other peoples," he wrote. "This is largely because our Jewish people is not rooted in a firm place of our own. We do not have a country of our own, with our own government, as other nations do." Gurwitz counted himself lucky to live "under a democratic government, which does not distinguish between Jews and non-Jews," but ultimately Texas, although it had provided a good home, could never be a homeland. "[T]he newcomers did not come here seeking Judaism," he observed. "That they had in their old home. They came to seek a livelihood." Yet, the more they worked toward

Texas Zionist Organization convention in Houston. *Houston Post*, January 4, 1911.
Photo courtesy of Hollace Ava Weiner, Clayton Library Friends, and
the Harris County Archives, Houston, Texas.

economic security, the more they sacrificed Jewish tradition: "neglect of
the sanctity of the Sabbath and Festivals, gradual ignoring of sacred Jewish
laws and customs, dereliction in providing a decent Jewish education for
children."[74]

When Gurwitz arrived, the Zionist movement forming in Texas was
aimed at exactly these kinds of identity issues rather than at the actual creation of a Jewish state. The flourishing Texas Zionist Organization (TZO),
founded in Houston in 1905 in the wake of Jacob de Haas' visit, reported
nearly one thousand members statewide by the end of its first year, a significant achievement in a state with just sixteen thousand Jews. Local groups—
TZO chapters and often also chapters of Hadassah, the Zionist women's
organization—appeared in all of the state's big cities and many smaller
towns. By 1911 Zionists had established ten Hebrew schools in seven cities
with student bodies ranging from 35 to 120 students.

Zionist leaders promoted the movement as a means of preserving Jewish identity both at home and worldwide. "There can be no true Jewish
culture and advancement without a Jewish land," stated TZO president
Louis Freed at a 1910 state meeting. "Only then will they feel a pride in
their language, traditions, history."[75] On this basis, too, the movement won

significant support from gentile leaders who recognized the importance of cultural preservation—if not the complex political goal of attaining Jewish national autonomy. Mayors and governors greeted TZO convention delegates, and in 1912 the TZO held its annual meeting in the chamber of the Texas State Senate, adorned for the occasion with the blue-and-white flags of the Zionist cause.

Great Britain's issuance of the Balfour Declaration in 1917 immediately altered the nature and purpose of Zionism worldwide, including in Texas. The Declaration promised England's support for the establishment of a Jewish state should the Allies claim Palestine from the Turks in World War I. Alexander Gurwitz welcomed the news as a "mystical balm" that "quickened the spirit of Jewry." Suddenly, he wrote, "there was the feeling that the long yearned for end to Jewish dispersion had begun" and that the Jews "were about to be re-settled in their own land, in the Fatherland called 'Eretz Yisrael,' the Land of Israel."[76] Although he lived in Texas, Gurwitz always looked beyond America, toward a Jewish future elsewhere. This sentiment was probably shared by hundreds of Jewish immigrants who made up the greater part of the membership of Texas Zionist groups.

For most Texas Zionists, however, the Balfour Declaration signaled not an imminent return to the biblical homeland, but a shift in the goals of their local organizations. With the prospect of a Jewish state made palpable overnight, activists stepped up their support of the cause and strengthened their local links to the international movement. Prominent Zionist leaders such as Vladimir Jabotinsky, Henrietta Szold, Chaim Weizmann, and David Ben-Gurion visited Texas cities as part of American lecture tours, and local affiliates sponsored a variety of dances, picnics, and other festivities to help raise the needed funds. As historian Stuart Rockoff observes, however, such events had less to do with establishing a national Jewish home than with achieving "the other central goal of the movement in Texas, the strengthening of local Jewish life." These events helped the state's tiny Jewish population "create a uniquely Jewish world that could withstand pressures of assimilation. . . . For many Texas Jews, Zionism was a means to ensure the survival of Judaism in the Lone Star State."[77]

As Texas Zionists became more active, however, many other Jewish Texans maintained the belief that Zionism, especially in this newly practical form, ran counter to Americanism and to the proper development of local communities. Religious leaders such as Rabbi Henry Barnstein of Houston, who was an early supporter of the TZO and its initial community programs, turned against the movement after the Balfour Declaration. A

Galveston observer remembered seeing Henry Cohen in 1917, fifty-four years old, just over five feet tall, clambering to the roof of the city's YMCA building to tear down the Zionist flag flying there in honor of the Declaration.[78] On another occasion, Mayor Isaac Kempner refused to permit the Star of David to fly over City Hall to mark "some celebration in Palestine." "I took the position," he remembered, "that only the Texas flag and the flag of the United States had flown or should be flown from our City Hall."[79] These acts of defiance were small but symbolic. Cohen and Kempner remained steadfast non-Zionists throughout their lives, and anti-Zionist sentiment remained strong among many Texas Jews well into the 1940s. However, the tide was turning. Kempner lost his bid for reelection in 1919 and claimed later, though perhaps facetiously, that "[i]f there is such a thing as an orthodox Jewish vote, it was in this election effectively invoked against me and contributed to defeating my aspiration."[80] For some Texas Jews, especially those of central European background like Cohen and Kempner, Texas itself was an acceptable, even preferable, Zion.

The conflict over Zionism was, of course, an international phenomenon, hardly restricted to Texas. Nor were Texans the only American Jews to imagine their home in exile as a Promised Land. In Texas, however, more than in most American places, the promise of Zionism collided with a frontier heritage that resonated long after the frontier itself had vanished. As diasporic Jews, Jewish Texans could not help but be aware of themselves as a peripheral community, far from both the American and global centers of Jewish history and culture. But as Texans, as frontier people, their main concern was with building an enduring home in the wilderness where they found themselves. Texas Zionists and non-Zionists differed only on the most effective way to do so. This emerging conflict over Zionism provided an impetus for Jews to define themselves in new ways, along lines of national rather than religious identity, even if there was little agreement about what exactly these new definitions should be.

✴

FOUR

Texas News for Texas Jews

In March 1910 a sixty-eight-year-old African American named Allen Brooks was standing trial in the Dallas County Courthouse when about two hundred whites stormed the court, overwhelming the seventy armed policemen and sheriff's deputies who tried to stop them. They seized the defendant, tied a rope around his neck, and hurled him from the courtroom's second-story window. As a crowd of more than two thousand people looked on, the mob dragged Brooks through the street, beating him viciously, tearing most of the clothes from his body, and almost certainly killing him. Then, at the downtown intersection of Main and Akard, in the middle of the day and in full public view, as lunchtime customers of the Palace Drug Store peered out through the windows, the mob passed the end of the rope over a lamppost and hoisted Brooks' body until it dangled about four feet over the street. Before the police arrived to cut the body down and take it to a hospital, the crowd had stripped the last of Brooks' clothing for souvenirs.[1] The next day, the *Dallas Morning News* insisted that the mob was moved not by "a lust for bloodshed nor by a desire to witness the torture of a fiend," but by "their contempt for the delays, reversals and failures of the courts."[2] Brooks' trial had only begun that day, a little more than one week from the date of his arrest.

Later that month, Houston's *Jewish Herald* ran a brief comment about the controversy generated by the event. "Murder, yes, lynching," wrote Edgar

Goldberg, the paper's founding editor, "is a crime to be condemned in the most stringent manner, and nothing, absolutely nothing, can be said in its defense."[3] Although it may seem natural that Goldberg commented on the exceptionally brutal attack, it was actually unusual for him to cover events, however momentous, that did not have a clear Jewish relevance.[4] The key to the item's appearance in the *Jewish Herald* is in the remainder of Goldberg's statement, in which he moderates his initial outrage. Although the story had no significance for his readers as Jews, it was a welcome opportunity for Goldberg to appeal to them as Southerners. Noting that "[t]he press from all over the country" was "commenting unfavorably upon the actions of some of the citizens of Dallas of recent date," Goldberg offered an apologist statement that could have come from many southern papers of the day. Seeking to explain the mob's anger toward Brooks, who was accused of assaulting the three-year-old daughter of his white employer, Goldberg explained that "[t]he sanctity of the home to our Southern citizens . . . is superior to the law" and that "[t]he people make the laws and the people can suspend the laws." In any case, he claimed, lynchings occurred in the North at least as frequently as in the South. "Each section has conditions to contend with that can not be governed to suit the like or dislike of the other section," he wrote. "The South is well able to take care of its own notwithstanding the comments of our Northern contemporaries."[5]

Unlike many Jewish editors of the time, Goldberg was not a rabbi. Managing the *Herald* was his profession and his sole livelihood—the paper was his "Pet Baby"—and he spared no effort to build its readership.[6] In this case, as in many others in his career, Goldberg sought readership by finessing the evolving frontiers that described Houston's Jews, defining his readers as heirs of a shared southern experience, and selecting his news coverage and editorial positions accordingly. As Texas modernized and its Jewish population became more urban, the frontier that had prevailed in the nineteenth century gave way to a new set of conditions more open to interpretation and even to manipulation. Goldberg built his career on his ability to tell Jewish Texans who and what they were and, at least as critically, who and what they were not.

Even as this Jewish community was growing rapidly and becoming increasingly integrated with Jews throughout the nation and the world, Goldberg emphasized Houston as a southern city, Texas as a southern state, and Texas Jews as distinct from other American Jews. Jewish journals of national circulation, particularly the *American Israelite* of Cincinnati and a variety of New York publications, offered a national perspective, often in-

cluding local news items from across the country, but Goldberg emphasized the particularly southern identity of his Texas readers and skewed his
coverage of state, national, and even international events accordingly. His
perception that he and his readers were native Southerners who shared a
core regional identification set the tone of the *Herald*'s early years, and his
success at keeping the paper alive for three decades until his death suggests
that he had gauged his readers' feelings correctly.

Goldberg clearly imagined his readers as acculturated Americans, although immigrants in Houston almost certainly read and subscribed to
the paper. The *Herald* published exclusively in English, except for the occasional transliterated Hebrew liturgical term, and the issue of immigration
was treated solely from the native point of view. A number of articles, for
instance, paternalistically described the experience of immigrants, identified as "The Other Half," and admonished readers not to mock the immigrants' accents. In another item, he explained that a Yiddish-language event
in Houston was well attended because the audience "wanted to listen to the
language of their childhood."[7] The *Herald*'s readers, that is, may not have
been born in America, but Goldberg assumed that they had accommodated
to the regional distinctions that had been so much a part of American history. He ran, on balance, far more national and international Jewish items
than distinctly southern or Texan ones—finding content to fill his pages
was always a challenge, and reprints from other papers were a staple—but
in covering Texas news a southern perspective strongly prevailed. Thus,
in 1909 he reprinted an article titled "The Southland" that celebrated the
myths of the Old South and the Lost Cause without a single mention of
Judaism, and the next year he ran a story on Jewish statesmanship that included a lengthy account of Judah P. Benjamin, a South Carolinian and
Louisiana senator who had held several cabinet posts in the Confederate
government.[8]

Goldberg's hyperbolic regionalism sometimes approached chauvinism.
In one notable instance, which will receive extensive treatment below, he
challenged the presumption of New York Jewish leaders (whom he disparaged as a "syndicate") to speak on behalf of American Jewry as a whole and
of southern Jews in particular.[9] To be sure, suspicion of New York's leading
role within American Jewry was common enough in Jewish communities
throughout the country, but Goldberg's inflated regional rhetoric was singular. In making an appeal to his readers' southern identity, Goldberg emphasized continually that Texas Jews were *not* New Yorkers, nor were they
Northerners or Easterners (terms he tended to use interchangeably), and he

presented the *Herald* explicitly as an alternative to the national Jewish press. "The Jews of Texas are interested in Texas just a little bit more than they are in Ohio or New York," he wrote in one early statement. "Matters of interest to the Jews of Texas can be more thoroughly disseminated through the columns of the *Jewish Herald* than any other medium."[10]

Goldberg's style of regionalism cut roughly along unspecific geographic lines, and he defined U.S. regions loosely and inconsistently. He occasionally referred to the state's western character, as when he published "The Last Trail of Jesse Bolande," a western adventure story with no Jewish significance whatsoever, and he carried Jewish items from Fort Worth and El Paso, cities more identified with Texas' western than its southern qualities.[11] In 1912, early in the paper's history, Goldberg added a permanent front-page heading identifying the *Herald* as "The Only Jewish Newspaper Published in the Southwest," later adjusted to read "The Oldest Jewish Newspaper Published in the Southwest" as competition developed.[12] He never overtly addressed the question of whether Texas was really in the South, nor whether it was western, southwestern, or a region unto itself. Indeed, he often seemed to want all of these attributes to exist together. Goldberg defined his readers as Southerners and Texans—*and* Westerners *and* Southwesterners *and* Americans *and* Jews—all at once or alternately, as circumstances warranted. He edited the *Herald*, he claimed, "in behalf of no particular faction of Jewry, but in the interest of the Jews of Texas as a unit. . . . 'Texas news for Texas Jews.'"[13]

An examination of how Goldberg exploited the presumed distinctiveness of Texas Jews and how he deliberately drew lines marking off differences between Jews in one place and those in another adds an important dimension to an ongoing scholarly debate about regional differences among American Jews.[14] At issue is the question of whether such differences exist or have ever existed. For every anecdote about kosher grits or drawling cantors, there is opposing evidence that Jewish communities in the South and West have always been immersed in the general currents affecting Jewish life throughout the nation. Goldberg's conspicuous use of southern regional rhetoric indicates that whether or not such distinctions can be confirmed through objective analysis of community activity, institutional behavior, or religious practices, they are quite real in the minds of individuals and in the self-identifications of groups. At the same time, Goldberg's approach suggests that regional differences, like the other frontiers that defined Jewish Texans, were shifting. Perhaps these differences had a real historical basis before the Civil War, but now they were pure rhetoric. Regional differences had become a nostalgic marketing device that spokesmen like Goldberg could deploy at will to define their group, to rally action around a shared sense of uniqueness, and, of course, to sell newspapers.

EGO

Although not a native Texan, Goldberg was a born Southerner with a southern sensibility that may have driven his effort to distinguish Texas Jews from their Yankee brethren. The future editor was born in Delta, a Louisiana village opposite Vicksburg, Mississippi, in 1876, the year that Democrats "redeemed" Mississippi from the Republican political dominance of Reconstruction. When Edgar was two, his mother died in a yellow fever epidemic; his father died five years later. The boy went to live briefly with his father's sister and her husband, a native Arkansan and Confederate Army veteran who had been wounded at the Battle of Fort Donelson in 1862. Unable to support an additional child, they sent him to live at the Jewish Children's Home in New Orleans, where he stayed until he was nearly fifteen. The Home, originally the Association for the Relief of Widows and Orphans, took in needy Jewish children from many southern states, and its blend of civic and ethical education, general studies, and liberal Judaism helped shape several generations of southern Jewish children. Goldberg remained grateful throughout his life for the opportunities that the Children's Home had given him, and he regularly encouraged his readers to support financially "that dearly beloved institution over in New Orleans that cares for the Jewish orphans of our fair Southland."[15] In the *Herald*'s first year, he committed the front page of six consecutive issues to an institutional history of the Children's Home in celebration of its fifty-fifth anniversary.[16] He was also a lifelong member and supporter of B'nai B'rith District 7, the southern branch of the international Jewish fraternal order and one of the Home's leading sponsors and advocates.

At fifteen, Goldberg reunited with his family and worked briefly as a jeweler's apprentice in Jackson, Mississippi, learning the engraving techniques he would later apply to printer's type. The family moved to Memphis, where Edgar took a job at the *Spectator*, a local Jewish newspaper, laying out type on the printing press. In 1899 the twenty-three-year-old left his family and traveled to St. Louis to work for the Sanders Engraving Company, where he remained for more than five years, dreaming of opening his own print shop. In St. Louis he met Esther Ruppin, daughter of a successful cigar merchant and first cousin of European Zionist leader Arthur Ruppin. The

Edgar Goldberg, ca. 1930.
Author's collection.

couple married in 1900, the first of their three daughters was born the next year, and soon the family relocated to Texas, the southern state with the largest Jewish population. Goldberg spent a few years as a reporter in the East Texas town of Lufkin, but the family found the lack of Jewish community there frustrating. In 1907, therefore, they moved to nearby Houston.[17]

Houston was undergoing dramatic changes in the century's first decade, benefiting from both the 1901 discovery of oil in Beaumont and the ongoing construction of a deepwater shipping channel to the Gulf of Mexico, which promised to make Houston one of the nation's busiest ports. The city's Jewish community also grew. Houston received some four hundred Galveston Plan immigrants directly from eastern Europe, more than any other Texas city, which added vitality and complexity to its Jewish facilities. Houston also received an influx of commercial and businesspeople abandoning Galveston in the wake of the 1900 hurricane that nearly destroyed the island city. The combination of the hurricane and the ship channel, in fact, assured that Houston permanently surpassed Galveston for commercial dominance of the Texas Gulf Coast. When the Goldbergs arrived in 1907, more than 2,500 Jews constituted some 4 percent of the city's population.[18]

Goldberg was confident that Houston, with its climate of expansion and commercial opportunity, could support its own Jewish newspaper. With Esther's help in the office, he opened the Herald Printing Company to publish the new paper and to operate a contract printing business as a hedge against insolvency. He began soliciting subscribers and advertisers among both Jewish and gentile business owners. A one-page trial issue in 1908 found a wide audience, and Goldberg prepared the first weekly issue of the *Jewish Herald* for the coming Rosh Hashanah, September 24, 1908. For nearly thirty years, until his death in 1937, Goldberg edited the paper, managed the Herald Printing Company, wrote many of the articles, and contributed a recurring column under the heading "EGO," a pseudonym he composed from his initials. The *Jewish Herald* was the state's first successful Jewish newspaper, and Goldberg had a unique opportunity to seek a readership and to define his adopted community along lines largely of his own choosing.

The Southern Jewish Press

The *Herald* was not the first Jewish paper in the South, nor even the first in Texas, and it was only the latest to exploit its readers' southern sensibilities. The *Jewish South*, a weekly edited first in Atlanta and later in New Orleans by Rabbi E. B. M. "Alphabet" Browne, provides the most useful comparison to the *Herald*'s regional approach. Browne billed his paper as "the only Jewish journal this side of 'Mason and Dixon's line'" and proclaimed in his October 1877 first issue that the paper would be "a Southern Jewish periodical preeminently." Browne observed that journals based on the East and West Coasts had limited circulation, while the only Jewish paper in the middle part of the country, Isaac Mayer Wise's *American Israelite*, had "too large a territory to oversee, and affairs nearer home will naturally obtain preference over items from the far South."[19] Considering Texas a southern state, Browne marketed the paper there, and Texas readers responded enthusiastically. Correspondents in Corpus Christi, Denison, Dallas, Calvert, and other Texas towns wrote frequently to the *Jewish South*, and Rabbi Jacob Voorsanger contributed "Lone Star Flashes," a regular report of Houston Jewish activities. In 1878 leading Jews from more than twenty-five Texas cities welcomed the paper's associate editor, Charles Wessolowsky, as he toured the state to drum up new subscriptions. From 1881 to 1883, Voorsanger took the helm of the *Jewish South* and published it in Houston, making it Texas' first Jewish newspaper.[20]

When the *Jewish South* ceased publication in 1883, Texas was without a Jewish journal until 1901, when the Dallas-based *Southwestern Jewish Sentiment* lasted a single year. During this period, although circulation data have

proven impossible to find, it is safe to assume that many Texas Jews subscribed to the *American Israelite*, a national paper that continued its tradition
of printing news and correspondence from Jews in every state. The *Texas
Israelite* was published in Fort Worth from 1908 to 1912, though Edgar
Goldberg seemed unaware of its existence when he began the *Jewish Herald*
the same year, envisioning his paper as a regular "Anglo Jewish weekly
which would chronicle the news affecting the Jews of Texas."[21] Eight pages
long and four columns wide, Goldberg's first issue contained an introductory message in which he offered the paper "to the people of Houston"
and asked the secretaries of local Jewish societies to pass on news of their
activities for him to report. "The columns of the Herald will be open at all
times," he promised, "to those who have anything to say that will be of
benefit to our co-religionists or community."[22] Although, as Goldberg later
noted, "we have not waxed rich" in the *Herald*'s publication, "and at times
I wonder if the effort is really worth while," he succeeded in attracting a
large enough readership to remain in operation through the difficult start-
up years.[23] The *Herald*'s estimated 1,150 subscribers in 1911 grew to 3,500
by 1920 and to a high of 6,600 in 1933. Circulation fell significantly during
the Great Depression, forcing Goldberg to curtail the paper's length, but it
survived that and many other crises.[24]

From his first issue, Goldberg offered an idealized portrait of a dynamic,
prosperous, and harmonious Jewish community. This issue detailed the
consecration of a new synagogue for Adath Yeshurun, the city's largest Orthodox congregation, including a description of the dedication ceremony
and speeches, a photograph of the congregation's rabbi, and a sketch of
the new building.[25] A smaller article in the same issue described the construction of Congregation Beth Israel's new Reform temple. Such even-
handedness became a hallmark. Two years later, Goldberg reiterated that
the *Herald* was not "the organ of any party within the creed and hence will
give publicity to all matters of news appertaining to Orthodoxy, Reform,
Zionism and Anti-Zionism, one as well as the other, regardless of whom
it may suit or may not suit."[26] As one of the nation's few non-rabbinical
editors of Jewish newspapers, Goldberg had no ideological axe to grind
and could cover the "Jewish news" without partisanship. "We have been
accused of being anti-Zionistic—of being Zionistic—of being too much in
favor of reform—and of giving only Orthodox news," he noted in 1910.
"Well, at any rate, we have not been accused of being un-Jewish."[27] When
divisions in the community occurred, Goldberg was often a voice for rec-
onciliation. When Adath Yeshurun split into factions over the confirmation

ceremony in 1911, for example, the *Herald* covered the conflict as it progressed through a failed arbitration proceeding and into the courts, and Goldberg urged the parties to avoid a trial because of the negative attention it could attract in the national Jewish press.[28] This moderate, inclusive approach put Goldberg in a position to comment on all Jewish community matters—and also targeted the largest possible readership.

At first, Goldberg struggled to find enough news of local interest to fill his pages. When short, he reprinted material from other Jewish newspapers, including features like "Jewish Women in New York"; "In Memory of Heine"; a sermon by a Baltimore rabbi; a feature story on the Baroness de Hirsch; and page after page of jokes and witty sayings. Meeting his commitment to cover "matters of interest to Jews in Texas in particular," however, the editor introduced a regular feature titled "Local Notes." Here Houston's Jewish citizens shared important events in their lives, from marriages and births to changes of address and family vacations.[29] Also, though columnists of national reputation were available for reprinting, Goldberg recruited local writers to contribute editorials. These included H. B. Lieberman, the cantor at Adath Yeshurun, who wrote many early opinions on matters of Jewish practice and identity, and Lena Lurie, an activist in Houston's Jewish charities, who commented on issues such as intermarriage, parochial schools, and "Jewish ostentation," as well as offering readers samples of her own short stories and poetry.[30] In later years, rabbis Samuel Rosinger of Beaumont and David Goldberg of Wichita Falls each wrote for the *Herald* on topics ranging from Jewish religious practice to international politics. Rosinger appealed on behalf of Leo Frank, the Atlanta merchant who had been falsely accused of murdering a young girl in 1913; applauded Woodrow Wilson's appointment of Louis Brandeis to the U.S. Supreme Court; and mourned the displacement of European Jews during World War I, while Rabbi Goldberg wrote often about the lasting effects of World War I on world Jewry, particularly the possibility of establishing a Jewish state in Palestine.[31] Although these leaders rarely commented on local events (a notable exception was Rabbi Goldberg's passionate warnings about the resurgent Texas Klan in the 1920s), their participation demonstrated to the *Herald*'s readers that Jewish thought and advocacy were alive and well in Texas and that Jewish issues of global importance had repercussions at home.[32]

The *Herald* also chronicled the growth of Texas Jewry's increasingly complex institutional structure. Rabbis came and went, cities formed new congregations and built synagogues, and a variety of clubs and organizations were started. The *Herald* promoted involvement in local charities like the Jewish Free Loan Society and the Jewish Women's Benevolent Society Charity Home, and Edgar Goldberg reported on the Jewish Literary Society and other local cultural organizations.[33] By reprinting items from other papers, Goldberg provided news from Reform and Orthodox rabbinical conferences, from meetings of Zionists and B'nai B'rith, and from gatherings of the American Jewish Committee and the National Council of Jewish Women. While covering these organizations' national and international activities, he also emphasized local and regional events. Meetings of the Texas Federation of Zionists and the Texas Zionist Organization, the Houston Council of Jewish Women, and District 7 of B'nai B'rith, the regional body that included Texas and in which Goldberg ardently participated as a member and an officer, all found notice in the *Herald*.

Goldberg's extensive coverage of the Galveston Movement further reveals his interest in finding and emphasizing the local angle in matters of national significance. Recognizing the certain economic benefit to Houston, Goldberg promoted the project enthusiastically, reprinting positive articles from Jewish and non-Jewish newspapers and inviting Galveston's rabbi, Henry Cohen, to report on his activities in support of the program.[34] In a January 1910 column, Superintendent Oscar Leonard, of the Jewish Educational and Charitable Association in St. Louis, encouraged diverting Jewish immigration from eastern cities and settling more immigrants in Texas. "It is well known," he remarked, "that Jews give an impetus to commerce and industry and for this reason they would be welcomed in many communities in this large state which waits for willing hands and alert minds to help it develop." He chastised Yiddish papers in New York that discouraged immigration to the interior on the grounds that "there were no synagogues there and [immigrants] would become estranged from the faith of their fathers." That, Leonard argued, "was an absurd thing to say and was dictated by selfishness and self interest." Leonard urged the *Herald*'s readers to tell their fellow Jews about Texas and to encourage them to migrate there. "If we relieved the congregation in the large cities," he concluded, "we shall surely have no 'Jewish problem' in America."[35]

Edgar Goldberg's comments on the Movement were brief and touched with a note of skepticism about the New York sponsors. He believed firmly in the project's goals in theory, but as actual immigrants began to arrive in Texas he questioned whether the movement's implementation would really benefit his city and state. Goldberg chided Jacob Schiff, for example, for pretending to act out of pure selflessness. "Jacob Schiff made two speeches in New York in the past week encouraging immigrants to come South," Goldberg wrote. "If the people he is urging to come South had any money we'd be tempted to ask what land company he had stock in." In a similar editorial in 1910, Goldberg reprimanded the Movement's leaders for sending immigrants into the South who were unskilled or unprepared to work. "There is more room for the Jew in Texas than any other state in the Union," he pointed out. "But the immigrant can't live on room. There is absolutely no difficulty to find work for those having occupations."[36] Despite these qualifications, Goldberg supported the Movement steadfastly, and throughout its duration, especially as it faced bureaucratic tangles and charges of inefficiency, he vigorously came to its defense.

Although his focus was always on Houston, even within his first year Goldberg set his sights on a larger, statewide readership. In December 1908, he ran an advertisement calling for representatives in other Texas cities to "take subscriptions and correspond for the Jewish Herald," and the following summer he introduced a "Texas News" page dedicated to items of Jewish interest from cities and towns around the state. By 1910, Goldberg could brag that the *Herald* had a statewide readership and "special correspondents at not less than fifteen [of the] most important points in the State."[37] Four years later, to reinforce his statewide appeal, he changed the paper's name from the *Jewish Herald* to the *Texas Jewish Herald*: "From the local publication which it was at its inception," he wrote, "[the *Herald*] has become the organ of all Jewry in Texas." He explained that he made the change on the advice of readers who had pointed out that the *Herald* was "as closely identified with Jewish interests in Dallas, Fort Worth, Waco, Austin, San Antonio, Galveston, El Paso, Beaumont, Corsicana, Tyler, Palestine and nearly all of the smaller towns in Texas as with Houston."[38] The idea that Jews in Galveston had anything in common with those in El Paso, which is just as close to Los Angeles, was debatable, but it was fundamental to Goldberg's marketing effort. Texas Jews were, as he had stated earlier, "a unit," a single readership best addressed by a Texas-based paper. The long list of towns reflected Goldberg's hope to appeal to a larger Texas Jewish community.

The *Jewish Ledger*'s long-standing presence in New Orleans may explain why Goldberg did not seek to expand his readership into other parts of the Old South, although his strong support of Louisiana institutions like the Jewish Children's Home and B'nai B'rith District 7 shows his personal identification with the region. Rather, he promoted circulation in Texas communities that were not already served by a regional Jewish paper, choosing to compete with the *Israelite* and the national New York journals rather

Banner from the *Texas Jewish Herald*, April 27, 1933.
Courtesy Michael C. Duke and the *Jewish Herald-Voice*, Houston, Texas.

than with a southern colleague. This strategy, however, did not prevent other editors from competing with him. It is likely, in fact, that the *Herald's* name change and Goldberg's urge to publicize his paper's statewide appeal were responses to the impending 1915 establishment of Fort Worth's *Jewish Monitor*. The *Monitor's* founding editor, Rabbi G. George Fox, claimed later to have started the paper in an effort to "spread information about matters of Jewish interest and to bring about closer cooperation among Texas Jews," though presumably not between himself and Goldberg.[39] The two papers competed for readers, writers, and advertisers, and they both claimed to be the oldest Jewish journal in the region. Although the *Herald* undisputedly preceded the *Monitor* by several years, Fox neglected to acknowledge it, crediting himself as the pioneer of Jewish journalism in Texas.

Like the *Herald*, the *Monitor* was an English-language weekly that covered national and international Jewish news as well as local issues. Like Goldberg, Fox recruited Texas rabbis to provide guest editorials, promoted assimilation and economic achievement, and spoke to readers as fully acculturated Americans.[40] Whereas Goldberg saw the whole of Texas as his field, Fox drew fewer borderlines, covering news and promoting circulation in Oklahoma, Arkansas, and Louisiana as well as in North Texas. Fox was conscious that the *Monitor* was a southern periodical—he once described it as "a real force in the South"—but he did not take a regional approach to the degree that Goldberg did.[41] If anything, Fox's outreach to communities outside Texas, particularly those in Oklahoma where an appeal to Dixie sensibility was largely irrelevant, indicates that Fox was more concerned with finding readers than with abiding by traditional regional boundaries.

Neither Fox nor Goldberg took as strongly regional a stance as "Alphabet" Browne had done in the *Jewish South*, but Fox's decision to turn northward for readers suggests that the *Herald* was already dominant through much of the state and that Goldberg's effort to appeal to his readers as Texans and as Southerners had been effective.

The Jewish Civil War

E. B. M. "Alphabet" Browne had set the *Jewish South* in opposition to the national leadership of Cincinnati's Isaac Wise. Goldberg looked to New York, then emerging as the center of American Jewish life, as a foil. In one extended episode, Goldberg relied heavily on regional rhetoric to assert that Jews in Texas and throughout the South stood outside the national structures that bound the American Jewish community together. He forged a symbolic frontier between his readers and New York Jews, and, from the southern side of that line, challenged the authority of national Jewish leaders and asserted his readers' right to speak on their own behalf and to pursue their own solutions to national Jewish problems. In place of self-designated Jewish leaders in New York, Goldberg promoted his friend and frequent editorialist, Houston lawyer Henry J. Dannenbaum, as a more suitable leader for American Jewry, publicity that Dannenbaum was more than happy to accept. Although not inherently important, the episode deserves to be described at length for the clarity in which it reveals Goldberg's manipulation of minor events to make a point about the Houston Jewish community's maturity and to promote to his readers a particular way of seeing themselves within the larger context of American Jewry.

The incident began in 1908 when New York's police commissioner, Theodore Bingham, published a report in the *North American Review* in which he associated criminality with foreignness. In New York neighborhoods where fewer native-born residents lived, he claimed, crime was more widespread. Russian Jews, who dominated the city's Lower East Side, represented one-quarter of the city's population, according to Bingham, but accounted for "perhaps half of the criminals."[42] The following year, *McClure's Magazine* presented a typically lurid account of the growing problem of "white slavery" in which George K. Turner described how a system of corrupt procurers, mostly Jews, seduced young immigrant women, also mostly Jews, and sold them into a life of degradation.[43] The association both writers made between Jewish immigration and urban vice, though wildly exaggerated, caught the attention of Jewish leaders in New York and elsewhere who feared it might damage the public perception of the nation's Jews.[44]

Prominent Jewish New Yorkers like attorney Louis Marshall of the American Jewish Committee and Jacob Schiff recognized a need to respond to such charges, but the fractious nature of New York Jewry prevented unified action. In particular, a rift existed between the Russian immigrant community and "uptown" Jews of German background, including Marshall and Schiff, who had immigrated earlier and had become prosperous and acculturated. The Yiddish press, speaking on behalf of the immigrant community, condemned the city's German Jews for their failure to address the white slavery charges and berated their approach as "assimilationist, timid, and disdainful of the immigrant Jews," even as they acknowledged their dependence upon these "men of influence" to direct the city's Jewish affairs. In response to the criticism, uptowners advanced a plan to organize a collective voice for all the city's Jews, a "New York Kehillah" derived from the eastern European tradition of *kehillah*, representative community leadership. Its purpose, according to Schiff, was to "further the cause of Judaism . . . and to represent the Jews of this city." The Kehillah president Judah Magnes claimed that the organization's regular meetings would help to forge a "Jewish public opinion."[45] Over the years, the Kehillah was active in reforming Jewish education, arbitrating labor disputes, and bridging the ideological gap between the city's Reform and Orthodox Jews.

Although the Kehillah represented a broad cross-section of the city's Jewish factions and institutions, it was dominated by Reform German Jews of a particular social status. Wealthy, genteel, and acculturated, they were respected members of both Jewish and gentile society. Some were rabbis and community activists, although the majority were lawyers and businessmen. When Bingham and Turner published their charges of Jewish involvement in organized prostitution, the Kehillah's central figures decided that it was best to downplay the problem rather than to attack the charges directly and visibly. In a well-publicized address, Magnes denied that the problem even existed, and other Kehillah members said nothing in the hope that their silence would render the problem invisible. This approach was also favored by representatives of the immigrant community who preferred that the whole matter disappear from public attention as quickly as possible.

Far from the city where most of the alleged offenses were occurring, Henry J. Dannenbaum, a dashing and successful Jewish prosecutor in Houston, saw an opportunity for idealistic action. Dannenbaum had been energetic in gaining support in Texas for the Mann Act, which opposed white slavery by prohibiting the transport of women across state lines for "immoral purposes." He had earned the respect of Jews and gentiles alike as a crusading crimefighter, and in 1915 Governor James Ferguson appointed him judge of the 61st District Court, the first Jew to sit on the federal bench in Texas.[46] A native Texan born to German immigrants, Dannenbaum was both rough and genteel, educated and well-mannered but with a frontiersman's directness. In speech and writing, he wrapped bold, often confrontational messages in a deliberately cultivated rhetoric that marked him as a true Houstonian, ambitious and capable but newly, somewhat uncomfortably, cosmopolitan.

In 1910, Dannenbaum wrote to the *Jewish Herald* criticizing the Kehillah for denying the existence of white slavery. "As if Jews have not enough trouble to fight prejudice from without," he wrote with typical flourish, "now comes a cancer from within to eat upon our morals and taint our good name." Dannenbaum felt that the Kehillah should attack the problem directly through a concerted program of prosecution, intervention, and public education and that Jewish leaders only demonstrated moral weakness by refusing to do so. "There is work to do for every decent man and woman in our ranks," he wrote. "Only cowards will shrink from the contest."[47] Dannenbaum had already initiated a series of meetings with Samuel London, an El Paso Jewish attorney who, after representing prostitutes, pimps, and procurers throughout the Southwest, claimed to know more about white slavery than anyone living. London approached federal investigators and offered to turn over his business records and to make his testimony available to prosecutors for a substantial fee. Anxious to secure this evidence, Dannenbaum sought a contribution of $3,700 from B'nai B'rith District 7 to purchase London's records, including the names of at least 1,200 of his contacts, and to provide him a salary while he gathered further intelligence from his former clients.[48] With London's records in hand, Dannenbaum approached the U.S. Justice Department and secured a position in New York as Special Assistant to the Attorney General charged with prosecuting violations of the Mann Act.

Dannenbaum's rapid ascent to national office enhanced his reputation among his fellow Jewish Texans and Southerners. As a sign of their respect, the members of B'nai B'rith District 7 elected Dannenbaum district president in 1911, a post he ceremoniously accepted and then immediately resigned because of his commitments in New York. Edgar Goldberg praised Dannenbaum in the *Herald* as "a man whose ability is unquestioned, whose loyalty and faith in the future of our people is inspiring, . . . [a] man without a blemish who is loved, honored and respected by all." In particular, the editor thrilled at the prospect of a local Jew, an officer in the regional B'nai B'rith, attaining national prominence. Dannenbaum's "acknowledged lead-

Judge Henry J. Dannenbaum, portrait made from a 1921 photograph. This portrait currently hangs in the 61st District Courtroom in the Harris County Civil Courthouse with those of other judges of the court. When the portrait gallery was commissioned in 1938, Dannenbaum's picture was left out, possibly due to anti-Semitism on the planning committee. It was added, with suitable ceremony, in 1997. Photograph courtesy of *Southern Jewish History*, used with permission of Glen A. Rosenbaum.

ership of the district comprising the Southern States," the editor wrote, "is but the stepping stone to the leadership of American Jewry."[49] Implicit in the exaggerated praise is Goldberg's belief that the South could produce spokesmen capable of standing on a national platform, that Jews living far from power centers like New York were not bound to let northern administrators speak for them. Indeed, as Goldberg was well aware, the South had already produced a number of Jewish leaders of national reputation, including former national B'nai B'rith president and Galveston native Leo N. Levi. Seeking renewed glory for his state and region, Goldberg placed the *Herald* firmly behind Dannenbaum's crusade.

To encourage the Kehillah to greater assertiveness, Dannenbaum corresponded frequently with several of its members while he was with the Justice Department in New York, but Judah Magnes explained to him that the Kehillah's members were "hard-headed men" who would not easily be moved to act.[50] Magnes declined to support Dannenbaum's idea of establishing a Lower East Side office to serve as a center for prosecution and public education, and he declined Dannenbaum's offer of information and financial support should the Kehillah ever establish a committee to combat white slavery. Dannenbaum returned to Texas late in 1911, disappointed but bearing a letter from the U.S. Attorney General stating that his efforts had been responsible for at least a dozen convictions.[51]

Soon after returning, Dannenbaum spoke at a regional B'nai B'rith meeting in New Orleans. In a wide-ranging and provocative address, Dannenbaum challenged U.S. diplomatic policy, asserting that the government should preserve a Russian trade treaty despite the tsar's crackdown on Jewish socialists. National Jewish leaders, including Kehillah members, had advocated abrogation of the treaty as a protest against Russian anti-Semitism, and Dannenbaum's condemnation of the move and apparent support for Russian authoritarianism outraged many of his listeners and others who later read the address. On the subject of white slavery, Dannenbaum insisted that the problem was getting worse: "The business has spread like a prairie fire until this night," he asserted, "when in the woman's night court of New York City and on gilded Broadway the majority of streetwalkers bear Jewish names." America's Jews, he continued, especially their self-proclaimed national leaders, were most responsible for the crisis. The Southerners of B'nai B'rith District 7 had distinguished themselves, he said, by their "brave and chivalrous and unselfish" purchase of Samuel London's business records, but their New York brethren had deserted them: "[P]leading, argument and threats have all fallen impotent at the feet of our leaders in the North."[52]

In making these charges, Dannenbaum ignored evidence of rampant Jewish prostitution in his own home state. He relied on Samuel London's evidence that Jewish women were being directed toward New York but overlooked the fact that London's clients—prostitutes and procurers—were Texans. Houses of prostitution, many with Jewish residents, operated freely in Galveston, Houston, Fort Worth, El Paso, and elsewhere in the state. Rabbi G. George Fox of Fort Worth claimed that as the Galveston Movement brought impoverished and dislocated Jews into the state, many were diverted into white slavery. Although Fort Worth was far from the coast, it "was an important railroad center, so that in a comparatively short time we found a large number of Jewish prostitutes in the city." Their reputation spread, and soon "ranchmen were heard to make remarks in hotels and drugstores about the 'Jew whores.'"[53] As noted earlier, these realities and the exaggerated rumors they inspired greatly hindered the ability of the Galveston Movement to recruit immigrants in Europe.

Equally willing to overlook the obvious, Goldberg took Dannenbaum's side. Even as the *Herald* disagreed with Dannenbaum on the treaty abrogation issue, the editor declared that "we do admire the courage and manliness of Mr. Dannenbaum in differing with what is supposed to be the great majority." Goldberg also reasserted the importance of southern Jewish leadership. "We admire him for upholding Southern Jewry and telling those of the East that we must be considered; that they cannot decide all questions and expect us to follow without regard to whether it is right or wrong." Dannenbaum was proof that the South, too, was capable of producing leaders of national quality. "Men of the type of Henry J. Dannenbaum are not only qualified to act and represent Southern Jewry," the *Herald* claimed, "but better qualified to act as leaders of all our people in the consideration of grave questions which confront us today."[54]

Needless to say, northern Jewish leaders reacted differently to Dannenbaum's address, dismissing the parvenu out of hand. B'nai B'rith national president Adolf Kraus referred to Dannenbaum as "a dangerous fool," to which Goldberg responded with sarcasm. "We trust that all members of the order among our readers will take notice," of Kraus' observation, "and shape their attitude accordingly."[55] B'nai B'rith headquarters in Chicago issued a disclaimer stating that Dannenbaum held no position in the national organization and that his New Orleans address did not reflect their views. An article in the *American Hebrew*, a weekly journal published in New York by Kehillah member Cyrus Sulzberger, described Dannenbaum's futile attempt to raise money among New York leaders and ridiculed his association with Samuel London, a lawyer "who has so little sense of honor as to take such clients in the first place and then sell them out." Titled, with apparent irony, "A Gentleman from Texas," the statement expressed particular disdain for Dannenbaum's stated wish in his New Orleans address "to speak [his] own mind without regard to New York or Chicago." Translated, the *American Hebrew* explained, this statement "evidently means without regard to the American Jewish Committee or the B'nai B'rith." The writer worried about the divisive speech's consequences, claiming that "if the Russian Government had secured the services of the gentleman from Texas, he would have earned his pay" and that B'nai B'rith District 7 should reconsider "whether it desires to retain a man of this kind in an official position in the Order."[56] In response, District 7 passed a unanimous resolution of support for Dannenbaum.

The *American Hebrew* article played right into the Texans' hands. Goldberg reprinted large extracts from it without comment, and the rhetoric on the editorial page grew still more strident in its attacks on the Kehillah. "Our own beloved Henry J. Dannenbaum," one editorial proclaimed, "has caused the displeasure of the syndicate who for years has been in absolute control of the Jewish voice and without whose authority no man dare move." Previously, the paper had simply defended Dannenbaum as a local hero, but it now blasted New York leaders who "dare strike at [him] because he honors truth and detests hypocrisy." Because Dannenbaum had "put aside fear and told the truth," the *Herald* claimed, "he is made the victim of an assault by the American Hebrew which is not alone false but maliciously written for the sole purpose of destroying his value to American Jewry and preserving the syndicate that they might continue to rule." Finally, regarding the suggestion to strip Dannenbaum of his standing in B'nai B'rith, the *Herald* advised the *American Hebrew* that "District 7 will not need the advice or assistance of the syndicate in determining who shall lead in this district." The *Herald* emphasized that Dannenbaum was a native Texan, "and District 7 is proud of its leader."[57] It must be noted here that Dannenbaum was writing regularly for the *Herald* during this period. Judging from the tone of these unsigned opinions, much more florid than Goldberg's plain style but bearing a strong resemblance to Dannenbaum's credited submissions, it seems likely that Dannenbaum wrote them himself.

The *Herald* proceeded to cover this peripheral conflict as if it were a national dispute of epic proportions. For four consecutive weeks, Goldberg dedicated the newspaper's front page to reprinting the correspondence between Dannenbaum and Kehillah president Judah Magnes, advising his readers to preserve these pages "as an historical record of a phase of American Jewish history."[58] Underscoring the regional animosities at play in the conflict, Goldberg termed the crisis a "Jewish civil war between the South and the North" and urged that it be "averted before the hostilities assume serious proportions."[59] The *Herald*'s attack on the Kehillah, however, was really a one-sided assault, with Goldberg and Dannenbaum flinging rhetorical grenades at an enemy scarcely aware it was at war. It is telling that the Galveston Movement, under the direction of Kehillah member Jacob Schiff, continued unabated throughout this "Jewish civil war," and that the "phase of American Jewish history" seems to have passed within a matter of weeks.

In July 1912, the issue of Jewish crime resurfaced when, only a few months after the *Herald*'s barrage against the Kehillah, a police officer killed a Jewish gangster named Herman Rosenthal on a New York street in broad daylight, and the national press reopened the issue of Jewish vice with renewed intensity. Faced with a public relations disaster, the Kehillah finally formed a committee to address the problem, and the coincidental timing gave the *Jewish Herald* a chance to gloat. Goldberg ran a story about the Kehillah's new Vigilance Committee on the front page, preceded by extracts from Dannenbaum's earlier New Orleans address and correspondence with

Magnes. The clear implication was that Dannenbaum had been vindicated. In another front-page article, Dannenbaum took a final shot at the Kehillah's tardiness and claimed the high ground for himself and for the newspaper that had supported him. "In no spirit of censure or 'I told you so,' does the Jewish Herald now publish these words," he wrote. "The New York Kehillah, under the splendid leadership of Dr. J. L. Magnes, has been awakened and is on the right track. . . . May they win the fight."[60]

What is most revealing in this story is Goldberg and Dannenbaum's insistence that regional Jewish identity should matter even where it clearly did not. Dannenbaum's condemnation of "our leaders in the North" and Goldberg's invocation of a "Jewish civil war" inserted regionalism into an issue where it otherwise would not have been a factor. Both men left unmentioned an important underlying reality: regardless of their claim of a regional divide among American Jews, Goldberg and Dannenbaum were absorbed in national American Jewish life and were seeking solutions for distinctively Jewish, not distinctively southern, problems. In doing so, Dannenbaum targeted Jewish vice, turned for support to a Jewish fraternal organization, sought an audience in New York with Jewish leaders, and used a Jewish newspaper as his platform. Regional animosity, the legacy of the Civil War, only entered the picture when Dannenbaum used it to secure the support of B'nai B'rith District 7 and when Goldberg employed it as a dramatic front- page device. To be sure, their use of regional Jewish identity as a marketing tool does not preclude its existence, but does suggest that it was becoming a matter of taste and style instead of a profound and continuing self-identification. In the hands of an opportunistic editor like Goldberg, region had become an exploitable resource, a set of imaginary lines that could be drawn and redrawn at will.

Beyond Regionalism

With the outbreak of World War I, the political ground shifted radically beneath Goldberg's feet. The Great War ravaged sections of Europe where large numbers of Jews lived and displaced hundreds of thousands. Refugees fled westward into Germany and Austria, crowding into shantytowns where they died in large numbers from starvation and disease. American Jews recognized a responsibility and organized charities to collect money for the relief of Jewish war victims. Many of these charities, representing a broad range of American Jewish ideologies, merged into the American Joint Distribution Committee, or "the Joint," and as stories of Jewish suffering proliferated, local agencies devoted to gathering donations sprang up throughout the United States. In many communities, this groundswell overwhelmed even the most rancorous differences that had existed among American Jews before the war. Zionist and anti-Zionist, Reform and Orthodox, and German and Russian Jews joined the campaign. Their underlying differences, of course, remained intact, and factional squabbles continued to erupt in American Jewish institutions, but the war provided a common outlet for common energies. In the midst of an international crisis, there was little enthusiasm for fabricated debates between southern and northern Jews. Goldberg now enthusiastically joined a philanthropic effort of national scope, devoting full pages of his paper to war relief advertisements and offering the *Herald* offices as a donation center. The reemergence in the 1920s of the Ku Klux Klan and, far worse, the rise of the Nazis in Germany showed still more clearly that divisions among Jews were superficial and meaningless in the face of genuine threats from outside.

Goldberg covered all of these issues as they developed throughout the 1920s and 1930s, acting as the *Herald*'s editor until his death in 1937. His emphasis on Texas Jewry remained central, but in these later decades, the *Herald* took a more universalist perspective. By the time of the transformative world crises of the 1940s, a new generation had taken the reins, and the *Herald* became a different kind of newspaper. David White, who had worked briefly under Goldberg as assistant editor but had left to start a competing paper, bought the *Herald* from Goldberg's widow, Esther, and combined it with his own, establishing the *Jewish Herald-Voice* in 1938. The new paper, which White billed as "The Jewish Herald's 31 Years Experience PLUS The Jewish Voice, The Vigor of Youth," was livelier, more modern, more politically liberal, and aimed at a younger readership.[61] White managed it for more than thirty years until his death in 1971. The newspaper is published and edited today by Joe and Jeanne Samuels, who took it over from White. At more than one hundred years old, the *Jewish Herald-Voice* is the longest-lasting Jewish paper in either the South or the West.

Edgar Goldberg's success in establishing and building the *Texas Jewish Herald* demonstrates the power of frontiers, the lines that distinguish one people from another, to form a group's identity. It was never necessary for Goldberg to clarify what exactly Texas, southern, western, or southwestern Jewry was, nor what made any of them unique. What mattered was that he differentiated Texas Jews from all other Jews, even if his standards and definitions changed, and by doing so he defined them as a distinct community that could be served by its own newspaper. The coloration of the difference depended on the circumstances and on whichever rhetorical approach would most effectively suit his purpose at the time. Edgar Goldberg showed how readily, and to what purposes, the shifting frontiers that Texas Jews used to define themselves could be manipulated to define and strengthen group identity. As the century wore on, however, Texas Jews were forced to realize that they were not the only ones with the power to fix the outlines of Texas-Jewish identity.

Dallas Klan No. 66 Drum and Bugle Corps parading at Klan Day, Texas State Fair, Dallas, October 24, 1923. From the collections of the Texas/Dallas History and Archives Division, Dallas Public Library, PA83–23/10.

FIVE

Texas Jews and the Ku Klux Klan

*J. D. Van Winkle, Grand Cyclops of the Dallas klavern, was having a won-*derful day. Standing at a podium on the State Fairgrounds, he addressed a crowd of fifteen hundred fellow Klansmen, many of whom had come from all over Texas and Oklahoma in chartered trains and automobile caravans to be part of his celebration: Klan Day at the Texas State Fair, October 24, 1923. The program was filled with speeches and spectacle in honor of his organization. The San Antonio and Wichita Falls delegations included brass bands to belt out patriotic songs. Rodeo riders performed in Klan regalia. At the grandstand in the evening, twenty hippodrome acts featuring acrobats, tumblers, and aerialists entertained the crowd until well after dark. Then, some seven thousand hooded Klansmen gathered for a cross-burning and initiation ceremony witnessed by more than twenty-five thousand non-Klan spectators. The "pageant," as the *Dallas Morning News* described it, "proved to be the most colorful and unique event and one of the most massive ever seen in the city of Dallas."[1]

The day's first event was virtually a personal tribute to Van Winkle, under whose leadership the Dallas klavern had raised about eighty thousand dollars to refurbish Hope Cottage, a Dallas home for orphaned and abandoned children. "We point to this completed institution," Van Winkle announced proudly as he prepared to present the check, "as a demonstration of the fact that we have been doing constructive work within the last eighteen months instead of indulging in river-bottom floggings, as our enemies would have the public believe." Behind him on the platform, an illustrious group laughed with him. His close friend, Imperial Wizard Hiram Evans, a Dallas dentist who had risen to the Klan's highest national office, had returned from his Atlanta headquarters for a triumphant homecoming. He was joined by a host of public officials, including Dallas Mayor Louis Blaylock, who praised the Klan "in its present period of greatness," and Judge Felix Robertson, who would soon make a strong showing as a pro-Klan candidate for governor. Flanking them were a flock of city commissioners, county officials, and state legislators who owed their offices to Klan support. Finally, in a position of prominence behind the speaker, sat Alex Sanger, the city's leading merchant and head of one of the state's premier retailing families, a respected civic leader, a member of the State Fair Board of Directors, and a founding member of Temple Emanu-El, the city's first synagogue.

With such an assemblage gathered behind him, Van Winkle could assure his listeners that "the day is yours, the city is yours—and I am glad to state that you are in a klan town."[2] Dallas *was* a Klan town. As many as thirteen thousand of its citizens were members of the "Invisible Empire," possibly the highest per capita participation of any city in the country. With just 4 percent of the Texas population, Dallas supplied some 13 percent of its Klansmen.[3] Not only was Imperial Wizard Evans a native Dallasite, but so were the National Vice Commander of the Women of the Ku Klux Klan and the Grand Titan of Texas, the head of the state organization. The current and future public officials arrayed behind Van Winkle at the Hope Cottage ceremony testified to the chapter's success at getting sympathetic candidates elected to local offices, and the attendance of Alex Sanger suggested that even the city's Jews found something to admire.

For many Texas Jews, however, the presence of a leading Jewish citizen at the head of an event celebrating the benevolent works of the Ku Klux Klan was, to say the least, ironic. Although it had tried to reinvent itself as a mainstream fraternal and patriotic organization, the Klan maintained a strict segregation that barred Jews, Catholics, and all nonwhites from membership. Klan leaders never openly encouraged violence against Jews, nor for that matter against anyone, but they promoted an agenda that explicitly questioned Jews' suitability as fellow citizens. Just hours after sharing the platform with Alex Sanger at Klan Day, in fact, Imperial Wizard Hiram Evans delivered an address at the Fairground's main plaza that confirmed Jewish fears about his organization's underlying agenda. With some seventy-five thousand Klansmen gathered to listen, many in full regalia, Evans proclaimed that Jews represented an "absolutely unblendable element" in American society. "Throughout the centuries," he declared, "there has been no country [the Jew] would or could call his home. . . . To him patriotism, as the Anglo-Saxon feels it, is impossible." Evans' contention was not that Jews were inferior or unacceptable as part of American society. On the contrary, he praised them as "law abiding," "of physically wholesome stock," "untainted by immoralities among themselves," "mentally alert," and "a family people." He condemned them, rather, for failing to integrate fully enough, for remaining separate and self-protective. "Their homes are not American, but Jewish homes," he said, "into which we can not go and from which they will never emerge for a real intermingling with America."[4] The previous year, Billie Mayfield, editor of a Houston Klan paper called *Colonel Mayfield's Weekly*, had expressed a similar opinion. "The Jew is not a citizen of this country," he wrote. "He is just an Inhabitant. . . . [Jews] come to America, the great melting pot of the world, with the avowed intention of never melting."[5]

The proposition that they were unpatriotic and "absolutely unblendable" outsiders presented Texas Jews with a new and potentially threatening situation. They had always been able to work their way into the state's power structure by virtue, in part, of their whiteness. Now the Klan suggested that the majority might reject them because they were not also Anglo-Saxon and Protestant and because they insisted on remaining even minimally unacculturated. To make matters more complicated, as part of the urban elite, many Jews felt compelled to support the Klan during its rise to political power despite its supremacist agenda, and many more chose quietly not to oppose it. When the Klan came briefly to dominate the state's Democratic Party, which was the only real political force in a one-party southern state, Jewish voters found themselves forced to choose between Klan-backed candidates whose policy views they could otherwise support or weak, obscure, even overtly anti-Semitic candidates who spoke out against the Klan. "Politics these days have ceased to operate on lines of principle and patriotism & Efficiency," wrote *Texas Jewish Herald* editor Edgar Goldberg to Galveston rabbi Henry Cohen at the height of the Klan's political influence, "but rather expediency."[6] As they selected candidates, Jewish Texans balanced competing new priorities that reflected deep conflicts over religious and ethnic identity.

The emergence of the Ku Klux Klan in Texas affected other minority groups more sharply than Jews. The Klan directed more hostile rhetoric at Catholics and more physical violence at African Americans. As Hiram Evans' Klan Day address attests, the group's attitude toward Jews was ambivalent at worst but generally respectful. Still, the Klan's rise to power on a platform that included anti-Jewish discrimination marked an important and threatening shift in the social status of Jewish Texans. For the first time, they awaited the acceptance of the Anglo majority and found it no longer immediately forthcoming. Since their arrival in the state, Jewish Texans had successfully managed a frontier existence, effectively adapting their self-definitions to changing circumstances. The results were beneficial relations with a variety of gentile Texans despite their religious differences. They had taken their place among whites with little fear of being perceived as anything but fellow Anglos. They had also constructed a distinctive local and regional sense of themselves as Texans while still identifying strongly with other American Jews and with world Jewry in general. Texas now had Jewish religious, social, and business institutions rivaling any in the country and operating alongside and in harmony with gentile establishments, and Jews had assumed prominent positions of civic leadership in every Texas city. Now the frontiers that defined who they were as a group, what they were and what they were not, were again being redrawn, but not by themselves. The new frontiers being established excluded them and threatened to divest them, on the basis of religious difference alone, of the social and economic gains they had made. This was the greatest threat to their collective security and the clearest anti-Semitism that they had faced since arriving in Texas.

The Second Klan

Anti-Semitism, though important in the Klan's 1920s agenda, had not been a part of the group's initial mission. The original Ku Klux Klan, founded in Tennessee in 1866, was little more than a motley collection of drunken Confederate veterans who felt that southern dignity and the virtue of southern women needed protection from the Republicans, carpetbaggers, and freedmen in their midst. Acting without organization or method during the Reconstruction years, they roamed the southern countryside terrorizing former slaves, Republicans, and northern sympathizers until dissolving in the early 1870s amid legislative and judicial efforts to repress their violent extralegal methods. The second, better organized, Klan was a secret society initiated in 1915 by an Atlanta traveling salesman named William Simmons. Simmons had been keenly affected by the release that year of

D. W. Griffith's *Birth of a Nation*, which romanticized the Reconstruction-era Klan, and he based the "Second Klan" on Griffith's nostalgic version of the southern past.

Simmons modeled the Klan's costumes on the ones in Griffith's film and invented, mostly from whole cloth, the mystical rituals, secret signs, specialized vocabulary, oaths, and initiation rites that gave the new Empire its hocus-pocus appeal. He imposed a strict institutional hierarchy, with himself at the top, along the lines of middle-class fraternal societies like the Masons and Odd Fellows (Simmons belonged to no fewer than twenty-five such societies). But, as historian Nancy MacLean writes, "Klansmen were not just Odd Fellows in robes and hoods."[7] Its motivating force, white supremacy, set the Klan apart from mainstream social clubs, and, unlike Reconstruction Klansmen, Simmons included Jews among the minorities he targeted. Simmons formed his group the same year that an Atlanta mob lynched Leo Frank, an innocent Jewish factory manager, in misdirected vengeance for the murder of a young girl who worked for him. The lynching remains the most notorious instance of anti-Semitic violence in American history, and it is likely that Frank's killers were among Simmons' first Klansmen.[8]

In the summer of 1920 Edward Clarke and Elizabeth Tyler, partners in an Atlanta public relations firm, joined Simmons to direct his publicity and membership drives. With their coaching, Simmons adopted a radically xenophobic posture emphasizing the theme of "100% Americanism," a vague standard that directed suspicion equally toward immigrants, ethnic minorities, and non-Protestants. At the conclusion of a speech to Georgia Klansmen in late 1920, the previously bland and mild-mannered Simmons methodically removed a pair of handguns from his pockets, unwrapped a cartridge belt from around his waist, and arranged them on a table before him. Then he drew a Bowie knife and plunged it into the tabletop, shouting, "Now let the Niggers, Catholics, Jews, and all others who disdain my imperial wizardry, come on!"[9] The audience rose to its feet, and Clarke and Tyler began spreading word of the new approach. In 1921, some two hundred new chapters appeared nationwide, boosting membership to nearly one million. At its peak in 1924, the order claimed as many as 4.5 million members, though it typically inflated its membership estimates.[10]

The growing Empire reached Texas in late 1920 in the person of Z. R. Upchurch, a Klan functionary who traveled to Houston to recruit new members at a United Confederate Veterans meeting. Within a few days there, Upchurch had mustered the numbers necessary to establish the first Texas chapter, Sam Houston Klan No. 1. Word spread quickly, and new chapters appeared in rapid succession. Within six months more than one hundred "klaverns" appeared in cities and towns across Texas, and by 1924 the state organization reached a peak membership of about two hundred thousand, a figure more than four times the state's entire Jewish population.[11] As elsewhere in the country, Texas Klansmen came from the respectable middle class of gentile society. "Many of America's good citizens were members," Edgar Goldberg recalled in 1933. "While many low liars and ignoramuses were also members of the Klan, many of the misguided were men of high standing and respectability."[12] Max Bentley, who wrote about the Texas Klan for *McClure's Magazine*, claimed that the initial roster of the Houston chapter "represented literally a glossary of Houston's *who's who*. The charter members were silk-stocking men from the banks, business houses and professions."[13] Duncan Aikman, a reporter for the *El Paso Times*, described El Paso Klansmen as "motor-car magnates, the insurance go-getters, the real-torian archdukes, the slap-on-the-back bankers, the high powered selling dervishes, [and] the dynamic contractors," a collection of "massed and gullible Babbittry."[14] The Klan drew its members from the solid, striving middle-class—from among Jewish businessmen's neighbors, customers, friends, and professional associates. These people had expressed little anti-Semitic feeling in the past, and Texas Jews had little reason to fear them. In fact, Jewish businessmen may have felt that they risked more by opposing such an organization and alienating the people on whom business depended than by finding a way to coexist peacefully.

Moreover, as membership rosters swelled, Klan organizers recognized that the nativist arguments that made the order popular in eastern states, where the economic effects of immigration were strongly felt, were harder to sell in Texas, where foreign-born white residents numbered less than 8 percent of the white population in 1920.[15] In 1923, the editor of *Colonel Mayfield's Weekly* noted the state's relatively small numbers of Catholics and Jews and shrugged off their voting strength.[16] Under these conditions, it was difficult for Texas Klan leaders to sell the idea that Jews, Catholics, and immigrants represented a serious threat to the white majority's way of life. "Although anti-Catholicism and anti-Semitism were important in the kluxing of the Southwest," observes historian Charles C. Alexander, "these prejudices were not as prominent in that region as in the East or Midwest." Although national leaders spoke often of the "unblendable" Jewish character, "outside of such eastern states as New York or New Jersey, anti-Semitism seems to have had only moderate appeal [to Klansmen]."[17] Instead, Alexander writes, the Klan in Texas was motivated less by nativism than by "a desire for social regulation," and Klan activity there became an "adventure in moral authoritarianism and politics."[18] Accordingly, Ralph Chase, who grew up in San Angelo, remembered the Klan there lashing out against "short skirts, demon rum, prostitutes, bathing-beauty contests, jazz, dancing, brief bathing suits, bosses who seduced their employees and women who smoked"—but not, conspicuously, Catholics or Jews.[19] Opposing such evils was a cause, ironically, that many Jews of a socially conservative bent could readily support, or at least choose not to oppose openly. As long as the Texas Klan avoided overtly anti-Semitic rhetoric, it did not seem to pose a real threat to the state's Jews.

However, Texas Klansmen speaking outside official channels did not refrain from verbal attacks on Jews. Klan papers in Houston and Dallas launched an unremitting assault on Jewish Texans, and newspapermen who had once seemed friendly turned against Jews with unsettling speed. As a *Houston Chronicle* reporter, Billie Mayfield had been on good terms with Houston's Jewish community. In one article, in fact, Mayfield described the significance of Yom Kippur and wished a "GOOD YONTIF" ("Happy Holiday") to "Jews around the world." He singled out several individuals, including Sol M. Oberndorfer, "prince of good fellows"; Izzy Greenberg, "with whom I work"; and Morris Levy, "my pal of years."[20] When he joined the Klan, however, and began editing its primary organ in Houston, Mayfield quickly and harshly turned against his former friends: "I haven't it in for the Jewish people," he wrote. "There are lots of good Jews in Houston and all over Texas; you find them with tombstones over their heads."[21] Perceiving an organized Jewish boycott of his advertisers (though it is unlikely any existed or was necessary), he began referring to Jewish merchants as "Kikes" and "hooks," condemning them for having "banded together to put a real American out of business who refuses to bow to their assumed superiority."[22]

Words are words, but beneath the rhetoric there was always the threat of actual physical attack. In Texas and elsewhere, the Klan enforced its vision of moral and racial order through violence and intimidation, but the Texas Klan distinguished itself by the ferocity and frequency of its attacks. The *Houston Chronicle* reported in the fall of 1921 that "Texas Klansmen have beaten and blackened more people in the last six months than all the other states combined," and one historian has calculated that the Texas Klan was responsible for more than five hundred "tar-and-feather parties and whipping bees, plus other threats, assaults, and homicides."[23] Despite Grand Cyclops Van Winkle's assertion on Klan Day that the Dallas klavern had no time for "river-bottom floggings," it was common knowledge that his klavern maintained a special "whipping meadow" along the Trinity River bottom where they dispensed their particular form of moral justice.[24]

In keeping with the Klan's moral agenda, the victims of such attacks were most often white Protestants whom Klansmen deemed guilty of some transgression. J. S. Paul, for example, was a white physician taken from his Beaumont home in May 1921, beaten almost to death, and covered with tar and feathers because he had allegedly performed abortions. In June, the Dallas Klan assaulted a white service station attendant for beating his wife. Other victims included whites believed to be gamblers, bigamists, adulterers, or drunks. In the summer of 1921, the *Fort Worth Star-Telegram* found that of fifty-two acts of coercive violence attributed to the Klan before August 1921, all but seven involved white Protestant victims.[25] This must have given some comfort to Jewish Texans. As long as the Klan kept its focus on the moral transgressions of fellow Protestants, Jews had little reason to worry. "[T]he Klan is a Protestant ailing and should be cured by the Protestant," Edgar Goldberg wrote in 1924 when criticized for his lax editorial stance against the Klan. "Preachments in a Jewish Newspaper & Pulpit to Jews would not reach the people affected."[26]

Still, a small number of Jews were among the Klan's early victims, and they were apparently singled out, to some degree, for their Jewishness. In March 1922, for instance, Manual Nussbaum, the twenty-two-year-old son of a wealthy Jewish family in Colorado County near Houston, was tarred and feathered for "despoiling a Gentile girl."[27] The same month, a group of hooded men charged into Philip Rothblum's Dallas house, took him outside, and beat him, apparently because he had been spotted associating with a black man.[28] These attacks closely resembled those perpetrated on white gentiles, but they were notably less brutal than assaults on non-white victims. In contrast, a party of hooded Dallas Klansmen led by future Wizard Hiram Evans kidnapped a black bellhop named Alex Johnson, whom they suspected of "pandering for white men and women," threw him into the back of a car, sped him out of town, flogged him severely, and branded the letters "KKK" on his forehead with acid. When they were finished, they took the unconscious and bleeding man back into Dallas and dumped him in the street in front of the hotel where he worked.[29] The relatively milder attacks on Nussbaum and Rothblum reflect the Klan's awareness that Jews, whatever their moral transgressions, were fellow whites.

Thus, for most Texas Jews the danger of physical violence from the Klan remained remote, and few took it seriously. More immediately threatening was the possibility that the Klan would organize boycotts against Jewish businesses. One Jewish resident of Corsicana remembered stickers placed in shop windows indicating that they were "Klan sanctioned, and stores without the stickers were to be boycotted. Of course, no Jewish stores were marked."[30] In 1923, the editor of the *Texas (100 Percent) American*, the Dallas Klan paper, warned a local Jewish tailor not to organize his industry against the Klan, "because if you do the Klan klothiers located all over the kountry might decide that Protestant scissors might better cut the garments they sell."[31] The threat of boycott was real enough that one unnamed Fort Worth Jewish storeowner was reported to have paid the Klan initiation fees for his employees so that other members would not withdraw their business.[32] Another Fort Worth merchant added the name of a Klan member he employed to his company's letterhead in the hope of discouraging boycotts.[33] The Dallas bakery owned by civic titan Julius Schepps paid the Klan membership dues for about fifty employees, perhaps to preserve gentile good will, though Schepps later claimed it was to help him keep watch on Klan activities.[34]

If the order's social organization was strong enough to threaten Jewish businesses, its tightening grasp on political power, which had always been open to Jews but to a lesser extent, was more frightening still. The Klan had enough pull in Dallas, Houston, and Austin to get downtown streetlights turned off for their night-time marches, giving the torch-lit events their requisite spookiness.[35] Dallas County residents suspected that both their sheriff and district attorney were active Klansmen—the *Dallas Morning News* referred to the pair as a "bedsheet sheriff" and a "river-bottom advocate"—and known Klan sympathizers occupied similar posts in counties and towns across the state.[36] Waco's mayor and Board of Police Commissioners, the DeWitt County (Cuero) judge and several jurors, and the Jefferson County (Beaumont) and Travis County (Austin) sheriffs were all Klansmen, as well as countless others.[37] Historian Norman Brown, who has written extensively on Texas politics during the Klan era, explains that Klansmen felt they had "immunity from punishment or even investigation" by virtue of the "district and county judges, district and county attorneys, justices of the peace, constables, police commissioners, chiefs of police, policemen, mayors, newspaper editors, and reporters" included among their members. Brown specifically cites Houston, where a Klan leader bragged that the order "ran things its own way," and Austin, where the Klan controlled both the city police force and the Travis County sheriff's office.[38] In addition to the numerous public officials on Klan membership rosters, many towns' general citizenry openly supported the Invisible Empire. In Lorena, south of Waco, hooded Klansmen with weapons concealed beneath their robes marched in violation of a prohibition by the McLennan County sheriff. When he tried to stop them, a riot ensued in which the sheriff and three others were injured and a spectator was killed. Five days later, the townspeople adopted a resolution that blamed the wounded sheriff for the fiasco.[39]

"Some of My Best Friends"

Jewish reaction to these developments was muted, in keeping with the relatively minimal threat that the Klan posed to Jewish lives and institutions. Whatever the Klan's rhetoric, its limited and isolated actions did not justify a sense of emergency to most Jewish Texans. On a personal level, Klansmen gave their Jewish neighbors little reason to fear them, and examples abound of cordial personal and business relations between Texas Jews and Klan members. When the Klan first marched in Houston in 1921, they wore robes and hoods bought from a Jewish manufacturer.[40] John Rosenfield, a Jewish reporter for the *Dallas Morning News* who later became its arts editor and one of the city's most influential cultural figures, began his career covering Klan picnics. Fred Florence, a leading Dallas banker, was a longtime friend of Zeke Marvin, head of the Texas Klan.[41] And during a Dallas recruitment drive, Klansmen visited Edward Titche, the Jewish head of the Titche-Goettinger department store, to invite him to join. Titche was obliged to explain why he could not, to which a Klansman replied that it was a shame—Titche would have made a fine recruiter.[42]

Fort Worth rabbi G. George Fox treated Klan members as the friends and associates they were, and when reports of Klan violence in his city began to surface, Fox expressed only mild dissatisfaction. "We had hoped," he said, "that the Ku Klux Klan would do some things that perhaps would add to the good and the glory of the nation . . . without infringing on the rights of others."[43] When word spread of a potential boycott of Jewish businesses, Fox went to his contacts inside the Klan and received their "absolute word" that no boycott would take place.[44] Upon the rabbi's acceptance of a Chicago pulpit in 1923, the Fort Worth Chamber of Commerce held a banquet in his honor "at which," Fox remembered, "the Texas head of the Ku Klux Klan presided, and a check was given me as a going-away present, with which I was to buy a new car when we got to Chicago."[45] Fox did speak out against the Klan in the abstract, and against its harsher methods, but he chose his words carefully and presented his criticism amicably. "Just

Rabbi G. George Fox in 1912 with wife Hortense Lewis Fox and son Samson George, who died in 1918. Courtesy Beth-El Congregation Archives, Fort Worth, Texas.

as my non-Jewish friends who say something against my co-religionists always assure me that their 'best friends are Jews,'" he wrote in a privately published circular, "so say I now to those who might feel that my words are directed against them, that among these false prophets are also some of 'my best friends.'"[46]

Fox's circular dissected the Klan's limited definition of "100% Americanism," emphasizing that Jews, Catholics, and the foreign-born were true patriots and that the Klan itself posed a graver threat to American values by its "injection of religious fanaticism into the body politic of our country."[47] Rather than single out minority groups for attack, he argued, the Klan should recognize that "[o]ur country has attained greatness because in it are mixed the best elements of many peoples, and multitudes of faiths."[48] In the *Jewish Monitor*, which he edited, Fox reassured his readers that the Klan only minimally threatened their place in American society: "The alleged prejudice against Jews in these organizations is exaggerated," he wrote, and "we can only make matters worse by consistently dwelling upon the unfortunate intrusion into the calmness of American life of racial and religious prejudice."[49] To him, the Klan's anti-Semitism was less important than the divisions it fomented among Americans.

Galveston rabbi Henry Cohen and his close friend Father James Kirwin, the leader of the island's Catholic community, led a more direct, though still muted and personalized, resistance. Galveston was a sophisticated and cosmopolitan city with a diverse population where the Klan had little support. Cohen and Kirwin were among the most esteemed men in town, and Cohen's son, Harry, published the afternoon paper, the *Galveston Tribune*. Nonetheless, the Klan managed to scrape together a Galveston chapter, and Cohen spoke against it whenever he could. At one public gathering, he harshly denounced a preacher in attendance who had explained from his pulpit why the Jewish people deserved the Klan's condemnation.[50] With Kirwin, the rabbi secured a promise from city officials to deny parade permits to Klansmen, and Cohen lobbied a local movie theater manager to cancel a screening of *Birth of a Nation*.[51]

In Dallas, where Klan influence was strongest and most malevolent, Rabbi David Lefkowitz of Temple Emanu-El was a more vocal and forthright opponent, devoting sermons, public speeches, and guest editorials to condemning the Klan. In 1920, the year the Texas Klan began its rise to prominence, Lefkowitz arrived in Dallas and soon signed the first call for a public meeting to rally opposition against the nascent organization. He was among the first members of the Dallas County Citizens League, which opposed the Klan on the political front. Lefkowitz also provided frequent encouragement to George B. Dealey, the publisher of the *Dallas Morning News* and the *Dallas Journal*, both of which lost subscribers over their bold anti-Klan positions.[52] In return, Dealey reprinted a sermon Lefkowitz delivered on the Friday following Klan Day at the State Fair. "[Hiram Evans] is a thousand times wrong," Lefkowitz said in reaction to the Imperial Wizard's claim that Jews were "an absolutely unblendable element." Lefkowitz pledged, "[He] has wrongly flouted my people, and I will not be silent." The rabbi's defense hinged on the principle that Jews, many of whom had fought and died defending democracy in World War I, were as loyal, patriotic, and American as anyone else.[53] In response to a reader's praise of the article, Lefkowitz remarked that he hoped that his "appeals to patriotism, common sense, and love of God" would "break the hold of the Klan upon a great many well-meaning people who were lured into it."[54]

Despite the rabbi's clear revulsion against the Klan, these comments are still remarkably accommodating. His defense focused on Jews' patriotism and Americanism, not on their Jewishness, their distinctiveness, or their right to be respected regardless of race or religion. Lefkowitz's reply to Evans' criticism that Jews did not blend sufficiently into American life was "Yes, we do," not "So what?" Accepting the Klan's self-description as a patriotic and benevolent organization rather than casting them as the thugs he knew they were, he let the Klan choose the grounds for the argument.

Like Fox, Lefkowitz preferred to emphasize the values that Jews shared with other Americans rather than to defend their differences. His efforts focused, therefore, on purging Klan influence from Dallas Masonic lodges, bastions of interfaith civility. The Klan recruited heavily among Masons, and Lefkowitz, himself a 33rd-degree member, observed that the Klan "got a good foot-hold and respectability through the fact that it had bored into the Masonic Lodge." While trying to discourage more Masons from becoming Klan members, he also worked to undermine the Klan's influence within Masonry itself. After a non-Klan Mason narrowly defeated a Klansman for district officer of the Dallas Lodge, Lefkowitz appealed to the crowd at the electoral meeting "in the well known thesis of good-will and fundamental religious attitudes." Challenging his gentile brothers in the Lodge, as Christians, to rethink their support for the Invisible Empire, he asked: "Do you believe in God and brotherhood and care of the widow and orphan? How do you square that with your actions relative to discrimination as to race and creed?" He pointed out that Jewish and non-Jewish Masons had all proven their patriotism, many on European battlefields, and deserved to be treated as equals. The address cleared the air, Lefkowitz later remembered, and was a "death blow" to Klan activity within the Masonic order.[55]

In these and other cases, Texas rabbis fought the Klan from within the shelter of white communal institutions and from positions inside their cities' power establishments. Cohen acted as one of the most respected men in Galveston, Lefkowitz as a high-ranking Mason among Masons, and Fox from almost within the Klan itself. They were all insiders, thoroughly acculturated to the American way of life and accepted in the halls of civic power. As such, they built their public resistance to the Klan on the premise that the Invisible Empire was only a danger to Jews insofar as it challenged the secular American values that Jews cherished as much as everyone else. Jews were patriots, these rabbis insisted, who had given their lives and fortunes for their country. In making their quiet stand against the Klan, these rabbis avoided even the appearance of a Jewish community organized for sectarian purposes, forging solidarity with like-minded gentiles rather than with one another. They answered the Imperial Wizard's charge that Jews were "unblendable" by insisting that they were in fact part of a white American consensus. Klansmen, they felt, not Jews, threatened that consensus by drawing lines between people where none existed. "That the Ku Klux Klan does not admit Jews bothers me little," Fox wrote. The real problem was "the constant injection into public life of the differences which are bound to exist, in a nation made up of so many different peoples as is ours."[56]

Burning Crosses

Although their religious leaders limited themselves to abstract arguments, many Texas Jews, especially in smaller communities, sensed that real trouble lay ahead, and whatever individual Klansmen (or rabbis, for that matter) might profess, the hooded crowds that turned out for rallies in dozens of cities and towns could not have been a comforting sight. The Klan's rise in the 1920s confirmed many Jews' fears about the unfriendly feelings that might lie beneath the genial surface of their relations with white Christian Texans. In Beaumont, for example, Carrie Chazan Leichtman recalled that "the community-at-large accepted our ability to serve the needs of the community," and "[t]here were no signs of overt anti-Semitism, although I remember that the undercurrent of anti-Jewish feeling was present."[57] Lionel Koppman, too, has written that anti-Semitism in Waco "was both open and hidden. Our neighbors were polite, but I don't recall ever having been invited into their homes."[58] Morris Zale, the self-professed "only Jew in town" in Graham, Texas, noticed that customers began to boycott his jewelry business in the months following the establishment of the local klavern. Zale held on until he witnessed a downtown parade and initiation ceremony. "When I saw that cross burning," he remembered, "I was scared to death." Zale fled Graham for nearby Wichita Falls, which had more Jews and a less active Klan, and there he built Zale's Jewelry into a Texas institution.[59]

Fear of gentiles' prejudice could have pushed Jews toward social identification with other racial and ethnic minorities who experienced more overt discrimination, but there is little evidence that this occurred in Texas. When living in communities with large African-American and Mexican-

American populations, Jews tended to feel part of white society, and, to a large degree, other whites invited Jews into their social circles. In fact, Texas' very diversity may have mitigated the differences among categories of whites. "We had a population of white, black, Mexicans, and Indians," Evelynn Lois Ray recalled of San Angelo, "and we all respected each other and showed it." As Jews, she said, her family was "never treated differently because there were too many different ethnic groups in San Angelo. There were business people, ranchers, farmers, oil men, Mexican pickers—everyone was different in his own way."[60] Such comments suggest that among whites, especially those of similar economic class, religious differences were less apparent than those among racial groups and between middle- and working-class Texans.

Although affiliating socially with whites, Texas Jews exhibited relatively little of the racial bigotry that often characterized white Texans, and many maintained business relations with black and Mexican-American employees and customers even if they did not commonly socialize with them. The Popular Store of El Paso, owned and managed by the Schwartz family, one of the city's original Jewish families, built success on the strength of its "one-price" policy, advertised on the store's billboards: "You pay what your neighbor pays. No discounts, no favorites. One price to all alike." The Popular was also the first major El Paso retailer to hire African-American floor workers, and Hispanics constituted the majority of the store's employees.[61] Albert Granoff, who began his Laredo retail business by selling Catholic pictures and religious items in Mexican-American neighborhoods, found that his Spanish-speaking clients were sympathetic and reliable customers, and he and his partner "became enthusiastic and worked more among the Mexican people than among the Negroes or whites."[62] Jimmy Wagner, a black Corpus Christi resident, suggested that minority customers treated respectfully remembered it and preferred to shop in Jewish establishments. Entering a Christian-owned department store to buy a pair of shoes, Wagner recalled that "[t]hey were not friendly. They said 'Boy. What you doin' here?'" Wagner walked out. "[I] went to Lichtenstein's, and was treated courteously. I remember that just as plain as day."[63]

However attentive they might have been to black and Latino acquaintances, Texas Jews always saw themselves as whites and remained conscious of the ethnic frontier that divided them. The state's peculiar racial algebra labeled everyone Anglo, African-American, or Mexican-American, so Jews could scarcely be anything else. "The schools were very segregated," remembered Julius Leshin of Robstown, in South Texas. "Through the sixth grade the Hispanic children attended a separate school, and the few black children attended a separate black school," while white children, including Jews like Leshin, attended the white school.[64] In Luling's segregated school district, not only did Milford Jacobs attend white schools, but his father, Leon, served as school board president. In the early 1920s, he oversaw the construction of "a nice brick school for the black children near the old Luling Jewish Cemetery." Students and their families were so pleased with the structure, Jacobs says, that when they dedicated the building "they had a picture in the Assembly Room of Booker T. Washington and one of Leon Jacobs on each side of George Washington's picture."[65] Though sympathetic to the racial minorities in their communities and treating them with somewhat more respect than did other whites, Texas Jews as a group did not identify with them or define themselves as a persecuted minority, despite the occasional slights they received from individual gentiles. On the contrary, Jews like Alex Sanger stood firmly within white business and social circles in positions of civic leadership. The Klan's rise, however, and its support from business, civic, and political leaders challenged that arrangement and forced Jews to reevaluate the degree to which they were really welcome.

Agonizing Choices: The Klan in Electoral Politics

When the Ku Klux Klan began influencing state and national affairs, the situation grew dire, and Texas-Jewish voters were forced to make difficult electoral decisions. Like white voters throughout the one-party South, Texas Jews were Democrats. Had there been no Klan, Jewish voters in Texas, as elsewhere, would have gone on voting for Democratic candidates and congratulating themselves on their successful Americanization and equal participation in the democratic process. By 1922, however, the Klan was backing successful gubernatorial campaigns in Georgia, Alabama, California, and Oregon in a national effort to put sympathetic candidates into office. As many as seventy-five members of the U.S. House of Representatives had received crucial support from the Klan, and a handful of U.S. senators, looking toward future elections, began cozying up to the organization. In Arkansas, the Klan was so powerful that it held its own unofficial primary before the regular Democratic primary to decide which of its members to support for the nomination.[66]

Few realms in the growing Klan empire, however, enjoyed Texas' exceptional political success. In many districts, popular anti-Klan incumbents, among them future Vice President John Nance Garner and future House Speaker Sam Rayburn, found themselves dangerously close to expulsion. In Dallas, the Klan helped make Edith Wilmans the first woman to serve in the Texas Legislature. In a Democratic-dominated state, moreover, the Klan's ability to wield its power in both parties was remarkable. San Antonio Klansmen stood behind a Republican candidate for local office who, with Klan help, defeated his Jewish Democratic opponent by about three thousand votes.[67] Most spectacularly, Texan Earle Mayfield, a nominee hand-picked by Imperial Wizard Hiram Evans, became the first candidate with known Klan support to win a seat in the U.S. Senate.

Mayfield's Klan-backed candidacy was the first of many to drive a wedge into Texas-Jewish identity. On his merits and experience, the candidate was perfectly acceptable, and in a normal year, most Jewish voters would probably have voted for him without thinking twice. Mayfield (who was unrelated to Klan newspaperman Billie Mayfield) was never a dues-paying member of the Klan, nor did he ever mention the group publicly during the campaign. However, because the organization was known to stand behind him, and because of the Klan's stated opposition to immigration and pluralism, as well as its anti-Semitic exclusiveness, Jewish voters hesitated before supporting Mayfield's candidacy. And once they hesitated, they instantly became *Jewish* voters, not fully blended into the mainstream but voting out of a distinctive set of concerns. In questioning Mayfield's candidacy, they drew a new division between themselves and Protestant voters who, whatever their personal feelings about the Klan, could vote with reasonable comfort for a candidate praised by Klansmen as the only "native-born white Protestant Gentile" in the race.[68] Here, then, is the most important consequence of the Klan years for Jews in Texas: forced to choose whether to identify themselves as whites in support of a respectable and qualified candidate or as Jews with separate, segregated concerns, they could no longer, it seemed, be both white *and* Jewish.

Earle Mayfield defeated six opponents in the 1922 Democratic primary, including three professed Klansmen and James Ferguson, the former governor who had been impeached and removed from office in 1917. "Farmer Jim" was a powerful spokesman for white laborers and farmers, who rewarded him with tenacious support, even backing him in a quixotic 1920 presidential race on his own American Party ticket. His rousing oratory, "a style of speaking that mixed bad grammar, folksy stories, sarcasm, and slander in about equal proportions," set a new standard for political speech in a state known before and after for its flamboyant public speakers.[69] Ferguson, the son of a circuit-riding Methodist preacher, took money from brewers and saloonkeepers and so opposed Prohibition, which the Klan supported. He ridiculed the wealthy and the urban elite and, in the judgment of an Austin newspaper editor, "purposely played ignorant to win the rural vote."[70] Beloved by the rural whites whose causes he championed, Ferguson's ruthless ambition, questionable ethics, and slick political tactics were a source of embarrassment for just about everyone else in the state, including its well-educated and urban Jewish population. By comparison, Mayfield seemed an acceptable if imperfect choice to most Democratic primary voters. The anti-Klan candidacy of Republican George Peddy gave the morally conscious Jewish voter some alternative, but Peddy was a bland and uninspiring candidate who, in a solidly Democratic state, had no chance of winning the general election. Loyalty to the Democratic Party had deep roots reaching back to Reconstruction, and many Texas voters, Jews and gentiles alike, would never consider voting for a Republican under any circumstances.

Not only the Klan, but also other Jews were forcing an unwelcome divergence between Jewish and mainstream white concerns. As the campaign progressed, national Jewish leaders pressured Texas Jews to act and vote in the name of Jews everywhere as they faced what leaders saw as a grave national political crisis. Louis Marshall, the nation's most prominent Jewish leader, wrote to Henry Cohen to urge him to take stronger action against Mayfield following his Democratic primary victory. Marshall presumed (wrongly, as it happens) that Mayfield was "conducting his fight on an anti-Catholic, anti-Jewish platform." If true, he continued, "it is not conceivable that [Jewish Texans] are indifferent. . . . Should Mayfield win, the K.K.K. would not refrain from carrying out its anti-Semitic policies." Marshall recognized that it would be inappropriate for him or for other non-Texans to intervene directly, so Texas Jews had an even greater obligation "to stand up for their manhood and to fight for the protection of their rights" by supporting Mayfield's Republican opponent.[71]

To Marshall's charge Cohen responded brusquely, "We are fighting the K.K.K. in our own way," referring presumably to his efforts with Father Kirwin to exert quiet personal pressure on city officials. Cohen assured Marshall that Texas Jews would vote overwhelmingly for Peddy of their own accord, and so "no organized campaign will be necessary." He went on to declare that he did not consider Mayfield an anti-Semite. "He is not the avowed candidate of the Klan," Cohen explained, "nor did he mention the Klan in his campaign." In closing, Cohen again assured Marshall that

Texas Jews were "alive to the possibilities and we are taking quiet precautions in the matter."[72] Cohen's position was grounded in the hard reality of the situation. Stubborn Democratic party loyalty would compel many Jewish voters to support Mayfield while others would cast ineffectual votes for Peddy, and Cohen believed that nothing he could do could alter the outcome. With the Klan in ascendancy, Jewish voters had little option but to follow the rabbi's lead and accept the inevitable. Mayfield would be their senator as well as the Klan's.

The 1922 Senate race was only the first of many statewide elections over the next decade in which Texas Jews faced the unsavory task of choosing the lesser from a field of evils. Like many other Texas Democrats, they resented and feared the Klan's intrusion into their party and hoped for a better alternative than voting Republican. Unfortunately, the only Democratic politician in Texas with the electoral strength to build opposition to the Klan into a viable campaign strategy was also the most widely despised—"Farmer Jim" Ferguson. However distasteful Jewish voters may have found Ferguson's personal style and dubious past, some viewed him as an acceptable alternative to Mayfield in the 1922 Democratic primary. In that campaign, Ferguson was the only candidate to make an issue of Mayfield's Klan ties, condemning the front-runner as the "crown prince of the Klan" and the pawn of a "hydra-headed monster."[73] Once, in a small East Texas town, Ferguson scolded a group of young Klan supporters in what a witness called "one of the most forthright statements I ever heard." Ferguson warned that "some of you young men who have been listening to the wrong people . . . will be talked into going with the crowd." They would eventually take actions, he said, "whipping a man or something worse," that would lead to "the penitentiary in Huntsville. Or it could be the electric chair." All this unnecessary pain, he concluded, would come "because you listened to some contemptible bigot."[74] His direct approach earned Ferguson allies among Jews and other anti-Klan Texans, and, with his eye on future campaigns, he continued his attacks on the Klan after losing the 1922 race. From his office in Temple, an agricultural community midway between Waco and Austin, he published the weekly *Ferguson Forum*, in which he constructed an image of himself as the greatest anti-Klansman in Texas. In early 1923, he moved the *Forum*'s headquarters to Dallas, the Klan's greatest Texas stronghold, a gambit he hoped would put him in a better position to run for governor in 1924. Besides being a Klan bastion, Dallas was also a retailing mecca with a wealth of potential advertisers that Temple, with its farming base, could never match. Looking toward the coming election, Ferguson hoped to count on support from Dallas' wealthy Jewish community in the epic anti-Klan battle he planned to stage.

Despite the inroads he had made with Jewish Texans, Ferguson managed within weeks of his arrival in Dallas to lose their trust. By his own account, he approached many of Dallas' leading Jewish merchants about advertising in the *Forum*, reminding them of his attempt the previous year to defeat a Klan-sponsored candidate. The response was tepid. One Jewish firm, Ferguson reported, bought $25 worth of ads, in exchange for which Ferguson bought $37.50 worth of floor covering—only to have the company refuse to buy more advertising. He accused another Jewish-owned company of spending $8 in the *Forum* on the same day that they bought $400 worth of ads in the *Texas (100 Percent) American*, the city's Klan paper.[75] A survey of the *American* during the months Ferguson was in Dallas reveals no advertisements by Jewish firms, suggesting that Ferguson was mistaken, that he misrepresented the incident, or that the editor of the *American* took $400 from a Jewish merchant and then never ran the purchased ads.

Ferguson responded to these perceived slights with a scathing *Forum* editorial, "The Cloven Foot of the Dallas Jew." In it, he described himself as "puzzled as well as disappointed" at the Jewish response to his requests for support, especially since he "had been criticized so bitterly for defending the legal right of the Jews," presumably a reference to his opposition to the Klan. Purchasing a few ads, he said, would have been a simple and painless way for Jewish merchants "to show some appreciation of the stand I had taken." When Ferguson prodded "one of the big Jew merchants" for an explanation, the merchant revealed that "the reason he could not give me any business was because of the political feature of The Forum and that because I had been so emphatic in my statements against the Ku Klux." At that point, Ferguson said, "I knew I was getting at the facts." In the remainder of the column, Ferguson outlined his belief that Jewish businessmen and the Klan had "hatched in Dallas an unholy alliance . . . whereby the Ku Klux are to get the big offices and the Big Jews are to get the big business." He warned his readers that if they bought anything from a "Jew store" they were "buying from the friend of the Ku Klux," a merchant who had "[surrendered] his religion to help his business." Ferguson vowed to "bust up this Ku-Jew-Klux Kombination if it is the last thing I ever do."[76] Ironically, the Klan condemned Jews for failing to assimilate sufficiently, yet Ferguson condemned them for accommodating their religious faith.

Rabbi Harry A. Merfeld, G. George Fox's successor as editor, responded to Ferguson's charges in Forth Worth's *Jewish Monitor*. Merfeld did not deny that Jewish merchants in Dallas had given the former governor the cold shoulder, but he argued that Ferguson had misinterpreted their reasons. Merfeld took strong objection to Ferguson's attack on Jewish character. "[A]sinine opinions to the contrary," he wrote, Dallas Jews were "honest, self-respecting citizens, 100 per cent Americans, if you please." The best way for them to prove their detractors wrong, he continued, was by "maintaining a dignified and gentlemanly demeanor, even in the face of unwarranted and unjustifiable vilification and abuse," and by "declining to support or foster in any way yellow journalism in whatsoever guise it may stalk." Finally, in a direct attack on Ferguson, Merfeld declared that Dallas Jews would refuse "in no uncertain terms to have fellowship with or to be identified in any way, however remote, with any movement sponsored by you and your kind."[77]

Ferguson was quick to parse Merfeld's words. "When he says that the Dallas Jews will not be identified with any movement sponsored by me," he wrote in a front-page *Forum* response, "he means that hereafter the Jews will not in any way approve . . . the opposition of the Forum to the Ku Klux." The editor also singled out Merfeld's use of a familiar phrase, remarking that "you now say that you are 100 per cent American," but "this 100 per cent talk, of course, is what the Ku Klux have put in your mouth to say."[78] Ferguson's argument that Jews' resistance to him was tantamount to donning hoods of their own made him unacceptable as a candidate to most Texas Jews, but the political climate of the time offered few alternatives.

The bitterness that Jewish voters continued to feel for Ferguson came to a head in the fierce gubernatorial campaign of 1924, the year after the publication of "The Cloven Foot." Ferguson entered the race in January, insisting that his prior impeachment did not bar him from running again for statewide office. When the Texas Supreme Court declared him ineligible, he offered his wife as a candidate to run in his place: "If the State has a Governor Ferguson," he declared, "we need not fall out about who signs on the dotted line."[79] Miriam A. Ferguson—whose initials soon earned her the nickname "Ma"—accepted her husband's platform as her own and let "Pa" do most of the talking. The Fergusons proposed several policy initiatives directed against the Klan, including a strict anti-mask law (which passed in 1925) prohibiting Texans from appearing in public with covered faces or in disguises of any kind. Masked participants, even in private meetings, could receive jail terms. The Fergusons also recommended requiring secret and fraternal societies to file their members' names with county clerks' offices for public scrutiny.

The Fergusons' chief opponent in the Democratic primary was Felix Robertson, a Dallas criminal district court judge and dues-paying member of the Dallas klavern, who had sat on the podium at the Hope Cottage dedication ceremony during the 1923 Texas State Fair. In its report of that event, the *Dallas Morning News* described Robertson as one of the "klan dignitaries" in attendance.[80] Robertson neither bragged about his participation in the order nor denied it. Expressing a support for moral law and order typical of Klan candidates, Robertson declared himself a prohibitionist and promised the "prompt, vigorous and impartial enforcement" of anti-liquor laws.[81] In addition, Robertson billed himself as a "praying judge" who advocated a renewed public focus on Christianity: "above all those ghastly ruins [of fallen civilizations] there stands but one thing," he said in a typical stump speech, "the rugged cross of Christianity, the cross on which our master was sacrificed."[82] His pledges to enforce the blue laws restricting the sale of merchandise on Sundays, to abolish immigration, and to suppress foreign-language newspapers made Robertson a candidate the Klan could wholeheartedly endorse—and one straight from the nightmares of Jewish voters.

At least in 1922 Jews had been able to comfort themselves with the belief that Earle Mayfield had never officially been a Klansman and was something more than a mouthpiece for the organization. Robertson, in contrast, made no secret of his allegiance to the Invisible Empire, and it was well known that the state's highest Klan officials had selected him. But the equally unthinkable alternative was to rally behind the author of "The Cloven Foot of the Dallas Jew." The choice also confounded non-Jewish voters, but they were more easily reconciled, especially as Ma's candidacy put some apparent distance between Pa and the governor's chair. "They say that Jim will run the state," said one former Ferguson opponent. "All right, I'd rather have it run by James and Miriam Ferguson than by Evans, Marvin, Butcher, Robertson and gang."[83] George B. Dealey, publisher of the *Dallas Morning News*, who had opposed Pa Ferguson as governor and remained among his harshest critics, also viewed the Klan as a greater evil than another Ferguson administration. The *News* supported Ma's election because it would "sound the death knell of the klan as a political power in this State."[84] Gentile voters had reservations about the Ferguson ticket, to be sure, but only Jews had faced the particular bigotry of which Farmer Jim was capable.

With infinite irony, Klansman Robertson recognized an opportunity and made a play for Jewish votes. His supporters distributed copies of "The Cloven Foot of the Dallas Jew," adding the caption "Ferguson Vents Spleen

Governors James E. "Pa" Ferguson and Miriam A. "Ma" Ferguson, ca. 1925.
The *San Antonio Light* Collection, UTSA's Institute of Texan Cultures, No. L-0827-G.
Courtesy of the Hearst Corporation.

on Jewish People."[85] The effort failed, however, as Robertson's strongest backers were unenthusiastic about recruiting Jews to their cause. In Houston, Dr. D. L. Griffith, pastor of Trinity Baptist Church, called a meeting of local clergymen to enlist their backing for Robertson. When asked why only Protestant clergy participated, Griffith replied that leaders of other denominations preferred not to attend, so he had not invited them.[86] Robertson himself, in his final speech of the primary season, alienated many of the Jewish voters he was trying to court by reiterating his call for a state government of "common sense, common honesty and Christianity."[87] Even so, with Ferguson, any Ferguson, in the race, the choice for most Jewish voters remained complex. Many probably found it easier to support Robertson, a Klan-backed candidate who *might* have been an anti-Semite, over Ferguson, an anti-Klan shadow candidate who clearly *was* an anti-Semite.

A number of statements in the *Texas Jewish Herald* reveal the degree of conflict that the Klan's influence in politics had caused in the Jewish electorate. Rabbi David Goldberg of Wichita Falls wrote in the *Herald* of the "vagueness and confusion" infecting politics even at the national level. "This is due to the note of insincerity and evasiveness injected by the Ku Klux Klan," he explained. "No one knows who is who and what one stands for."[88] In a related editorial, the rabbi responded incredulously to a reader's question: "Should a Jew oppose the Klan?" The question itself, he said, is "evidence of the confusion which the advent of the hooded organization has brought into the minds of otherwise clear thinking people." Of course Jews should oppose the Klan, he answered, "and that [is] because the Klan [has] placed the Jew in opposition to itself."[89]

For most Texas voters, the Ferguson ticket offered the best hope of ridding the state of an organization with which they were losing patience. When the primary was over, Ma Ferguson had defeated Robertson by nearly one hundred thousand votes statewide in the largest tally ever polled in a Texas election up to that time. Even in urban counties where Klan support was strongest, Ma polled surprisingly well. The loss signaled the beginning of the end for the Texas Klan. "After Robertson was beaten," remembered a former member, "the prominent men left the Klan. The Klan's standing went with them."[90] But, with the November general election still ahead, the organization was not quite finished.

To oppose Miriam Ferguson, the Republicans nominated George Butte, a mild-mannered law professor who, though vocal in his opposition to the Klan, was far less so than Farmer Jim. Jewish voters were again faced with a complicated choice, and their ambivalence appears clearly in the pages of the *Texas Jewish Herald*. In October, just weeks before the general election, Butte supporters purchased a half-page of the *Herald* in order to reprint Ferguson's "Cloven Foot" editorial in full. Beneath it, the advertisement announced that Butte was "an eminently qualified, broad-minded man interested in the welfare of every citizen of Texas, without regard to race or creed."[91] Perhaps due to that position, Texas Klansmen rallied only half-heartedly behind the Republican in a last-ditch hope to defeat the Ferguson ticket. The Klan's limited but visible involvement in the Butte campaign was more than many Jews could stand, and the Fergusons pushed to bring Jewish voters back into their camp. One week after the Butte advertisement appeared in the *Herald*, Harris County Democrats sponsored a larger announcement "[c]ordially inviting our Jewish friends to vote and see that all of their friends vote for Mrs. Miriam Ferguson," who was "the Democratic Nominee and Anti-Klan."[92] The involvement of the hooded order in Texas politics had not only deepened the division between Jews and white gentiles, but it had also fragmented the Jewish electorate. Those who supported Butte had betrayed party and regional allegiance to vote with the Klan, but those who stayed with the Democrats and Ferguson had accepted a proven anti-Semite.

In the end, to no one's surprise, Ma Ferguson was elected easily. Butte's loss dealt a deathblow to the Texas Klan, and interest in the group vanished. Only nine months earlier, the Houston chapter had sponsored a huge initiation ceremony on Main Street, but by December the Fort Worth chapter had trouble building even moderate excitement for a parade. As the *Houston Press* reported, "the public is about fed up with the klan."[93] Both *Colonel Mayfield's Weekly* and the *Texas (100 Percent) American* folded, along with klaverns across the state. The organization lingered at the local level in many cities for the next year or so but was no longer an avenue for political action. The order's fate was sealed in 1926 when Attorney General Dan Moody, who had risen to fame by fighting the Klan in the courts, defeated Ma Ferguson and served two terms as governor. Moody finally gave voters an opportunity to support a reputable and likable Democrat who was untainted by a corrupt past, personal ambition, or vindictiveness. As quickly as it had started, the era of the Texas Klan ended.

Though brief, the period of Klan power had a significant impact on Texas Jewry, adjusting the internal frontiers that defined it. Throughout their history, Jewish Texans had manifested an almost unquestioned commitment to acculturation. They had made every effort to prove themselves worthy fellow-citizens and to downplay the ethnic and religious differences that distinguished them from the gentiles whose respect, friendship, and business they desired. In their own eyes, they were as native to the Lone Star State as anyone else, and they had continually emphasized their patriotism, military service, and civic leadership so that gentiles might see them as they saw themselves.

However, the Klan's success at finding a willing gentile audience and at infiltrating state and local governments revealed that complete acceptance was not forthcoming. The Klan's popularity threw into relief the fundamental differences between Jews and other Texans, differences that had always existed but had been smoothed over by accommodationist and commercially oriented Jews. Jews were Anglos, perhaps, but they could never be Anglo-Saxons, nor could they become Protestants without ceasing to be Jews. As long as they kept their Jewish identity, they would never be American enough for the Klan or for the public that supported it. The Klan's foray into Texas politics had drawn a clear line between Jews and other Texans that ended their long effort to prove their worthiness to gentiles. Along with other developments in Texas and far beyond it, the Klan experience helped set Texas Jews on a path toward greater Jewish self-awareness, assertiveness, and involvement with Jewish issues and institutions worldwide. At the same time, they experienced an ideological clash at home that shook the state's largest Jewish community and split its oldest synagogue. As the global crises of the twentieth century began to unfold, Houston Jews turned on each other.

SIX

Traditional Judaism and
the Beth Israel Revolt

"The miraculous story of a people's struggle against tyranny, a story that was thousands of years in the writing, is told in one inspired phrase—from Egypt to Texas." Thus the authors of the *Golden Book of Congregation Adath Yeshurun,* in celebration of their Houston synagogue's fiftieth anniversary in 1941, imagined a straight line from the ancient history of the Jewish people to their eventual home in Texas. Symbolically equating tsarist Russia, from which many of them had fled, with biblical Egypt, they likened their experience to that of Moses, recalling their own "providential escape" that revealed "the same truth that the Israelites of old saw in the wonders of the exodus." Like the flight from Egypt, theirs was a prophetic journey of both material and spiritual liberation, "[f]rom oppression to freedom, . . . from broken body and spirit to the joyous worship of God," a journey that had once again assured the survival of Jewish life. For these writers, their escape to freedom ended in Texas, whose "wide and open spaces . . . symbolized the unrestrained welcome that America extended to those who were seeking a new home." They felt part of Texas history, noting proudly that "a Jewish name is . . . immortalized among the martyrs of the Alamo and several others are mentioned in the course of the struggle for freedom from Mexican rule." When Texas achieved independence, they remarked, "the adventuresome spirit of the Jew thrilled with other Texans at the establishment of the Lone Star Republic."[1]

However, few members of Congregation Adath Yeshurun had Texas ancestors, and the degree to which they fit in among the state's gentiles— or among its Jews, for that matter—was doubtful. Unlike Texans born in the state or in other parts of the South or West, most were immigrants from eastern Europe, or the children of immigrants, who had come via New York and other northeastern American cities. Moreover, although the majority of Jewish Texans had established Reform Judaism as the dominant form of worship, Adath Yeshurun was an Orthodox synagogue whose members and their ancestors had defied religious reform and resisted the urge to accommodate their religion to the requirements of secular society. Adath Yeshurun's traditional form of Judaism, closer in style to that of eastern Europe than was common among Houston Jews, emphasized Hebrew as the language of prayer rather than English or German, traditional liturgical dress and dietary restrictions, separation of the sexes in the synagogue, and strict adherence to Sabbath observance. The state's Reform majority, in contrast, descended from central Europeans with roots in the Enlightenment culture of Germany and Austria, had established communities and religious institutions modeled after those of gentiles, and had sought to secure a place for themselves within secular American society. In defining who they were on the Texas frontier, they had emphasized their whiteness, their southernness, their Americanness, their commercial spirit, and their civic mindedness—all factors they shared with the majority culture. Now, as the growing strength of congregations like Adath Yeshurun demonstrated, new arrivals held different views about Jewish religious practice and national identity, and they were just as devoted to carving out a place for themselves in Texas society.

The new migration of Jews, with its origins in Poland and Imperial Russia, brought a stronger insistence on Jewish distinctiveness. Their ancestors, victims of frequent pogroms, had been ghettoized in the Russian Pale of Settlement and impoverished by legal restrictions on their ability to pursue the professions and to acquire property. When they arrived in America, therefore, the distinctions between them and gentiles were sharper. They were more skeptical of gentile good will and they were less anxious to be fully incorporated into American life than the central Europeans who preceded them. They spoke Yiddish—as their parents' first language if no longer their own—and they were heirs to a rich tradition that formed the spiritual and cultural core of eastern European Jewry but put them at odds with both gentile Americans and with American Reform Judaism. They were also typically Zionists, devotees of the idea of settling a permanent Jewish homeland in Palestine, an idea whose time on the international stage had finally come just as these immigrants were reaching Texas in large numbers. More than any other issue, Zionism drove a wedge between new arrivals and native Texas Jews who saw Jewish nationalism as a threat to their status in America, opening them to the charge of dual loyalty. Texas-Jewish communities clashed and ruptured over the question of Jewish nationalism, reinforcing divisions between native and newcomer, Reform and Orthodox, and German and Russian.

After the Galveston Movement ceased operation in 1914, few Jewish immigrants arrived in Texas directly from Europe, so most of the eastern European Jews arriving in Texas after World War I had first spent several years in New York or other eastern cities. By the time they arrived in Texas, they were no longer greenhorns but Americans. They had gained experience in the arts of democracy, capitalism, and community development, and when they challenged native Texans for leadership of their communities they had a powerful and immediate impact. The dispersion of "New York Jews" to smaller cities in the South and West had been a common phenomenon for decades, and the newcomers were making their presence known in many parts of the country. In California, for example, Jews from eastern cities preferred to build new traditionalist alternatives to the state's older Reform institutions rather than to accommodate themselves or to compete for power within those already in place.[2] Atlanta's Jewish community was reshaped by such a large influx of northern Jews after the Civil War that by 1896, despite the large numbers of eastern European immigrants arriving in the city, the majority of the city's Jews were native-born Americans.[3]

For native Texas Jews, the newcomers were alien and their ideas threatening. In 1950, a Dallas parent, angry that Sunday school students were wrapping holiday gifts in the blue and white of the Israeli flag, exclaimed, "We're being taken over by another wave of immigrants"—by which she meant New Yorkers.[4] As Irving Goldberg, born in Port Arthur and later a Dallas attorney and federal judge, observed, "These new people from out of the state were more traditional in religion, more conscious of their Jewishness, more learned in Jewish concepts, and more desirous of Jewish grouping and ingathering." Their presence in Dallas and the increasing influence they wielded within the Jewish community led to changes in Dallas synagogues' worship services, especially as Conservative Judaism gained in numbers and as Reform temples, competing for new members, became more Conservative. In addition to such institutional changes, Goldberg described "other impingements" for which the newcomers were responsible. These included the opening of "a kosher delicatessen within walking distance of a Neiman-Marcus store in a fashionable part of the city"; some amount of "self-segregation by Jews in public schools"; "problems arising from the observance of Jewish holidays in relation to attendance and public schools"; and, Goldberg remarked, "[s]ome who are native to Dallas now know a bagel when they see one." Goldberg's observations, while anecdotal, support his conclusion that a new sense of religious identity was forming in his city on the Jewish frontier. "All of these factors," he wrote, "have made the community more conscious of being Jewish, more identifiable as a group."[5]

Texas Jewry remained on the geographical periphery of American Judaism, but the Jewish spiritual center, marked by religious traditionalism and a deep personal and communal sense of Jewish identification, came to Texas. When it arrived, however, native Texans opposed it. They fought back not only against the migrants themselves but also against what they represented—American and world Jewry's broad global drift toward stronger ethnic and religious identification and Zionist nationalism. Protective of their tradition of acculturation and rapprochement with gentiles, watchful of their social status, and perhaps even fearful of gentile reaction should Texas Jewry become too visible or too "pushy," natives resisted the newcomers' efforts to reshape their communities and institutions. They drew battle lines around local customs that emphasized modernization, Americanization, and acculturation, and they worked energetically to hold those lines against all challenges.

This was the first clear fissure to appear within the Texas-Jewish community. Once relatively unified in contrast to gentiles and to other Jewish communities, Texas Jews now stood arrayed along a frontier that divided them from one another. The friction culminated in Houston with the "Beth Israel Revolt" of 1943, when the state's largest and oldest congregation split over Zionism and its congregants' right to practice Judaism in more traditional ways. In this and in many less damaging instances, Jewish Texans turned against each other, fighting for control of Jewish institutions and communities. To be sure, strain between German and Russian Jews was a hallmark of the American Jewish experience, and schisms in American Jewish congregations were the norm, not an exception. Most communities throughout the nation struggled to reconcile newcomers' needs with those of community leaders who had been there since the beginning. In this national context, however, the Beth Israel Revolt stands out for its virulence, its national visibility, and the starkness with which it displayed ideological divisions among American Jews. Reform Jews and traditionalists contested the meaning of Judaism and fought over the power to define themselves, and until world developments of the 1940s gave them common cause again, these conflicts tore both large and small communities apart.

Establishing a Traditional Presence

Certainly traditional Judaism was not new in Texas, but its impact was slight until the "New York Jews" began to arrive in greater numbers in the interwar years. Houston's Congregation Beth Israel had begun as an Orthodox institution in 1859 but switched to a Reform service soon after the Civil War and eventually became a bastion of classical Reform. The state's largest cities, and many small ones, maintained a continuous traditional Jewish presence. In several communities, traditional Jews were numerous enough to break from the Reform congregations and to establish Orthodox, or later Conservative, synagogues. These include congregations Agudath Jacob of Waco (1888), Agudas Achim of San Antonio (1889), and Adath Yeshurun of Houston (1891). Fort Worth's Ahavath Sholom, founded in 1892, offered its traditional liturgy several years *before* a Reform congregation was formed in the city, and B'nai Abraham of Brenham, organized in 1885, served that small community as its only Jewish congregation for nearly a century. Where congregations could not be sustained, traditional worshipers gathered *minyans* whenever possible and employed *schochtim* (plural of *schochet*, kosher slaughterers) even if only a segment of the community took advantage of their services. Furthermore, by the early twentieth century Houston, Dallas, and San Antonio had Talmud Torahs, schools where Hebrew language and literature, including some Talmudic interpretation, was imparted to the sons of traditional Jews in the eastern European method.

Because of the relatively small number of Orthodox Jews in Texas, however, much of the burden of preserving traditional Judaism rested on the shoulders of especially dedicated individuals. Rabbi Ya'akov Geller, who immigrated from Galicia in 1892, and his wife, Sara, were a focal point of traditional Jewish belief, first in Galveston and later in Houston. According to a family biographer, Sara remained "undaunted by the ridicule of members of the community who considered her old fashioned." She proudly retained her European style of dress, "including hair covering, despite the warm Texas climate." She periodically changed the color of her wig to suit her advancing age, "indicating that her purpose was a religious act, not [for] cosmetic reasons." Sara and her husband maintained a home described as "a transplantation of European Jewish life on American soil," which served as "an oasis for many European Jews who yearned for a link to the Shtetl of their past."[6] Their son, Abram, remembered that their home "was a haven for all kinds of Jews: Rabbis, Cantors, schochtim, businessmen, meshulachim [authorized charity collectors], schnorrers [freeloaders], beggars and new immigrants coming to Texas, to the 'Goldina Medeena' [Golden Land]." During the years of the Galveston Movement, the Gellers opened their home to the more traditionally observant immigrants, providing them with kosher accommodations until the trains to their next destinations arrived. "To this day," Abram remarked in 1988, "I meet people who tell me their first kosher meal in America was cooked by my mother."[7]

The Jewish scholarly tradition also found a home in Texas, though with moderate institutional support it too depended on the efforts of dedicated students and teachers. When the Conservative congregation in San Antonio, Agudas Achim, opened its Talmud Torah around 1920, the director was a New Yorker named Saul Epstein. "He was an excellent pedagogue," recalled Hebrew teacher Alexander Gurwitz, "and he taught the children 'Hebrew in Hebrew,' that is, translating the Hebrew text into simpler Hebrew, rather than into English or Yiddish." Epstein also established a "Hebrew speaking club" so adults could gather regularly to converse in the ancient language. "It was a spiritually uplifting and exhilarating experience," wrote Gurwitz, "and sheer joy." When Epstein returned to New York, however, the school closed and the speaking club disbanded.[8]

Rabbis also maintained Jewish scholarship in Texas. Heinrich Schwarz of Hempstead, a Talmudically trained scholar, writer, and linguist, directed a small family-run *shul* and offered guidance to other Jewish scholars in the state. Jacob Voorsanger, a rabbi in Houston in the 1880s and later in San Francisco, made regular trips to Hempstead to study with Schwarz. Voorsanger described his mentor in the *American Israelite* as "one of the best Jewish scholars in the country. . . . The constant flow of wisdom that proceeds from his lips is of exceeding benefit."[9] Rabbi Ya'akov Geller helped to organize a small Talmudic study circle in Galveston, and in 1927 Abraham Schechter of Houston's Orthodox Congregation Adath Yeshurun formed the Kallah of Texas Rabbis, an organization of rabbis from across the state who met regularly "for the purpose of exchanging views along the lines of Jewish scholarship."[10] The Kallah published the papers presented at its meetings, which included subjects such as Talmudic exegesis, Jewish history, and interpretations of Jewish ethics. "The contents of this volume," wrote Rabbi Samuel Rosinger of Beaumont in his foreword to one such collection, "represent only a drop in the ocean of Jewish scholarship, but in the Texan desert a small canteen of water often serves as a life saver."[11]

Along with these spiritual and scholarly connections to traditional Judaism, a number of small organizations dedicated to the preservation of secular Jewish identity appeared in Texas. Many retained elements of the radicalism that was a staple of eastern European Jewish politics. Around 1930, Hebrew teacher Alexander Gurwitz noted the presence in San Antonio of a group he disparagingly regarded as "Jews without a synagogue . . . the Socialist Yiddishists, the secular Jews." Because "the religious core of Judaism was not for them," Gurwitz wrote, they needed "no synagogue for themselves, nor a Religious School for their children." They had organized several secular institutions in San Antonio, most of which, according to Gurwitz, "were affiliated with the *Poale Zion* (Workers of Zion, the Socialist Zionist Party), or the *Arbeiter Ring* (Workmen's Circle)." Gurwitz disdained these Jews' lack of religious devotion, but he applauded their social and cultural involvement. "These 'radicals,'" he wrote, "were passionate devotees of Zionism. They collected, and gave, much money for the cause of Zion Rebuilt." They also "took leading roles in the attempts to rescue our poor Jewish brothers and sisters trapped in the post-[First] World War European trap" and had in fact taken "leading roles in all of our Jewish institutions— except the synagogues, of course—with commendable zeal and generosity. Their wives took part in every communal charity endeavor, be it Jewish or general."[12]

Similar organizations existed in other Texas cities. Waco Jews chartered a Workmen's Circle in 1912, which sponsored charitable efforts on behalf of European victims of World War I, consumptive hospitals, immigrant aid, and settlers in Palestine. A Ladies' Auxiliary formed in 1931 to support similar efforts.[13] In Galveston, Freida and Itzik Weiner were founding members of an *Arbeiter Ring*, most of whose members had been Bundists in Russia. Freida was the chapter's first secretary, held local and regional offices in the organization for some sixty years, and subscribed to the *Jewish Daily Forward*, the socialist Yiddish-language newspaper published in New York. In later years, she traveled in Texas encouraging the preservation of the Yiddish language, formed several Yiddish-speaking groups for adults and children in the Houston area, and helped establish Yiddish-language classes at the Houston Jewish Community Center.[14]

Eva Green of Houston also brought her leftist politics and native Yiddish with her to Texas. Although her son Louis recalled that "[s]he was not an

ardent ritual observer and did not hold us to such practices," she had received a great deal of Jewish education and "knew her Hebrew well—reading, writing and using this beautiful language in the synagogue." Eva was
active in the "center-core of the left wing of the Democratic Party and even
of a then strong Socialist party," and once took her young son to meet Norman Thomas, the six-time Socialist Party presidential candidate. Although
"quite liberal as regards the secular world," Louis wrote, Eva "could actually be grouped with that large immigrant group who sought consolation
in not relying on a God which had failed them the past 300–400 years and
relying on their own efforts to bring about change."[15]

Organizations with their roots in eastern European politics or Orthodox
Jewish practice were quite small, however, in comparison to the dominant
Jewish communal institutions. Freida Weiner estimated that, at its peak of
activity between 1910 and 1930, the Galveston *Arbeiter Ring* had about 25
members, the Houston branch 70 or 80, and the Dallas branch, the state's
largest, about 100 members and its own building, which housed a small
synagogue and religious school.[16] In comparison, Dallas' Temple Emanu-El
boasted about 275 congregants in 1919, while by 1931 Houston's Congregation Beth Israel operated a religious school with 375 students.[17] The arrival
of traditional Jews in ever-larger numbers, however, enhanced the available
resources and facilities for Orthodox religion and social life.

New Immigrants and Native Texans

Between 1910 and 1920, Texas' Jewish population nearly doubled, and by
1940, it grew almost another 50 percent, a total increase from about 16,000
to roughly 50,000 by the outbreak of World War II.[18] Whether direct from
Europe as part of the Galveston Movement or passing through centers of
Jewish religion and culture like New York, these new arrivals brought with
them a sense of Judaism seldom seen in Texas before. "At home, in the small
shtedtl [or *shtetl*, small eastern European town with a large Jewish popula-
tion] in Lithuania where he lived, he was a respectable, pious Jew," wrote
Alexander Gurwitz, himself a devoted traditionalist, of his brother-in-law,
Solomon Lifshutz of San Antonio. "No, more than pious, he was a religious
fanatic. He brought to America all of his small town ways, casting none of
them into the ocean on the trip over. In fact, he gathered up all of the old
world obsolete nonsense which the other passengers left on the ship, made
a package of them, and brought them with him, intact, to America!"[19]

Written in Yiddish, Gurwitz's account of his life in San Antonio is one

Alexander Ziskind Gurwitz, ca. 1925.
Courtesy of Dr. Neil Gurwitz.

of the best sources available on traditional Judaism in Texas. It provides a
detailed picture of the religious and institutional changes occurring because
of the influx of Orthodox and Conservative Jews into San Antonio. Gurwitz described in rich detail—and with caustic Yiddish irony—the growth
of his community from the outpost of Judaism that he found upon his arrival in 1910 to a condition that he felt was, at least, better. When he first
came to San Antonio, the city offered few opportunities for the practice
of traditional Judaism. "The synagogue was closed all week, for there was
never a Daily *Minyan*," he wrote. "If someone had a *yahrzeit* [anniversary
of a loved one's death], or was in mourning, and he wanted to recite the
Kaddish [mourner's prayer], he was obliged to go up and down 'Jerusalem
Street,' [where the Jewish stores were located]. There he could gather ten
men for *Minchah* [afternoon] and *Ma'ariv* [evening] Services." Gurwitz also
described the dearth of trained Jewish clergy in the city. One man, Reb Solomon Solomon, he said, performed every ritual function, serving as a cantor, *schochet*, services leader, *mohel*, wedding officiant, and Hebrew teacher.
Gurwitz lamented San Antonio's lack of a *Rav*, an ordained Orthodox rabbi,
but he acknowledged with barely concealed bitterness that there really was
no need: "Ritual questions nobody had, and rabbinical arbitration they did
not need, and obscure points of Jewish law they cared nothing for." Solomon provided "all the skills that the Jewish community required."[20]

Twenty-five years later, Gurwitz was able to describe Agudas Achim, the Conservative congregation, as the largest in San Antonio, offering *minyan* twice daily and traditional Friday evening services. This was still not enough for Gurwitz, but he acknowledged that "the fact is that there is a Service daily—something we did not have [before]." A Talmud Torah, where Gurwitz taught for many years, provided Hebrew lessons under the guidance of trained instructors, and plans for a Jewish Community Center were under discussion. With the addition of these facilities, Gurwitz looked to the future with "very real hope that the Jewish upbringing of our children may prosper and thrive."[21]

Although this influx of Jews with more traditional beliefs provided the numbers necessary for new Jewish institutions, communities struggled to find ways to balance the newcomers' wishes and needs with entrenched religious practices. Particularly in small towns that could not afford multiple congregations, rabbis and worshipers had to seek compromise. Gurwitz provides an insightful description of such arrangements:

> In the small towns further out from San Antonio, there are small numbers of Jews. Nevertheless, in each of these country towns, the Jews are divided as they are in our city: Traditional Jews and German Jews. Since they cannot afford to have two synagogues, and two rabbis, most of them have one synagogue, in partnership, with one Rabbi serving both theological groups. In order not to discriminate, the Rabbi stands at the Ark, but the worshipers are seated at each side of the synagogue. The Rabbi addresses each side, in turn, and delivers his sermons accordingly.
>
> On Rosh Hashanah and Yom Kippur, however, the Rabbi has his work cut out for him. For the German Jews he conducts the Service without a hat, and he faces them during the entire Service. Then he puts on his yarmulke, turns to the other side, faces the Ark, and conducts the Orthodox Service. After this, he turns to the center, so that he is addressing both sides, and he delivers his sermon to both sides simultaneously![22]

This is, perhaps, an extreme case, if not a deliberate exaggeration, but certainly creative compromise was necessary in small communities throughout Texas. In Brownsville, for instance, lay leader Sam Perl, who guided a diverse congregation with members from Mexico, Russia, and New York, described his temple as having "a mixed congregation—some of them of the reformed branch—many from the conservative and some from the orthodox—so we conduct our service in a manner that will be pleasing to most of them."[23]

In other cases, compromise was less successful. When the question of building a synagogue—"the 'shul' problem," as Reform resident Albert Granoff described it—arose in Laredo in 1936, conflict immediately erupted between Reform and Orthodox members of the congregation. "The Reform group wanted to put the question to a vote, but the outnumbered Orthodox group was against it," Granoff remembered. "The Orthodox group suggested we take in new members, but the Reform group caught on. They knew that these new members would be the newcomers to America, and they were all Orthodox." Eventually, the Reform group, which had contributed more money to the cause than their Orthodox counterparts, resolved to build a Reform temple and to pay off their Orthodox members with cash toward a future synagogue of their own. Orthodox members of the community resented Granoff's efforts to raise money for the Reform temple, and when Granoff invited a member of the Orthodox group to speak at the dedication ceremony as a gesture of goodwill, Reformers in the community turned against him as well.[24] Differences between the two groups proved difficult, if not impossible, to resolve.

Even within traditional synagogues, rabbis and lay leaders had difficulty maintaining the strictest standards among their members. Creeping accommodation to American ways obliged some rabbis and congregations to enforce Jewish law and tradition among their unwilling members. In 1920, the directors of Temple Beth-El, the Reform congregation in San Antonio, passed a resolution requiring members to "observe the New Year and Day of Atonement by keeping their places of business closed on said holidays," closures that business owners had once performed voluntarily.[25] Similarly, in 1936, Rabbi J. M. Rosenberg of Waco's Conservative Congregation Agudath Jacob sent a letter to his congregants explaining his new policy of requiring them to sit *shiva* for members who had died, to attend their families during the required period of mourning. It was possible, he wrote, to appoint "several people in our community . . . to act as professional mourners," but it was preferable that "there should be a more friendly spirit existing in our community and that there should be present several members of our Congregation on every sad occasion." To facilitate this, the rabbi and the congregation's board of directors decided that "the secretary shall place the name of every member in a container and the president will withdraw six names every time a death occurs in our community."[26]

These examples suggest that even as newcomers with a more profound sense of themselves as Jews were arriving, many native Texas-Jewish families were becoming more acculturated. Isaac Kempner, whose father Harris was one of the founders of Temple B'nai Israel in Galveston, described himself in 1953 as coming from a "decidedly Jewish" background that was changing over time: "All grandparents lived kosher," he wrote on an autobiographical survey form, "but my father and mother embraced Reform Judaism." None of Kempner's children, he reported, had converted away from Judaism, but three had intermarried with Christians.[27] Galveston's Rabbi Henry Cohen, whose commitment to Reform Judaism seemed to grow steadier as he aged, declined numerous job offers from larger congregations around the nation, at least once because "he had left British Conservative Judaism for American Reform and didn't want to go back to cap and tallis."[28] Equating his style of Reform Judaism with a non-Zionist ideology, Cohen complained that "[y]ear after year, the Freshmen admitted to the Hebrew Union College are of Orthodox parentage, bound up in Zionism." His objection was not that students raised in Orthodox homes sought Reform pulpits, but that acceptable changes in ritual were "often over-shadowed by nationalistic tendencies to which I am utterly opposed. To my thinking, the College should uproot them!" Cohen concluded that Isaac Wise, the founder of the college, had rightly emphasized *"American Judaism."*[29]

Zionism and Anti-Zionism at Beth Israel

The connection Cohen made between Orthodox Judaism and Zionism was a logical one. Most of the traditional Jews entering Texas brought with them a passion for Jewish nationalism, and their presence in customarily non-Zionist communities was a source of great tension. The 1943 "Beth Israel Revolt" dramatically reflects the crises that occurred on a smaller scale within many Texas synagogues as a result of the changing Jewish population. As World War II raged and patriotic sentiment ran high, Houston's Congregation Beth Israel, the state's oldest and largest Reform congregation, divided over Zionism and, as many long-standing congregants saw it, the threat that Jewish nationalism posed to American national loyalty. In addition, the dispute included a disagreement over whether the temple should condone traditional forms of Jewish religious practice that some felt promoted an antiquated view of Judaism that set it outside the American mainstream. Newer members, many of whose families had recently arrived from eastern Europe, saw no conflict between Jewish nationalism and American patriotism and insisted that a Jewish institution must look and act like a *Jewish* institution. The Beth Israel Revolt was rooted in the attempt by two groups to define Judaism by defining themselves in contrast to one another. New members' needs, expectations, and political views differed markedly from those of the native Texans, whose rigid defense of their accustomed ways and tenacity in defining the newcomers as outsiders tore the congregation apart.[30]

Hundreds of these new arrivals were drawn to membership in Beth Israel for reasons other than agreement with the leadership. The population of Houston nearly tripled between 1920 and 1940, and Congregation Beth Israel grew with it.[31] Its membership of 309 families in 1920 more than doubled to 807 in 1943, necessitating the construction of new religious school buildings and cemetery facilities. During that period, the congregation outgrew its temple twice.[32] Beth Israel was by far Houston's largest synagogue, its only Reform group, and the city's most socially prestigious Jewish organization, a factor that appealed to the middle-class second-generation Americans arriving in the city. Many of the newcomers had become active in northern Reform congregations before moving to Houston and joining Beth Israel, and they soon confronted the truism that what New Yorkers call Reform looks more like what Southerners call Conservative.

Many of the new congregants were also attracted to Beth Israel, despite differences in their ideological and ritualistic views, by the involvement of Rabbi Robert Kahn, the son of a progressive Jewish family in Iowa who started as assistant rabbi in 1935. Young, eloquent, and dynamic, Kahn was hired to strengthen the congregation's religious school and youth activities, and he attributed Beth Israel's growing number of traditional members to the fact that "the children of orthodox Jews were being sent because it was a good religious school and they were getting from the Talmud Torah what they wanted." In contrast to the lay leadership and to senior rabbi Henry Barnston, Kahn described himself as a cultural Zionist, a supporter of the advancement of Jewish religious and cultural institutions in Palestine as a means of recreating a center of Jewish life and learning. "I believed that somehow, a concentration of Jews living in Israel, and therefore, not having to [adapt] to another's culture, another's civilization, could recreate the kind of things that led to the prophets, led to the Talmud, led to the great flowering of Jewish intellectual and spiritual civilization."[33] In line with this view, Kahn introduced more Hebrew language study into Beth Israel's curriculum and emphasized Jewish solidarity, the belief that "all Jews are responsible, or [are] comrades one to another." Among older temple members, however, opposition to this approach was clear. One mother complained to the rabbi, insisting that "I'm not going to be responsible for all Jews. Don't teach that to my children." Kahn was surprised to discover as later events unfolded "how deep this sentiment was."[34] Indeed, Beth Israel's president, Leopold Meyer, described his congregation as "uncompromising and unalterably Reform in manner of worship and definitely non-Zionist ideologically."[35]

Temple leaders, intent on preserving the acculturationist tradition of Reform Judaism, saw a grave danger in the influx of traditionalist and Zionist members. Generally fearful of losing control of their congregation, they were especially appalled at the newcomers' devotion to political and cultural Zionism, which these leaders saw as linked to traditional Jewish practice. They understood that if traditional practice gained a foothold at Beth Israel, so would Zionism, and the combination could threaten the unity that they had long nurtured between Jews and non-Jews. Thus, they set themselves firmly against both.

Israel Friedlander, a former congregational president, was a leading spokesman for the temple's native Texan majority. He explained that the problem originated with "[f]orces and influences outside of the Congregation membership, some local and some national," who "sought to control the future of Beth Israel Congregation." Their goal, he continued, "was not American Reform Judaism, to which our efforts have been and are dedicated, but to [Jewish] nationalism." They sought "to swerve the destiny of Beth Israel toward a rapprochement with traditional or conservative Judaism and, of course, in the interest of political Zionism."[36] It was clear to Friedlander and other temple leaders that they had to prevent such a power shift from occurring.

The ideology Friedlander shared with the majority of Beth Israel's members accorded with increasingly outmoded definitions of "classical Reform." In 1885, when large numbers of traditional Jews from eastern Europe were beginning to arrive in the United States, American Reform rabbis, most of whom had been trained by Isaac Wise of Cincinnati, gathered in Pittsburgh to formulate a set of principles to guide the future of American Reform. They ratified a statement, the Pittsburgh Platform, which provided a touchstone for lay and clerical leaders of American temples for a generation. The Pittsburgh Platform legitimized a tendency in the United States to match Jewish religious practices to gentile patterns, making Judaism superficially indistinct from Christian worship and permitting congregations to determine the relevance of traditional requirements on their own rather than by reverting to biblical or Talmudic authority. Thus, the American Reform rabbinate gave its official sanction to informal clerical dress, lenient dietary laws, and services held on Sundays so as to accommodate Saturday commerce. Regarding the nascent movement to establish a Jewish political state, these rabbis declared unanimously, "[W]e consider ourselves no longer a nation but a religious community, and therefore expect neither a return to Palestine . . . nor the restoration of any of the laws concerning the Jewish state."[37] In other words, a belief in Judaism was a religious choice that coexisted with other religious alternatives in a pluralistic society. It was not a distinct national, ethnic, or racial identity. When the Zionist movement began to catch hold in the late nineteenth century and to arrive in America on ships full of eastern European immigrants, this view of American Reform compelled opposition to it.

Support for Zionism grew nevertheless, especially following the Balfour Declaration of 1917, which promised British support for a Jewish state. Accordingly, the national institutions of American Reform Judaism began to shift toward the ideas of Jewish nationality and a Jewish homeland. In 1931, a survey reported by the Union of American Hebrew Congregations (UAHC) found that "despite the traditional opposition of Reform Judaism to Zionism in the past, we find one member of every five families enrolled in the Zionist Organization of America or Hadassah [the Zionist women's organization]."[38] Although these groups remained weak in peripheral areas like Texas, the emergence of Nazism fueled a nationwide shift in their direction. The membership of Zionist organizations climbed from 807,000 in 1935 to nearly 1.5 million by 1945. To the authors of the Pittsburgh Platform, modernized religious practice, Americanism, and non-Zionism were all of a piece, all expressions of the wish to identify with the American mainstream rather than with a separate Jewish nationhood. Under the influence of a new eastern European majority, however, American Jewry was coming around to the idea that it was possible to be both loyal American citizens and supporters of Jewish national sovereignty.

In response to this changing attitude, the Central Conference of American Rabbis (CCAR) met in Columbus, Ohio, in 1937 to endorse a revision of the Pittsburgh Platform. The Columbus Platform rejected the earlier doctrine, restoring the primacy of traditional Jewish practices. It was most significant, however, for its ringing endorsement of cultural Zionism, proclaiming that the "rehabilitation of Palestine" offered "the promise of renewed life for many of our brethren," and so "[w]e affirm the obligation of all Jewry to aid in its upbuilding as a Jewish homeland by endeavoring to make it not only a haven of refuge for the oppressed but also a center of Jewish culture and spiritual life."[39] The delegates stopped short of explicitly favoring the formation of a sovereign Jewish state, but the drift toward that view was implicit in their language. Many delegates thus felt compelled to oppose the Platform, which passed by a single vote, whereas the non-Zionist Pittsburgh Platform fifty years earlier had been sustained unanimously. Far from achieving a settlement, the Columbus meeting exposed a growing rift within the American rabbinical community over the Zionist issue.

The bitterness of that division was further revealed in 1942 when Rabbi Louis Wolsey of Philadelphia convened a meeting of non-Zionist Reform rabbis in Atlantic City to protest the Zionist drift in the CCAR and to plan a response. Nearly eighty participants, identifying themselves as "Rabbis in American Israel," signed a statement endorsing the "universalism" of Judaism and expressing concern that the "absorption of large numbers in Jewish nationalistic endeavors" tended "to reduce the religious basis of Jewish life to a place of secondary importance." Although they offered "unstinted aid" to their brethren already in Palestine, they were "unable to subscribe to or support the political emphasis now paramount in the Zionist program." The rabbis feared, in particular, that "Jewish nationalism tends to confuse not only our coreligionists but our fellow citizens of other faiths in regard to our place and function in society."[40] They were concerned, that is, that gentiles would think them less American (and therefore, presumably, less welcome in America) if Zionists persisted in describing the Jewish people as a separate nation. A later "Statement of Principles" reiterated that position, asserting that "American Jews reject the idea of Jewish nationalism" and "desire no other homeland, political or otherwise, than the United States and no other citizenship, actual or emotional, than American citizenship."[41] By the end of 1942, the group had organized formally as the American Council for Judaism (ACJ), incorporated in New York, and adopted a constitution. By 1946, following a national membership drive, the ACJ had established local chapters across the country and regional offices in Richmond, Chicago, Dallas, and San Francisco.[42]

The ACJ drew its support from around the nation, but it was especially strong in the South and Southwest. By one account, half of the members of the ACJ's board of directors came from southern or southwestern communities, despite the relatively tiny number of Jews in those regions.[43] A 1943 ACJ membership list shows that some 40 percent of the organization's members lived in southern states, particularly in Texas, which had more

ACJ members than any other state. Houston alone had twice as many as New York State and more than any other American city except Philadelphia.[44] ACJ members, moreover, were among the most prominent Jews in Texas communities and included several leading rabbis. Houston's Henry Barnston, Dallas' David Lefkowitz, and San Antonio's Ephraim Frisch attended the Atlantic City meeting and signed the Statement of Principles. Henry Cohen of Galveston declined to attend because of his advanced age but sent a supportive telegram to the conference endorsing its goals.[45]

Henry Barnston, chief rabbi at Beth Israel since 1900, was especially vocal in his support of the ACJ's mission, drafting a letter to the delegates in Atlantic City in which he stated that "the day when Zionism was launched was one of the most tragic in Jewish history." Identifying Judaism as a separate nation, he wrote, "will not fit in with the Anglo-Saxon civilization amidst which we live and may forever brand us as strangers in a strange land." He also contended that Zionism was practically treason in wartime, or at least might look so to gentiles, and that Jews could better expend their efforts on demonstrating their loyalty to the United States. American rabbis, he wrote, would do well to "bring some pressure to bear upon the younger Rabbis to enlist as Chaplains" and to refrain from endorsing "idealistic papers on peace when the Nation is engaged in total war and its continued existence depends upon winning that war."[46] Other Houston Jews shared Barnston's concern about appearing divided in their national loyalty. Diane Ravitch, an historian and educator, grew up in Houston in the 1940s and 1950s before moving to New York. Her fellow Houston Jews, she remembered, "experienced great insecurity about whether they had dual loyalty. It meant a lot in Texas to be patriotic, and there always seemed to be some doubt about whether Jews were fully committed as Americans. The Houston Jews I knew tried extra hard to show that they were as patriotic as non-Jews."[47]

If Zionism, with its implicit suggestion of Jewish national identity, was a minority view in Houston, it was common enough to sow discord in the community. Beth Israel's young assistant rabbi, Robert Kahn, received an invitation to the ACJ's initial meeting, but as a professed "pro-Zionist" he declined to attend and wrote to many of the delegates expressing his opposition to their actions. Israel Friedlander, the former temple president, later described the "anomalous position" into which Kahn's actions had put the congregation: "[I]ts senior rabbi, Dr. Henry Barnston, a life long avowed opponent of Zionism, divide[s] the pulpit with a militant Zionist," who "publicly throughout the country condemn[s] the judgment and the position of the rabbis signing the Atlantic City statement of principles, of which number Dr. Henry Barnston, his senior colleague, was one."[48] For Friedlander, Jewish nationalism was un-American, but he wisely stopped short of questioning Kahn's patriotism: Kahn was then serving as a U.S. Army chaplain in the South Pacific. Friedlander's statements do suggest, though, the antagonism that he and other Beth Israel leaders felt toward Kahn.

The Basic Principles

The event that triggered Congregation Beth Israel's split was Henry Barnston's announced retirement as senior rabbi in May 1943. Robert Kahn, who had entered military service with the understanding that he would return to his duties at Beth Israel when the war was over, was the most likely successor, and he wanted and expected the position. An ally of Kahn's in the congregation, however, later claimed that Kahn never stood a chance, that the temple's non-Zionist leadership had deliberately forced Barnston into retirement in order to replace him with not only a younger but also a non-Zionist rabbi—an ideological demand Kahn clearly did not meet.[49] Whatever their reasons, the temple board of trustees rejected Kahn quickly, before even receiving recommendations for other candidates. They carefully expressed a "sympathetic attitude" toward him and noted without much enthusiasm that he had served "generally satisfactorily" as assistant rabbi. However, they concluded, he was in New Guinea and so "was not available" for the job. More to the point, and in spite of claiming to want a younger rabbi, they stated that Kahn was too inexperienced to handle the spiritual leadership of a congregation as large as Beth Israel and too young to associate with the "more mature leadership" of the city's churches.[50] After a brief search, the board offered the job to Hyman Judah Schachtel of West End Congregation in New York, an ACJ member and just four years older than Kahn.

When congregants met in August 1943 to approve the new appointment, it was clear that Zionism had become the main source of contention within the congregation, and that opinion had coalesced into support for either Kahn or Schachtel. The meeting erupted into noisy debate, both sides assuming that the approval of a rabbi amounted to a permanent statement of the temple's Zionist policy. Despite the efforts of Zionist participants to turn the meeting to their advantage, they were clearly in the minority, and the assembled congregants voted 346 to 91 to offer the position to Schachtel. As a courtesy, the vote was recorded as unanimous, but the debate had exposed divisions within the congregation that would prove irreconcilable.

Army chaplain Robert Kahn in 1942
with tallis draped over his lieuten-
ant's uniform. Courtesy of Hollace
Ava Weiner.

Leopold Meyer, the temple's president, expressed outrage after the
meeting, not only at the "character of the claptrap" that Kahn's supporters
had presented but also at the parliamentary tactics employed to subvert the
board. To him, "the Zionist ideology was hopelessly incongruous with the
temper of Beth Israel as well as incompatible with doctrines and precepts of
Reform Judaism as fostered within our Temple." Perceiving a need to limit
membership to those with more compatible views, he appointed a Policy
Formulation Committee with Israel Friedlander as chair to draft a set of
"Basic Principles" for the congregation. The committee then recommended that the temple require new membership applicants to subscribe to the
Principles in order to obtain full membership privileges. Those who refused
to sign could join as "Associate" members but would not be eligible to vote
in congregational matters.[51] Current members would not be required to
approve the Principles.

On September 7, 1943, Friedlander's committee presented a seven-point
draft of the "Basic Principles" to the board, which adopted them after some
minor discussion and rewording. Following an utterly uncontroversial confirmation in Principle No. 1 of the oneness of God and the responsibility of
Jews to "worship and to serve Him," the Principles plunged into the issue
of Zionism and Jewish nationalism, clarifying the board's view that there
was no place in their congregation for a philosophy that they believed ran
counter to the spirit of Reform Judaism and to American values:

PRINCIPLE NO. 2. We are Jews by virtue of our acceptance of Judaism. We consider ourselves no longer a nation. We are a religious community, and neither pray for nor anticipate a return to Palestine nor a
restoration of any of the laws concerning the Jewish state. We stand
unequivocally for the separation of Church and State. Our religion is
Judaism. Our nation is the United States of America. Our nationality
is American. Our flag is the "Stars and Stripes." Our race is Caucasian.
With regard to the Jewish settlement in Palestine we consider it our
sacred privilege to promote the spiritual, cultural and social welfare of
our co-religionists there.[52]

The Basic Principles also reiterated support for a number of elements
of classical Reform Judaism. Among other things, they declared that Beth
Israel "reject[ed] the religious obligatory nature" of the "rabbinical and Mosaic laws which regulate diet, priestly purity, dress, and similar laws"; provided the board the sole power to determine the nature of temple ritual and
ceremonies; recognized "the complete religious equality of woman with
man"; and favored minimal use of Hebrew in its worship services.[53] Largely
a restatement of the obsolescent 1885 Pittsburgh Platform, the document
showed that Beth Israel's leaders were anxious to present themselves to the
world as patriotic, unequivocal, and fully acculturated Americans. Although
non-Zionism had been a test in the selection of a new chief rabbi, the Basic
Principles went further, calling into question the choices congregants made
freely in their own daily lives and religious behavior and barring from full
membership any Jew who conformed to traditional practices. The debate
at Beth Israel had evolved into a fundamental disagreement over future
congregants' freedom to practice their faith within the temple according to
their own consciences.

Supporters of the Basic Principles, a strong majority of the congregation, also drafted a three-part resolution for members to consider. This
statement condemned, in turn, the three dominant institutions of Reform
Judaism in the United States—the Union of American Hebrew Congregations (UAHC), the Central Conference of American Rabbis (CCAR), and
the Hebrew Union College (HUC)—for the "growing deviation of organized American Reform Judaism from the ideals and pattern which were
established at its founding under the leadership of Isaac M. Wise." Over
the previous twenty years, they claimed, changes within Reform had set
in motion "forces which do not belong to the new world of emancipation

and promise, but which are attuned to and a part of the old world's concept of segregation and despair for Jewish life."[54] In defending the fifty-year-old tradition of classical Reform, Beth Israel's members claimed to speak for the future, while the "obstructionists" in their congregation were fighting for a vision of Judaism that they felt amounted to an outmoded and un-American clannishness despite its growing popularity. Beth Israel's resolutions reflected the temple's readiness to segregate itself from other American Jews in order to avoid segregating itself from other Americans.

Supporters and opponents of the Basic Principles called for a meeting of the whole congregation to vote on the document and to debate the proposal to make signing it a requirement for new membership. On November 23, some 800 members, a remarkable 50 percent of the congregation's full voting strength, attended the meeting and cast ballots. Opponents of the measure, labeling themselves "dissenters," were concerned that Beth Israel was neglecting the true historical mission of Reform Judaism—to change with changing times and to tolerate differences of opinion. "I have no quarrel with the political Zionists though I do not accept their views," said William Nathan, a former temple trustee, "[and] I say without fear of contradiction that I shall not quarrel with the views entertained by any Jew." Nathan expressed astonishment, therefore, that the board would seek "to impose upon any member of this Congregation whatever be his beliefs the set and frozen norm of an inelastic credo." Judaism, he continued, "has been amended time and time again, and is in a constant state of flux and change. Its eternal quality is dynamic rather than static. . . . Our prophets and our seers have taught that each generation raises up its own saviors, and solves in its own way its own problems." Finally, Nathan raised the specter of Nazism, pointing out that for all its supporters' professed Americanism, the Basic Principles was a quasi-fascist document that "bears all the earmarks of 'Made in Germany.'"[55]

When discussion was concluded, the membership voted 632 to 168 to support the Basic Principles and the resolutions condemning the UAHC, CCAR, and HUC. This outcome was disastrous for the congregation. In April 1944, from his South Pacific post, Robert Kahn submitted his resignation to Beth Israel, citing not so much his opposition to the Principles themselves, which he characterized as "a rather poorly written hodge-podge of theology, anti-defamation, anti-Zionism, and anti-Orthodoxy," but the requirement that they be the *sine qua non* for temple membership.[56] *This*, Kahn said, was un-American. Within two months, more than two hundred dissatisfied Beth Israel members left the congregation to form Temple

Emanu-El, and they invited Kahn to serve as head rabbi upon his return. The charter of the new congregation clearly articulated its origin in the division of the older temple: "Judaism is a religion of perpetual growth and development," it read, and "the power of the synagogue for good depends, in part, upon the inherent right to freedom of thought and speech of both its members and its pulpit."[57]

"The Shame of Houston"

Every American Jewish community struggled over Zionism, but no other congregation's internal conflict drew as much national attention as Beth Israel's. It was one of the last temples to insist on adherence to the 1885 Pittsburgh Platform, and its dispute also stood out from other, less rancorous disagreements because of the Basic Principles, a Houston novelty. Beth Israel's national reputation suffered from its moment in the limelight as it became a target for Jewish commentators across the country. With the exception of a few scattered supporters, mostly Southerners and ACJ members, condemnation was widespread. Solomon Freehof, national president of the CCAR, noted insightfully that Beth Israel's effort to defeat orthodoxy had led it to implement an orthodoxy of its own.[58] Austin rabbi Abram Goodman wrote to William Nathan, who soon left Beth Israel to join the founders of Emanu-El, that "nationally the Houston congregation has received a terrible black eye. Everybody is talking about their action in offending Jews who were not of the same opinion."[59] The Basic Principles evoked such intense anger that the American Jewish Congress, the national Jewish advocacy organization, accused the temple of composing "a set of 'Nuremberg laws,'" a fearful metaphor that *Time* reprinted for national consumption.[60] And Stephen Wise, the nation's most renowned Reform rabbi and a fiery orator on liberal causes, asserted in an article titled "The Shame of Houston" that the Basic Principles "virtually affirmed the second-rate Americanism" of observant Jews. By discriminating between traditional and nontraditional applicants, Wise wrote, "the Jewish Grand Inquisition of Houston" had committed an "evil and self-damning deed" that was an expression of "their unwisdom and bigotry."[61] The irony was devastating. Beth Israel's leaders had sought to protect Reform Judaism as an expression of American democracy but ended by inviting comparison to Nazism and the Spanish Inquisition. In defending the liberal mission of Reform Judaism, Beth Israel imposed a new kind of orthodoxy; in its attempt to defend American values, it produced an exclusionary and anti-democratic doctrine.

Despite the furor, the Basic Principles were never fully enforced, though they remained official policy at Beth Israel until 1968, when Schachtel wrote to historian Jacob Rader Marcus that "[w]hile these principles have de facto been forgotten for many years," they finally "were eliminated and revoked without a dissenting voice" at an annual meeting of the congregation.[62] The episode, however, exposed a number of ironies at the heart of Jewish life in Texas. After Beth Israel's decades on the frontier of American Jewry, when they finally sought to define themselves as defenders of core Jewish values, they showed themselves to be still on the fringe of American Jewish life, arraying themselves so as to see other American Jews as their opponents and traditional Judaism as the enemy. Conditions around the world were rapidly changing, American Jewry was changing, even Houston was changing, but Beth Israel fled from those changes, preferring to remain remote, isolated, and righteously indignant. Just five years later, Israel achieved its national sovereignty, and Jews around the world, including in Texas, rallied to its support.

SEVEN

Texas Jews Respond to
the World Crises of the 1940s

The Beth Israel Revolt was a moment of intense reaction in which Texas Jews resisted the changing tides of Jewish life in the middle twentieth century, but it brought home to Jewish Texans the deep and significant changes affecting Jewish identity around the world. Despite its self-consciousness as a frontier community, Texas Jewry was, and really had always been, part of a Jewish community of global scope, and international events had an impact in every corner of the Jewish world, including Texas. This was especially true in the 1940s, when the Holocaust, World War II, and the establishment of Israel shaped Jewish communities everywhere in profound and permanent ways. The influx of more traditionally religious Jews had already changed local communities in Texas, and now world events of incalculable importance encouraged Jewish Texans to cultivate stronger institutional and spiritual connections with Jews from other places. Native Texas Jews could no longer avoid a Jewish universalism that pressed upon them a solidarity with Jews around the world. Concerted action in the face of world events drew pluralistic communities together as well, locating and strengthening a common core of Jewish identity that mitigated differences of denomination, language, national origin, economic class, and length of time in the community. Judge Irving Goldberg of Dallas, for example, observed "an affirmative alliance between all Jews" in his city, an "admixture of the old and new, harmoniously harnessed, [which] did an effective job in the crises of our times."[1]

The Holocaust, the war, and the creation of Israel affected Texas Jews directly and personally, drawing them out of the self-conscious isolation that had long characterized their lives in Texas. Evident and growing German anti-Semitism moved them to collect funds for the support of European Jews and later to bring Holocaust refugees and survivors to safety in Texas. Support for the American war effort unified fractious urban Jewish communities, while smaller communities strained their resources to provide a Jewish environment to servicemen from all over the country stationed at nearby military bases. After the war, Israel's creation as a true Jewish geographic and cultural center provided a new sense of spiritual meaning and identity shared with Jews around the world. Texas was still far from the geographic centers of American and international Jewish life, but the internalized frontiers that had kept Jewish Texans at a distance from Jews elsewhere were steadily eroding.

Taking the Children Out of Hell

The Nazis' organized mass murder of European Jews did not begin intensively until 1942, but intimations of what was to come were felt long before, even in Texas. As early as 1928, Houston's *Texas Jewish Herald* reported on the "Anti Semitic Hooliganism" of German "Hitlerites."[2] As the threat gathered, editor Edgar Goldberg regularly provided news of Nazi activities and the party's increasing power. The *Herald* had always included clips of national and international Jewish news, especially about the evolution of Jewish institutions in Palestine, but Nazism provided Goldberg with an emotional *cause célèbre* that he exploited fully, both as a matter of conscience and as a way to sell newspapers in the dark days of the Great Depression. By the early 1930s, Nazi activities were such a fixture in the *Herald* that Goldberg began to receive complaints. "One of my friends says you give too much space to the Nazis—you should lay off them," he wrote in late 1933. "Well I'd like to! But when 600,000 [German] Jews can do nothing but wait the coming of death and when the insidious serpent multiplies in our midst—some one should awaken Jewry."[3]

Goldberg was fearful that Nazism's success in Germany could hearten American anti-Semites, and in a strongly worded front-page story under the dramatic headline "When Hitler's Nazis Come to Houston!" he admonished his readers that they were not as secure as they felt. He quoted a *Houston Chronicle* article that hinted at "organized activities under way [in Texas] to stir hatred of the Jews and to advance Nazi principles." He described an incident the previous week at Houston's docks, where police were called onboard a German vessel after a dispute regarding "the propriety of the ship's crew marching through Houston downtown streets with a Nazi flag." The police prevented the action, but they accepted pro-Hitler pamphlets, printed in English, from the crewmen. Goldberg warned his readers of the outcome if such a demonstration had been permitted to occur:

> Were the Nazis allowed to parade down Main Street, just what do you think would happen? Well Levy's is the outstanding business institution in the city. Theirs would be subject for first attack! What would follow? Well Sakowitz Bros. hold an enviable position among the business institutions of Houston, as do Battelstein, Weingarten, Ben Wolfman, Dollarhite-Levy, the Smart Shop, Lechenger, Becker, Gordons Jewelers, would have to pay their toll for being Jews. Yet who among them in this city is doing anything to fight the anti-Semitic tendency?[4]

Goldberg may have sacrificed some credibility by suggesting that the best course of action for these business leaders was for each to "subscribe for a hundred copies of the Herald to go to leading non-Jews for propaganda purposes."[5] He was vindicated a few months later, however, when he reported the founding of a new anti-Semitic journal in Houston, the *Nationalist*. In its first issue, it urged its readers to "[p]ut the Jews in their places" and observed that "Germany has shown the way in persecuting them."[6] Throughout the 1930s Goldberg and his editorial successor at the *Herald*, David H. White, as well as Jewish editors in Dallas, San Antonio, and Fort Worth, printed countless articles and editorials about the Nazis, anti-Semitism in Europe and in the United States, and American responses to these developments.

As news of the Nazi terror proliferated, American Jews became concerned about the problem of sheltering the hundreds of thousands of Jewish refugees fleeing Europe. In contrast, non-Jewish Americans were conspicuously negligent in addressing the tragedy in Nazi Europe, and thousands of Jews who could have been saved by immigrating to the United States were denied entry. Between 1933 and 1941, some 112,000 Jews from Germany, Austria, and Czechoslovakia found refuge from the Nazi regime in the United States, but this figure represents only a fraction of the number legally entitled to enter the country under the nation's immigration quota system.[7] During the war years, only 21,000 Jewish refugees entered the United States, some 10 percent of the number that could have been admitted under the existing quotas.[8]

The reasons for this failure are complex, but at the heart of the problem was a fundamental anti-immigration sentiment among Americans, including many in the government, that overwhelmed whatever compassion they may have felt for Hitler's victims. In the midst of the Depression, Americans were not prepared to accept countless displaced, impoverished immigrants who might compete with them for scarce jobs and public assistance. That the refugees most in need of rescue were Jews did not help their case, either. By 1940, the American Jewish Committee determined that anti-Semitism in America had reached an unprecedented level: nearly half of those responding to a national poll agreed that Jews already exercised "too much power" in the country and should not be allowed to augment their numbers.[9] Popular anti-Jewish commentators like Father Charles Coughlin, whose syndicated radio program reached millions, linked Jews—however paradoxically—with both Communism and an imaginary international banking conspiracy, painting them as an internal menace that threatened American security. Coughlin strenuously opposed immigration measures that would increase Jewish numbers, and as one of the most popular personalities on American airwaves, his opinion carried influence with the public.

Although no evidence suggests that anti-Semitic sentiment was stronger in Texas than elsewhere in the nation, Texas congressmen were among the staunchest advocates of the restrictionist immigration policies that prevented more Jewish refugees from finding safety in the United States, and it is a safe guess that their nativist views carried a measure of anti-Semitism. In 1931, eleven out of seventeen Texas congressmen voted in support of a proposal to freeze immigration into the United States for two years, with a single exception for relatives of immigrants already in the country.[10] The bill was ultimately defeated, but its support in the Texas delegation demonstrated the representatives' restrictionist leanings.

The most prominent restrictionist in the Texas delegation was Martin Dies Jr. of Beaumont, one of the most vocal conservatives in Congress and the first chairman of the House Un-American Activities Committee (HUAC). During his fourteen years in Congress, from 1930 to 1944, Dies was a passionate opponent of the New Deal, labor unions, and immigration, and he argued consistently for an isolationist approach to foreign affairs. "If the majority of the German people want Adolph Hitler," Dies proclaimed on the House floor in December 1931, "it is none of our business, and we should be content to administer our own affairs without interfering with those of other countries."[11] Two years later, in the course of a House debate on immigration policy, Dies expressed his view in no uncertain terms: "We must ignore the tears of sobbing sentimentalists and internationalists, and we must permanently close, lock and bar the gates of our country to new immigration waves and then throw the keys out."[12]

In 1936, Dies condemned immigrants already in the country for sending money earned in the United States to their families overseas and for holding jobs that "rightfully belonged" to Americans. Tying immigration to the political radicalism of which he was a sworn enemy, he declared that immigrants were "the backbone of communism and fascism," bringing alien standards into the country and forcing the United States into involvement in European affairs.[13]

Dies never condemned Jews publicly and openly, but there was an implicit anti-Semitism in his condemnation of European immigration and of political radicalism. Moreover, in the course of the HUAC hearings over which he presided, he let others speak for him, sitting by passively while witnesses read extended anti-Semitic diatribes into the official record. Dies represented an especially conservative district for seven terms, but his failure to win a seat in the U.S. Senate in statewide elections in 1941 and 1957 indicates that his isolationist views were not shared by the majority of Texas voters outside his district. Still, his visibility in Congress and the national attention he received could not have given hope to Jewish Texans waiting for their government to recognize the urgency of the European situation and to act.

Even well-meaning gentiles offered little encouragement. Mollie Cohen, the wife of Rabbi Henry Cohen, expressed annoyance when a gentile acquaintance stopped by to "commiserate with them on the fate of their coreligionists." As the friend expressed his concern, Mollie "turned on him and said, 'Yes, it is too bad. Why don't you Christians do something about it?'"[14] Although some gentiles expressed support, most demonstrated little or no awareness that European Jews were suffering. City papers rarely covered European issues, let alone European Jews, and the press in rural areas, where most Texans still lived, generally ignored international events altogether.[15]

In Texas, as throughout the United States, the public failed to notice the cause of European Jewry, let alone to rally behind it. Jewish individuals and organizations, however, found ways both inside and outside the requirements of the law to save as many lives as possible. As a result, hundreds of refugees found safety in Texas, though their exact number is impossible to determine. Because efforts to transport refugees to America were unofficial and often illegal, they are mostly undocumented. Although international organizations like the Hebrew Immigrant Aid Society (HIAS) helped refugees navigate the American immigration process, they then passed them on to family members or to local branches of the Jewish Family Service to see to their adjustment and survival in their new homes. HIAS can therefore provide no information on how many refugees settled in any particular place, nor on what happened to them once they left the Society's care.[16] Nor are statistics on prewar refugees to Texas available at the National Holocaust Memorial Museum or the Holocaust research centers in Dallas and Houston.[17]

However great their numbers, refugees arriving in Texas found a Jewish community ready to help. In the state's large cities, refugees' needs provided an impetus to achieve a level of organization that had been impossible before, and communities established citywide Jewish federations to reach across the barriers between organizations and agencies. The Jewish Community Council of Metropolitan Houston, the Jewish Federation of Social Services in Dallas, the Jewish Federation of San Antonio, and the Jewish Federation of Fort Worth, all in place by the late 1930s, provided assistance to immigrants, facilitated support for the Jewish poor, and organized the collection of funds for refugee relief in Europe. Jewish Federations also contributed money to national organizations such as the American Jewish Committee and the Anti-Defamation League of B'nai B'rith that combated anti-Semitic speech and activity.[18]

Anecdotal evidence also suggests the outlines of a heroic, if impromptu, rescue program in which Texas Jews and non-Jews cooperated to bring hundreds of central European Jewish refugees into Texas. One compelling though scantily documented case may have involved Lyndon Johnson, then a young Hill Country congressman. In 1938, Jim Novy, a Jewish Austinite and Johnson's friend and constituent, traveled to central Europe to visit family. Johnson provided a letter for Novy to present to the American embassy in Poland requesting help in bringing Novy's friends and relatives from Poland and Germany to Texas. Johnson's office arranged the necessary affidavits for the rescue, at Novy's expense, of forty-two people from Germany and Poland. Two years later, Novy and Johnson expanded their effort, arranging for hundreds of Jewish refugees to enter Texas through Cuba, Mexico, and South America in order to circumvent American immigration quotas. Many of these were housed throughout the state in training camps of the National Youth Administration (NYA), a New Deal agency of which Johnson had been Texas state director and over which he still kept a close watch.[19]

LBJ never spoke publicly about these activities, nor is there any written evidence of his role. Researchers, moreover, have been unable to identify any of the refugees he reportedly helped or to confirm the involvement of the NYA, which, if true, was illegal. But in December 1963, just a month after the Kennedy assassination, President and Mrs. Johnson attended a dedication ceremony for Congregation Agudas Achim in Austin at which Jim Novy gave the introductory address. Novy described the rescue effort in detail, saying of Johnson, who sat by silent but smiling, that "[w]e can't ever thank him enough for all those Jews he got out of Germany during the days of Hitler."[20] Lady Bird later reported that after the dinner "person after person plucked at my sleeve and said, 'I wouldn't be here today if it weren't for him. He helped get me out.'"[21]

In addition to Novy, other Texas Jews went to great trouble and expense to rescue family members facing persecution in Europe. Nathan Klein of Houston began his rescue effort in 1934 by signing an affidavit for one of his wife's relatives who hoped to enter the country as part of that year's quota. Required by U.S. immigration law for admission under the quota, the affidavit certified that Klein would bear financial responsibility for the woman, assuring that she would not become a burden to the country after her arrival. Following her safe passage to Texas, Klein began receiving requests for similar documents from other family members in Europe, some distantly related, then from friends of family members, and then from mere acquaintances. He continued signing affidavits, guaranteeing financial security in Texas for any who asked. As a further assurance to federal authorities, Klein deposited money into bank accounts he opened in the immigrants' names to show that the refugees had financial means. Klein eventually made such guarantees for roughly one hundred people, most of whom were total strangers to him, leading his banker to wonder if he was trying to save every Jew in Europe.[22]

Klein was only one of many Houstonians willing to make such commitments. Rabbi Robert Kahn recalled a campaign in Houston to gather as many affidavits as possible. Kahn signed several himself and then began recruiting others to follow his lead, arguing that if he could afford to sign them on his salary, they could, too. "I did a *minyan*," Kahn said. "I did ten. Then I thought I'd done enough. But I realized later that I should have done many more."[23]

Maurice Schwartz, founder of the Popular Store, and his brother Nandor made a similar effort in El Paso. Beginning in 1939, with children coming first in small groups, the brothers arranged transportation to Texas for upwards of one hundred Hungarian family members, mostly nieces and nephews, and navigated the legal immigration requirements on their behalf. The Schwartzes had family spread throughout Texas, many of whom took responsibility for new refugees as they arrived. When the Hungar-

Jim Novy, left, with President and Mrs. Lyndon Johnson, at the dedication ceremony for Congregation Agudas Achim, Austin, Texas, December 30, 1963. Photograph by Yoichi Okamoto. Courtesy of the Lyndon Baines Johnson Presidential Library, Austin, Texas.

ian quota was filled, the Schwartzes sought ways to bring family through Mexico, a complicated procedure that cost a great deal of money and effort. To that end, the brothers managed a fund at the Popular Store to which their American family members could contribute. Through their efforts, family members were removed from Europe to America, educated, and integrated into the Popular's workforce.[24]

With these efforts underway, Texas Jews still despaired over how little they could do. After a 1939 *Reader's Digest* article about Henry Cohen appeared in European translations, the rabbi began receiving letters from European Jews asking him to help them leave as he had helped Russian refugees during the Galveston Movement. The letters came in increasing numbers "until thirty or forty of them in the morning's mail were not unusual." In great detail, frightened writers described the dangers they faced and the circumstances they were frantic to escape: "mothers begging him to take their children out of hell; whole families, grown childish in their desperation, asking to be removed bodily to America." Cohen's biographers relate how he sat down to respond each time, in any one of a multitude of European languages, that there was nothing he could do. "The laws of this country have changed since the days of the [Galveston Movement]," he explained. "You must wait your turn in the quota." Eventually, he was obliged to publish a statement in European newspapers saying that he was unable to help, and the flood of letters abated. Cohen's inability in the face of U.S. law to help these desperate people remained one of the tragedies of his life.[25]

The War

The reverberations of the Holocaust in Texas diminished the conceptual distance between Texas Jews and Jews elsewhere. The destruction of European Jewry and the hardships and triumphs of refugees could not be ignored as somebody else's problem. Similarly, World War II presented a crisis in which Texas Jews, regardless of any lingering sense of remoteness they might feel, were compelled to participate. The war provided opportunities for community organizations to expand social action efforts that were already underway, many having been initiated to provide support for Jewish refugees of the First World War. Marguerite Meyer Marks of Dallas, for example, had long been involved in community organization on behalf of a number of nonsectarian causes while remaining an active member of the Dallas chapter of the National Council of Jewish Women (NCJW). As an NCJW member, she was involved in a campaign to provide free meals to the city's poor children. "It was characteristic of the Jewish women," she wrote, "to see the need and find the way to feed the hungry children of whatever conviction."[26] As a child in Galveston, she had learned from her mother's example "to abandon provincial Sisterhood in order to ally [herself] with a larger National Council of Jewish Women" that pursued projects of national and international scope.[27] As the European situation worsened, Marks spoke for peace, giving a radio address in 1936 and forming the Texas State Committee on the Cause and Cure of War out of a coalition that included the Business and Professional Women, the Federated Council of Church Women, the Temple Emanu-El Sisterhood, the NCJW, the American Association of University Women, the PTA, the YWCA, and the Woman's Christian Temperance Union. In 1941, Marks was asked to join the National Committee on International Relations and Peace, and throughout the war years she organized civil defense activities, promoted the sale of war bonds, and established kindergartens for the children of women working in defense factories.[28]

In Texas' large cities, Jews mobilized with other Texans to prepare for and support the nation's war effort. Henry Jacobus headed the Dallas USO and fed soldiers at his home. Many Dallasites volunteered with the Red Cross, serving in a variety of capacities. Valerie Aronoff worked in the news office, and Louise Mittenthal, Adlene Nathanson, and Olga Mae Schepps drove for the Red Cross Motor Corps Unit, transporting soldiers who arrived at Love Field bound for veterans' hospitals or military bases in the area. Dorothy Lewis had worked for the Red Cross since 1931, caring for World War I veterans, and she again went to work, knitting and sewing, preparing surgical dressings, and assembling service kits. Members of the Temple Emanu-El Sisterhood, led by Seline Roos, arranged a sewing circle to produce clothing for the Red Cross. The Jewish Community Center hosted dances and set up cots to accommodate servicemen on furlough in Dallas. On Saturdays, Rosalee and Bernice Cohn brought the men breakfasts of lox, bagels, and cream cheese.[29]

Although large cities' Jewish communities had greater means and human resources to contribute to the war effort, the conflict reached deeply into rural areas as well. As the nation's defense structure grew during the war, the government built or upgraded military bases in Texas, often in rural areas, where more than 1.2 million troops and some 200,000 airmen were trained.[30] Of these, thousands were Jewish. In fact, the Jewish military presence on a base often exceeded, sometimes significantly so, the Jewish population of nearby towns. "A most happy memory," remembered Evelynn Lois Ray of San Angelo, "was that when World War II was being fought, we could at last start dating because we were not allowed to date non-Jews, and the war meant there were Jewish servicemen available for dating."[31] Besides such social aspects, the sudden surge in Jewish population posed a challenge to local Jewish communities who felt obliged to provide Jewish fellowship to the servicemen stationed nearby. Rabbi Sidney Wolf of Corpus Christi, where the expansion of the Naval Air Station roughly doubled the city's population, volunteered to serve the base as an auxiliary chaplain, welcomed Jewish servicemen into his home, and performed weddings for them in his parlor.[32] Lena and Leon Aron served Passover Seder at their Nacogdoches home for Jewish soldiers and Women's Army Auxiliary Corps members (WAACs) stationed nearby. To their guests, a Texas Seder offered some surprises. "When young Mr. Aron read the Hebrew passages in his warm Texas drawl," remembered WAAC Clarice Pollard from Brooklyn, "the unaccustomed inflections fell on our northeastern ears for the first time and caused hilarity. . . . We pressed our lips together to hold back our laughter, until we could no longer stifle our reactions."[33]

Abilene's Jewish community provides a case study in local responses to the needs of Jewish servicemen and women. Camp Barkeley, located eleven miles southwest of town, became one of the state's largest military installations during World War II, serving as headquarters for the Forty-fifth Infantry Division and as a POW camp for German prisoners. At its peak, it had a population of fifty thousand, far exceeding the wartime population of Abilene itself.[34] Abilene's Jewish community, consisting of thirteen families, found itself host to "hundreds of Jewish boys" and "welcomed them by entertaining at their homes and providing Jewish services at various halls in the town."[35] As the camp's Jewish population increased, townspeople recognized the need for a *shul* and an opportunity to build one. Committees formed to plan the synagogue and to raise funds, half of which came from the small Jewish community. Gentile citizens, believing that all American soldiers should have a place to pray before going overseas, contributed the rest.[36] Abe Levy, a retailer in nearby Sweetwater, donated a Torah to the congregation, and Temple Mizpah was opened in time for High Holiday services in 1942.[37]

The Ladies' Auxiliary of Temple Mizpah was especially active in creating social and religious opportunities for Camp Barkeley's Jewish soldiers. In September 1942, they served High Holiday meals to approximately 250 soldiers and sponsored suppers every other Sunday for 200 to 400. Mrs. Mary Elias, Auxiliary president, attended every Jewish wedding at the temple that involved servicepeople, and she and her husband acted as surrogate parents for many couples far from home. Under her leadership, the Auxiliary provided wedding feasts for Jewish couples married in the temple. The Auxiliary also organized parties for Chanukah and Purim and, most spectacularly, prepared Passover Seder meals for hundreds of participants. In 1944, working closely with representatives of the New York–based Jewish Welfare Board, the Auxiliary prepared a kosher Seder for more than eleven hundred soldiers in a Camp Barkeley mess hall. "New dishes, new pots and pans were used and the mess hall was completely repainted and cleaned," records the Temple Mizpah memory book. "Kosher food arrived from sources as far away as New York, Chicago and Dallas. Temple Mizpah women's auxiliary was in charge and those few women prepared and served the entire Seder." The women worked for two weeks to prepare twenty-five hundred homemade matzo balls with chicken soup and all the trimmings.[38] "It is hardly believable that so much can be done in so little a community," wrote the parents of a Brooklyn soldier who had attended services at Temple Mizpah.[39]

After the war, the bases shrank or closed—Camp Barkeley was deactivated in 1945—and the large numbers of soldiers who had temporarily transformed Jewish life in Texas rural communities disappeared. Texas Jews, however, could not return to their sense of isolation from world problems. Almost immediately, they stepped in to ease the arrival of Jewish "displaced persons," including many survivors of the concentration camps who sought refuge in Texas. Between 1945 and 1951 the United States took in about 350,000 European Jews, who settled in communities across the country.[40] As with prewar refugees, it is impossible to determine the number of survivors who settled in Texas, but there are many examples of Texas Jews and gentiles reaching out to help them. In 1946, Rabbi Sidney Wolf of Corpus Christi organized a banquet to raise money for displaced European Jews, and he invited the city's mayor, Robert Wilson, to address the crowd. "[I]n a subdued and moving voice," Wolf remembered, the mayor "pledged $5,000 in memory of his beloved son who had lost his life on the battlefields of Europe . . . whereupon it seemed as if the whole crowd rose en masse to its feet to follow the Mayor's example." The banquet raised more than $125,000.[41] Placement of refugees in Texas communities required collecting affidavits to certify that new arrivals would not become public charges, and many Texas individuals and organizations provided them in quantity, as they had done for refugees before the war. By one account, the Weingarten grocery store chain alone made one thousand affidavits available to the Hebrew Immigrant Aid Society.[42]

National organizations such as the United Service for New Americans asked local communities to assume support of refugees, and Texas communities accepted that responsibility. In 1950, for example, the Jewish Family Service and the Jewish Welfare Federation of Dallas met to discuss ways of integrating an additional ninety-six refugee families into their community.[43] Two years later, the same group issued a plea to the public to help the "New Americans" among them. According to a pamphlet, "109 families have already been settled in Dallas [and] 25 more will come in 1952. . . . Fresh dollars are needed to start new lives for them." A list of groups benefiting from recent fundraising included the Dallas Refugee Service Program.[44] In Laredo, representatives of the New York Association for New Americans, affiliated with the United Jewish Appeal (UJA), asked local Jews to look after immigrants crossing the Mexican border into Texas. "Whenever these people came to Laredo and asked for Jewish help, they were always referred to me," recalled Albert Granoff, who operated a retail establishment that conducted business on both sides of the border. "[New York directors] gave me permission to spend as much money as I needed in order to help these people," Granoff wrote in his memoirs. "All I had to do was to present them with a bill at the end of the month and it was paid without question." He was able to help many of the refugees solve whatever immigration, transportation, or personal problems they had, "and those whose problem could not be solved, I sent back to New York, where the UJA helped them." In several cases, Granoff assisted Jews who were moving in the other direction, passing through Laredo to join family in Mexico. In later years, Granoff remembered these activities as "a profound and enriching satisfaction."[45]

For many Holocaust survivors seeking refuge in the United States, Texas seemed a remote and unfamiliar destination. Some saw this as an advantage. Sam Silberman, awaiting transport from a displaced persons camp in Europe, specifically requested Texas, a place he had heard of and thought was still a frontier with plenty of opportunity.[46] For others, however, Texas seemed a lonely and forbidding prospect. Arnold and Rebecca Spanner, Auschwitz survivors who met and married in a displaced persons camp in Germany, were skeptical about being relocated to Corpus Christi, a place neither of them had ever heard of. They were both from large cities—she from Lodz, Poland, and he from Berlin—and both had lost their entire families in the concentration camps. Worried about living in a strange and faraway town that appeared on few maps of the United States, they arrived in Corpus Christi to find that their final destination was actually McAllen, an even smaller community in the Rio Grande Valley near the Mexican border. They learned later that the small Jewish community in McAllen had specified to relocation authorities the kind of refugees they believed would be best able to adapt to life there. "[I]t required one young couple, not rigidly orthodox," writes Dorothy Rabinowitz, who interviewed Rebecca Spanner in the 1970s, "who could therefore probably adjust to a place that was not, after all, one of the centers of Jewish life in America, a town where kosher food was not available around the block." McAllen had chosen the Spanners, Rabinowitz explains, "and there, whether they wished to go or not, they went."[47]

During the long drive from Corpus Christi to McAllen, the Spanners and their hosts maintained a near-total silence, unable to communicate effectively in Yiddish, Polish, German, or English. It was after eleven o'clock at night when they arrived:

> In wintertime, McAllen's houses darkened early; furthermore, they looked to the couple as though they had no one living in them. No

chink of light was visible; no sound came from them. Where were they being taken, Rebecca had asked her husband in a whisper. "A *dorf* [a very small village, a backwater]" she answered herself, having received no reply from her husband, who was busy staring into the darkness, looking for clues in the outsides of the few shuttered houses they passed. "A *dorf*," she maintained again, whereupon her husband turned and whispered in Polish not to worry, no one would force them to stay if it didn't work out for them here.[48]

Rebecca had been prepared to settle anywhere, "but now that the time had come, her heart sank to see how tiny and remote a place they were to live in, how far from cities and people." She had grown up in the second largest city in Poland and "had all along seen herself coming to a city or, at the least, a large town."[49]

On arriving in McAllen, however, the Spanners were touched by the generosity of its sixty or so Jewish families, who provided them with a five-bedroom home, much more space than they would have had if they had settled in a larger community. The Jewish Community Service paid the rent on the house and covered the couple's medical costs, and McAllen's Jews provided so much in the way of food, clothing, and other necessities that Rebecca was embarrassed to accept it. Rebecca befriended an older woman whom she came to address as "Aunt Sarah," "a Texas born and bred local schoolteacher, whose Yiddish was fluent and impeccable," who coached Rebecca tirelessly in English. Sarah comforted Rebecca in her "pure, almost literary kind" of Yiddish, "which she had learned from her parents and somehow managed to preserve, though there had not been anyone to speak Yiddish with in McAllen for many years." She told the young refugee that "since the people in McAllen spoke only one language and she, Rebecca, spoke three—none of which was English, it so happened—that it was not she but the other people who should be feeling self-conscious."[50] When, several years later, the Spanners were obliged to move to Houston, Rebecca was sorry to leave McAllen, but in Houston she was able to play the same role for new refugees that McAllen's Jews had played for her.[51]

Mike Jacobs, another Auschwitz survivor, was relocated to Dallas where he had an adjustment experience that differed greatly from Rebecca Spanner's, though he had similar doubts about Texas' remoteness. Jacobs had spent two years in the Auschwitz and Mauthausen concentration camps and survived a five-day death march in freezing weather. During the war he lost his entire immediate family—both parents and five siblings—as well as more than eighty extended family members. He remained in Germany for six years after the war, teaching athletics and running a small shop. In 1951, the Jewish Joint Distribution Committee (JDC) and HIAS helped him move to Dallas. When he applied for the required papers to immigrate to the United States, an American official told him that he should avoid New York, where there were few openings for teachers, and look instead to Texas. "In New York there is a big forest of trees," the official explained. "If you were to go and be in the middle of the forest, you would get lost and not know how to get out. I'm talking about people." When Jacobs looked blank, the official laughed and told him that he was going instead "to the biggest state in the United States." Jacobs remained dubious: "I still had no idea what he was talking about," he later remembered, "but I guessed it was okay."[52] Jacobs' friends offered only discouragement when he told them that he was going to Dallas:

> They looked at me. "Mendel, you are crazy! . . . Why not New York, Baltimore, Chicago, Philadelphia, where more of the displaced people are going? They speak the language you can understand. You are crazy to go to Texas. Don't you watch the movies? No sidewalks, people coming out of beer joints, shooting each other?"[53]

Jacobs brushed off their concerns. "Guys, what are you worried about?" he asked. "When I get to Dallas, Texas, I will buy me a horse and saddle and ride, too."[54]

The JDC arranged his transportation to New Orleans, where representatives of the Jewish community met him at the port. They gave him a shower, a meal, and fifteen dollars for expenses and led him to the train. Harry and Chaya Andres, who spoke Yiddish, met him at the Dallas station and took him to a boarding house in a South Dallas neighborhood that had a large Jewish population. The Dallas Jewish Family Service provided $125 for his first month's rent and expenses. "I did not feel comfortable getting an allowance," Jacobs wrote later, "so that was the last time I received money from the Jewish Family Service."[55] Instead, he worked briefly as a landscaper, a skill he had learned at a Nazi work camp. During his years in Dallas, Jacobs organized and coached youth soccer leagues and opened a scrap metal business with his wife Ginger in 1954. In an English-language class at SMU, Jacobs, required to give a five-minute extemporaneous speech on "something you know about," spoke for an hour about Auschwitz, prompting classmates to invite him to speak at their church. He continued making reg-

Mike Jacobs, second from right, sharing plans for the Dallas Holocaust Memorial Center
with Elie Wiesel, third from left, January 13, 1982. Wiesel was in Dallas speaking for the Jewish
Federation Drive. Also pictured, left to right, are Max Glauben, Jack Altman, Sam Szor,
and Ann Sikora. Courtesy of the Dallas Jewish Historical Society.

ular speaking engagements. "I promised [in the camps] I would go and talk
about the Holocaust to as many people as possible. . . . Since then, I have
never stopped speaking and bringing the message of what one human can
do to the other when we are silent and complacent." Since that first speech,
Jacobs has addressed "schools, universities, community colleges, churches,
synagogues, eating-disorder groups, therapists, and people at risk."[56]

Jacobs' efforts at public education led him to spearhead the creation of
the Dallas Holocaust Memorial Center, the first such facility in the nation,
which opened in 1984. "It had long been a dream of mine to have a place
where we Holocaust Survivors could gather and memorialize our loved
ones," he explains in his memoirs. "As I developed my idea, I decided that
we should build a memorial center for Holocaust studies, which would
include a memorial room wherein we could have memorial stones on the
wall."[57] The Jewish Community Center provided space for the facility. Jacobs convinced other survivors in the community that the plan was worth-
while, and they began raising funds and selecting architects. As the capping
achievement, Jacobs went to extreme effort to locate a European boxcar
that had been used for the transport of Jewish prisoners and to arrange its

shipment to Dallas to stand as a permanent exhibit at the Center. The Dallas Holocaust Memorial Center served as a model for similar facilities in Houston and El Paso, as well as in other communities around the United States.[58]

United Jewish Appeal

Mike Jacobs was also an active Zionist—he served as area chairman for Israel Bonds, and the Zionist Organization of America once named him Man of the Year—which is not surprising in a person whose Holocaust experience so shaped his life and character.[59] The destruction of European Jewry led directly to the 1948 establishment of Israel, and the memory of the Holocaust inspired much of the support that Israel received in its early years from Jews and gentiles around the world. As the Holocaust and World War II unfolded, Texas Jews naturally underwent a gradual but definite change in their feelings toward Zionism. Traditionally, Jewish Texans were acculturationists who had long and consistently opposed the notion of a Jewish state with its suggestion of a separate, distinct Jewish nationhood. But as the Beth Israel Revolt demonstrated in 1943, Texas Jewry had strong and growing undercurrents of sympathy for a Jewish Palestine that echoed sympathies around the world.

As Israeli independence neared, Texas rabbis urged their congregations to take a less provincial view of Jewish affairs and to involve themselves in Israeli development. By bending with the times and pushing their congregations to do the same, these rabbis helped to prevent confrontations like the one that tore Beth Israel apart in 1943. David Lefkowitz of Dallas' Temple Emanu-El, for example, had long been opposed to the idea of a Jewish state and had joined the anti-Zionist American Council for Judaism. Unlike Beth Israel's unwavering anti-Zionist stand, Lefkowitz's view was more nuanced, more sensitive to the inflections of opinion within his congregation. "A Jewish congregation," he wrote to his son-in-law, the banker Fred Florence, "should neither come out for or against Zionism, but rather for Judaism, which is the uniting principle of all congregations."[60] After the 1948 creation of Israel, the Jewish Welfare Federation of Dallas, a regular fundraiser for the United Jewish Appeal and other Jewish causes, met to plan a fundraising drive for the new nation. One participant took a traditional isolationist stance, arguing that Dallas Jews preferred to keep their money in Dallas. Lefkowitz spoke in favor of the United Jewish Appeal and insisted that the drive continue.[61]

Similarly, Beaumont's Rabbi Samuel Rosinger pushed his acculturation-ist and politically conservative congregation toward active Zionism and a broader range of Jewish activism, even when they put up resistance. Ros-inger had long sympathized with the Zionist movement—Henrietta Szold, the founder of Hadassah, was his classmate at the Jewish Theological Sem-inary—and he encouraged his congregants to form Zionist organizations. When Szold visited "wild and wooly Texas" in 1912, Rosinger supported her effort to establish Hadassah chapters in the state, even though he felt that "with her modesty, simplicity, and naturalness, she was not cut out for propaganda work . . . especially in this borderland of civilization." Her tour, however, "was a success of the most enduring kind," and Rosinger remarked that the chapters she organized in many Texas towns, including Beaumont, "have made vital contributions to the work of healing and re-demption to which she dedicated her life."[62] In the late 1940s, Rosinger vis-ited Israel and met Prime Minister David Ben-Gurion, to whom he bragged that "[w]hen I came to my congregation, they were anti-Zionists, but I con-verted them to Zionism." Ben-Gurion replied that this was "only the begin-ning of the task incumbent upon you. When you return home, you have to convert them to be Israelis."[63]

Anti-Zionism remained a powerful force in Texas-Jewish communities, however, even after Israel's existence was an accomplished fact. "Probably my most unpleasant experience in my seven years in Fort Worth," wrote Rabbi Milton Rosenbaum, "was having to deal with anti-Zionist Jews." These congregants "saw Zionism as a threat to their acceptance as true Americans," he wrote, "subjecting them to the charge of dual loyalty." They regarded the rabbi's efforts on behalf of Israel "as an attack upon their mis-conceived 'nativism.'" Though incredulous about an opinion that seemed to him "especially senseless in view of the facts that a great many Jews had already found refuge in Palestine after World War II [and that] in 1948 the State of Israel had come into existence," Rosenbaum tried to understand their feelings. "They were decent people," he wrote. "Some were multi-generational Texans. They were well accepted by their neighbors. Texas was far away from the horrors of Europe. Why did someone have to rock their comfortable boat?"[64] Diane Ravitch, an education scholar who grew up in Houston in the 1940s, noted lingering ambivalence toward Israel in that city as well. While overt anti-Zionism had waned by the 1950s—she only learned years later that her rabbi, Hyman Schachtel, had been a prominent anti-Zionist—neither was pro-Israeli sentiment particularly strong. "I knew next to nothing about Israel," she recalled. "I was aware of its existence, but dimly. There wasn't anything like the intense involvement that one gets growing up in New York. I don't think I ever met anyone, as I was growing up, who had been to Israel or who had any interest in going there."[65] Nor was Rosenbaum able to sway his Fort Worth congregation entirely toward Zionism, but the "course of events," he claimed, "eventually numbed the fervor of their opposition as history simply passed them by."[66]

Despite such lingering doubt among Texas Jews about the propriety of a Jewish state, anecdotal evidence attests to the strong support many Jewish Texans felt for Israel. Walter Cohen, who left his home in Lubbock to fight with the Israeli liberation force, is a rare but compelling example of a Texas Jew who went to extremes in support of the new state. In 1947, Cohen was a World War II veteran haunted by memories of the war and the Holocaust: "That tragic loss had made a tremendous impact upon me, just one generation removed from Europe," Cohen wrote. "Without question, the Holocaust was probably the most important factor in my decision to become a volunteer in Israel." Reading the *Dallas Morning News*, "with its anti-Zionist persuasion, and all the unfriendly letters-to-the-editor," strengthened his resolve to fight. Lubbock's rabbi, Joseph Kermin, had been a member of the Palestinian Jewish Brigade during World War I and referred him to appropriate contacts. Cohen offered his service in the Israeli war for independence and received an assignment to fight in an armored brigade in the Galilee. After the war, he traveled back to Israel at least six times.[67]

Most Texas Jews, however, limited their pro-Israeli action to advocacy and fundraising, though these efforts were extensive and far-reaching. Herbert Mallinson of Dallas co-chaired the southwestern region of the Joint Distribution Committee and served as Texas State Chairman of the National Refugee Service. After his death in 1941, his sister Reba Wadel took over his campaign, becoming national chairwoman of the Women's Division of the United Jewish Appeal, which collected money for Israeli and American Jews. Jewish newspapers in Texas also promoted fundraising efforts. "This is not just Charity," the *Jewish Herald-Voice* asserted in a full-page advertisement for the United Jewish Campaign of Houston in 1942. "This is a campaign to DECIDE the destiny of a people!"[68]

In Dallas, these and similar efforts strengthened the solidarity that the war and the refugee crisis had already forged in the Jewish community. Whereas the city's German and Russian Jews had lived and socialized in separate communities, revolving around the Reform and Conservative synagogues, fundraising for Israel drew both into a common cause. Soon after the war, the city's Jewish country club, the Columbian, which had been an appendage of the Reform congregation, began admitting more Orthodox and Conservative members.[69] Judge Irving Goldberg wrote that "[a]s the lives of Dallas Jews became more complicated and as they became more intimately involved with the more cosmic issues presented to the American and world Jewish community," the Jewish Federation, which represented Dallas Jewry as a whole, became the vanguard of Jewish activism. As long as "the primal demand upon Dallas Jewry relates to Israel and to national causes," he wrote, "local tensions between and among Jews in Dallas will have little influence upon the effectiveness of the Federation."[70]

As their support for Israel grew, many Texas Jews began making the journeys there that became a hallmark of American-Jewish identification. Albert Granoff traveled to Israel in 1953 and described its profound impact on his sense of himself as a Jew. "You have no idea what impression Tel-Aviv made on me," he recalled in his memoirs. "To see a Yiddish policeman talking Hebrew to passers-by, to see Hebrew signs all over the streets. Wherever you are and wherever you go nothing but Jewish faces; some speaking Hebrew, some Yiddish, and others in English and many other languages. It had a tremendous effect on me."[71]

Bertha and Charles Bender provide a particularly colorful example of Texas-Jewish support for Israel. Bertha, born in Lithuania, and Charles, from Odessa, Russia, met in 1911 at a Zionist meeting in Portsmouth, Virginia, where Bertha was the Zionist Organization's secretary; they were married the next year. Ambitious and energetic, Charles imagined better opportunities in Texas than on the East Coast, so the couple traveled to Dallas in 1912, where he established the Star Bottling Company and founded the Texas Young Zionists of Dallas. They went to Lubbock a few years later to operate a retail store, then moved to Breckenridge in 1919 to open the Bender Department Store, which they operated together until 1953. Lacking a synagogue in West Texas, Charles helped to organize Breckenridge's Temple Beth Israel in 1929 and served as its first president.[72]

The couple became deeply devoted to Texas—"we were destined to grow together," Bertha said of her adoptive state—and Charles took to wearing elaborate western costumes, including neckties with pictures of oil rigs and cowboy boots embossed with the Star of David.[73] Bender's ostentatious outfits made an impression during his frequent visits to Israel. The *Jerusalem Post* described "America's famous 'Cowboy Zionist' from Breckenridge, Texas" as "colourful in dress and striking in personality." Bender's "sweeping sombrero, his lurid shirts and his distinctive cowboy boots, decorated with blue-and-white Magen David," the paper reported,

Charles and Bertha Bender in Israel. Texas Jewish Historical Society Collection, Center for American History, University of Texas at Austin, CN 12115.

"have already attracted widespread attention on the streets of Haifa and Tel Aviv."[74] "We always visited with Prime Minister David Ben Gurion," Bertha claimed, "and he dubbed my husband Charles as 'The Jewish Cowboy from Texas.'" Other Israelis delighted Charles by referring to him as "'Tex" or "Little Tex."[75]

As the *Jerusalem Post* was careful to point out, however, "there is more to Charlie Bender than just the cowboy pose." The Benders had sent both of their sons to school in Israel, and as president of the Southwest Zionist Region and in his efforts to promote Israel Bonds, Bender was "hailed as a master salesman for Israel." In 1957, the Benders' large donation built the Charles and Bertha Bender Laboratory, which provided facilities for aeronautics research in Israel. The *Post* praised Charles as "a sincere and deeply devoted Zionist who has already done much for the country."[76]

Charles Bender was an especially colorful example of a common phenomenon: Texas Jews, steeped in the provincial concerns of their Texas lives, who were nevertheless focused on global Jewish events. Earlier Jewish Texans had often imagined themselves as isolated and distinct from Jews elsewhere in the world: "Pardon me for having forgotten the [Jewish] New Year," wrote El Paso's Ernst Kohlberg to his German family in September 1876, "for one is not reminded of it here."[77] As late as the 1950s, Diane Ravitch recalled, Jewish education in Houston provided little sense of religious identification. "My Jewish education was limited to Sunday school in our Reform temple," she wrote. "We learned a smattering of Jewish history. I was so poorly educated as a Jew that I didn't know how poorly educated I was."[78] The critical events of the 1940s, however, were forcing Texas Jews to peer out from behind their provincial curtains to see a Jewish world that was rapidly changing. World War II, the Holocaust, and the establishment of Israel turned their attention away from the local concerns that had underscored their separateness and differences from each other and from Jews elsewhere. These crises, in fact, *became* local concerns as immigrants from around the country and around the world entered their communities bringing complex new perspectives. Global events proved that Texas Jews were no longer as isolated as they had once thought.

Sit-in protest at Weingarten's Grocery Store #26 on Almeda Street in Houston, March 4, 1960. A protester is reading the March 7, 1960, edition of *Time*, which featured a cover photo of Kenyan statesman Tom Mboya. *Houston Post* Collection, Houston Metropolitan Research Center, Houston Public Library, RG D6–00131.

EIGHT

"Are You Going to Serve Us?"

TEXAS JEWS AND THE BLACK CIVIL RIGHTS MOVEMENT

*The first sit-in to challenge racial segregation in Texas public accommoda-*tions occurred at a Jewish-owned store in Houston's predominantly black Third Ward. Following the example of nonviolent protesters in North Carolina and Georgia, about thirty-five African-American students from Texas Southern University gathered around the campus flagpole on Friday afternoon, March 4, 1960, and then marched to Weingarten's Grocery Store #26 nearby on Almeda Road. Weingarten's was a strategic choice. Not only did it operate a whites-only lunch counter in spite of its primarily black clientele, but the Weingarten's chain of about thirty stores was also a local institution.[1] Its Jewish owner, Joseph Weingarten, esteemed for his social and charitable work, sat on the governing boards of several area hospitals and had been honored by B'nai B'rith and the National Conference of Christians and Jews for his civic activities. He had recently met with several European heads of state and with Pope John XXIII to discuss world peace, a cause he had adopted as a personal crusade after a visit to Israel.[2] Yet Weingarten's corporate policy, under his personal management, was to belittle a large number of his customers by refusing them service and employment while profiting from their patronage in their own neighborhoods. The hypocrisy was too pungent for the protest's organizers to ignore.

At the store, several students took seats at the counter, prepared either to be served or to be arrested. The few customers already sitting at the counter quietly left, allowing the protesters to occupy all thirty seats. One of the protest leaders, Eldrewey Stearns, rushed to a pay phone to contact police and media, who promptly arrived and prepared for trouble, though none was to occur. Store officials also appeared and invited some of the protesters to a private meeting upstairs, where they tried to work out a quiet solution. For the students, however, negotiation was impossible. "Are you going to serve us or are you not?" one asked. "I don't think you can afford not to—you've got too much money involved." When the students refused to leave, company officials shut the counter down rather than serve them, but the protesters kept their seats, quietly reading newspapers and magazines until 8:30 that evening, soon before the store closed for the day. The following morning, they resumed their sit-in at Weingarten's, while another group of protesters occupied the soda fountain at a nearby drug-store, which also immediately closed the counter.[3] The next week, about 150 TSU students, inspired by these early successes, ventured out of the Third Ward to challenge downtown stores on Main Street.[4]

Within a few days, sit-in demonstrations had spread to lunch counters throughout Houston and to the City Hall cafeteria. Rabbi Hyman Judah Schachtel of Temple Beth Israel and attorney Leon Jaworski served on the forty-one-member Citizens' Relations Committee that negotiated a two-week truce between storeowners and protesters. Finally, virtually by order of the committee, counters throughout the city were integrated—quickly, completely, and with little public recognition. In the same way, Houston had already integrated many of its municipal facilities, including golf cours-es (in 1950, under court order), the public library (in 1953), and the city bus system (in 1954), without much public notice. Most of Houston's stores and restaurants, as well as its public parks, beaches, and swimming pools, were integrated by 1963 due to quiet but persistent protests like that at Weingarten's.[5]

The Weingarten's demonstration illustrates an important irony of the American civil rights era: even as many Jews became deeply involved in the movement, inspired by the ancient Jewish commitment to social justice and by an ultimate concern for self-protection, others were part of the seg-regationist system the protesters sought to destroy. In Texas, every major retail store in every major city except Fort Worth was Jewish-run. These included Joske's and Frost Brothers in San Antonio; Sakowitz's, Weingar-ten's, Battlesteins, and Foley Brothers in Houston; Lichtenstein's in Corpus Christi; Levine's and Kruger's Jewelry in Austin; the Popular Store in El Paso; and Titche-Goettinger, Sanger Brothers, E. M. Kahn, A. Harris and

Company, and Neiman-Marcus in Dallas. Jewish owners and managers were thus directly affected by segregation law and became its enforcers. None of their stores employed black salesclerks until the early 1960s, and as in gentile-owned stores, black customers were admitted, if at all, only into separate areas of the store. They were prohibited from trying on merchandise or using in-store restaurants, lunch counters, and restrooms. Eddie Bernice Johnson, an African-American congresswoman from Dallas, tried to buy a hat at A. Harris soon after arriving in the city in the 1950s. "I was told that I could not try on hats or shoes," she remembered later. "They had to measure my head and then go over and measure the hat."[6] Stanley Marcus, head of Neiman-Marcus and one of Dallas' civic giants for sixty years, later admitted that such practices were "designed to discourage black patronage" in order to make the stores more appealing to white customers.[7]

As throughout the South, however, many Jewish merchants in Texas were deeply ambivalent about segregation and their participation in it. An ethnic minority in a society that valued adherence to the status quo, Jews felt great pressure to conform, and undoubtedly many Jews, fully blended into southern life, sincerely approved the dominant ideologies. In any case, those who opposed segregation mostly kept their opinions to themselves. According to a 1959 opinion poll, Jews were much more likely than the majority of white Southerners to support civil rights initiatives, but only 15 percent of the general population *believed* that Jews were in favor of integration. Fully 67 percent had no idea how their Jewish neighbors felt about the issue.[8]

Jewish Texans, like Jews elsewhere in the South, tended to be more attuned to the problem of racial prejudice than other whites. Socially and commercially part of the white majority but still, as the Klan's ascendancy in the 1920s had demonstrated, different and less acceptable than white Christians, they held a peculiar place in the South's racial order. The long history of anti-Semitism, held in collective memory if rare in actual experience, conditioned them to be sensitive to social discrimination based on ethnic or cultural differences, and they were more likely to question the fairness of segregation than were white gentiles who had not suffered such prejudice.

Texas Jews' small numbers and great success in becoming part of the business establishment made them vulnerable and gave them much to lose, and so their response to racial inequality was muted. When they acted, they did so in a reactionary way: they moved when circumstances initiated by others (protesters or the courts) made them move. But once moved, their response was prompt and genuine. Jewish civic and business leaders led the way, though they generally did so behind the scenes and without drawing public attention to their activities. Jewish businesspeople pressured gentile friends and associates to use their greater civic clout. Rabbis served as moral guides for their communities, speaking to Christian as well as Jewish audiences, and serving on municipal boards and steering committees to guide their cities through the difficult but inevitable changes of integration.[9] Secular and religious Jewish leaders sought to encourage communication among whites and between white and black citizens, in order to promote a peaceful and, above all, inconspicuous transition to a desegregated society. By the 1960s, a generation after the resurgent Ku Klux Klan had reminded them that they were not, after all, just like other Texans, Texas Jews had become the consummate outsider-insiders. The civil rights era called on them to serve Texas communities through the application of distinctly Jewish conscience and well-tuned intergroup diplomacy.

Racial Middlemen

As the civil rights movement began to unfold, the unique role that southern Jews could play became apparent. El Paso's Rabbi Floyd Fierman told his congregation after *Brown v. Board of Education*, the Supreme Court's 1954 school desegregation decision, that Jews must be involved in the social changes that were to come. "The Jew is frequently called a middleman," he explained in his handwritten sermon notes. "By middleman it is meant that he stands midway between the producer & the consumer." The financial metaphor, however, also had "a cultural significance"—Jews had mediated between competing cultures throughout their history. "Economically, culturally, also religiously & racially he is a middleman," Fierman explained. In a new era, "farsighted Jewish lay leaders & rabbis are concerning themselves with a relationship that has been haunting America: the relationship of the brownskin man & the whiteskin man & the Jew here again is fulfilling an historical role."[10] Standing along a conceptual frontier that divided them from their neighbors and, in a sense, excused them from the South's painful history of racism and violence, Jews sought the middle ground, fashioning means of improving themselves and their communities without plunging into the extremism of either side. No longer anxious to make a place in Anglo Texas society, Jews now found that their differences provided a unique perspective and opportunities to lead.

In Texas, Jews managed this balancing act carefully and successfully. Even as Jewish retailers were the most visible segregators, African-American activists praised rabbis for their loyalty to the civil rights cause. Peter Johnson, the self-described "first legitimate civil rights worker to be sent to the southwest," considered Rabbi Levi Olan his mentor in Dallas, calling him "one of our strongest supporters."[11] San Antonio activist Claude Black made a similar observation about Rabbi David Jacobson, praising him as "a friend to the black community when white friends were scarce."[12] Although it may appear that the Jewish community was divided, with rabbis offering the moral direction while retailers and businessmen protected the status quo, this was not the case. Even within the civic and commercial establishment, Jews pushed for change with a subtle combination of firmness and compromise, nudging others along but yielding when necessary to keep the peace. The Jewish community was not so much divided between those who supported integration and those who did not as between those who were anxious to speak against it immediately and those who preferred to wait for more favorable circumstances.

This Jewish cautiousness in the matter of civil rights had its roots in many generations of adaptation to southern life and cultural mores. Since the years immediately after the Civil War, when Jewish peddlers and merchants first began arriving in the southern states, they maintained a relatively cordial relationship with African-American customers, treating them with a respect uncommon among white retailers of the time. Jewish sellers extended credit to black buyers and let them try on clothing before paying for it, a practice that black customers appreciated, perhaps especially because all knew that it made the merchandise unacceptable to most white buyers. These customers appreciated, too, Jews' willingness to bargain, to offer lower prices even at a loss, in order to maintain their patronage.

To be sure, such policies were not entirely altruistic. It was good business strategy to find and exploit a market that gentile merchants were underserving. As Stephen Whitfield has explained, Jewish merchants in the South were "more interested in customers than in customs of racial discrimination, more committed to making sales than to making trouble, more worried about inventory than about integration."[13] Early in the twentieth century, many Jewish shopkeepers hired black employees, in part to provide them employment, but mostly to draw black customers into the store. If the clientele failed to materialize, the employees were often let go.[14] Similarly, Jewish merchants broke with white custom and advertised in African-American newspapers, a practice that, despite its egalitarian overtones, clearly served their own commercial needs as well. In treating black customers courteously, therefore, Jews put business ahead of racial principle—a move available to them as outsiders that their gentile competitors, more firmly tied to the region and to southern history, could not, or would not, make.

By the mid-twentieth century, though, the Texas oil boom, the Second World War, and the subsequent economic prosperity created a growing class of wealthy white purchasers much in demand as customers. As retail competition intensified, and as Jewish merchants reaped the benefits of the boom, they became more protective of their white clientele. With segregation hardening throughout the South, Jewish-owned stores became bastions of racial prejudice. Paradoxically, the same business sense and flexible racial views that had allowed Jews to cultivate friendly relations with black customers now made them devoted segregationists. With no clearly articulated principles regarding race and no long involvement in the social conflicts and contracts that created Jim Crow, Jewish merchants simply went with the flow, with whatever policies best served their business interests year to year. By the 1950s, that meant unqualified segregation.

The degree to which Texas Jews adopted the racial mores of their white contemporaries can be glimpsed in the observations of eastern European immigrants who, on first entering Texas communities, were shocked by the treatment of African Americans and at local Jews' willingness to permit it. Mike Jacobs, an Auschwitz survivor, had been in Dallas only a week when he boarded a public bus in 1951:

> On paying my bus fare, I went to an empty seat toward the back of the bus. The bus driver stopped the bus and waved toward me. I thought he was waving to the black people for the black people to get off the bus. He stopped at the next stop, again motioning, and I still did not know what was going on. He then started yelling and did not move the bus. A man who had just gotten on the bus came in and talked to the bus driver as he pointed to the back of the bus. The man then came over to me and introduced himself in English. When I shrugged my shoulders, he realized I didn't speak English. He then asked me in Yiddish if I spoke Yiddish. I answered "Yes" in Yiddish, and he then told me that I was not allowed to sit in the back of the bus; the back of the bus was for the black people. He showed me a sign on the bus saying the front was for whites and the back was for blacks. I really couldn't understand what the difference was. . . . He then said, "Go to the front, don't make any trouble," as the bus had still not moved.[15]

Jacobs refused to change seats, saying, "no one can force me." When the man asked again, Jacobs got off the bus and walked the rest of the way. More notable than Jacobs' ignorance about the segregation laws is the complicity in them shown by another Jewish passenger.

Part of the Establishment

When Jewish owners were the direct enforcers of segregation, they made shopping at Jewish-owned stores painful and embarrassing for black customers, many of whom recall the experience with bitterness. Bettie M. Patterson, a black public school teacher, remembered Houston in the 1950s as a place "filled with segregation, police brutality, white supremacy, and inferior schools," and she experienced discrimination most personally on public buses and in the city's famous department stores. "My friends and I loved to look at all the pretty things they had in Sakowitz, Neiman Marcus [which opened a Houston store in 1955] and Battlestein," she wrote, "but we hated how they treated us. From the moment we entered, . . . a store security person would obviously follow us around as if we had no rights to look nor purchase the merchandise." Some black customers, she said, pretended to be shopping for their white employers in order to buy from these stores with less trouble. "I was really glad when Sakowitz and Battlestein went out of business," she said, "and hope I will live to see Neiman Marcus do the same."[16]

Jewish merchants might have had personal reservations, but they were not prepared to disavow the social requirement of segregation. In 1953, seven years before nonviolent protests began in Texas, W. J. Durham of the Dallas Citizens' Committee to Abolish Discrimination against Negro Women in Dallas Department Stores approached Morton Sanger of E. M. Kahn's and convinced him to talk to other storeowners about their practice of "discriminating against Negro women in the sale of merchandise." Sanger's fellow retailers, including Stanley Marcus, "would not meet with the members of [the] committee [to] discuss the matter," Durham reported. Consequently, Sanger chose to leave Kahn's segregation policy in force. His competitors' reluctance to change their guidelines, he said, "left the management of the Kahn store to choose between two classes of business—white trade and trade from Negro citizens. Therefore, I can do nothing about the racial discrimination policy in force at the Kahn store."[17] Sanger may have been sympathetic to the protesters but was disinclined to be a test case. If no one else would go first, neither would he, and Dallas stores remained segregated until the early 1960s.

Dallas retailers were concerned about the impact that desegregation could have on their white clientele, but they were also reluctant to counter the official segregationist policy of the Dallas Citizens Council, whose self-appointed members one writer described as "a collection of dollars represented by men."[18] Not to be confused with the segregationist White Citizens Councils of many southern cities, the Dallas Citizens Council was formed to facilitate the city's successful effort to attract the 1936 Texas Centennial Exposition and to oversee its planning, building, and execution. After the Centennial, leaders formed an official and semi-permanent committee of twenty-two members, all powerful businessmen, who together set long-term goals for the city, selected and influenced officeholders, and unilaterally directed civic affairs. They operated the annual Texas State Fair (largely to their own profit); planned the location and design of freeways and neighborhoods, office buildings, and parks (largely to accommodate their personal and corporate investments); and oversaw the racial segregation and gradual desegregation of their city. Under their guidance, Dallas came to maturity in the 1950s as a well-oiled, conservative commercial machine.

Not only were Jewish businesspeople wary about challenging such powerful interests, but some participated directly in their activities. Two of the Dallas Citizens Council's long-time members were Jewish: Julius Schepps, a wholesale liquor distributor, member of every synagogue in town, and de facto leader of the Jewish community; and Fred Florence, president of Republic National Bank, former director of the Texas Centennial Exposition, treasurer of Temple Emanu-El, and son-in-law of Emanu-El's rabbi, David Lefkowitz. A 1964 list, following an apparent expansion of the Council's membership, showed 238 members, of whom 23 were Jewish. Stanley Marcus was one of only nine members of the "inner circle of leadership."[19] Other Dallas Jews—such as Herbert Marcus, Stanley's father and Neiman's founder; Arthur Kramer, A. Harris and Company president; John Rosenfield, the *Dallas Morning News* arts editor; and advertising executive Sam Bloom—were not officially Council members but were close to those who were and exercised great influence in the city's public affairs. Moreover, Jews headed both Temple Emanu-El and Republic National Bank, two of the six Dallas institutions that Sam Bloom later identified as "the great philosophical nurseries" of the city's commercial class.[20]

Jewish leaders' contributions to Dallas civic and cultural life were most obvious in support of the fine arts. John Rosenfield, Herbert and Stanley Marcus, and Arthur Kramer, in particular, were pivotal in establishing and supporting the Dallas Symphony Orchestra, the Dallas Civic Opera, and several local theatrical companies.[21] Thus, at a 1966 meeting of the Panel

Four members of the Dallas Citizens Council at a 1953 luncheon. The group examines
a letter addressed only to "Neiman-Marcus, Texas," successfully delivered by the post office.
Pictured, left to right, are Ben Wooten, president of First National Bank; Stanley Marcus,
president of Neiman-Marcus; Fred Florence, president of Republic National Bank; and R. L.
Thornton, chairman of the board of the Mercantile National Bank and later mayor of
Dallas and founder of the Citizens Council. Photograph by Johnny Hayes, *Dallas
Times-Herald*. From the collections of the Texas/Dallas History and Archives
Division, Dallas Public Library, PA76-1/20091.

of American Women, one discussion question was, "Why are Jews the cultural leaders of Dallas?"—not "*Are* Jews the cultural leaders of Dallas?"[22] As
in commercial life, the Dallas arts world was segregated, and here too Jews
not only acquiesced to the racial reality but also helped actively to uphold
it. In 1961, for instance, the Metropolitan Opera of New York announced
that it would no longer appear at the Music Hall on the Dallas Fairgrounds
because of its segregated seating arrangement. In defense, Rosenfield wrote
that black operagoers sat in the back of the auditorium not because of race
but by choice, a consequence of their unwillingness to donate to the opera
company or to purchase season tickets. "Negro interest in high-priced
events never has been rampant," he observed. "If the interests of the cul-
tured Negro . . . are genuine to the extent of wanting to hear the best opera
from a very good seat, one could tell him how to go about it." Rosenfield
suspected, instead, that African Americans only wished to attend the opera
"to 'test' segregation [rather] than to patronize the arts."[23] This view, of
course, ignored the economic realities of black life in Dallas in the 1950s,
not to mention the ruinous cycle of segregation itself.

Pressure behind the Scenes

Even after the Supreme Court's 1954 decision in *Brown v. Board of Education*, which ordered school integration and provided a moral basis for desegregation in all other areas, Dallas leaders, including Jews, were cautious and recommended a wait-and-see approach. The civic leadership only acceded to the requirements of *Brown* in 1961—and then only in the face of a direct federal court order and after exhausting every judicial avenue for appeal. By then, other southern towns and cities had demonstrated the disastrous potential of massive resistance. At a 1956 riot in Mansfield, southeast of Fort Worth, police stood aside while hundreds of white protesters surrounded the public high school to block access to black students, strung up effigies, fought with observers, and stopped cars at the town limits to prevent civil rights advocates from entering. The next year, in Little Rock, Arkansas, federal troops were needed to calm violence that erupted in what had been a placid and moderate white community. Rather than risk such possibilities, Dallas leaders, ever conscious of their city's reputation and of maintaining its commercial viability, decided to accept the inevitable and honor the court ruling. Integration of Dallas schools, however minimal, needed to take place quickly and quietly.

To that end, influential Dallas Jews mobilized to play a key role in the long effort to desegregate not only the city's public schools but also its arts facilities, public transportation, and shopping centers. Back in 1953, when black protesters had urged Jewish owners to integrate their stores, retailers ran for cover. Now, with a federal order in place and the writing clearly on the wall, they led the effort to desegregate the city's public accommodations. After all, these men—more so than the land developers, investors, and corporate heads on the Citizens Council—had direct contact with the daily conditions of Dallas life. They served customers of all classes and all races, and they understood intimately the requirements of selling and of building commercial enterprises. The retailers were in a position to see both the big picture—long-term plans and hopes for their city—and the details—the day-to-day operations of their stores and banks. The high representation of Jews in this category and in positions of direct influence on the Dallas Citizens Council gave them a unique opportunity to influence their city's integration policy as it unfolded.

Another probable reason that Jews were at the forefront of the belated effort to integrate Dallas was that even the most successful and powerful among them had suffered religious discrimination and had some sensitivity to the feelings of the segregated. Julius Schepps, for example, easily the city's most widely admired Jewish citizen, could not join the Dallas Country Club. Sanguine about the slight, he often retold a story about how a member once invited him out for a round of golf, then urged Schepps to join the club. "Fine idea there, pal," Schepps told him. "[W]hy don't you run upstairs to the office and fetch me a membership application?" He never heard from the man again.[24] Ordinarily, Schepps and his wife, who was not Jewish, refused invitations to social events held at facilities that discriminated against Jews, including the Dallas Country Club, often to the consternation of close gentile friends whose celebrations the Scheppses declined to attend. "I wish to remain honest with both of you because our sincere affection for you makes it rather hard for me to give our reason," Julius explained on one such occasion. "We just do not attend functions at Northwood, Dallas Country Club, Brook Hollow or the Petroleum Club owing to the fact that our Faith does not qualify for membership."[25]

With such experiences as a regular reminder of their own glass ceiling, Jewish merchants like Schepps were ambivalent about their place in Dallas' segregated system. Leon Harris, a longtime manager at A. Harris and Company, writes that even as Jewish merchants embraced segregation as a necessary evil, they "often had a bad conscience about refusing to serve blacks."[26] Jewish storeowners were thus among the first to acquiesce to court orders and to protesters' demands when civil rights demonstrations began. Harris' claim suggests, in fact, that they may have been waiting for a pretext to do what their consciences demanded all along. Or, it must be granted, they may simply have recognized that injunctions and picket lines were worse for business than were black customers. In either case, they integrated their stores before gentile retailers and other Dallas businesses did.

Stanley Marcus has described the speed with which Neiman's and other Dallas department stores abolished their racial policies once a federal court had ordered the city's public schools to desegregate in 1961. "We all agreed that children should not be the first to meet desegregation," he wrote, "but that the adult community needed to desegregate itself beforehand." Marcus issued an "executive decision" ordering his salespeople to cease discriminatory sales practices and to open employment immediately to black applicants. Concerned that the store's staff would not go gently, Marcus arranged training meetings "to break through generations of prejudice, to give us confidence that black customers would be served in our stores well and graciously." Several white customers canceled their charge accounts rather than buy from black salespeople, but most soon reopened their ac-

Julius Schepps, right, with Dallas mayor R. L. Thornton, 1958. UTSA's Institute of
Texan Cultures, No. 074–0617. Courtesy of the Dallas Jewish Archives
Committee of the Julius Schepps Community Center.

counts.[27] Neiman's restaurant, the Zodiac Room, was one of the first fine restaurants in Dallas to open its doors to black diners.[28] In smaller cities, Jewish-owned firms like the Popular Store in El Paso and Lichtenstein's in Corpus Christi were the first in town to employ black salespeople and to end the unequal treatment of black customers.[29]

In Dallas, Julius Schepps chaired a Citizens Council subcommittee tentatively described as the Committee to Work with Negro Leaders, which worked behind the scenes to facilitate the desegregation not only of Jewish-owned stores but also of all public accommodations in the city. "We have had no professional interference," he wrote in response to a query about the committee's work, "and the community has accepted the Committee's behavior in the manner in which it has handled its integration problem. It takes hard work and it is a continuous effort on the part of the Committee composed of seven Negroes and the seven Whites."[30] Reports submitted to Schepps from various civic and commercial groups indicated that progress was being made. "In each meeting," one wrote, "practically all of those present have indicated their willingness to allow us to quietly, without publicity, notify the Dallas Negro Community that food service in restaurants, cafeterias, drive-ins, and motels in Dallas will be integrated beginning Wednesday, June 26 [1963]."[31] The absence of publicity was essential: another report confirmed that as part of the arrangement made between the committee and Interstate Theatres, "[t]here is to be no publicity whatever attached to the matter."[32] As a result, Schepps' role went largely unnoticed. A *Dallas Morning News* editor wrote to thank him for "the tremendous job you have done and are doing in the current problem of the races," but noted that it was "evident you do not seek credit."[33]

Dallas at the Crossroads

The relative ease with which merchants integrated their stores demonstrated that change was possible and that white Texans could accept desegregation with equanimity. Community leaders were hopeful that school desegregation could likewise be accomplished without the turmoil that had attended it in Little Rock and elsewhere. In this effort, too, Jewish leaders worked behind the scenes to encourage Dallasites to accept the inevitable and to avoid the open conflict that could damage the city's commercial appeal. At the forefront of this effort was Sam Bloom, head of one of the city's leading advertising agencies and twice president of Temple Emanu-El, who had served at President John F. Kennedy's request on national desegregation and equal employment initiatives. Bloom, along with Stanley Marcus and others, determined that a public relations campaign, focused on the perils of massive resistance, would pave the way for desegregation in Dallas. Their hope, Bloom later explained, was to create an atmosphere in which citizens could "get up and advocate for [desegregation] without being . . . politically shot down or ostracized in the community."[34] Bloom and Marcus had been silent on the matter until the city's legal appeals ran out, but once desegregation was clearly the law they became leaders in making the transition as smooth as possible.

Bloom produced a twenty-minute documentary film, *Dallas at the Crossroads*, a propaganda masterpiece directed squarely at the city's white population. No African American appears on the screen, and the word "desegregation" does not occur until nearly halfway into the film. The emphasis in the opening minutes is on images of Dallas as a modern paradise: grandparents cooing over babies, young couples moving into new suburban homes, the State Fair, a Cub Scout meeting. "We call our city 'Big D,'" a speaker explains, "because it is big-hearted, open-handed, both friendly and progressive."[35] Such was the filmmakers' hope and expectation.

Soon, however, the scene changes to Little Rock, where an angry mob shouts and threatens the unseen black students trying to enter Central High School. The focus is on faces contorted with rage. "This is the face of hate," explains the narrator, now revealed as Walter Cronkite. "This is the face of man-made destruction." A series of local authorities follows Cronkite to assert that Dallas must desegregate peaceably. A doctor describes the psychological harm that violent parental behavior can do to children. A law professor in a courtroom explains the judicial process, concluding that "[v]iolence cannot change a decision rendered within these walls." A judge, looking fixedly into the camera, declares that despite the opinions of any individuals, desegregation is the law and that "[d]isagreement must not be expressed by violence." The mayor, a union leader, and the editors of both daily newspapers follow with similar remarks. Violent individuals may exist, Cronkite resumes, but they "will stand alone." To emphasize that point, the city police chief promises that whatever views individual officers hold, they will rigorously enforce the law. Bloom inserted grainy footage of a police chase, followed by the incarceration of a young, white, male prisoner who sits in his cell with his head in his hands. The film closes as "America the Beautiful" plays over scenes of waving flags, weddings, and Boy Scout parades.[36]

The Dallas Citizens Council screened *Dallas at the Crossroads* all over the city to neighborhood groups, schools, churches, and corporate employees. Bloom and his associates shrewdly made no overt claim that integration was good, nor that it would benefit the city's black community. They did not play the film for black audiences. The message, aimed at white Dallasites, was that desegregation was certain and that violence in response to it would only harm the city's reputation and discourage its growth and commercial development. This middle road, supporting desegregation in practice while remaining ambivalent about it in theory, was typical of Jewish business and civic leadership in Dallas and other Texas cities. It was a conspicuously political and commercial appeal rather than a moral one.

A City's Conscience

At the same time, however, the Jewish clergy in Dallas, especially Levi Olan of Temple Emanu-El, was making the moral case for integration. Born in Ukraine, Olan grew up in Rochester, New York, in an Orthodox, Yiddish-speaking home. He developed an early passion for scholarship, language, and learning, as well as a compulsion to question authority, which later drew him away from the traditional Judaism of his childhood toward Reform practice. Olan completed his rabbinical training at Hebrew Union College in 1929 and served a Reform congregation in Worcester, Massachusetts, for twenty years, earning a reputation as an outspoken political liberal and advocate of the social component of Judaism. "I was a liberal economically and politically," Olan later explained in an interview. "Of course, I had one rule: that is that I always preached the social message . . . from a Jewish religious point of view."[37] When Temple Emanu-El representatives approached him in 1948 seeking a replacement for their retiring mainstay, David Lefkowitz, Olan wavered before accepting a pulpit in a region so conservative and so dominated by Christian fundamentalism. "You won't last a day," one friend advised him. "If you get up and spout some of your things you'll be out on your ear."[38] Olan was also unsure whether he could make a home in a city untouched by Jewish culture as he understood it. On an earlier visit, he had asked Lefkowitz where he could go in Dallas for a good bagel. The older rabbi replied, "What's a bagel?"[39]

In the end, Olan decided that not only could he survive in Dallas, but that he would also have an opportunity there to be an ambassador of Jewish culture and social values in a region on the verge of blossoming. "My answer to [the naysayers]," he later told an interviewer, "was 'It's very easy to stand for [liberal] things in New England. . . . The real place to stand for them is where they are challenged, and if you're really going to do anything about them, that is the place to do it."[40] Along with his pulpit at Emanu-El, Olan took over from the retiring David Lefkowitz a weekly radio program that quickly became Olan's own. These radio addresses, later televised, won Olan recognition and respect in the city's gentile community as well as among its Jews: one Baptist Sunday School teacher proclaimed the rabbi to be "the best preacher in Dallas."[41] His sermons were straightforward in their message but erudite and thoughtful in their substance and argument. "[I]n his more fiery and extravagant sermons," wrote journalist David Ritz, "he might drop as many as many as 40 or 50 names—Kafka, Malraux, Tillich, Tolstoy, Faulkner, Spinoza, Sartre, de Tocqueville, Cardinal Newman—sending your poor mind reeling, taking your breath away. He was an Old Testament prophet, a consummate performer, with substance and clarity at the base."[42]

Olan first encountered his congregants' resistance on racial matters in 1959 when a young African American approached him wishing to convert to Judaism and to join the temple. Olan counseled him through conversion, but when he recommended the man to the congregation, they refused him membership. Atlanta segregationists had recently bombed the Reform temple there, allegedly in response to remarks by the rabbi, and the "leadership of the Temple was frightened," Olan recalled.[43] Six months later, after fears had subsided, they complied with the rabbi's wishes and integrated their temple. "I was a kind of person who didn't hem and haw," Olan said later. Indeed, his eagerness to use the radio to challenge the status quo and his recognition that racial segregation was one of Dallas' major problems were both apparent in one of his first broadcast sermons. Olan the newcomer was dismayed to see signs proclaiming "for whites only" on public restrooms. "[T]hat got me," he said. "So I preached a sermon on the radio on the race issue." The response was largely hostile. "My phone rang that afternoon. Someone says to me, 'Go back where you came from.'"[44] Olan continued raising the issue throughout the 1950s, however, taking pains to place it in a moral context that demonstrated its urgency and importance. In a 1959 letter, he explained that the "moral issue from my point of view is a clear one, segregation is a vestige of slavery, and is highly immoral. No one who believes in one God can believe in discrimination amongst His children."[45] Drawing on his moral authority as a clergyman in a city and region that cherished church affiliation, Olan took a religious view of an issue other Jewish leaders tried to keep strictly secular. He cast segregation not in the political, legal, and economic terms of *Dallas at the Crossroads*, but

Rabbi Levi Olan, second from left, with Dr. Martin Luther King Jr., who was in Dallas for a voter registration rally at Fair Park, January 4, 1963. Also pictured are Rev. H. Rhett James, left, and Rev. J. A. Stanfield. From the collections of the Texas/Dallas History and Archives Division, Dallas Public Library, PA2005–4/3.1.

in the moral terms of Dr. Martin Luther King Jr. and of the biblical prophets. While secular Jewish leaders stressed that integration was unavoidable, Olan argued that it was just.

Olan, frequently described as the "conscience of Dallas," spoke out with conviction on issues that made many of his listeners cringe. While Jewish business leaders campaigning for school desegregation sat in his congregation, Olan blasted their efforts as insincere tokenism, motivated by commercial rather than ethical interests.[46] After the 1963 assassination of President Kennedy, when most Dallasites worried that the nation would blame their city for the tragedy, Olan told his congregation that it was, in fact, their fault. They had been silent in the face of degrading jokes and vicious insults directed at Kennedy and his administration; they had permitted others to label Kennedy a traitor and a Communist agent; and they were thus guilty, along with "the deranged sick soul that fired the gun." Even those "who could never assassinate" had helped to "[create] the passionate hatred which does."[47]

Four and a half years later, Olan responded to the death of Dr. King, whom he had met in Dallas in 1963, by warning his radio listeners that "we seem to be a very violent nation" to whom retribution would surely come. The only solution was for whites to overcome their prejudices and recognize human beings' fundamental unity. "More important than anything else in the world today," he said, "is the recognition, the acceptance, and the living by the basic natural fact that humanity is one. . . . [Racial discrimination] is both immoral and blasphemous." Olan also took the opportunity to criticize the Vietnam War, placing it in the same moral context. "Can we go on dropping Napalm on little children and burn them alive and not pay a price for doing it?" he exclaimed. "Can we reduce the houses of innocent people to rubble and escape the penalty? If this is a moral universe, we shall pay a bitter price."[48] Years later, Olan claimed that such comments made him unpopular with his congregants and with non-Jews. "Did you receive a lot of flack from taking a stand like that?" asked an interviewer in 1983. "That's an understatement," Olan responded.[49]

Juanita Craft, one of Dallas' most outspoken and successful civil rights activists, described the gulf she perceived between the city's black and Jewish communities. "They [Jews] accepted us, you know, as far as meetings and things of that sort," she recalled in an interview, "but they don't put themselves to any trouble to meet us, and we don't put ourselves to any trouble to meet them."[50] Olan, however, insisted that Jews shared with African Americans a common experience of slavery, diaspora, and social isolation, and, in addition to goading his listeners with speeches and sermons, he directed his Emanu-El congregants into concrete action to benefit Dallas' other minority communities. In particular, he sought fair housing for a black population with 21,500 households but only 14,800 available segregated rental units. Claiming that housing was a fundamental human right, Olan made the acquisition of federal housing dollars for Dallas a cornerstone of his preaching.[51] Beginning his call for fair housing as early as 1950, Olan arrived at the importance of the issue long before even King did.

Other Dallas Jews were already at work, behind the scenes as usual, trying to improve living conditions for the city's African Americans. Emanu-El member Louis Tobian was chairman of the Dallas Housing Authority and helped oversee the construction of low-income housing developments as well as public utilities and streets to serve these new communities. Jerome Crossman, another congregant, headed the Chamber of Commerce Inter-Racial Housing Committee, whose members included Tobian and Fred Florence of Republic National Bank. With foundation funding, Crossman's group established the neighborhood of Hamilton Park, purchasing 170 acres in North Dallas and helping to build 750 homes for middle-class African-American families displaced by the expansion of Love Field Airport in 1951. Although still segregated, and surrounded on all sides by afflu-ent white suburbs, the neighborhood was an island of African-American middle-class achievement and a point of pride for the black community.[52]

Olan pushed his congregants to build on these efforts. After his admon-ishment that a religious community "should have a concern for the welfare of human beings" and should find a way to put their benevolent feelings into action, the temple's newly appointed Community Affairs Commit-tee, led by Hortense Sanger and Billie Stern, recommended that Emanu-El should "develop a pre-school for disadvantaged children, providing skilled professional leadership and adequate equipment, in a [suitable] neighbor-hood."[53] Olan appealed to the congregation for funds and quickly raised 60 percent of the necessary $25,000. Temple members also volunteered time preparing the Rhoads Terrace Housing Project school, which opened in September 1965 with twenty-nine students, aged four and five, and a staff of professional teachers. About one hundred women from the temple pre-pared and served lunches, escorted the children on weekly field trips, and assisted in the classrooms.[54] Olan urged the Dallas school board to institute public kindergartens, which the city did not have at that time, "in those areas of the community where the need for them is most acute, and where parents cannot afford tuition in such private institutions as already exist and thrive in the more prosperous areas of the city." In 1971, the school board finally did so.[55]

Olan was hardly alone among Texas rabbis in promoting a moral, even a prophetic approach to the civil rights struggle, nor was he the only one to argue that this view should be expressed in action. In Houston, Rabbi Moshe Cahana of Conservative Congregation Brith Shalom spoke fre-quently about the need to improve race relations. After participating in the 1963 Birmingham protests, he helped to organize the Metropolitan Houston Conference on Religion and Race, an interfaith clerical commit-tee. "Religion has always had something to say about the moral questions of society," Cahana told the group at Houston's Christ Church Cathedral in June 1963. "Religion is the best instrument to shed light on the social questions of each generation. Why then does not the pulpit identify itself openly and actively with the Negro fight for justice, equality and decent relations?" Cahana cited the names of biblical prophets—as well as that of Jesus—to make his case that people of every faith share the responsibility for racism. "Segregation and prejudice are not God's will and the scriptures condemn them," he said. "It is a sin, and the time has come to stop sinning. The time has come to confess and repent."[56] The Reverend Thomas Griffin of University Christian Church seconded Cahana's comments, noting that blacks' resentment at clerical inaction was growing. Griffin also criticized Jews in the business community who continued to oppose efforts to integrate Houston. "The feeling of the Negro," he observed, "is not limited to the Christian church," but many blacks "are appalled by the gap between the basic teachings of Judaism and the practice of the business world."[57] Representatives of other Protestant and Catholic churches rose to make similar addresses. The interdenominational language at the meeting emphasized not only the Conference's overt goals but also that Cahana was part of a constellation of people and faiths that he hoped could unite in common cause.

In San Antonio, Rabbi David Jacobson promoted integration and fair treatment of both black and Mexican-American citizens. Jacobson took an early role in advancing race relations when, as a member of the public library's board of directors, he supported the 1949 desegregation of city libraries. This role led him to attend fundraisers for Henry B. Gonzales, a city councilman and later congressman who was the city's most prominent activist for Mexican-American equality and for desegregation. Jacobson also invited black clergymen to his home and to speak from his pulpit at Temple Beth-El. In March 1960, Jacobson and other clergymen met with San Antonio business leaders to begin discussions about desegregating their stores and restaurants. All except Joske's, which was no longer under Jewish management, agreed to do so peacefully and immediately rather than face imminent NAACP-led protests. In these matters, Jacobson was a bridge-builder and mediator, seeking "accommodation and compromise without sacrifice of principle."[58]

After the integration of the city's lunch counters—to which Joske's also capitulated after three months—Jacobson began a series of visits to restaurants around the city to urge them to integrate their facilities. Sometimes arriving alone and speaking to the manager about the moral necessity of integration, other times arriving with a black friend, taking seats, and insisting on being served together, Jacobson put on the pressure in a firm but cordial way.[59] By February 1962, thirteen restaurants had opened their doors to black customers, and Jacobson had been personally involved in integrating at least four of them. He recalled later that a top official of the Luby's Cafeteria chain, which the rabbi had helped integrate in San Antonio, thanked him for making him do what he knew he should: "I didn't want to [integrate]," Jacobson quoted him saying, "but I've discovered how right you were, and we should have done it on our own long ago."[60]

Even if their actions often worried their congregants, Olan, Cahana, and Jacobson could afford to be moral leaders because they stood at the head of large, wealthy, and secure Jewish communities. Outside major Texas cities, however, where Jews did not enjoy the same status and civic influence, their approach to matters of race was more conservative. Milton Rosenbaum, a native New Yorker who served Fort Worth's Beth-El Congregation from 1949 to 1956, provided a useful summary of his congregants' social and racial attitudes. He noted that the Jewish community itself, at that time numbering no more than twenty-five hundred people, was distinctly insular: "[M]any people there were related to each other," and so "there seemed little room for newcomers to Fort Worth [and] many newcomers found the community cold. You were either socially 'in' or 'out.' Probably because of my position, Thelma and I were generally 'in' and found the community most hospitable."[61]

Rosenbaum remained an outsider, however, in his views on the pressing matter of civil rights. The opinions Fort Worth Jews expressed about race were especially troubling to him, and his response, following a strategy like that of Jewish civic leaders next door in Dallas, was threatening to his more conservative congregants. "I regarded myself as a middle of the road liberal but felt strongly about the indecency of racial prejudice," he wrote. "For some in my congregation that marked me as a radical, especially when I explained that since things would inevitably change, they might have a hard time in later years justifying their current attitudes to their children."[62]

However, with time Rosenbaum discovered that the "racial attitudes of Texas Jews were . . . more complicated than they first appeared." He distinguished between public and private opinions, observing that "[p]ublicly there was a strong urge to be approved by non-Jewish neighbors. Therefore, I learned, many Jews publicly expressed the same biases that they thought their neighbors held." In their private relations with blacks, though, "their relationships were far more personal and less socially distant than those of Jews in the North toward African Americans." Indeed, when the civil rights movement altered the legal landscape, opening doors to black Texans, "Texas Jews particularly often accepted them more readily than did their Northern counterparts. To me, these changes in attitude and behavior shown by Texas Jews were an antidote to my earlier Northern smugness and sense of moral superiority."[63] Rosenbaum's observations bear out the idea that Texas Jews, although careful not to offend their white gentile neighbors' sensibilities, adjusted to the inevitability of racial equality not only in advance of other Texans but also, Rosenbaum believed, ahead of other Jews.

Like Rosenbaum, Texas Jews were typically neither insiders nor outsiders, neither fully a part of the communities in which they lived nor fully apart from them. In earlier periods, as when the Ku Klux Klan rose to prominence in the 1920s, such ambiguity troubled Jewish Texans. Throughout their history, they have consistently sought the acceptance of the non-Jewish majority and insisted that they were equally part of Texas society. In the civil rights era, for the first time, their difference from other whites, so long minimized, excused, and explained away, found its purposefulness. That they were not, in fact, part of mainstream white society, that they were connected to it only through business and civic life but not through the historical roots that led to Jim Crow, gave Jews both the perspective and the credibility necessary to lead their communities in a new direction. They were not, by any means, the only group to join the civil rights struggle—indeed, many Christian leaders preceded them—but on the whole their unusual social position gave them unusual opportunities. Although their role in the desegregation crisis was minimal, proportionate to their small numbers, the effect of their involvement on their communities was deep and far-reaching. In later years, with the benefits of outsiderness proven and with the civil rights movement's inspiring successes becoming familiar, Texas Jews no longer thought of themselves as an endangered minority dependent on Christian tolerance. They were, rather, a minority with a voice, with power, purpose, and wealth, and the decades following the 1960s would find them no longer seeking the shade of Christian goodwill but building ways of life in Texas that were distinctly and unabashedly Jewish.

NINE

Interior Frontiers

Led by its dynamic high-tech industry, particularly by the legendary success of Dell Computer, the city of Austin grew tremendously in the 1990s—about 41 percent according to the U.S. Census.[1] "Thirty-five thousand people, the equivalent of a fair-sized town, moved here last year alone," a *New York Times* reporter wrote from Austin in 2000. "And in the last five years, Austin has produced or acquired 17,000 new millionaires." In addition to the business opportunities such a climate afforded, newcomers were drawn to the city's vaunted quality of life. "With its bars, bands and barbecue joints, its lakes, parks, low crime and temperate winters," the *Times* reporter wrote, "Austin is a lifestyle mecca that attracts all kinds."[2]

Quality of life, however, is not the same for everyone. In 1995, IBM decided to transfer about 900 employees from Boca Raton, Florida, to Austin, raising serious concerns for many of the approximately 150 Jewish families asked to relocate. Boca Raton, as the *Austin American-Statesman* reported, had more than 116,000 Jewish residents who constituted 16 percent of the city's population. It had eighteen synagogues; fourteen Jewish day schools and child-care centers; a selection of kosher markets and restaurants; and a public school system that closed on the High Holidays. Austin, in contrast, had only 6,000 Jews, representing a little more than 1 percent of the city's population; two synagogues (neither of them Orthodox); two Jewish day-care centers; and no Jewish schools or kosher food stores. IBM's Jewish employees worried about the lack of an Orthodox *shul*, about the distances between residential neighborhoods and synagogues, and about the lack of educational facilities for their children. "You meet people here who have never met a Jew or don't know they have," said a representative of the Jewish Federation of Austin. "That will be strange to [the newcomers]."[3]

The IBM transferees were part of an influx that raised Austin's Jewish population from about 5,000 in 1990 to 13,500 in 2000.[4] Congregation Beth Israel, the city's oldest and largest Reform temple, grew from 400 member families in 1991 to more than 700, straining available facilities and forcing the Sunday School to hold classes "in every available space: the rabbi's office, the chandeliered boardroom, even the bride's and groom's dressing rooms."[5] This growth, and the subsequent variety of denominational preferences, provided the impetus and the means to form new Jewish institutions in Austin such as Kol Halev, an independent, nondenominational congregation with about 120 member families, founded in 1997.

The cultural effects of the population increase were also profound. Austin began hosting a Jewish Book Fair and a Jewish Film Festival, and in 1998, a large grocery chain opened a butcher shop and café offering a variety of kosher foods and meats. A Jewish day school, providing a full religious and secular curriculum, opened in 2000 at the new Dell Jewish Community Center (DJCC). The forty-acre campus, named for patrons Michael and Susan Dell, also houses two congregations and provides a wealth of activities and programs for Jews and non-Jews. During the 2000 presidential race, George W. Bush rented the DJCC for several events, running into trouble only when his campaign wanted to celebrate their Super Tuesday primary victories by serving the press corps a pork barbecue, which the DJCC refused to permit.[6]

These developments suggest that Austin and other major Texas cities are no longer marginal Jewish communities. Mirroring the postwar growth of other Sunbelt locales, the Jewish populations of Dallas–Fort Worth, Houston, San Antonio, and Austin are booming, and the newcomers enhance the diversity and richness of Jewish life. Numbering more than 130,000, the Texas-Jewish community is larger than those of Michigan, Georgia, Virginia, or Missouri, and Houston and Dallas have larger Jewish communities than Pittsburgh, Seattle, or Cincinnati. More Jews live in Texas today than in any other southern state except Florida and any other western state except California.[7]

This growing population has brought many inducements of modern Jewish life to Texas, and Texas-Jewish institutions have become more sophisticated and diverse. Dallas, Houston, and San Antonio support local

Jewish historical societies, and the Texas Jewish Historical Society, founded in 1980, has more than 750 member families statewide. The nation's first Holocaust Museum was established in Dallas in 1984 and was followed by museums and research centers in San Antonio (1990), El Paso (1992), and Houston (1996). All of the state's major cities and many smaller towns maintain Jewish charitable foundations and community centers. Houston's *Jewish Herald-Voice*, founded in 1908, is one of the country's longest-running Jewish newspapers, and the Dallas, San Antonio, and Fort Worth communities support their own weeklies. Dozens of B'nai B'rith groups and twenty chapters of Hadassah are active in large and small communities throughout Texas; Houston's Hadassah chapter is the city's largest women's organization. There are Hillel Centers at nearly fifty college and university campuses statewide; organized Hasidim in Austin, Dallas, El Paso, Fort Worth, Houston, Plano, and San Antonio; and a bagel shop in Abilene.

This expansion has also helped to dissolve the provincialism that once characterized Texas Jewry. State law now excuses Jewish public school students from class on religious holidays. Jewish Texans have led the most important national Jewish organizations, and thousands of Soviet, Russian, and Israeli Jews have moved to Texas cities. Sixty percent of Houston's Jewish households report having at least one member who has visited Israel, and the Anti-Defamation League regularly flies Texas congressmen to the Middle East to help assure the delegation's political support for the Jewish state.[8] Texas Jewry today is, in short, a modern, self-conscious, globally integrated, socially active, and spiritually rich community.

Despite this modern reality, however, Texas Jewry still possesses a deep-rooted sense of its own implausibility. Jewish Texans emphasize their peripherality from Jewish centers and their difference from other American Jews. The frontier, that is, remains a defining experience. English professor Adam Newton, for example, a Bronx native then teaching at the University of Texas at Austin, observed that his work at the Austin Hillel helped him feel "'somewhat less *bamidbared*,' Hebrew for 'in the wilderness.'"[9] Sheldon Zimmerman, the former rabbi of Temple Emanu-El, told the Dallas Jewish Historical Society in 2002 that their city was "removed from major centers of Jewish population, activity, education and culture. This is *not* the heartland of Jewish life. In fact, many Dallas Jews feel isolated from the rest of the Jewish world." He quickly corrected himself, noting, "I'm not talking about today. Things have changed. I'm talking about the Dallas that was," but his spontaneous use of the present tense seems significant. In any case, he went on to link specific qualities of Dallas Jewry today to its "isolated" origins.[10]

Zimmerman and Newton are originally New Yorkers and so may be forgiven for making the inevitable comparison to home, but native Texans also seem haunted by the strangeness of their situation and their distance from other Jews. *Texas Monthly* writer Mimi Swartz, for instance, suggested that her San Antonio family's tendency to secularize and assimilate "has to do with Texas, its myths and its demands. 'Are there any Jews in Texas?' I am still asked by people on the East Coast." Here Swartz could have commented on the intractable provincialism of "East Coast" Jews but does not. Instead, she sees their question as a reflection on Texas Jewry, casting the questioners' skepticism back upon herself and her contemporaries. She realizes that "[i]n just a generation or so, we have ceased to be exotics," but she attributes her family's neglect of Jewish religious faith to a conflict with something inherent in Texas culture. "[E]ach generation wanted to be Jews and each generation wanted to be Texans, and in their own way they tried to strike a balance so that both identities could be passed on. Mine is the story of the price paid for trying to have it both ways."[11]

These examples attest to the frontier's durability as a way of describing not only the Texas-Jewish past but also its present. The frontier idea, so often shaped and reshaped in Texas-Jewish consciousness to a variety of purposes, seems now a permanent sense of distinctiveness that even newcomers adopt as readily as synagogue membership. This development is in part a product of demographic realities, particularly the apparent unattractiveness of Texas as a postwar destination for Jewish Sunbelt migrants, but it also comes from a deliberate act of imagination by Jewish writers who have emphasized the frontier experience and Texas Jews' estrangement from the rest of the Jewish world. In their work, quite simply, the frontier has become Texas-Jewish identity itself.

The Buckle of the Sunbelt

Like the rest of the South and Southwest, Texas has experienced rapid population growth since World War II due to the arrival of hundreds of thousands of new Texans from northern and midwestern states. This growth is part of a general postwar population shift to the Sunbelt, in particular to its exponentially growing cities: Atlanta, Miami, Los Angeles, Phoenix, Houston, Dallas–Fort Worth, and San Antonio. The Sunbelt's explosive growth is largely attributable to increased federal spending in the region on defense and other industries, the perception of a favorable business climate, and the elusive and hard-to-define "quality of life" the region affords—made possible by air conditioning.[12] Northern servicemen stationed in southern and western states during the war were often surprised to discover such a pleasant environment in these alien regions, and as heavy federal invest-ment in defense manufacturing fueled sustained economic growth, thou-sands of veterans moved south and west. Texas, straddling the two regions, benefited from all of these developments. In the decades between 1950 and 2000, the Texas population grew more than 170 percent, with the greatest increase occurring in its largest metropolitan areas. San Antonio's popula-tion became almost three times what it was, while Dallas and Houston each grew about fourfold.[13]

Jews were a significant part of this Sunbelt migration. In 1940, nearly 70 percent of the nation's Jews lived in the Northeast, some 46 percent just in New York State. Another 19 percent were in the Midwest, mostly in Chi-cago, while only 7 percent of the American Jewish population lived in the fourteen Sunbelt states. A change was underway by 1950: the Northeast's share of the nation's Jews had fallen to 67 percent and the Midwest's to 14 percent, while the Sunbelt's share nearly doubled to 13 percent. By 2000, a major shift had clearly taken place, as only 46 percent of American Jews now lived in the Northeast, with just 27 percent remaining in New York State, and about 11 percent in the Midwest. One-third of the nation's Jew-ish population lived in the Sunbelt states. In the same period, Texas' Jew-ish population grew from just under 50,000 in 1950 to about 130,000, an increase of 160 percent.[14]

Jewish migrants to Texas have also followed the Sunbelt pattern by moving into the suburbs. About 96 percent of Jewish Texans live in met-ropolitan areas, but, for example, 82 percent of Houston's Jews live in the suburban or exurban parts of the city.[15] Older congregations have followed a common national pattern, moving away from their central city origins, as Houston's Beth Israel and Dallas' Emanu-El both did in the 1950s. More re-cently, new congregations representing a variety of denominational views have been formed in exurban areas. These include Beth Shalom, a Reform congregation in Arlington, between Dallas and Fort Worth; Conservative Congregation Anshai Torah in Plano, north of Dallas; and Shaar Hashalom of Clear Lake (Conservative) and Beth Shalom (Reform) in The Wood-lands, both outside Houston. The enormous population growth has been felt dramatically in this upsurge of Jewish institutions and in the resulting richness and diversity of Jewish communal life in Texas.

From a national perspective, however, it is clear that Texas lies outside the major streams of postwar Jewish migration. "Eighty percent of all Jews moving south after the war settled in Miami," writes Deborah Dash Moore, "and 70 percent of all Jews heading west landed in Los Angeles."[16] Jewish population figures, expressed as a proportion of the total population, confirm Moore's perception of two channels of Jewish migration away from New York to California and Florida. Between 1940 and 2000, as Jewish New Yorkers were moving cross-country, the proportion of Jews to non-Jews rose markedly in the states where most of them settled. In California, the Jewish population rose from 2.3 percent of the state's total in 1940 to more than 4 percent ten years later, settling at about 3 percent by 2000. Florida saw its Jewish community grow even more dramatically, from 1.1 percent of the state's total in 1940, past a 1980 high of 4.7 percent, to settle just below 4 percent in 2000.[17] California and Florida were growing quickly, but Jews were arriving in even greater numbers than gentiles, driving up the Jewish proportion of the total population.

This was not the case in Texas, where Jewish in-migration lagged far behind that of non-Jews. Despite their increasing numbers, the Jewish proportion of the Texas population *fell* between 1940 and 2000, dropping from 0.8 percent to 0.6 percent of the state's total, a level much lower than either California or Florida.[18] Texas ranks second among all the states in total population but has only the tenth largest Jewish population. Massachusetts, with a fraction of Texas' general population, has more than twice the number of Jews.[19] Texas cities have grown significantly and contain stronger Jewish communities than they did even a decade ago, but they are hardly Jewish centers like New York and South Florida, nor do they provide the breadth of Jewish life available in Los Angeles, Chicago, or Boston. Given that the Texas climate, economy, and cost of living compare well to those of many other states, why did Texas never receive a comparable Jewish influx? Deborah Dash Moore attributes the appeal of Los Angeles and Miami to "the particular lure of a leisure lifestyle" those cities offered.[20] If she is right, then Texas must have lacked that reputation among Jews seeking to relocate. It seems, in fact, that something about Texas was actually repelling them.

Several social and demographic realities may provide answers. Certainly the dominance and visibility of Christianity, especially Evangelicalism, made Texas less appealing for Jewish migrants than other destinations. In 1961, journalist John Bainbridge reported the familiar observation that Texas had "more churches per capita" than any other state, "a ratio between population and places of worship that . . . is even higher than . . . Ireland."[21] While the accuracy of the statement is doubtful, it explains the popular perception that Texas is unusually church-oriented. More recently, Sheldon Zimmerman described Dallas as "one of the most highly Christian-identified places in the world," where "within the first ten minutes of your conversation, people will say, 'Well, what church do you go to?'"[22] Despite Texas Jewry's enormous postwar growth, it is still a small island in a vast Christian sea. Its respectable Jewish population of 130,000 vanishes behind the state's 4.5 million Southern Baptists and 4.3 million Catholics.[23] Even in the cities, where Jewish institutional presence is strongest, that of gentiles overwhelms it. In the Houston metropolitan area, for example, 21 Jewish congregations provide the state's greatest variety of Jewish worship options, but they exist alongside 952 Evangelical, 339 mainline Protestant, and 106 Catholic churches.[24] However appealing its climate and economy, Texas is the capital of Jesusland, and this reputation must have made some Jews unwilling to move there.

Another factor is that more Texans live in rural areas than do residents of either California or Florida, the Sunbelt states with which Texas best compares. In 1950, as the Sunbelt migration began, about 63 percent of the state's population lived in urban areas, roughly the same as the national average. Florida was slightly more urbanized, at 66 percent, and California much more so, at 81 percent. Fifty years later, 83 percent of Texas' population was in cities. In comparison, the 2000 national average and Florida's urban population rate were both about 89 percent, and California's was nearly 95 percent.[25] For potential Jewish in-migrants who were entirely urban in their lifestyle and occupational choices, these social and demographic realities must have been a deterrent.

Finally, the state's politics may have made Texas unappealing to Jewish migrants. American Jews are disproportionately progressive in their political views, and Jewish candidates have won statewide election in California, Florida, New York, Illinois, and many other states throughout the country. Texas, in contrast, has always been a deeply conservative political landscape with little Jewish participation in state politics. Only one Jewish candidate has ever been elected to statewide office, Democratic Supreme Court Justice Rose Spector in 1992. In 2006, Kinky Friedman ran a credible independent campaign for governor, and Houston attorney Barbara Ann Radnofsky ran as a Democrat for U.S. Senate. Both were soundly defeated by Republican incumbents in the general election. In 2008, San Antonio Republican Joe Straus was named Speaker of the House, one of the most powerful offices in Texas government, but he was placed there by his fellow state legislators, not by the general electorate. Jewish politicians have had greater success at the municipal level. Galveston has had three Jewish mayors, the first in 1853, and Dallas has also had three, all women. Jews have served in respectable numbers in both houses of the Texas legislature since Texas was a republic, but only Martin Frost of Dallas has been elected to the U.S. Congress. Thus, in smaller urban and suburban settings Jewish candidates have done well, but they have been invisible in larger electoral districts where voters' conservative and rural natures come more into play.

Given the conservative political climate, the predominance of evangelical Christianity, and the persistently rural aspect of Texas culture, postwar Jews seeking better lives in the South or West might reasonably have imagined that Texas would provide less developed city life, smaller Jewish communities, and a power structure more at odds with their views than other destinations. As the example of the IBM transferees indicates, these and similar concerns are dissuading factors that may prevent Jews from moving to Texas even today. Texas has therefore not experienced a boom in Jewish population comparable to those in other Sunbelt states and remains outside the awareness of "mainstream" American Jews. Native Jewish Texans, aware of this neglect, learn to see themselves as peripheral even as their population grows and their communities provide a greater range of Jewish activities. This impression is reflected and reinforced, furthermore, in popular fictional writings about Texas Jewry. It is, in fact, the prevailing theme in every published work about Jewish Texas.

Frontiers in Texas-Jewish Fiction

Creative writers have explored the complications of Texas-Jewish identity in a variety of fictional works, and the unifying theme of these works is the frontier, the perceived differences between Texas Jews and those elsewhere. Texas Jewry is the subject of a surprising wealth of literary works in several genres: no fewer than seven works for young readers, two novels, a short story collection, a literary memoir, two stage plays, two series of detective novels together consisting of nearly twenty-five volumes, and a work of apocalyptic science fiction.[26] In these works, Texas Jews struggle to find a place for themselves and to define themselves in contrast to non-Jewish Others. They are marginal characters, whose peculiar identities give them special status and special insight. Many of the books take place in a recognizably frontier setting, but even those with more modern settings focus on the lines dividing Texas-Jewish characters from "real" Texans or from "real" Jews. These stories are built around the characters' efforts to bridge those gaps while maintaining their religious authenticity and personal integrity. Texas is no longer a frontier state, and Texas Jewry is no longer a peripheral community, but negotiating frontiers remains the essential metaphor of Texas-Jewish life.

Few of these works' protagonists are native Texans—most arrive in the state either from Europe or from cities in the American North—and they explicitly contrast their circumstances in Texas with the more profoundly Jewish communities they left behind. "In Russia," one of Jan Siegel Hart's characters observes to her children, "their lives had centered around their religion and the *shul*." In their new home in Dublin, Texas, however, they are isolated and alone. "Since there were no other Jewish families in Dublin," she adds, "much less a *shul*, they could not enjoy the friendships and feeling of belonging which develop when people are members of a group."[27] Similarly, the protagonist of Amy Hest's young-adult novel, *The Private Notebook of Katie Roberts, Age 11* (1995), regrets her family's move from New York to West Texas after her father's death in World War II and her mother's subsequent remarriage. "I miss my old bed in my old room in New York City," Katie confides to her diary. "I HATE living on a ranch in the middle of nowhere! . . . There are no neighbors nearby. No subways. Not a single tall building. I LIKE CITIES NOT WILDERNESS, AND I AM NO PIONEER!"[28]

Like other Texas-Jewish writers, Hart and Hest emphasize the strangeness of their Jewish characters' situation by placing them in the remotest possible surroundings. Few works take place in a modern suburban setting, despite the fact that the vast majority of today's Jewish Texans live in metropolitan areas. Instead, stories that occur in cities are set in a past before the development of Jewish institutions, while those taking place in more modern eras are set in isolated rural communities where few Jews live. Dede Fox Ducharme's *The Treasure in the Tiny Blue Tin* (1998), for instance, set in Houston, and Lois Ruby's *Swindletop* (2000), set in Galveston and Beaumont, take place in urban settings but in the early twentieth century, when Jewish institutions were rudimentary. In contrast, Hest's *Katie Roberts* and Mark Harelik's play *The Legacy* (1997) are set after World War II but in rural West Texas, where the protagonists are the only Jews. By either strategy—remoteness of time or remoteness of place—these authors put their Jewish characters where they seem out of place, where Jewishness becomes a sign of distinction and difference, and where they will be more likely to run into the emblematic frontier images of Texas culture.

In this, they follow the example of Isadore, the German-Jewish protagonist of David Carb's 1931 novel *Sunrise in the West,* who, in the late nineteenth century, wishes to find "the wildest part of the mythical, uncivilized, Western Empire" and so buys a railroad ticket to "a village called Dallas," the last stop on the line. Disappointed with what he finds in Dallas, Isadore writes to his mother in New Orleans, "There's no cowboys here and everybody rides slow like at home and don't make no noise. . . . The books and the fellers I heard talking before I left didn't tell the truth."[29] Intent on locating the real frontier, Isadore heads west to Fort Worth, where he finds everything he is looking for. "I sure like Fort Worth. It's got cowboys and everything. It's just like the books and people said."[30] Like Isadore (and his author, Carb), the creators of fictional works about Texas Jewry travel far afield to find the frontier they expect Texas to provide.

The point of all of this imposed isolation is to explore the difficulty of preserving Jewish faith and identity in a setting that provides no help in doing so, where Jews must be self-reliant, courageous, and tough-minded in order to survive. These, of course, are the virtues most in demand in mythic Texas, and the isolated Texas frontier proves an effective external setting for the inner conflicts of assimilation, faith, and cultural continuity. Playwright Mark Harelik, who has written and produced two plays about the Texas-Jewish experience, has most explicitly examined the conjunction of the outward Texas landscape and the inward struggle for Jewish survival and continuity. His 1985 play, *The Immigrant,* tells a story of assimilation— how Haskell Harelik, the playwright's grandfather, settled in small-town Texas. Haskell learns English, makes gentile friends, and accommodates his identity to the expectations of his neighbors and the demands of making a living in the rural South.

Harelik envisions Texas as a place of great personal risk but equally great economic opportunity, and his characters face the classic choice between religious faith and secular success. Haskell, as it happens, values economic opportunity more than the preservation of Jewish tradition, and as Seth L. Wolitz has observed of the play, Haskell's ability to make a good living is so powerful an inducement that he all but forgets his origins, experiencing in Texas a "new centering" based on "the self-realization of his personal accomplishment, his business." For Haskell, home becomes, not his place of origin, his family, or his religious identity, but the geographical site of his personal achievement: "Haskell's identity," writes Wolitz, "is Texanized to the place and site of his accomplishment."[31]

Harelik does not let his grandfather's accommodation pass unremarked.

As Haskell carries on about the material benefits of his life in Texas, his wife, Leah, complains of the compromises they and their children are forced to make. "For my baby, there is no life here," she tells her husband. "Yes, of course I can learn to live in a different house. I learn a different language. I can say Howdy, grow cactus in a front yard." But her child, born in Texas, will not have her sense of Jewish history and will lose something in the bargain. "To cover his head, do I buy a cowboy hat?" Leah asks sarcastically. "Pointy boots, big belt buckle? He'll fit right in, huh?"[32] Leah fears that to "fit in" this way would be tantamount to becoming something other than a Jew. Haskell may comfort himself with his material achievements, but Leah sees the frontier, geographically and conceptually, as a threat to the preservation of Jewish identity.

Harelik's 1994 play, *The Legacy*, is a fuller and richer exploration of the difficulties of maintaining Jewish tradition in such a frontier. Harelik confronts the problem of authenticity, of whether the forms Judaism necessarily takes in a remote environment can provide anything meaningful to its adherents. Here the Estanitsky family lives in an isolated house in the West Texas desert in 1962. Harelik has chosen to set his story in the remotest possible corner of the state, an environment one character describes as "the wilds of Texas" and a "wasteland."[33] When the play opens, twelve-year-old Nathan is studying for his *bar mitzvah*, the coming-of-age ceremony for thirteen-year-old men, by listening to phonograph records of his grandfather, Hillel, reciting Hebrew prayers and telling stories in Yiddish. We learn later that Hillel, who died long before, made the records for his grandson on a home recording machine. As the first Estanitsky to venture into the wilderness, Hillel was intimately aware of the hardships his descendants would face, and he planned to make his legacy, his Jewishness, available to them in a form that he hoped would last forever. But Nathan neither understands nor appreciates the Hebrew and only "memorizes that voice syllable by syllable and mumbledy by bumbledy and just hopes somebody'll figure it out later."[34] Nathan's father David, Hillel's son, is also entirely ignorant of the Hebrew language and of Jewish tradition, though he insists that his son undergo the training he never did. "[P]robably thanks to me," he tells a visiting rabbi, "we're all feeling a little stranded out here, and I want Nathan to have this."[35] David treasures his parents' Sabbath candlesticks, though the family no longer uses them, as well as old family photographs and his father's recordings. These are the legacy he hopes his son will inherit.

Rabbi Bindler, visiting the Estanitsky home to help Nathan prepare, tries to encourage David to reconsider the meaning of the process he is forcing on his son. Bindler explains that Nathan is mimicking prayers in his grandfather's eastern European-inflected Hebrew, not in modern Hebrew pronunciation. When David insists that "we think it's important that he learn it the way Pop did it," Bindler cannot understand their wish to preserve an accent while neglecting the prayers' content. "Jewishness is not a few fond memories of your father," he explains. "It's an entry into a way of life. That's where 'Jewishness' is."[36] David and Nathan remain unmoved.

In the remainder of the play, Harelik further reveals the flaws in David's thinking and pushes the story to a powerful conclusion. David's wife, Rachel, is facing impending death from cancer, and she asks Bindler to explain why God causes her to suffer. He offers her only the assurance that her illness is not a divine judgment. Seeking some source of hope, Rachel converts to Christian Science. When, suddenly filled with joy and faith, she asks David to accompany her to church, he refuses to do so:

> You know I've spent my whole life here trying to fit in. But there
> comes a point, for me and Nathan, when we have to do something to
> define ourselves and that something is, we don't pray with them. We
> don't go to church with them. Not because it's bad, but because there's
> got to be a separation somewhere.[37]

David has compromised every element of Jewish ritual and is utterly without faith, but when pushed to the wall he finally draws a line around his Jewish identity and defends it. With the positive content of his faith reduced to nothing, he defines himself in the negative: he is a Jew because he will not be a Christian. Such line-drawing is characteristic of frontier life. In remote West Texas, where Jews are such an extreme minority that the question of self-identification is central, the setting itself becomes a frontier in which the basic composition and definition of Jewish identity are explored. The frontier's suitability as a metaphor for the inner complexities of Jewish identity is, in fact, the reason it figures so prominently and repetitively as a theme in Texas-Jewish fiction.

The Case of the Jewish Cowboy

The frontier also provides an underlying theme in the mystery novels of Kinky Friedman (eighteen titles between 1986 and 2005) and Sharon Kahn (six titles since 1998). Unlike the works considered so far, these series featuring Texas-Jewish detective protagonists are set in a contemporary context. Kahn's takes place in the fictional Austin-area community of Eternal, and Friedman's in a variety of settings from Kerrville, Texas, to Greenwich Village, New York. Instead of a geographical reality or a meeting-ground between cultural groups, the frontier appears in these works as an internal marker that makes the Texas-Jewish detective somehow odd or distinctive. The idea that Texas Jews are a marginal people, whose unique perspective gives them special insight, lends itself to the construction of detective protagonists, and both Friedman and Kahn exploit the notion of Texas-Jewish eccentricity to give their characters appeal and interest.

The apparent implausibility of Texas-Jewish identity fulfills a number of the mystery genre's stylistic requirements. The success of detective novels, especially those that feature a protagonist who reappears in successive volumes, depends upon a central character who is sufficiently likable, quirky, and recognizable to maintain the reader's interest from one book to the next. Although close enough to events to see them clearly and having personal access to all the suspects, the detective must also seem "normal" enough that readers never truly suspect that he or she may be guilty of the crimes under investigation. Since the days of Sherlock Holmes and M. Dupin, mystery writers have created detectives who are interesting and memorable without being threatening or criminally suspicious. Some have traits such as distinctive physical characteristics, dressing in especially formal or especially informal ways, enjoying strange hobbies, or drinking, eating, and smoking with abandon.[38] Modern fictional detectives, notes one critic, have taken a variety of unconventional forms, including "a Navajo (Tony Hillerman), an Afrikaner working with a Bantu (James McClure), a central Australian aborigine (Arthur Upfield), a Chicano (Rex Burns), a male homosexual (Joseph Hansen), a lesbian (M. F. Beal), a dwarf, a child, a machine."[39] A Texan Jew could easily be added to this list.

Friedman and Kahn in fact belong to a mystery subgenre, works featuring Jewish detectives. In Harry Kemelman's books, for example, Rabbi David Small makes his Jewishness, especially his Talmudic training, a basic part of his crime-solving process. Faye Kellerman's books feature the husband-and-wife team of Peter Decker and Rina Lazarus, an Orthodox couple who solve crimes while struggling to maintain a traditionally religious home and family. Judaism is a deep part of who these characters are, what they think about, and how they approach their vocations. In contrast, Friedman and Kahn represent their characters' Jewishness as less essential, less about core identity. Rather, it is a superficial character quality that, especially when blended with "Texanness," creates a distinctive individual clearly set apart from everyone else in the fictional world. Working in a genre that does not permit subtle exploration of complex issues, these authors depend heavily on preconceived notions about Texas, Jewishness, and their peculiar potential combinations and contradictions. The frontiers of Texas-Jewish identity provide the necessary marginality to make successful fictional detectives.

For Friedman, writing is only one facet of a career as a country singer, political commentator, gubernatorial candidate, and all-around professional celebrity Texan. During his musical career, Friedman was as famous for his flamboyant self-presentation as for his songs, and during this stage, he developed the swaggering, cigar-chewing character that later became his quasi-autobiographical detective hero. "The Kinkster" is a fictionalized version of himself—or at least of his real-life persona—and is suitably hard-boiled and cynical, though occasionally revealing an inner soft-heartedness through ruminations about lost loves, good cigars, and old friends who have "gone to Jesus."[40] A Jew in cowboy garb who wears a broad black hat over a mass of curly hair he calls his "Hebrew natural";[41] a drinker who slugs Jameson Irish Whiskey from an "old bull's horn shot glass";[42] an inveterate cigar smoker who carries extra stogies in the ammunition loops of a hunting vest; an amateur private investigator who keeps two telephones on his desk connected to the same line so that, when both ring simultaneously, it "[makes] the calls sound important";[43] a former cocaine addict and almost-famous country-western musician, the Kinkster easily joins the ranks of eccentric fictional investigators. And, as a self-professed "Texas Jewboy," an ambiguous personal identity that allows him to stand outside the action, he can observe it with the requisite detachment.

In contrast to other Jewish detectives, including Sharon Kahn's Ruby Rothman, the fictional Kinky Friedman reveals almost nothing of a traditional Jewish consciousness. In fact, in one of the few passages in the novels dealing specifically with religious faith, he shows himself to be more ecumenical, even agnostic, than Jewish. "Let us pray," he suggests to his cat in a moment of existential crisis, and the two bow their heads. After beginning, "Dear God, Jesus, Buddha, or L. Ron Hubbard, please help us," he then explains, "I didn't really expect to hear from L. Ron Hubbard. And Buddha hadn't spoken to anyone in years. But I did hope that God or Jesus might be more forthcoming." Receiving no response, he determines that "either they didn't exist, they didn't care, or they were both autistic."[44] In a later moment, he considers prayer again but opts against it. "I said to hell with it," he explains. "Let the good Christians around the world pray for my eternal soul."[45] The Kinkster's sense of his Jewish identity is without an authentic religious component.

In a secular sense, however, the narrator does identify himself as a Jew, and self-consciously "Jewish" language pervades the novels. He describes one character, for example, as wearing "off-lox-colored slacks"; another is a partner at a New York law firm called "Schmeckel & Schmeckel"; and the family dog back home on the ranch is characterized as a "Jewish shepherd."[46] On the other hand, Friedman greatly diminishes the significance of his persona's Jewishness by setting most of the novels in New York. In a city where Jews are a large part of the population, his "Texanness," not his Jewishness, sets him apart. Other Jews among his New York associates often remark on their cowboy friend's place of origin. "Head 'em up. Move 'em out," one says to him as they set off to investigate a lead, "[i]n the language of your people."[47] The narrator himself makes much of his blended personality, and the apparent incongruity of a Texas Jew provides the basis for many of his one-liners. Asked by a friend when he might play another concert at the Lone Star Café, Kinky replies, "Probably on a cold day in Jerusalem, pal," adding that "I missed performing there like I missed having a mescal worm in my matzo-ball soup."[48]

Unexpected juxtapositions like these show that the narrator thinks of himself as both a Texan and a Jew, but they confront neither as a meaningful category of identity. They are, rather, a means for the author to present his detective hero as a marginal figure, one who is both an insider and an outsider, at home in his environment but not truly of it. As a Texan and a Jew, he is partly at home and partly detached from both Texas and New York and from the people who more fully inhabit those environments. In the first novel, the narrator remarks on the comments he receives walking through Greenwich Village in his cowboy hat. "People would be yelling 'Hey, Tex' and 'Cowboy!' You never could tell if they were being derisive or just curious and exuberant, but personally, I never did like it much."[49]

When the narrator returns to the Texas fold, however, as when he joins Willie Nelson on his tour bus in *Road Kill*, he is equally out of place. His old friends in Willie's entourage remind him that he is no longer really one of them. "You're some kind of big detective up in New York," one teases. "Why don't you start detectin'?"[50] Kinky does not fully belong to Texas or New York, to ecumenicism or Judaism. As a Texas Jew, he defines himself, and lets others define him, in terms of what he is not, and so he is always a step removed from present company.

Friedman's ambiguous status provides one of *Road Kill*'s key themes. Although his Texas-Jewishness is not the story's turning point, the marginality that it imparts to him helps him to solve the crime. Willie Nelson, shaken by some unknown recent event, calls Kinky in New York to invite him aboard the tour bus. Kinky's place within Willie's traveling clan is that of insider and outsider, old friend of the star but, as one crew member says, "not on the payroll, working for him."[51] Kinky describes Willie's world, what he calls "Nelson's superstructure," as a series of concentric circles, with the "Family" at the center—Willie, his wife, and his closest confidantes. Outside lay "the periphery . . . folks he was close to" who were not intimates.[52] Trying to place himself within that system, Kinky admits that he, a fellow musician on whom Willie felt comfortable calling for help in a crisis, was nevertheless part of the periphery. "I was having a hard time defining my role, if, indeed I had one, within the Willie Nelson Family," he explains. "As an outsider, I couldn't quite see [that something was wrong], but I was at the same time enough of an insider to feel it taking place."[53] This dual perspective later gives Kinky the unique vantage point he needs to be able to solve the mystery.

Ruby Rothman, the detective protagonist of Sharon Kahn's six mysteries, is also both an insider and an outsider. Like Kinky, Ruby is a straight shooter who casts an ironic eye on everyone around her and keeps herself at a distance from those whose motives she mistrusts. Most of Friedman's stories take place on the streets of Greenwich Village, but Kahn's remain closer to home, focusing on the members of Ruby's congregation, Temple Rita, in the fictional bedroom community of Eternal, Texas. Temple Rita's members and social and religious activities provide much of the novels' narrative action, as well as a number of their murder victims and suspects. In Kahn's stories, a self-conscious Texas-Jewishness is always present: one book even begins with the mysterious death of a famous scholar of Texas crypto-Jews.

Eternal is itself a marginal community, lying several miles outside Austin but close enough that many of its residents live and shop in the city. Kahn explicitly describes it as a frontier community lying on a natural boundary between geographic regions:

> The town of Eternal is topographically schizophrenic. The half where
> I live lies in the flat plain that leads eastward to the heart of the Old
> South in Louisiana and Mississippi. The other half, literally popping up
> from one street to the next, is a hilly, roller-coaster route to the Old
> West of New Mexico and Arizona.[54]

The members of Eternal's small Jewish community are also divided between those who wish to see the congregation adopt modern, sophisticated

Austin author Sharon Kahn. Photo ©
Gina Evans. Courtesy of Sharon Kahn.

ways and others who are more interested in preserving tradition. As Ruby
notes wryly, however, "that doesn't mean Jewish tradition." When temple
members hire a new rabbi, tradition means that "the candidate's ancestors
put the first stone in a temple building somewhere in Texas in the nineteenth century."[55] At the same time, it is important to the Jews of Eternal
that they not stray too far from Jewish custom, however idiosyncratic their
interpretation. Of the town's two bagel shops, for example, they prefer The
Hot Bagel, owned by a Lebanese New Yorker "whose mother gave him
a salami end to teethe on," to Kulberg's Deli, "run by Jewish expatriates
from Brooklyn" whose "collective cultural memory apparently faded when
they crossed the Texas border."[56] The Kulbergs' actual Jewishness does not
offset the perception that they have over-assimilated, so that a less acculturated Lebanese deli owner can provide a more authentic Jewish menu.

In this environment, Ruby Rothman fights a constant battle to avoid
both extremes. She herself is a marginal figure in the community. Although
part of the group—"These are good people," she writes a friend, "and
they're my people"—she is often doubtful about their sincerity and wary of
entangling herself in their congregational squabbles.[57] Ruby is the widow of
Temple Rita's previous rabbi, whose mysterious death draws her into the
world of amateur sleuthing in the series' first book. When the congregation is slow to replace him, Ruby finds herself obliged to serve as "almost

clergy," a rabbinical stand-in at social functions.[58] She detests the role. Committed to the temple and to her faith, yet without an official position, Ruby is both an insider and an outsider, one of the group but a step apart from it.

The issue of Jewish authenticity runs through Kahn's books, expressed in concerns such as whether Ruby's East Texas birth and upbringing invalidate her Jewish credentials. "I don't even think you're bona fide Jewish," a friend teases her, describing her as "an East Texas ex-rebbitzen who grew up on collard greens." Ruby explains that her grandfather came to America through Galveston and settled "where the horse died." When her friend asks how she survived marriage to a rabbi, she says that she "learned more Yiddish expressions the first year of marriage than I had known my whole life before." If a congregant called for a Jewish recipe, she consulted a cookbook kept by the telephone. "But to tell you the truth," she says, "I never did get the hang of seasoning anything that didn't have a little East Texas / West Louisiana tang to it."[59] Using food as a metaphor for identity—as she regularly does throughout the books—Kahn creates a character who is a blend of "Texan" and "Jewish" qualities.

In the same way that she acknowledges a difference between the kind of food she prefers and "real" Jewish cooking, Ruby recognizes the Texas-seasoned Judaism practiced in Eternal, and she frequently resists the cheapness with which her fellow congregants treat Jewish tradition. Thus Ruby, the "East Texas ex-rebbitzen," becomes the defender of a respectful, traditional outlook and comments relentlessly on her fellow congregants' bad taste. The debate over the selection of a new rabbi illustrates Ruby's skepticism about the approach taken by most of Temple Rita's members. Of the factions she identifies, she approves of only one, the view of the temple president that the successful candidate should represent authentic Jewish values. Ruby admired her husband because "as rabbi he was more interested in people than in pronouncements or decibel levels." In contrast, a group of congregants "now wants something different," someone with "charisma" who "should also look like a rabbi, whatever that means." Others prefer a candidate "with tradition," but, Ruby notes, they seem uncertain whether that means Jewish or Texan tradition. After meeting a candidate at the "Jews and the Old West Conference," one supporter of this view remarked that the rabbi was "wearing the most beautiful pair of eelskin cowboy boots you ever saw in your life. The Star of David was etched on 'em." The rabbi "told me he almost never takes 'em off his feet. Think of what that says about a man. I had tears in my eyes."[60] Ruby condemns this group's shallowness, observing caustically, "Looks are not a priority" for them, but "being a good ol' boy is."[61] They have let their sense of themselves as Texans overwhelm their sense of Jewish meaning, and so they have become ridiculous to her.

Similarly, Ruby defends the sacredness of the Passover Seder when her congregational nemesis, Essie Sue Margolis, wants to prepare an "Ecumenical Diet Seder" that will be both nondenominational and nonfattening. When one character remarks that the Seder "is such a universal occasion," Ruby recoils. "Yes and no," she muses. The themes of freedom and slavery are universal, "but I can't think of a more in-group occasion myself. This is the night, after all, when we recount the boils of our enemies, promise next year in Jerusalem, and re-create the tears and mortar from those sentimental old days when we were plastering bricks for the Pharaoh." It was a rough history, she says, "but it's ours, and we're still here."[62]

Ruby finds Essie Sue and her cohorts bemusing and troubling because they draw Jewish practice too far from its center, its roots in the non-Texan Jewish past. They have accommodated Texas and American culture to such a degree and are making such an attempt to be absolutely democratic and ecumenical that they are cheapening and damaging something Ruby holds sacred. A Texas Jew herself, a peripheral figure, Ruby nevertheless casts herself as the guardian of essential Jewish values. As a protector of traditional Jewish belief (and a crime-fighter), she becomes the narrative's ethical center, a figure who is beyond reproach and so can help restore the ethical continuity of the fictional world. Skeptical of everyone around her, Ruby is the first to suspect foul play and the first to take steps to achieve a just outcome.

Because so many of Ruby's associates—including most of the murderers and most of the murdered—are also Texas Jews, she remains an outsider among outsiders. Whether she is the quirkiest among them or the only reasonable one depends on one's interpretation. Ruby is, in her own first-person narrative, the calm eye of the storm seeking to preserve order and an authentic display of Jewish dignity and pride. Kahn's satirical style also keeps Eternal's Jewish population at a humorous distance that prevents the reader from identifying with them too closely or seeing them as anything but interesting oddballs with a shocking ability to befriend people soon to meet with mysterious accidents. Kahn is herself a long-time Texan and a former rabbi's wife, but the entertainment value of her books depends upon a now-familiar presumption: Texas Jewry is essentially an untenable, humorous, even unsightly combination of disparate elements, and the characteristics on the Texas side of that frontier constantly threaten to overpower those on the Jewish side.

All of these literary examples reveal that the frontier, the conceptual space in which different groups compete with one another for dominance and define themselves in opposition to one another, remains a central theme in Texas-Jewish life as in its fiction. Despite Texas Jewry's growth in population and complexity, despite its participation in national Jewish networks and in American demographic trends, the frontier has never disappeared from the self-definitions of Jewish Texans. Its outward manifestations having faded, the frontier has simply moved inside, becoming the indispensable element of an emerging Texas-Jewish identity.

✳

Conclusion

*The main purpose of this book is to go beyond the biographical and photo-*graphic interest of earlier studies of Texas Jewry to a more general interpretive level. Texas-Jewish history is well documented but, until now, largely unexplained, leaving a reader with the impression that what the Jewish people have done in Texas is without meaning or is meaningful only to genealogists, antiquarians, and Texas Jews themselves. On the contrary, the Jewish experience in Texas embodies a number of crucial themes in Jewish and American history that should be explicitly noted, and I hope that this work makes a contribution to these larger fields by using Texas-Jewish history to illuminate new ways of thinking about some very old issues.

Because Jews are so community- and family-oriented, all Jewish history is local history. Jewish life always occurs *here*, in some specific place, and it always takes on shades and colorings unique to its particular setting. Thus, American Jewish historians have tended to emphasize regionalism, how Jews in the South, or the West, or in New York, differ from one another. This book, too, reads the Jewish life of one such place. However, in the light of a powerful interpretive framework, the frontier, which is applicable in so many contexts, it is possible to see how much Jewish life in Texas shares with other American Jewish experiences. In fact, the frontier is a common, unifying force behind Jewish history everywhere. The first European Jews to settle in Palestine, with the eventual hope of establishing a

Jewish state there, were called *halutzim*, frontiersmen. Examining the frontier idea closely reveals what many Texas Jews, both now and in the past, might have been reluctant to admit: Texas Jewry is not unique, nor is it more or less than Jewries elsewhere, but it typifies the fundamental nature of Jewish life wherever it occurs.

The idea that all Jewish experiences are equally valid has been a key motivation of this study. Since the earliest stories of the Jews, including those collected in the Bible, Jewish history has been understood as circular: from their origin point in Jerusalem, Jews were forced into exile across the globe, but they have returned or will eventually return to Jerusalem to fulfill their true destiny. By this interpretation, everything that occurs in the interim—while the Jews are rootless, wandering, and exiled—is unimportant. The Diaspora is a temporary existence, and the scattered Jews of the world will either return to their true history in Israel or will be lost to Judaism forever. In either case, their experience while in the Diaspora is irrelevant, even if it should last for thousands of years. Many earlier studies of diasporic communities have reinforced this idea by documenting the declension of Diaspora Jews, the many ways in which acculturation, assimilation, and accommodation have destroyed their sense of themselves as a distinct ethnic and religious entity.

This study shows that Jewish survival in the Diaspora is not only possible but also offers opportunities for Jewish identity to evolve into new, meaningful forms. I do not mean to suggest that Texas Jewry represents a Jewish experience as deep or as rich—as centered—as that which has existed in places like Jerusalem, New York, or eastern Europe. The Texas Jewish community is too small and relatively indistinguishable from its gentile neighbors to justify such a comparison, nor has it produced the arts, language, and self-conscious worldview that mark mature and self-identified communities. This book demonstrates, however, that a beginning point has perhaps been reached, that Jewish Texans have achieved a critical mass of population and an institutional vitality that may permit the development of a true Texas-Jewish culture.

Whether or not this happens, the Jewish community of Texas illustrates the possibility that Jewish religion and identity are not fated for destruction in the Diaspora. Instead, they continue to thrive, often in surprising and unfamiliar ways made possible only by the Diaspora. Texas Jewry provides an example of cultural adaptation and survival in a remote place that may serve as a model for future studies of Jews in other frontier settings. Furthermore, as the diasporic idea takes hold among scholars of African,

Chinese, English, Irish, and other ethnic groups as a way of describing how they have spread across the face of the earth, stories like those told here may show how ethnicity and traditional identification can survive in innovative ways and in unexpected places. As Jews have made themselves at home in Texas while retaining many of the characteristics that make them different from other Texans, other ethnic and religious groups may do the same in other diasporic places.

As a work of American history, this book engages the continuing redefinition of the idea of the frontier, a term that has been much disparaged in recent years as fundamentally racist and imperialistic. As Frederick Jackson Turner originally used it, to denote a meeting point between civilization and savagery, it deserves to be disparaged. As employed here, however, I believe it is a useful way to understand the intersection and confrontation of cultures in a crossroads like Texas. Defined as an imagined space of cultural interaction where differences collide, groups encounter one another, and cultural boundaries must be devised and continually revised, the frontier remains an evocative and eminently useful idea. As an internal rather than an external reality, it provides a powerful metaphor for the cultural collisions that American pluralism inevitably produces and for the new forms of cultural expression and group identity that emerge from those collisions. In this sense, the frontier is a much larger idea than Turner knew: it explains the very process through which American culture is produced out of its constituent parts. It thus remains, as Turner knew it to be but for a different reason, essential to understanding the making of American identity.

The story of the Rope Walker, with which I began, is a fitting way to conclude. In his few, tense moments over the streets of Corsicana in 1884, he stood in the balance between extremes—between one building and the next, between control and chaos, between sky and earth. After his fall, he lay dying in a hotel bed, balanced again between extremes—outsider and insider, Jewish and Christian, life and death. The Rope Walker's story, while true, is also a fable about the fluidity of identity, about the impossibility in any frontier of being all one thing or the other. It finds a suitable setting in the Jewish history of Texas. Where the frontier was an enduring reality of life, Texas Jews poised themselves on the high wire between identities, daring to be, as much as possible, everything at once.

NOTES

Prologue

1. I compiled the story of the Rope Walker from Nancy Ashburn, "Tombstone Seals Secret of Peg-leg Ropewalker," *Corsicana Daily Sun* (October 30, 1988); Robert C. Campbell, "Walk Into Oblivion," *Denver Post Rocky Mountain Empire Magazine* (December 11, 1949): 3; Ernest Joseph, "Rope Walker's Tombstone," Texas Jewish Historical Society Records [TJHS], Center for American History [CAH], University of Texas at Austin, Box 3A170, Folder 1; and Frank X. Tolbert, "A Better Memorial for 'Rope Walker'?" *Dallas Morning News*, n.d., TJHS Box 3A170, Folder 1.

Introduction

1. Andrea Chambers, "It's Elementary: Shooting from the Lip, Cocky Kinky Friedman Has a Talent for Music and Mysteries," *People Weekly* 28 (November 9, 1987): 117.
2. Quoted in Abraham Schechter, *The Kallah: An Annual Convention of Texas Rabbis*, 17.
3. Shmuel Geller, *Mazkeres Ahavah: Remembrance of Love*, 33.
4. Fanny Sattinger Goodman, "'In the Beginning': The Jewish Community of El Paso, Texas," 1.
5. Ava F. Kahn, ed., *Jewish Life in the American West: Perspectives on Migration, Settlement, and Community*, 13.
6. Fredrik Barth, ed., *Ethnic Groups and Boundaries: The Social Organization of Culture Difference*, 15.
7. T. R. Fehrenbach, *Seven Keys to Texas*, 2.

8. Henry Cohen, "Henry Castro, Pioneer and Colonist," 41. On the complications of identifying Castro as Jewish, see Bryan Edward Stone, "On the Frontier: Jews without Judaism," 23–24.
9. Cohen, "Henry Castro," 41.
10. Walter K. Kohlberg, *Letters of Ernst Kohlberg, 1875–1877*, 14.
11. Sander L. Gilman, "The Frontier as a Model for Jewish History," 1.
12. Deborah Dash Moore, *To the Golden Cities: Pursuing the American Jewish Dream in Miami and L.A.*, 1–2.
13. For the record, there are no mountains in Lubbock. "Jewish Texans Commemorate Holocaust . . . Texas-Style!" *The Onion* (February 12, 1997), www.theonion.com/content/node/39219, accessed May 28, 1997.
14. "Louis" to the Editor, *Jewish South* (May 16, 1879).
15. Betty Ewing, "A Delight at 101: Bertha Bender's Life was Destined to Grow with the State She Adopted," *Houston Chronicle* (September 6, 1989).
16. Seth L. Wolitz, "Bifocality in Jewish Identity in the Texas-Jewish Experience," 187.
17. Wolitz, 200, 188, 187–188, 188.
18. Gilman, 11, 12, 11.
19. Frederick Jackson Turner, "The Significance of the Frontier in American History," 2, 3.
20. See, most notably, Patricia Nelson Limerick, *Legacy of Conquest: The Unbroken Past of the American West*, and Richard White, *"It's Your Misfortune and None of My Own": A New History of the American West*.
21. Patricia Nelson Limerick, "What on Earth is the New Western History?" 85–86.
22. Gilman, 14.
23. Stephen Aron, "Lessons in Conquest: Towards a Greater Western History," 128.
24. Kerwin Lee Klein, "Reclaiming the 'F' Word, or Being and Becoming Postwestern." Page numbers within this article were not included in the on-line text retrieved from InfoTrac on July 4, 2000.
25. Gloria Anzaldúa, *Borderlands/La Frontera*, 3, ix.
26. Gilman, 22.
27. Penny Diane Wolin, *The Jews of Wyoming: Fringe of the Diaspora*, 152, 156.
28. Judith Geller Marlow, "My Wandering Roots," 121–122.
29. Marlow, 122–123.
30. Marlow, 124.
31. Material on Friedman comes from an earlier essay, which provides further discussion of his cultural significance. See Bryan Edward Stone, "'Ride 'Em, Jewboy': Kinky Friedman and the Texas Mystique." Used with permission.
32. Alice Wightman, "Real Kinky," *@Austin* 1 (1997): 34; Bill Mann, "Are You Ready for Kinky Friedman and the Texas Jewboys?" *Melody Maker* (December 8, 1973).
33. Lester Bangs, review of *Sold American*, *Rolling Stone* 137 (June 21, 1973): 63.

34. Mann.
35. Wightman, 36.
36. Bangs, 63.
37. Kinky Friedman, "Ride 'em, Jewboy," *Old Testaments & New Revelations* (Fruit of the Tune Music, 1992), originally recorded 1973.

Chapter One

1. For the history of the Carvajal family and colony, see Martin A. Cohen, "The Autobiography of Luis De Carvajal, the Younger"; Martin A. Cohen, *The Martyr*; Seymour B. Liebman, *The Enlightened: The Writings Of Luis de Carvajal, El Mozo*; Seymour B. Liebman, *The Jews in New Spain: Faith, Flame and the Inquisition*; Harriet and Fred Rochlin, *Pioneer Jews: A New Life in the Far West*; Richard G. Santos, *Silent Heritage: The Sephardim and the Colonization of the Spanish North American Frontier, 1492–1600*; and Alfonso Toro, *The Carvajal Family*.
2. Toro, 167–168.
3. Toro, 234–235.
4. Toro, 402.
5. For the history of the Castaño de Sosa expedition, as well as a strong defense of Hispanic claims of crypto-Jewish descent in New Mexico, see Stanley M. Hordes, *To the End of the Earth: A History of the Crypto-Jews of New Mexico*. Hordes does not address similar claims in Texas.
6. See, for example, Carlos Montalvo Larralde, "Chicano Jews in South Texas"; Richard G. Santos, "Chicanos of Jewish Descent in Texas"; Santos, *Silent Heritage*.
7. Henry Cohen, "Settlement of the Jews in Texas," 139; Natalie Ornish, *Pioneer Jewish Texans*, 132; Ruthe Winegarten and Cathy Schechter, *Deep in the Heart: The Lives and Legends of Texas Jews, a Photographic History*, 7.
8. S. J. Isaacks, "The Isaacks Clan in America and Texas," www.geocities.com /astromood/ISAACKSc.html, accessed April 28, 2005.
9. Ibid.
10. Constitution of the United Mexican States (1824), www.constitution.org /cons/mexico/constit1824.htm, accessed March 29, 2007.
11. Randolph B. Campbell, *Gone to Texas: A History of the Lone Star State*, 110, 113.
12. Cathy [Schechter] to Ruthe [Winegarten], Ginger [Jacobs], and Jimmy [Kessler] (February 11, 1987), TJHS Box 3A173, Folder 3; Henry Cohen, "Settlement of the Jews in Texas," 139; I. Harold Sharfman, *Jews on the Frontier*, 254.
13. Texas Declaration of Independence.
14. Constitution of the Republic of Texas.
15. See, for example, Constitution du Texas, *Archives Israelites de France* 7 (1846): 654; Isaac Leeser, "The Prospect," *Occident* 4 (September 1846): 270.
16. Although no single study has focused exclusively on this hub-spoke community arrangement, several have touched on it. See Leonard Rogoff, *Homelands: Southern Jewish Identity in Durham and Chapel Hill, North Carolina*; William Toll,

242

The Making of an Ethnic Middle Class: Portland Jewry over Four Generations; and Lee Shai Weissbach, Jewish Life In Small-Town America: A History.

17. Henry Cohen, "Settlement of the Jews in Texas," 143–147.

18. Henry Cohen, "Settlement of the Jews in Texas," 146.

19. Daniel N. Leeson, "In Search of the History of the Texas Patriot Moses A. Levy"; Saul Viener, "Surgeon Moses Albert Levy: Letters of a Texas Patriot."

20. Marquis James, The Raven: A Biography of Sam Houston, 196.

21. M. K. Wisehart, Sam Houston, American Giant, 109.

22. Archie P. McDonald, ed., Hurrah for Texas! The Diary of Adolphus Sterne, 1838–1851, xii.

23. Winegarten and Schechter, 9.

24. Harriet Smither, "Diary of Adolphus Sterne," 139–140n.1; Bertram Wallace Korn, The Early Jews of New Orleans, 206n.54.

25. Korn, The Early Jews of New Orleans, 206.

26. Gloria Frye, "Eva Catherine Rosine Ruff Sterne (1809–1897)," 235.

27. Amelia W. Williams and Eugene C. Barker, eds., The Writings of Sam Houston, 1813–1863, v. 1, 478n.3. M. K. Wisehart states that Adolphus and Eva served together as Houston's godparents, though he provides no evidence of it. Wisehart, 114.

28. McDonald, x.

29. Ibid.

30. James, 204.

31. McDonald, xi.

32. McDonald, 4, 175; Korn, The Early Jews of New Orleans, 206n.55.

33. McDonald, 50.

34. McDonald, 62.

35. McDonald, 175. Here and below, grammatical and spelling errors are Sterne's.

36. McDonald, 186.

37. McDonald, 26.

38. McDonald, 212, 247.

39. McDonald, 103, 177.

40. McDonald, 114.

Chapter Two

1. Isaac Leeser, "The Prospect," Occident 4 (September 1846): 271.

2. [Isaac Leeser], "The Importance of Missions," Occident 11 (May 1853): 85–86. The congregation to which Leeser referred is probably Beth Israel in Houston, which was not chartered until 1859 but may have held informal worship services earlier.

3. E. Wolff to Isaac Leeser (December 31, 1850), Isaac Leeser Papers, Jacob Rader Marcus Center of the American Jewish Archives, Cincinnati Campus, Hebrew Union College–Jewish Institute of Religion [AJA].

4. Isaac Jalonick to Isaac Leeser (May 28, 1853), Isaac Leeser Papers, AJA. Transcription as in original.

5. Ibid.

6. *American Israelite* (October 17, 1873).

7. "United States Historical Census Data Browser," http://fisher.lib.virginia.edu /census, accessed December 20, 2002; Union of American Hebrew Congregations, *Statistics of the Jews of the United States*, 29–30; American Jewish Historical Society, *American Jewish Desk Reference*, 35; Jacob Rader Marcus, *To Count a People: American Jewish Population Data, 1585–1984*, 211–217; *American Jewish Year Book* 3 (1901–1902): 58 and 16 (1914–1915): 376. In annual volumes since 1899, the *American Jewish Year Book* has provided the best available population data on American Jewry, but these are rough and notoriously inexact estimates. In many cases when no new data were available, the *Year Book* reprinted figures year after year, thus it is impossible to gather even estimated data for most specific dates. In these calculations, as hereafter, I have used *Year Book* figures for the closest available year. In this case, where 1900 figures do not exist, I have used 1905 data printed in a 1915 historical table.

8. D. W. Meinig, *Imperial Texas: An Interpretive Essay in Cultural Geography*, 65.

9. Eric L. Goldstein, *The Price of Whiteness: Jews, Race, and American Identity*, 2, 1. For an equally discerning interpretation of another white ethnic group's complicated journey to whiteness, see Noel Ignatiev, *How the Irish Became White*.

10. Elaine Maas, "Jews," 141.

11. *Houston Telegraph* (March 7, 1855), reprinted as "Houston, Texas, Hebrew Benevolent Association," *Occident* 13 (July 1855): 199–200.

12. "Leon and H. Blum," *The Handbook of Texas Online*, www.tshaonline.org /handbook/online/articles/LL/dhlhf_print.html, accessed July 2, 2004.

13. Carol Tefteller, "The Jewish Community in Frontier Jefferson," 5, 4.

14. See Ava F. Kahn, ed., *Jewish Voices of the California Gold Rush: A Documentary History, 1849–1880*; Ava F. Kahn and Ellen Eisenberg, "Western Reality: Jewish Diversity During the 'German' Period"; and Toll, *The Making of an Ethnic Middle Class*.

15. Deborah R. Weiner, *Coalfield Jews: An Appalachian History*, 1.

16. M. Seeligson to Isaac Leeser (June 19, 1853), Isaac Leeser Papers, AJA. Capitalization as in original.

17. Steven Hertzberg makes a similar point in reference to Atlanta in *Strangers Within the Gate City: The Jews of Atlanta, 1845–1915*, 22.

18. Jacob de Cordova, *Lecture on Texas Delivered by Mr. J. De Cordova . . .*, 24–25.

19. Clive Webb, *Fight Against Fear: Southern Jews and Black Civil Rights*, 2. For further discussion of slavery and southern Jewry, though with minimal attention to Texas, see Bertram Wallace Korn, *Jews And Negro Slavery in the Old South, 1789–1865*.

20. Gary Alan Ratkin, "The Jews in Houston and Galveston, Texas during the Civil War," 4.

21. Winegarten and Schechter, *Deep in the Heart*, 20.

22. Osterman materials, TJHS Box 3A167, Folder 1; Winegarten and Schechter, 23.

23. Anne Nathan and Harry I. Cohen, *The Man Who Stayed in Texas: The Life of Rabbi Henry Cohen*, 120.

24. Julius Henry, "The Making of an Abolitionist," 169–170.

25. Harry Landa, *As I Remember*, 19.

26. Harold M. Hyman, *Oleander Odyssey: The Kempners of Galveston, Texas, 1854–1980s*, 13.

27. Quoted in Donald Day, "The Americanism of Harris Kempner," 126.

28. *Houston Transcript* (September 30, 1867), reprinted in *American Israelite* (October 18, 1867): 6.

29. *Dallas Herald* (January 22, 1876), quoted in Elizabeth York Enstam, *Women And The Creation Of Urban Life: Dallas, Texas, 1843–1920*, 50.

30. Elizabeth Hayes Turner, *Women, Culture, and Community: Religion and Reform in Galveston, 1850–1920*, 8.

31. Louis Schmier, ed., *Reflections of Southern Jewry: The Letters of Charles Wessolowsky, 1878–1879*, 101.

32. Jacob Voorsanger [under pseudonym Koppel Von Bloomborg], "Lone Star Flashes," *American Israelite* (June 23, 1882): 419.

33. William Levy, "A Jew Views Black Education: Texas—1890," 359, 352–353.

34. Levy, 354.

35. Kohlberg, *Letters of Ernst Kohlberg*, 14, 39.

36. Kohlberg, 29.

37. Kohlberg, 29, 31, 40, 44.

38. Winegarten and Schechter, 18.

39. J. O. Dyer, "Life of Early Galveston As Told by Storekeeper," *Galveston Daily News* (December 18, 1921).

40. Information on the Dyers and Ostermans comes from Henry Cohen, "Settlement of the Jews in Texas," 147–149; Winegarten and Schechter, 10, 18; Ornish, *Pioneer Jewish Texans*, 171–173, 246–248; and from materials collected in TJHS Box 3A167, Folder 1.

41. "Will of Rosanna Osterman.—Extracts Pertaining to Charitable Bequests, etc.," appendix to Cohen, "Settlement of the Jews in Texas," 153–156.

42. "Hebrew Burial Ground," *Galveston Daily News* (August 31, 1852); *Occident* 10 (October 1852): 366.

43. "Ceremonial at Galveston," *Occident* 10 (August 1852): 380–381.

44. "Ceremonial at Galveston," 382–383, 381.

45. *Occident* 10 (April 1852): 58–59.

46. *Occident* 18 (April 1860): 24.

47. Cohen, "Settlement of the Jews in Texas," 147.

48. *Galveston Daily News* (October 8, 1859).

49. Information on Lewis Levy was compiled from papers collected in TJHS Box 3A165, Folder 7 and Box 3A166, Folder 1. See also Leeson, "In Search of the History of the Texas Patriot Moses A. Levy." Moses Levy was Lewis' brother.

50. Levy materials, TJHS Box 3A166, Folder 1.

51. Winegarten and Schechter, 21; Levy materials, TJHS Box 3A166, Folder 1.

52. Jacob de Cordova, *Texas: Her Resources and Her Public Men*, 64.

53. Helena Frenkil Schlam, "The Early Jews of Houston," 38–46.

54. *American Israelite* (November 18, 1859): 159.

55. *Occident* 17 (March 15, 1860): 306.

56. M. Seeligson to Isaac Leeser (November 1851). Isaac Leeser Papers, AJA.

57. Landa, 14, 26.

58. *American Israelite* (May 23, 1856): 374.

59. Susanne Parker, "Shema Israel: The Reform Jewish Movement in Marshall"; Audrey Daniels Kariel, "The Jewish Story and Memories of Marshall, Texas," 197; *Die Deborah*, 6 (October 12, 1860): 59.

60. "United States Historical Census Data Browser," http://fisher.lib.virginia.edu/census, accessed December 20, 2002.

61. Meinig, 75.

62. On the Sangers, see Gary P. Whitfield, "Confederate Stories: The Sanger Brothers of Weatherford, Dallas, and Waco," and Rose G. Biderman, *They Came to Stay: The Story of the Jews of Dallas*.

63. Union of American Hebrew Congregations, *Statistics of the Jews of the United States*, 29–30.

64. Of these early communities, Fort Worth was a frequent exception to the normal pattern. See Hollace Ava Weiner, "Tied and Tethered (*"Geknippt und Gebinden"*): Jews in Early Fort Worth."

65. *Jewish South* (December 5, 1879).

66. Cathy Schechter, "Shalom, Y'all," *Texas Highways* (August 1990): 52; Hollace Ava Weiner, "The Mixers: The Role of Rabbis Deep in the Heart of Texas," 291–292; *Jewish South* (January 18, 1878). See also Steven Fox, "On the Road to Unity: The Union of American Hebrew Congregations and American Jewry, 1873–1903," 145–193.

67. *Jewish South* (December 5, 1879).

68. *American Israelite* (September 17, 1880): 93.

69. "M. R." to the Editor, *Occident* 17 (September 8, 1859): 144.

70. *American Israelite* (November 1, 1900), reprinted as "From Kempen, Poland to Hempstead, Texas: the Career of Rabbi Heinrich Schwarz," 132–133; Hollace Ava Weiner, *Jewish Stars in Texas: Rabbis and Their Work*, 3–20.

71. For detailed studies of small Jewish communities that experienced similar limitations, see Weissbach, *Jewish Life in Small-Town America*; Rogoff, *Homelands*; and Weiner, *Coalfield Jews*.

72. *Jewish South* (July 11, 1879); *Jewish South* (August 1, 1879).

73. Daniel Frosch, "Unto the Seventh Generation," 2: 29.
74. *Jewish South* (December 26, 1879).
75. *Jewish South* (September 13, 1878).
76. Frank Wagner, untitled biography of David Hirsch; Frank Wagner to Bryan Stone (September 1, 1995). See also Fanny Weil Alexander, "Charles and Sarah Weil."
77. Kohlberg, 28.

Chapter Three

1. David Geffen, "A Sentimental Journey—Early Zionist Activities in the South— The Diary of Jacob de Haas' Trip in 1904," 161–162.
2. Geffen, 167, 165, 161.
3. Geffen, 168, 166, 164, 166.
4. Geffen, 168.
5. Jacob de Haas to Lillian de Haas (December 24, 1904), Jacob de Haas Papers, AJA Microfilm 1336.
6. Geffen, 168.
7. "U" was for unity and "M" for morality. "'Possum and Tater Feast was a Howling Success," *Waco Daily Times-Herald* (December 21, 1904).
8. Geffen, 168.
9. Ibid.
10. "Waco, Texas," *The Handbook of Texas Online*, www.tshaonline.org/handbook /online/articles/WW/hdw1.html, accessed September 14, 2001.
11. Ava F. Kahn, ed., *Jewish Life in the American West*, 53.
12. Sophie Trupin, *Dakota Diaspora: Memoirs of a Jewish Homesteader*, 1, 35.
13. *Asmonean* (June 28, 1850).
14. Ibid.
15. See, for example, M. Levy to the Editor, *Jewish South* (September 5, 1879); M. Schwartz to the Editor, *American Israelite* (August 8, 1879).
16. Louis Schmier, ed., *Reflections of Southern Jewry*, 86–87.
17. Such appeals were by no means unique to Texas. See, for example, Robert Alan Goldberg, *Back to the Soil: The Jewish Farmers of Clarion, Utah, and Their World*.
18. Isaac Herbert Kempner, "My Memories of Father," 57.
19. See Harold M. Hyman, *Oleander Odyssey*, 114, 207ff.
20. Lionel M. Schooler, "Mitchell (Michael) Louis Westheimer (1831–c.1910)."
21. Patrick Dearen, "Home on the Range: Mayer Halff's Cattle Empire," 56–57.
22. Jacob Voorsanger (under pseudonym Koppel Von Bloomborg), "Lone Star Flashes," *American Israelite* (June 23, 1882).
23. Samuel Joseph, *History of the Baron de Hirsch Fund: The Americanization of the Jewish Immigrant*, 288.
24. Ibid.

25. Ibid.

26. Gabriel Davidson and Edward A. Goodwin, "A Unique Agricultural Colony," 2.

27. Joseph, 134–135; Gabriel Davidson, *Our Jewish Farmers and the Story of the Jewish Agricultural Society*, 24–25; "Colonists and Colonization," *The Menorah* 38 (March 3, 1905): 185.

28. Robert I. Kahn to Jacob R. Marcus (June 5, 1959), AJA Small Collection 2375; author's interview with Robert I. Kahn, October 7, 1995.

29. "Director Loeb Plans to Bring Kaufman Jews Here," *Jewish Herald* (September 4, 1913).

30. Ibid.

31. Quoted, for instance, in Bernard Marinbach, *Galveston: Ellis Island Of The West*, 173.

32. Cyrus Adler, ed., *Jacob H. Schiff: His Life and Letters*, vol. 2, 113.

33. Peter Romanofsky, "'To Rid Ourselves of the Burden': New York Jewish Charities and the Origins of the Industrial Removal Office, 1890–1901," 331.

34. Jacob Schiff to Mayer Sulzberger (September 27, 1906), Galveston Movement Records, AJA.

35. Jacob Schiff to the manager of the Transcontinental Passenger Association (December 22, 1909), in Adler, vol. 2, 105.

36. Jacob Schiff to Simon Wolf (December 29, 1890), quoted in Gary Dean Best, "Jacob H. Schiff's Galveston Movement: An Experiment in Immigrant Deflection, 1907–1914," 43.

37. Marinbach, xiv.

38. Jacob Schiff to Israel Zangwill (November 21, 1905), quoted in Best, 46.

39. Best, 50.

40. Eli N. Evans, *The Provincials*, 99.

41. For more on the Industrial Removal Office's activities, in particular those in Texas, see Hollace Ava Weiner, "Removal Approval: The Industrial Removal Office Experience in Fort Worth, Texas."

42. Jacob Schiff to Israel Zangwill (August 24, 1906), in Adler, vol. 2, 97–98.

43. Jacob Schiff to Israel Zangwill (October 25, 1906), in Adler, vol. 2, 99.

44. Morris Waldman to David Bressler (November 5, 1906), Galveston Immigration Plan Records, American Jewish Historical Society [AJHS].

45. Jacob Schiff to Israel Zangwill (August 24, 1906), in Adler, vol. 2, 97–98; Morris Waldman to David Bressler (November 5, 1906).

46. Jacob Schiff to Israel Zangwill (August 24, 1906), in Adler, vol. 2, 97.

47. Jacob Schiff to Israel Zangwill (October 25, 1906), in Adler, vol. 2, 99.

48. Henry Cohen is the most written-about Jewish Texan, the community's one folk hero, and his many biographies offer a rich mixture of fact and legend. See, especially, Henry Cohen II, *Kindler of Souls: Rabbi Henry Cohen of Texas*; A. Stanley Dreyfus, *Henry Cohen: Messenger of the Lord*; Jimmy Kessler, *Henry Cohen: The*

Life of a Frontier Rabbi; and Anne Nathan and Harry I. Cohen, *The Man Who Stayed in Texas*.

49. Henry Cohen, "The Galveston Movement: Its First Year," 114.

50. Cohen, "The Galveston Movement," 115–116.

51. Alexander Ziskind Gurwitz, "Memories of Two Generations," vol. 2, 208.

52. *American Israelite* (September 3, 1914).

53. "Jewish Immigrants," *Galveston Times* (July 2, 1907). See also Cohen, "The Galveston Movement."

54. Cohen, "The Galveston Movement," 119.

55. "Jewish Immigrants," *Galveston Times* (July 2, 1907).

56. *Houston Post*, reprinted as "Texas Has Room," *Jewish Herald* (September 24, 1908).

57. Oscar Leonard, "Come to Texas," *Jewish Herald* (January 6, 1910).

58. "The Galveston Movement," *Jewish Herald* (October 24, 1912).

59. Hyman, 242.

60. Jacob Schiff to Henry Cohen (January 8, 1907), Henry Cohen Papers, AJA.

61. Quoted in Hyman, 243.

62. Jacob Schiff to Henry Cohen (January 8, 1907), Henry Cohen Papers, AJA.

63. David Bressler to Israel Zangwill (October 7, 1907), quoted in Marinbach, 23.

64. Waldman's handwritten comments on a pamphlet published by ITO Central Emigration Bureau for all of Russia in Kiev (1907), in Marinbach, Photoplate 20.

65. Marinbach, 23; "Statistics of Jewish Immigrants Who Arrived at the Port of Galveston, Texas During the Years 1907–1913 inclusive, handled by Jewish Immigrants' Information Bureau of Galveston, Texas," 11, Henry Cohen Papers, AJA.

66. David Bressler to Clement I. Salaman (November 20, 1907), quoted in Marinbach, 23.

67. "Statistics of Jewish Immigrants."

68. Ibid.

69. See, for example, an anti–Galveston Movement article in the *Jewish Daily Forward* and the request by J. Jochelman of the German *Hilfsverein* to Morris Waldman (October 23, 1907) to explain the situation so "that we might be able to protest most strongly against those insinuations," Galveston Movement Records, AJA. For details on the charges against the Galveston Movement, especially as they relate to business and social conditions in Galveston, see Hyman, 244–248. According to Hyman, the Kempner family's use of prison labor in their sugar operations gave credence in some circles to the rumor that the Galveston Movement, which the Kempners actively supported, was to be a source of similar labor.

70. See Esther Panitz, "In Defense of the Jewish Immigrant (1891–1924)."

71. Hyman, 246.

72. Marinbach, 173.

73. Ibid.

74. Gurwitz, vol. 2, 249–251.

75. Stuart Rockoff, "Deep in the Heart of Palestine: Zionism in Early Texas," 95, 97.

76. Gurwitz, vol. 2, 253.

77. Rockoff, 102.

78. Abram L. Geller to *Jewish Press* (August 13, 1980), TJHS Box 3A171, Folder 3. Geller apparently mistitled the newspaper he was addressing: the Jewish paper in Fort Worth is called the *Texas Jewish Post*.

79. I. H. Kempner, *Recalled Recollections*, 58.

80. Ibid.

Chapter Four

1. "Dallas Mob Hangs Negro from Pole at Elks' Arch," *Dallas Morning News*, March 4, 1910; Brian Anderson, "1910: Historical Eyesore; Lynching Turned Downtown Centerpiece into Disgraceful Reminder," www.dallasnews.com/s /dws/spe/2002/hiddenhistory/1901-1925/070002dnhharch.441b518d.html, accessed July 3, 2002.

2. *Dallas Morning News* (March 4, 1910).

3. *Jewish Herald* (March 17, 1910).

4. Edgar Goldberg was my great-grandfather. For a survey of topics covered in the *Herald* during the Goldberg years, see Bryan Edward Stone, "'Texas News for Texas Jews': Edgar Goldberg and the *Texas Jewish Herald*." Much of this chapter previously appeared in this article and in Bryan Edward Stone, "Edgar Goldberg and the *Texas Jewish Herald*: Changing Coverage and Blended Identity." Both are used with permission.

5. *Jewish Herald* (March 17, 1910).

6. Henry Jacob Horowitz, "Just a Reflection," 316.

7. *Jewish Herald* (July 15, 1909; March 17, 1910; February 29, 1912).

8. Anna Bashear, "The Southland," *Jewish Herald* (March 5, 1909); "The American Jew as Statesman," *Jewish Herald* (February 17, 1910).

9. *Jewish Herald* (February 1, 1912).

10. "About the Herald," *Jewish Herald* (July 1, 1909).

11. *Jewish Herald* (January 28, 1909).

12. *Jewish Herald* (February 15, 1912 and May 22, 1924).

13. *Jewish Herald* (July 28, 1910).

14. For the outlines of this debate, see Mark K. Bauman, "A Century of Southern Jewish Historiography," and Mark K. Bauman and Bobbie Malone, "Directions in Southern Jewish History."

15. Edgar Goldberg, "EGO," *Texas Jewish Herald*, January 6, 1927.

16. *Jewish Herald* (December 10, 1908 through January 14, 1909).

17. Author's interview with Edna Friedberg, June 25, 1994.

18. *American Jewish Year Book* 16 (1914–1915): 354; "United States Historical Census Data Browser," http://fisher.lib.virginia.edu/census, accessed December 20, 2002.

19. "Salutatory," *Jewish South* (October 14, 1877).

20. Janice Rothschild Blumberg, "Rabbi Alphabet Browne: The Atlanta Years," 28.

21. Quoted in "Editorial Comment," *Jewish Herald-Voice, Passover Eightieth Anniversary Edition* (April 2, 1988): 4.

22. "Salutatory," *Jewish Herald* (September 24, 1908).

23. Edgar Goldberg to Henry Cohen (July 8, 1924), Henry Cohen Papers, Box 3M241, CAH.

24. *N. W. Ayer & Son's American Newspaper Annual*, volumes for 1910 through 1945.

25. "Adath Yeshurun Synagogue Dedicated," *Jewish Herald* (September 24, 1908).

26. *Jewish Herald* (June 9, 1910).

27. *Jewish Herald* (February 10, 1910).

28. *Jewish Herald* (July 25, 1912).

29. *Jewish Herald* (June 9, 1910); "Local Notes," *Jewish Herald* (August 12, 1909).

30. Mrs. B. Lurie, "Intermarriage," *Jewish Herald* (June 23, 1910); "Parochial Schools," *Jewish Herald* (August 18, 1910); "That Beaumont Ad for a Rabbi," *Jewish Herald* (May 26, 1910); and "Jewish Ostentation," *Jewish Herald* (July 28, 1910).

31. Samuel Rosinger, "Do Your Duty By Leo Frank," *Texas Jewish Herald* (December 17, 1914); "Louis D. Brandeis," *Texas Jewish Herald* (February 3, 1916); and "Jews and the War," *Texas Jewish Herald* (September 3, 1914). David Goldberg, "Pertinent Questions," *Texas Jewish Herald* (September 30, 1920) and "If We Were to Keep to the Point," *Texas Jewish Herald* (July 26, 1923).

32. David Goldberg, "Up in the Air," *Texas Jewish Herald* (June 26, 1924) and "Should a Jew Oppose the Klan?" *Texas Jewish Herald* (August 21, 1924).

33. Although such organizations were usually called "Hebrew Free Loan" societies, the *Herald* reported the founding of a "Jewish Free Loan Society." *Jewish Herald* (January 14, 1909).

34. See, for example, "The Galveston Movement: Movement to Divert Jewish Immigration from New York is Interesting," *Jewish Herald* (November 12, 1908), original credited to "H. J. Haskell in Kansas City Star"; Henry Cohen, "The Galveston Immigration Movement," *Jewish Herald* (February 5, 1909).

35. Oscar Leonard, "Come to Texas," *Jewish Herald* (January 6, 1910). Leonard's affiliation is provided later in "The Settlement of the Immigrant," *Jewish Herald* (January 8, 1914).

36. *Jewish Herald* (February 10, 1910).

37. *Jewish Herald* (December 31, 1908; August 19, 1909; and July 28, 1910).

38. *Texas Jewish Herald* (November 26, 1914).

39. G. George Fox, "The End of an Era," 283.

40. Hollace Ava Weiner, *Jewish Stars in Texas*, 95.

41. Fox, 283.

42. Theodore A. Bingham, "Foreign Criminals in New York," 383.

43. George Kibbe Turner, "The Daughters of the Poor," 45–61.

44. For a balanced study of the actual incidence of Jewish prostitution in American cities, see Edward J. Bristow, *Prostitution and Prejudice: The Jewish Fight Against White Slavery, 1870–1939,* 162.

45. Arthur A. Goren, *New York Jews and the Quest for Community: The Kehillah Experiment, 1908–1922,* 28, 51, 58.

46. *American Hebrew* (October 15, 1915); *Houston Post* (August 24, 1940). For a more complete biographical treatment of Dannenbaum's many social and judicial activities, see Glen Rosenbaum, "Portrait of a Judge."

47. Henry J. Dannenbaum, "That White Slave Traffic," *Jewish Herald* (May 12, 1910).

48. Bristow, 271.

49. "Henry J. Dannenbaum," *Jewish Herald* (May 4, 1911).

50. J. L. Magnes to Henry J. Dannenbaum (August 25, 1911), printed in *Jewish Herald* (March 21, 1912).

51. Bristow, 275.

52. "That 'Big Problem': Extracts from New Orleans B'nai B'rith Day Address By Henry J. Dannenbaum," *Jewish Herald* (February 1, 1912).

53. Fox, 280. See also Bristow, 179, which cites several reports by Texas vice inspectors.

54. "Editorial," *Jewish Herald* (January 18, 1912).

55. "The B'nai B'rith and Henry J. Dannenbaum," *American Hebrew* (February 9, 1912); *Jewish Herald* (December 5, 1912).

56. *Jewish Herald* (February 1, 1912); "A Gentleman from Texas," *American Hebrew* (January 26, 1912); *Jewish Herald* (May 16, 1912).

57. *Jewish Herald* (February 1, 1912).

58. *Jewish Herald* (February 22, 1912).

59. *Jewish Herald* (February 8, 1912).

60. *Jewish Herald* (August 29, 1912, and September 11, 1912).

61. *Jewish Herald-Voice* (January 7, 1938).

Chapter Five

1. "Great Throngs Participate in Colorful Klan Initiation at Fair Park," *Dallas Morning News* (October 25, 1923).

2. "Hope Cottage Is Dedicated By Klan," *Dallas Morning News* (October 25, 1923).

3. Kenneth T. Jackson, *The Ku Klux Klan in the City, 1915–1930,* 79, 265–266n.12.

4. "Imperial Wizard of Klan Says Immigration America's Big Problem," *Dallas Morning News* (October 25, 1923).

5. *Colonel Mayfield's Weekly* (February 25, 1922).

6. Edgar Goldberg to Henry Cohen (July 8, 1924), Henry Cohen Papers, Box 3M 241, CAH. Capitalization as in original.

7. Nancy MacLean, *Behind the Mask of Chivalry: The Making of the Second Ku Klux Klan*, 11.

8. Ward Greene, "Notes for a History of the Klan," 242–243; MacLean, 12.

9. David M. Chalmers, *Hooded Americanism: The History of the Ku Klux Klan*, 32–33.

10. Stanley Frost, *The Challenge of the Klan*, 142.

11. Max Bentley, "The Ku Klux Klan in Texas," 16; *American Jewish Year Book* 31 (1929–1930): 304.

12. Edgar Goldberg, "EGO," *Texas Jewish Herald* (November 9, 1933).

13. Bentley, 14–15.

14. Duncan Aikman, "Prairie Fire," 214.

15. Charles C. Alexander, "Crusade For Conformity: The Ku Klux Klan In Texas, 1920–1927," 28.

16. *Colonel Mayfield's Weekly* (November 24, 1923). When Klan commentators like Mayfield spoke of Catholics, they generally meant white, rather than Hispanic, Catholics. Klansmen rarely acknowledged the state's Mexican-American population. Even their comments about the dangers of immigration tended to focus on European immigration and took little notice of migration across the southern border.

17. Charles C. Alexander, *The Ku Klux Klan in the Southwest*, 25–26.

18. Alexander, "Crusade for Conformity," iv.

19. Ralph Chase, "A Genial Company of Friends."

20. Billie Mayfield Jr., *Chroniclings of Billie.*

21. *Colonel Mayfield's Weekly* (December 31, 1921).

22. *Colonel Mayfield's Weekly* (February 25, 1922).

23. *Houston Chronicle* (October 4, 1921); Chalmers, 42.

24. "Hope Cottage Is Dedicated By Klan," *Dallas Morning News* (October 25, 1923); Chalmers, 42.

25. *Fort Worth Star-Telegram* (August 28, 1921). In an unpublished master's thesis, Danny Lee Ahlfield, who agrees that the Texas Klan practiced "social regulation" rather than overt racism, provides an important caveat: "One disturbing factor in accepting this thesis is the possibility that it is skewed through source selectivity. That is to say, there is no insurance that the white-controlled press reported every action the Klan took against blacks." Ahlfield adds, "Klan actions based primarily on racial prejudice might not have been reflected in that manner in the white press." Danny Ahlfield, "Fraternalism Gone Awry: The Ku Klux Klan in Houston, 1920–1925," vi.

26. Edgar Goldberg to Henry Cohen (July 8, 1924), Henry Cohen Papers, Box 3M241, CAH. Capitalization as in original.

27. *Colonel Mayfield's Weekly* (March 18, 1922).

28. *Dallas Morning News* (March 8 and March 9, 1922). For a detailed analysis of the

Rothblum incident, see Rosalind Benjet, "The Ku Klux Klan and the Jewish Community of Dallas," 145ff.

29. Alexander, "Crusade for Conformity," 40; Jackson, 67.

30. Tommy Stringer, "A Most Unlikely Canaan: A Brief History of the Corsicana Jewish Community," 13.

31. *Texas (100 Percent) American* (June 8, 1923), quoted in Linda Elaine Kilgore, "The Ku Klux Klan and the Press in Texas, 1920–1927," 178. The writer's idiosyncratic spelling, replacing c's with k's, was, according to Kilgore, "an integral part of the mystery which added to the appeal of the organization."

32. Alexander, "Crusade for Conformity," 55.

33. Hollace Ava Weiner, *Jewish Stars in Texas*, 97.

34. Marilynn Wood Hill, "A History of the Jewish Involvement in the Dallas Community," 53.

35. Occasionally, this dramatic touch had unintended consequences. "Although the turning off of the street lights aided in the effect of the parade," reported the *Austin American* after a large Klan procession in 1921, "many persons not close to the line of march had difficulty in reading the signs because of this lack of light." *Austin American* (September 3, 1921).

36. Jackson, 72.

37. Chalmers, 41.

38. Norman D. Brown, *Hood, Bonnet, and Little Brown Jug: Texas Politics, 1921–1928*, 58.

39. Alexander, "Crusade for Conformity," 51–53; Bentley, 19; Chalmers, 41.

40. Bentley, 14.

41. David Ritz, "Inside the Jewish Establishment," *D, The Magazine of Dallas* 2 (November 1975): 53–54.

42. Ritz, 54.

43. *Jewish Monitor* (February 3, 1922), quoted in Weiner, *Jewish Stars in Texas*, 96.

44. Weiner, *Jewish Stars in Texas*, 97.

45. G. George Fox, "The End of an Era," 289.

46. G. George Fox, "Who Is 100 Per Cent American?" 1.

47. Fox, "Who Is 100 Per Cent American?" 4.

48. Fox, "Who Is 100 Per Cent American?" 6.

49. *Jewish Monitor* (May 12, 1922), quoted in Weiner, *Jewish Stars in Texas*, 97.

50. Anne Nathan and Harry I. Cohen, *The Man Who Stayed in Texas*, 254–258.

51. Weiner, *Jewish Stars in Texas*, 74.

52. Gerry Cristol, *A Light in the Prairie: Temple Emanu-El of Dallas, 1872–1997*, 99.

53. *Dallas Morning News* (October 25, 1923).

54. Quoted in Cristol, 100.

55. Ritz, 54 and Cristol, 100. Hollace Ava Weiner describes a similar *contretemps* between Rabbi Maurice Faber of Tyler and that city's Masonic chapter in Weiner, *Jewish Stars in Texas*, 45.

56. Fox, "Who Is 100 Per Cent American?" 6.

57. Quoted in Howard V. Epstein, *Jews In Small Towns: Legends And Legacies*, 668.

58. Lionel Koppman, "What I Remember," 3.

59. Tommy Stringer, "The Zale Corporation: A Texas Success Story," 9–12. See also Lauraine Miller, "The Zale Story: Diamonds for the Rough," 152.

60. Quoted in Epstein, 676, 678.

61. Floyd S. Fierman, *The Schwartz Family of El Paso: The Story of a Pioneer Jewish Family in the Southwest*, 19, 48.

62. Albert L. Granoff, "To America with Love," 64.

63. Hollace Ava Weiner, "Rabbi Sidney Wolf: Harmonizing in Texas," 130.

64. Quoted in Epstein, 670.

65. Quoted in Epstein, 663.

66. Chalmers, 3.

67. Brown, 118–119.

68. Quoted in Chalmers, 43.

69. Brown, 96.

70. Quoted in Brown, 96.

71. Louis Marshall to Henry Cohen (September 20, 1922), Henry Cohen Papers, Box 3M240, CAH.

72. Henry Cohen to Louis Marshall (October 5, 1922), Henry Cohen Papers, Box 3M240, CAH.

73. *Fort Worth Star-Telegram* (August 13, 1922).

74. Stanley Walker, *Texas*, 30.

75. Jim Ferguson, "The Cloven Foot of the Dallas Jew," *Ferguson Forum* (March 15, 1923).

76. Ibid.

77. Harry A. Merfeld, "Pathetic Not the Word," *Jewish Monitor* (March 23, 1923).

78. Jim Ferguson, "The Big Jew Gets Mad," *Ferguson Forum* (April 5, 1923).

79. Quoted in Brown, 216.

80. "Hope Cottage Is Dedicated By Klan," *Dallas Morning News* (October 25, 1923).

81. Quoted in Brown, 213–214.

82. Quoted in Brown, 216.

83. Quoted in Brown, 229. This commentator refers to Imperial Wizard Hiram Evans, candidate Felix Robertson, and Zeke Marvin and George Butcher, two state Klan officials.

84. *Dallas Morning News* (August 17, 1924).

85. *Dallas Morning News* (August 15, 1924) and *Texas (100 Percent) American* (August 8, 1924).

86. Ahlfield, 87.

87. *Dallas Morning News* (August 23, 1924), quoted in Brown, 238.

88. David Goldberg, "Up in the Air," *Texas Jewish Herald* (June 26, 1924).

89. David Goldberg, "Should a Jew Oppose the Klan?" *Texas Jewish Herald* (August 21, 1924).
90. Quoted in Alexander, *The Ku Klux Klan in the Southwest*, 199.
91. *Texas Jewish Herald* (October 23, 1924).
92. *Texas Jewish Herald* (October 30, 1924).
93. *Houston Press* (December 5, 1924), quoted in Ahlfield, 110.

Chapter Six

1. *The Golden Book Of Congregation Adath Yeshurun, 1891–1941*, 15–16.
2. Ava Kahn, ed., *Jewish Voices of the California Gold Rush*, 36.
3. Steven Hertzberg, *Strangers Within the Gate City*, 97, 99.
4. David Ritz, "Inside the Jewish Establishment," *D, The Magazine of Dallas* 2 (November 1975): 111.
5. Irving L. Goldberg, "The Changing Jewish Community of Dallas," 83, 87.
6. Shmuel Geller, *Mazkeres Ahavah*, 32–33.
7. Geller, 47–48.
8. Alexander Ziskind Gurwitz, "Memories of Two Generations," vol. 2, 236. *Ivrit b'ivrit*, or Hebrew in Hebrew, is a method of immersive Hebrew language study with roots in eastern Europe. It has remained popular in the United States and has had a recent resurgence among Jewish educators.
9. Jacob Voorsanger [under pseudonym Koppel Von Bloomborg], "Lone Star Flashes," *American Israelite* (October 19, 1880).
10. Geller, 28; Abraham Schechter, *The Kallah*, 11.
11. Samuel Rosinger, ed., *The Kallah: An Annual Convention of Texas Rabbis, Year Book 5696*, 1.
12. Gurwitz, vol. 2, 277–278. Definitions in parentheses, as in subsequent quotations from Gurwitz, are from the original, provided by the translator.
13. *Congregation Agudath Jacob Golden Jubilee Year Book, 1884–1934*, 29–30.
14. Phyllis Weiner, "Freida Weiner"; "Freida Weiner—The 96 Years Young Dynamo," *Jewish Daily Forward* (November 7, 1986), and Susan Ganc, "Vos Machstu, You-all—or—Yiddish in Houston," *Jewish Herald-Voice* (April 2, 1988), clippings in TJHS Box 3A167, Folder 3.
15. Louis Green, untitled family history.
16. Ruthe Winegarten, notes from interview with Freida Weiner (May 2, 1988), TJHS Box 3A167, Folder 3.
17. Gerry Cristol, *A Light in the Prairie*, 78–79; Anne Nathan Cohen, *The Centenary History, Congregation Beth Israel of Houston, Texas, 1854–1954*, 47.
18. *American Jewish Year Book* 13 (1911–1912): 267; 26 (1924–1925): 575; and 42 (1940–1941): 228.
19. Gurwitz, vol. 2, 224.
20. Gurwitz, vol. 2, 215–217.

21. Gurwitz, vol. 2, 276, 281.

22. Gurwitz, vol. 2, 279–280.

23. Harriet Denise Joseph, "The Brownsville Jewish Community: From Generation to Generation," 5–6.

24. Albert L. Granoff, "To America with Love," 169–171.

25. Minutes of Temple Beth-El (August 1920), quoted in William Sajowitz, "History of Reform Judaism in San Antonio, Texas, 1874–1945," 68.

26. J. M. Rosenberg to Members of Agudath Jacob (November 10, 1936), Congregation Agudath Jacob (Waco) Papers, AJA.

27. Isaac H. Kempner, "Response to American Jewish Archives Autobiographical Questionnaire" (February 9, 1953), AJA Small Collections.

28. Anne Nathan and Harry I. Cohen, *The Man Who Stayed in Texas*, 281.

29. Henry Cohen to Israel Friedlander (June 10, 1942), Henry Cohen Papers, AJA.

30. For more on Zionism in Texas and the Beth Israel Revolt, see Stuart Rockoff, "Deep in the Heart of Palestine: Zionism in Early Texas," and Howard R. Greenstein, *Turning Point: Zionism and Reform Judaism*, 51–71.

31. The population of Harris County, which Houston dominates, was 186,667 in 1920 and 528,961 in 1940. U.S. Census, as reported in "United States Historical Census Data Browser," http://fisher.lib.virginia.edu/census, accessed January 30, 2003.

32. Cohen, *Centenary History*, 40, 53.

33. Louis J. Marchiafava and David Courtwright, interview with Robert I. Kahn, 22.

34. Author's interview with Robert I. Kahn, October 7, 1995.

35. Leopold Meyer, "Report of the President on Behalf of the Board of Trustees," in *Annual Report, Congregation Beth Israel, Houston, Texas*, 24.

36. Israel Friedlander, "Report of the Policy Formulation Committee" (May 30, 1944), 1–2, Congregation Beth Israel (Houston) Papers, AJA.

37. Quoted in Greenstein, 19.

38. Abraham Franzblau, *Reform Judaism in the Large Cities—A Survey*, quoted in Greenstein, 26.

39. Quoted in Greenstein, 29.

40. Untitled declaration of principles (June 22, 1942), Louis Wolsey Papers, AJA.

41. "Statement of Principles," American Council for Judaism Papers.

42. "An Inventory to the American Council for Judaism Collection," American Council for Judaism Papers, AJA.

43. Carolyn Lipson-Walker, "'Shalom Y'all': The Folklore and Culture of Southern Jews," 117.

44. "Membership List" (November 30, 1943), American Council for Judaism Papers, AJA.

45. "Report of Replies for Atlantic City Meeting" (May 27, 1942), and telegram,

Henry Cohen to Louis Wolsey (June 1, 1942), American Council for Judaism Papers, AJA.

46. Henry Barnston to The Convention of American Rabbis (May 26, 1942), Louis Wolsey Papers, AJA.

47. Diane Ravitch, "The Educational Critic in New York," 390.

48. Israel Friedlander, "A Chronological Listing of Bibliographical Events and Circumstances Which Led to the Creation by Beth Israel Congregation of a 'Policy Formulation Committee,'" (May 30, 1944), 10, Congregation Beth Israel (Houston) Papers, AJA.

49. William M. Nathan to Jacob R. Marcus (December 13, 1954), Congregation Beth Israel (Houston) Papers, AJA.

50. "Members of Congregation Beth Israel" (August 4, 1943), Congregation Beth Israel (Houston) Papers, AJA.

51. Meyer, "Report of the President," 23–24.

52. "Basic Principles of Congregation Beth Israel, Houston, Texas. Adopted at a special meeting of the membership of the Congregation, held November 23, 1943," Congregation Beth Israel (Houston) Papers, AJA.

53. Ibid.

54. "Resolution Adopted by the Members of Hebrew Congregation Beth Israel of Houston, Texas (An American Reform Congregation) at a Special Meeting of the Congregation Held on November 23, 1943," appended to letter from Leopold L. Meyer to Adolph Rosenberg (January 12, 1944), Congregation Beth Israel (Houston) Papers, AJA.

55. William M. Nathan, "Mr. President and Members of Beth Israel" (November 23, 1943), Congregation Beth Israel (Houston) Papers, AJA.

56. Robert Kahn to Board Members of Congregation Beth Israel (March 1, 1944), Congregation Beth Israel (Houston) Papers, AJA. The *Jewish Herald-Voice* reprinted Kahn's letter in its entirety as "Chaplain Robt. I. Kahn Tenders His Resignation to Temple Beth Israel," *Jewish Herald-Voice* (April 13, 1944).

57. *Congregation Emanu El, Houston, Texas: The First Fifty Years, An Adventure of the Spirit, 1944–1994* (Houston, 1994).

58. Solomon Freehof to Leopold Meyer (March 15, 1944), in Friedlander, "Report of the Policy Formulation Committee," Exhibit 2-X.

59. Abram V. Goodman to William Nathan (December 13, 1943), Congregation Beth Israel (Houston) Papers, AJA.

60. "Judaism in Houston, Texas," *Congress Weekly* (November 19, 1943), in Friedlander, "Report of the Policy Formulation Committee," Exhibit 2-E; "Storm Over Zion," *Time* (January 17, 1944): 38.

61. Stephen S. Wise, "The Shame of Houston," 5.

62. Hyman Judah Schachtel to Jacob R. Marcus (December 9, 1968), Congregation Beth Israel (Houston) Papers, AJA.

Chapter Seven

1. Irving L. Goldberg, "The Changing Jewish Community of Dallas," 84.

2. "The German Police and Anti Semitic Hooliganism in Germany," *Texas Jewish Herald* (October 25, 1928).

3. Edgar Goldberg, "EGO," "When Hitler's Nazis Come to Houston!" *Texas Jewish Herald* (December 7, 1933).

4. Ibid.

5. Ibid.

6. "New Anti-Semitic Sheet In Houston," *Texas Jewish Herald* (January 4, 1934).

7. Howard M. Sachar, *A History of the Jews in America*, 485.

8. David S. Wyman, *The Abandonment of the Jews: America and the Holocaust, 1941–1945*, x.

9. Sachar, 478.

10. Kathryn Diane Cain, "'In Your Own State, In Your Own Community': Jewish and Non-Jewish Texans' Reactions to the Early Days of the Holocaust, 1933–1939," 53.

11. *Congressional Record* (December 18, 1931): 845–847, quoted in Cain, 56.

12. Quoted in Arthur Morse, *While Six Million Died: A Chronicle of American Apathy*, 145.

13. *Congressional Record* (March 10, 1936): 1367–1368, quoted in Cain, 57.

14. Nathan and Cohen, *The Man Who Stayed In Texas*, 306–307.

15. Cain, 48.

16. My thanks to Valery Bazarov of HIAS, who spoke to me at length about the difficulty of recovering statistics on Jewish refugees in the 1930s and 1940s.

17. I corresponded, for example, with Barbara Fagin of the Dallas Holocaust Memorial Center and Martin Goldman of the U.S. Holocaust Memorial Museum in Washington, D.C., neither of whom could provide figures on refugees to Texas. "There is no way for sure to know when they came, if [Texas] was the first place they went to, etc.," Mr. Goldman wrote in an e-mail. He was able to tell me that there are about nine hundred Holocaust survivors currently living in Texas, but it is, of course, impossible to derive from that figure any estimate of how many arrived in Texas in any particular era. Leslie Wagner of the Dallas Jewish Historical Society uncovered some materials relating to Jewish survivors arriving in Dallas after the war but could not locate statistics on prewar refugees.

18. Cain, 66.

19. Robert Dallek, *Lone Star Rising: Lyndon Johnson and His Times, 1908–1960*, 169–170; Claudia Anderson, "Lyndon B. Johnson: Friend to the Austin Jewish Community," 26. Both of these accounts rely on original research by Louis Stanislaus Gomolak, "Prologue: LBJ's Foreign Affairs Background, 1908–1948."

20. Quoted in Dallek, 170.

21. Lady Bird Johnson, *A White House Diary*, 28.

22. Lorraine Wulfe to "Ruthie" (September 20, 1994), author's collection, provided by Robert I. Kahn.

23. Author's interview with Robert I. Kahn, October 7, 1995.

24. Fierman, *The Schwartz Family of El Paso*, 34. For details on another El Paso effort, orchestrated by Polish immigrant Emil Reisel, see Mimi Reisel Gladstein and Sylvia Deener Cohen, "El Paso: The Wild West Welcomes Holocaust Survivors."

25. Nathan and Cohen, 316–317.

26. Marguerite Meyer Marks, "Integration of the Jew and the Non-Jew in Dallas."

27. Marguerite Meyer Marks, "Memoirs of My Family."

28. Winegarten and Schechter, *Deep in the Heart*, 153.

29. Cristol, *A Light In The Prairie*, 130–132.

30. "World War II, Texans In," *The Handbook of Texas Online*, www.tshaonline .org/handbook/online/articles/WW/qdw2.html, accessed July 1, 2002.

31. Epstein, *Jews in Small Towns*, 677.

32. Weiner, "Rabbi Sidney Wolf," 128.

33. Clarice F. Pollard, "WAACS in Texas during the Second World War," 64.

34. "Camp Barkeley," *The Handbook of Texas Online*, www.tshaonline.org/handbook /online/articles/CC/qbc2.html, accessed July 2, 2002; "Abilene, Texas," *The Handbook of Texas Online*, www.tshaonline.org/handbook/online/articles/AA /hda1.html, accessed July 2, 2002.

35. Mrs. Leonard Goldblatt to unknown addressee (February 4, 1946), TJHS Box 3A169, Folder 3.

36. Mrs. Leonard Goldblatt; Roy A. Jones II, "Returning Respect: Jewish Families of Temple Mizpah Donate Jeweled Curtain to MOA [Museums of Abilene]," *Abilene Reporter-News* (November 7, 1992).

37. Suzanne Campbell, interviewed in Brian Cohen, dir., *At Home on the Range: Jewish Life in Texas (Beyond the Big Cities)*; *Temple Mizpah: 50 Years Remembered*, 9.

38. *Temple Mizpah*, 12–13.

39. Mr. and Mrs. M. Lustberg to Temple Mizpah (October 6, 1943), in *Temple Mizpah*, 14.

40. Leonard Dinnerstein, *America and the Survivors of the Holocaust*, 283–284.

41. Quoted in Weiner, "Rabbi Sidney Wolf," 128.

42. Ruthe Winegarten, notes from interview with Eva Silberman (May 1988), TJHS Box 3A169, Folder 6; Winegarten and Schechter, 212.

43. Irving L. Goldberg and Mrs. Jack Woolf to Boards of Directors, Jewish Welfare Federation and Jewish Family Service (June 13, 1950), Levi Olan Papers, AJA.

44. "Channel Your Giving Along These Lines" (1952), Jewish Federation of Greater Dallas Records, Dallas Jewish Historical Society Archives.

45. Granoff, "To America with Love," 179.

46. Winegarten, notes from interview with Eva Silberman.

47. Dorothy Rabinowitz, *New Lives: Survivors of the Holocaust Living in America*, 114.

48. Rabinowitz, 115–116.

49. Rabinowitz, 116.

50. Rabinowitz, 118–119.

51. Rabinowitz, 124.

52. Mike Jacobs, *Holocaust Survivor: Mike Jacobs' Triumph Over Tragedy, a Memoir*, 132–133.

53. Jacobs, 133.

54. Ibid.

55. Jacobs, 137.

56. Jacobs, 141–142.

57. Jacobs, 144.

58. See, for example, Waveney Ann Moore, "From Despair, Hope: Building on an Idea," *St. Petersburg Times* (February 15, 1998) on the creation of the Tampa Bay Holocaust Memorial Museum and Educational Center. On the El Paso Holocaust Museum and Study Center, see Gladstein and Cohen.

59. Winegarten and Schechter, 161.

60. Quoted in Cristol, 140.

61. Cristol, 140.

62. Samuel Rosinger, "Deep in the Heart of Texas," 125–126.

63. Rosinger, 137–138.

64. Milton Rosenbaum, "Remembering Fort Worth," 7.

65. Ravitch, "The Educational Critic in New York," 390–391.

66. Rosenbaum, "Remembering Fort Worth," 7–8.

67. Walter Cohen, "1948–1949: A Volunteer Looks Back," 1–2; Walter Cohen, "Statement by Walter Cohen."

68. *Jewish Herald-Voice* (March 18, 1942).

69. Cristol, 142.

70. Goldberg, "The Changing Jewish Community of Dallas," 93–94.

71. Granoff, 224.

72. Bertha Bender, "I Remember When."

73. Betty Ewing, "A Delight at 101: Bertha Bender's Life Was Destined to Grow with the State She Adopted," *Houston Chronicle* (September 6, 1989).

74. "Cowboy Zionist," *Jerusalem Post* (September 11, 1957).

75. Ewing; Merlon Montgomery Jr., "Charlie Bender—A Man To Remember," *Breckenridge American* (August 4, 1970).

76. "Cowboy Zionist."

77. Kohlberg, *Letters of Ernst Kohlberg*, 39.

78. Ravitch, 391.

Chapter Eight

1. "Negroes in Sit-Down at 2d Houston Store," *Houston Chronicle* (March 5, 1960); Thomas R. Cole, *"No Color Is My Kind": The Life of Eldrewey Stearns and the Integration of Houston,* 26; Gregory Curtis, "The First Protester," *Texas Monthly* (June 1997): 7.

2. "Joseph Weingarten," *The Handbook of Texas Online,* www.tshaonline.org /handbook/online/articles/WW/fwe15.html, accessed July 12, 2002; Cole, 26; Winegarten and Schechter, *Deep in the Heart,* 212.

3. "Negroes in Sit-Down"; Cole, 1, 29; Curtis, 7.

4. Cole, 40.

5. "165 Years of Historic Houston."

6. Quoted in Jim Schutze, *The Accommodation: The Politics of Race in an American City,* 87.

7. Stanley Marcus, *Minding The Store: A Memoir,* 369.

8. Clive Webb, *Fight Against Fear,* 44.

9. For discussions of the rabbinic role in southern civil rights activity, see Mark K. Bauman and Berkley Kalin, eds. *The Quiet Voices: Southern Rabbis and Black Civil Rights, 1880s to 1990s.*

10. Floyd S. Fierman, "The Jew and the Negro," Floyd S. Fierman Papers, AJA.

11. "'The Jewish Role in Desegregating Dallas': Meeting of the Dallas Jewish Historical Society, January 6, 1998."

12. Karl Preuss, "Rabbi David Jacobson and the Integration of San Antonio," 146.

13. Stephen J. Whitfield, "Commercial Passions: The Southern Jew as Businessman," 353.

14. Arnold Shankman, *Ambivalent Friends: Afro-Americans View the Immigrant,* 120, 122.

15. Mike Jacobs, *Holocaust Survivor,* 137–138.

16. Bettie M. Patterson, "My Neighborhood in the 1950s and 1960s," http://hti .math.uh.edu/curriculum/units/1999/04/99.04.04.pdf, accessed March 16, 2009. This document is included online in a public school curriculum. The original source is unknown.

17. Michael Phillips, *White Metropolis: Race, Ethnicity, and Religion in Dallas, 1841– 2001,* 146.

18. Warren Leslie, *Dallas Public and Private* (1964), quoted in Schutze, 58.

19. Marilynn Wood Hill, "A History of the Jewish Involvement in the Dallas Community," 81.

20. Schutze, 57. Schutze is paraphrasing Bloom's original remark.

21. David Ritz, "Inside the Jewish Establishment," *D, The Magazine of Dallas* 2 (November 1975): 108; Dorothy Jacobus, "Growing Up in Dallas," 2; John Bainbridge, *The Super-Americans,* 142.

22. Hill, 120n.105.

23. Quoted in Schutze, 97.

24. Ritz, 109.

25. Julius Schepps to Mr. and Mrs. James F. Chambers Jr. (September 24, 1965), Julius Schepps Papers, AJA.

26. Leon Harris, *Merchant Princes: An Intimate History of Jewish Families Who Built Great Department Stores*, 127.

27. Marcus, 368–369.

28. Craig Hines, "American Wonder in the Heart of Texas," *Houston Chronicle* (January 26, 2002).

29. Floyd S. Fierman, *The Schwartz Family of El Paso*, 48; Hollace Ava Weiner, "Rabbi Sidney Wolf," 130.

30. Julius Schepps to Jim Dunnington (July 17, 1963), Julius Schepps Papers, AJA.

31. Dallas Restaurant Committee for Peaceful Integration to Julius Schepps, n.d., Julius Schepps Papers, AJA.

32. "1963, May 28th," Julius Schepps Papers, AJA.

33. Jack B. Krueger to Julius Schepps, June 19, 1963, Julius Schepps Papers, AJA.

34. Interview with Sam Bloom by Joan Loeb and Gerry Cristol (March 26, 1974), quoted in Gerry Cristol, *A Light in the Prairie*, 187.

35. *Dallas at the Crossroads*, Dallas Public Library.

36. Ibid.

37. Levi Olan, *Levi Olan: Oral History Interviews*, 16–17.

38. Levi Olan interviews (1972, 1974), quoted in Cristol, 156.

39. Ritz, 111.

40. Derro Evans, "Rabbi Levi Olan: A Conversation," *Sunday Magazine, Dallas Times Herald* (October 11, 1970), and James Street, "Dazzling Dallas," *Holiday* (March 1953): 102–119, quoted in Weiner, *Jewish Stars in Texas*, 219–220.

41. Adolphus Cummings to the Editor, *Dallas Morning News* (November 8, 1984), quoted in Cristol, 184.

42. Ritz, 111.

43. Quoted in Webb, 206.

44. Olan, *Oral History Interviews*, 16.

45. Quoted in Ritz, 111.

46. Weiner, *Jewish Stars in Texas*, 229.

47. Levi Olan, "In Memoriam—President John F. Kennedy," Notes for Address (November 25, 1963), Levi Olan Papers, AJA.

48. Levi Olan, "From Birmingham to Memphis," Notes for Address (April 28, 1968), Levi Olan Papers, AJA.

49. Olan, *Oral History Interviews*, 30–31.

50. Phillips, 147.

51. Weiner, *Jewish Stars in Texas*, 228.

52. Cristol, 189.

53. Temple Emanu-El Board Minutes (January 29, 1963), quoted in Cristol, 190; Report of the Temple Emanu-El Pre-School Project (November 23, 1965), quoted in Cristol, 191.
54. Cristol, 191–192.
55. Quoted in Cristol, 192.
56. Moshe Cahana, "Confession and Repentance," Address to Metropolitan Houston Conference on Religion and Race (June 25, 1963), in "Proceedings of the Steering Committee," Metropolitan Houston Conference on Religion and Race Papers, AJA.
57. Ibid.
58. Preuss, 146.
59. Preuss, 149.
60. Quoted in Preuss, 149–150.
61. Milton Rosenbaum, "Remembering Fort Worth," 2–3.
62. Rosenbaum, 5.
63. Rosenbaum, 5–6.

Chapter Nine

1. In 1990, Austin had a population of 465,622, which grew to 656,562 by 2000. *The World Almanac and Book of Facts, 2003*, 403.
2. Helen Thorpe, "Austin, We Have a Problem," *New York Times* (August 20, 2000).
3. Juan R. Palomo and Stephen Pounds, "Dearth of Jewish Amenities Worries IBM Transferees," *Austin American-Statesman* (November 20, 1995).
4. *American Jewish Year Book* 91 (1991): 218, and 101 (2001): 270.
5. Congregation Beth Israel homepage, www.bethisrael.org, accessed March 9, 2003; Starita Smith, "Jewish Congregations Consider Dell Campus 'Wonderful,'" *Austin American-Statesman* (May 27, 1997).
6. Max Garrone and Anthony York, "Republicans Rebuff Bush," *Salon*, http://archive.salon.com/politics2000/feature/2000/03/16/trail_mix/index.html, accessed March 10, 2003. For more on Austin Jewry and the creation of the Dell JCC, see Cathy Schechter, "Forty Acres and a Shul: 'It's Easy as Dell.'"
7. *American Jewish Year Book* 106 (2006): 159–160, 184–185.
8. Jewish Federation of Greater Houston, "2001 Study of the Jewish Community of Houston," www.jewishdatabank.org, accessed October 16, 2006.
9. Nathan Levy, "Seeking Unity in the Age of Diversity," *Austin American-Statesman* (May 12, 1996).
10. Sheldon Zimmerman, Speech to the Dallas Jewish Historical Society.
11. Mimi Swartz, "The Promised Land," *Texas Monthly* (April 1994): 109. Similarly, the rabbi of San Antonio's Temple Beth-El told an audience in 2004 that "[w]hen I visit family and friends up north and tell them that I live in Texas,

their instantaneous response is: 'Gee, I didn't know that there were any Jews down there.'" From "The Uniqueness of Texas Jews: Sermon given April 30, 2004, by Rabbi Samuel M. Stahl," www.beth-elsa.org/sms043004.htm, accessed January 6, 2009.

12. Richard M. Bernard and Bradley R. Rice, eds., *Sunbelt Cities: Politics And Growth Since World War II*, 11.

13. *The World Almanac and Book of Facts, 2003*, 399; "Texas: Population of Counties by Decennial Census, 1900 to 1990," www.census.gov/population/cencounts /tx190090.txt, accessed February 19, 2003; "American Fact Finder," http:// factfinder.census.gov, accessed February 19, 2003.

14. *American Jewish Year Book* 43 (1941–1942): 656; 52 (1951): 17–21; 101 (2001): 259– 260; and 106 (2006): 159–160. Following the U.S. Census Bureau, the "Northeast" includes Maine, New Hampshire, Vermont, Massachusetts, Connecticut, Rhode Island, Pennsylvania, New Jersey, and New York; the "Midwest" includes North Dakota, South Dakota, Nebraska, Kansas, Minnesota, Iowa, Missouri, Wisconsin, Illinois, Michigan, Indiana, and Ohio. Following Bernard and Rice (p. 7), the "Sunbelt" consists of North Carolina, South Carolina, Georgia, Florida, Alabama, Mississippi, Tennessee, Arkansas, Louisiana, Oklahoma, Texas, New Mexico, Arizona, and California.

15. *American Jewish Year Book* 106 (2006): 184–185; Jewish Federation of Greater Houston, "2001 Study of the Jewish Community of Houston," 37.

16. Deborah Dash Moore, *To the Golden Cities*, 27.

17. *The World Almanac and Book of Facts, 2003*, 399; *American Jewish Year Book* 43 (1941–1942): 656; 52 (1951): 17–21; 81 (1981): 172; and 101 (2001): 259–260.

18. Ibid.

19. *American Jewish Year Book* 106 (2006): 159–160.

20. Moore, 27.

21. John Bainbridge, *The Super-Americans*, 19, 329.

22. Zimmerman, Speech to the Dallas Jewish Historical Society.

23. "Church Affiliation Change: 1990 to 2000," *Texas Almanac 2006–2007*, 520–521.

24. Association of Religion Data Archives, www.thearda.com/mapsReports, accessed October 10, 2006.

25. U.S. Census Bureau, "Table 1. Urban and Rural Population: 1900 to 1990," www .census.gov/population/censusdata/urpop0090.txt, accessed October 30, 2006; "Rural Population as a Percent of State Total By State, 2000," www.nemw .org/poprural.htm, accessed October 30, 2006.

26. The works under consideration are Max Apple, *Roommates*; David Applefield, *Once Removed: A Novel*; Barbara Barrie, *Lone Star*; David Carb, *Sunrise in the West*; Dede Fox Ducharme, *The Treasure in the Tiny Blue Tin*; Kinky Friedman, *Greenwich Killing Time* and subsequent titles; Mark Harelik, *The Immigrant* and *The Legacy*; Jan Siegel Hart, *Hanna, the Immigrant, The Many Adventures of Minnie*, and *More Adventures of Minnie*; Amy Hest, *The Private Notebook of Katie Roberts, Age 11*; Sharon Kahn, *Fax Me a Bagel* and subsequent titles; Lois Ruby, *Swindle-*

top; Jake Saunders and Howard Waldrop, *The Texas-Israeli War: 1999*; and S. L. Wisenberg, *The Sweetheart is In: Stories*.

27. Hart, *The Many Adventures of Minnie*, 63.

28. Hest, 8.

29. Carb, 335–336, 340.

30. Carb, 342.

31. Seth L. Wolitz, "Bifocality in Jewish Identity in the Texas-Jewish Experience," 198–199.

32. Harelik, *The Immigrant*, 39.

33. Harelik, *The Legacy*, 6, 7.

34. Harelik, *The Legacy*, 2.

35. Harelik, *The Legacy*, 33.

36. Harelik, *The Legacy*, 34.

37. Harelik, *The Legacy*, 63–64.

38. In compiling these observations, I have relied on Robin W. Winks, ed., *Detective Fiction: A Collection of Critical Essays*, especially the essays by W. H. Auden, George Grella, and Robin Winks.

39. Winks, 8.

40. Kinky Friedman, *Armadillos and Old Lace*, 3.

41. Kinky Friedman, *Road Kill*, 17.

42. Friedman, *Road Kill*, 25.

43. Friedman, *Road Kill*, 26.

44. Kinky Friedman, *Elvis, Jesus and Coca-Cola*, 6.

45. Friedman, *Elvis, Jesus and Coca-Cola*, 124.

46. Friedman, *Greenwich Killing Time*, 16; Kinky Friedman, *The Love Song of J. Edgar Hoover*, 43; Friedman, *Armadillos and Old Lace*, 24.

47. Friedman, *Elvis, Jesus and Coca-Cola*, 55.

48. Friedman, *Greenwich Killing Time*, 16.

49. Friedman, *Greenwich Killing Time*, 33.

50. Friedman, *Road Kill*, 92.

51. Friedman, *Road Kill*, 70.

52. Friedman, *Road Kill*, 104.

53. Friedman, *Road Kill*, 92.

54. Sharon Kahn, *Fax Me a Bagel*, 11.

55. Kahn, *Fax Me a Bagel*, 17.

56. Kahn, *Fax Me a Bagel*, 24, 22.

57. Kahn, *Fax Me a Bagel*, 17.

58. Kahn, *Fax Me a Bagel*, 13.

59. Kahn, *Fax Me a Bagel*, 24–25.

60. Kahn, *Fax Me a Bagel*, 39.

61. Kahn, *Fax Me a Bagel*, 16–17.

62. Sharon Kahn, *Never Nosh a Matzo Ball*, 59.

BIBLIOGRAPHY

Archival Collections

American Council for Judaism Papers (Manuscript Collection 17). Jacob Rader Marcus Center of the American Jewish Archives, Cincinnati Campus, Hebrew Union College–Jewish Institute of Religion [AJA].

Cohen, Henry Papers (Manuscript Collection 263). AJA.

Cohen, Henry Papers. Center for American History, University of Texas at Austin [CAH].

Congregation Agudath Jacob (Waco) Papers (Small Collection 12655). AJA.

Congregation Beth Israel (Houston) Papers (Manuscript Collection 132). AJA.

de Haas, Jacob Papers (Microfilm 1336). AJA.

Fierman, Floyd S. Papers (Manuscript Collection 649). AJA.

Galveston Immigration Plan Records (Record Group #I-90). American Jewish Historical Society [AJHS].

Galveston Movement Records (Small Collection 3845). AJA.

Jewish Federation of Greater Dallas Records. Dallas Jewish Historical Society Archives.

Leeser, Isaac Papers (Manuscript Collection 197). AJA.

Metropolitan Houston Conference on Religion and Race Papers (Small Collection 2850). AJA.

Olan, Levi Papers (Manuscript Collection 181). AJA.

Schepps, Julius Papers (Small Collection 10825). AJA.

Texas Jewish Historical Society Records, 1838, 1884–1996 [TJHS]. CAH.

Wolsey, Louis Papers (Manuscript Collection 15). AJA.

References

Adler, Cyrus, ed. *Jacob H. Schiff: His Life and Letters*. Garden City, N.Y.: Doubleday, Doran and Company, 1928.

Ahlfield, Danny Lee. "Fraternalism Gone Awry: The Ku Klux Klan in Houston, 1920–1925." Master's thesis, University of Texas at Austin, 1984.

Aikman, Duncan. "Prairie Fire." *American Mercury* 6 (October 1925): 214.

Alexander, Charles C. "Crusade for Conformity: The Ku Klux Klan in Texas, 1920–1927." PhD dissertation, University of Texas at Austin, 1959.

———. *The Ku Klux Klan in the Southwest*. Lexington: University of Kentucky Press, 1966.

Alexander, Fanny Weil. "Charles and Sarah Weil." TJHS Box 3A167, Folder 3.

American Jewish Historical Society, *American Jewish Desk Reference*. New York: Random House, 1999.

American Jewish Year Book. Philadelphia: Jewish Publication Society of America, 1899–present.

Anderson, Claudia. "Lyndon B. Johnson: Friend to the Austin Jewish Community." *Among Friends of LBJ* 70 (January 2003): 24–27.

Annual Report, Congregation Beth Israel, Houston, Texas. Houston, 1944.

Anzaldúa, Gloria. *Borderlands/La Frontera*. San Francisco: Aunt Lute Books, 1987.

Apple, Max. *Roommates*. New York: Warner Books, 1994.

Applefield, David. *Once Removed: A Novel*. Oakville, Ont.: Mosaic Press, 1996.

Aron, Stephen. "Lessons in Conquest: Towards a Greater Western History." *Pacific Historical Review* 63 (May 1994): 125–147.

Bainbridge, John. *The Super-Americans*. New York: Holt, Rinehart and Winston, 1972 [1961].

Barrie, Barbara. *Lone Star*. New York: Delacorte Press, 1990.

Barth, Fredrik, ed. *Ethnic Groups and Boundaries: The Social Organization of Culture Difference*. Boston: Little, Brown and Co., 1969.

Bauman, Mark K. "A Century of Southern Jewish Historiography." *American Jewish Archives Journal* 59 (2007): 3–78.

Bauman, Mark K. and Berkley Kalin, eds. *The Quiet Voices: Southern Rabbis and Black Civil Rights, 1880s to 1990s*. Tuscaloosa: University of Alabama Press, 1997.

Bauman, Mark K. and Bobbie Malone. "Directions in Southern Jewish History." *American Jewish History* 85 (September 1997): 193–195.

Bender, Bertha. "I Remember When" (November 1983). TJHS Box 3A164, Folder 2.

Benjet, Rosalind. "The Ku Klux Klan and the Jewish Community of Dallas, 1921–1923." *Southern Jewish History* 6 (2003): 133–162.

Bentley, Max. "The Ku Klux Klan in Texas." *McClure's Magazine* 57 (May 1924): 11–21.

Bernard, Richard M. and Bradley R. Rice, eds. *Sunbelt Cities: Politics and Growth Since World War II*. Austin: University of Texas Press, 1983.

Best, Gary Dean. "Jacob H. Schiff's Galveston Movement: An Experiment in Immigration Deflection, 1907–1914." *American Jewish Archives* 30 (April 1978): 43–79.

Biderman, Rose G. *They Came to Stay: The Story of the Jews of Dallas.* Austin: Eakin Press, 2002.

Blumberg, Janice Rothschild. "Rabbi Alphabet Browne: The Atlanta Years." *Southern Jewish History* 5 (2002): 1–42.

Bristow, Edward J. *Prostitution and Prejudice: The Jewish Fight Against White Slavery, 1870–1939.* New York: Schocken Books, 1983.

Brown, Norman D. *Hood, Bonnet, and Little Brown Jug: Texas Politics, 1921–1928.* College Station: Texas A&M University Press, 1984.

Cain, Kathryn Diane. "'In Your Own State, In Your Own Community': Jewish and Non-Jewish Texans' Reactions to the Early Days of the Holocaust, 1933–1939." Master's thesis, Southwest Texas State University, 1998.

Campbell, Randolph B. *Gone to Texas: A History of the Lone Star State.* New York: Oxford University Press, 2003.

Carb, David. *Sunrise in the West.* New York: Brewer, Warren and Putnam, 1931.

Carrington, Evelyn M., ed. *Women in Early Texas.* Austin: Jenkins Publishing Company, 1975.

Chalmers, David M. *Hooded Americanism: The History of the Ku Klux Klan.* Durham: Duke University Press, 1987.

Chase, Ralph. "A Genial Company of Friends: Presented to the Texas Jewish Historical Society" (March 13, 1993). TJHS Box 3A173, Folder 1.

Chyet, Stanley F., ed. *Lives and Voices: A Collection of American Jewish Memoirs.* Philadelphia: Jewish Publication Society of America, 1972.

Cohen, Anne Nathan. *The Centenary History, Congregation Beth Israel of Houston, Texas, 1854–1954.* [Houston, 1954.]

Cohen, Brian, dir. *At Home on the Range: Jewish Life in Texas (Beyond the Big Cities).* New York: Carousel Film and Video, 1999.

Cohen, Henry. "The Galveston Movement: Its First Year." *Western States Jewish History* 18 (January 1986): 114–119.

———. "Henry Castro, Pioneer and Colonist." *Publications of the American Jewish Historical Society* 5 (1897): 39–43.

———. "Settlement of the Jews in Texas." *Publications of the American Jewish Historical Society* 2 (1894): 139–156.

Cohen, Henry, II. *Kindler of Souls: Rabbi Henry Cohen of Texas.* Austin: University of Texas Press, 2007.

Cohen, Martin A. "The Autobiography of Luis De Carvajal, the Younger." *American Jewish Historical Quarterly* 55 (March 1966): 277–318.

———. *The Martyr.* Philadelphia: Jewish Publication Society, 1973.

Cohen, Walter. "1948–1949: A Volunteer Looks Back." TJHS Box 3A172, Folder 5.

———. "Statement by Walter Cohen." TJHS Box 3A164, Folder 4.

Cole, Thomas R. *"No Color Is My Kind": The Life of Eldrewey Stearns and the Integration of Houston.* Austin: University of Texas Press, 1997.

Congregation Agudath Jacob Golden Jubilee Year Book, 1884–1934. Waco: Congregation Agudath Jacob, 1934.

Congregation Emanu El, Houston, Texas: The First Fifty Years, An Adventure of the Spirit, 1944–1994. Houston, 1994.

"Constitution of the Republic of Texas, The. March 17, 1836." In Wallace, *Documents of Texas History,* 105.

Cristol, Gerry. *A Light in the Prairie: Temple Emanu-El of Dallas, 1872–1997.* Fort Worth: Texas Christian University Press, 1998.

Dallas at the Crossroads. Dallas Film Council, 1961. Dallas Public Library.

Dallek, Robert. *Lone Star Rising: Lyndon Johnson and His Times, 1908–1960.* New York: Oxford University Press, 1991.

Davidson, Gabriel. *Our Jewish Farmers and the Story of the Jewish Agricultural Society.* New York: L. B. Fischer, 1943.

Davidson, Gabriel and Edward A. Goodwin. "A Unique Agricultural Colony." Reprinted from *The Reflex* (May 1928). AJA Small Collection 2375.

Day, Donald. "The Americanism of Harris Kempner." *Southwest Review* 30 (Winter 1945): 125–128.

de Cordova, Jacob. *Lecture on Texas Delivered by Mr. J. De Cordova, at Philadelphia, New York, Mount Holly, Brooklyn and Newark. Also a paper read by him before the New York Geographical Society, April 15th, 1858.* Philadelphia: Ernest Crozet, 1858.

———. *Texas: Her Resources and Her Public Men.* Philadelphia: J. B. Lippincott, 1858.

Dearen, Patrick. "Home on the Range: Mayer Halff's Cattle Empire." In Weiner and Roseman, *Lone Stars of David,* 50–63.

Dinnerstein, Leonard. *America and the Survivors of the Holocaust.* New York: Columbia University Press, 1982.

Dreyfus, A. Stanley. *Henry Cohen: Messenger of the Lord.* New York: Bloch Publishing, 1963.

Ducharme, Dede Fox. *The Treasure in the Tiny Blue Tin.* Fort Worth: Texas Christian University Press, 1998.

Enstam, Elizabeth York. *Women And The Creation Of Urban Life: Dallas, Texas, 1843–1920.* College Station: Texas A&M University Press, 1998.

Epstein, Howard V. *Jews in Small Towns: Legends and Legacies.* Santa Rosa, Calif.: Vision Books International, 1997.

Evans, Eli N. *The Provincials.* New York: Atheneum, 1980.

Fehrenbach, T. R. *Seven Keys to Texas.* El Paso: University of Texas at El Paso Press, 1986 [1983].

Fierman, Floyd S. *The Schwartz Family of El Paso: The Story of a Pioneer Jewish Family in the Southwest.* El Paso: University of Texas at El Paso Texas Western Press, 1980.

Fox, G. George. "The End of an Era." In Chyet, *Lives and Voices,* 274–309.

———. "Who Is 100 Per Cent American?" Fort Worth: Temple Beth-El [Beth-El Congregation, n.d.].

Fox, Steven. "On the Road to Unity: The Union of American Hebrew Congregations and American Jewry, 1873–1903." *American Jewish Archives* 32 (November 1980): 145–193.

Friedman, Kinky. *Armadillos and Old Lace*. New York: Bantam, 1994.

———. *Elvis, Jesus and Coca-Cola*. London: Faber and Faber, 1993.

———. *Greenwich Killing Time*. New York: Beech Tree Books, 1986.

———. *The Love Song of J. Edgar Hoover*. New York: Ballantine, 1996.

———. *Old Testaments & New Revelations*. Fruit of the Tune Music, 1992 [1973].

———. *Road Kill*. New York: Ballantine Books, 1997.

"From Kempen, Poland to Hempstead, Texas: the Career of Rabbi Heinrich Schwarz." *Western States Jewish History* 19 (January 1987): 132–133.

Frosch, Daniel. "Unto the Seventh Generation." TJHS Box 3A164, Folder 8.

Frost, Stanley. *The Challenge of the Klan*. Indianapolis: Bobbs-Merrill, 1923.

Frye, Gloria. "Eva Catherine Rosine Ruff Sterne (1809–1897)." In Carrington, *Women in Early Texas*, 233–237.

Geffen, David. "A Sentimental Journey—Early Zionist Activities in the South—The Diary of Jacob de Haas' Trip in 1904." *Forum on the Jewish People, Zionism and Israel* 34 (Winter 1979): 161–171.

Geller, Shmuel. *Mazkeres Ahavah: Remembrance of Love, A Biographical Account of Rabbi Yaakov and Sara Geller and Family*. Zichron Yaakov, Israel: Institution for Publication of Books and Study of Manuscripts, 1988.

Gilman, Sander L. "The Frontier as a Model for Jewish History." In Gilman and Shain, *Jewries at the Frontier*, 1–25.

Gilman, Sander L. and Milton Shain, eds. *Jewries at the Frontier: Accommodation, Identity, Conflict*. Urbana: University of Illinois Press, 1999.

Gladstein, Mimi Reisel and Sylvia Deener Cohen. "El Paso: The Wild West Welcomes Holocaust Survivors." In Weiner and Roseman, *Lone Stars of David*, 239–254.

Goldberg, Irving L. "The Changing Jewish Community of Dallas." *American Jewish Archives* 11 (April 1959): 82–97.

Goldberg, Robert Alan. *Back to the Soil: The Jewish Farmers of Clarion, Utah, and Their World*. Salt Lake City: University of Utah Press, 1986.

Golden Book of Congregation Adath Yeshurun, 1891–1941, The. Houston: Congregation Adath Yeshurun, 1942.

Goldstein, Eric L. *The Price of Whiteness: Jews, Race, and American Identity*. Princeton: Princeton University Press, 2006.

Gomolak, Louis Stanislaus. "Prologue: LBJ's Foreign Affairs Background, 1908–1948." PhD dissertation, University of Texas at Austin, 1989.

Goodman, Fanny Sattinger. "'In the Beginning': The Jewish Community of El Paso, Texas" (1970). AJA Histories File.

Goren, Arthur A. *New York Jews and the Quest for Community: The Kehillah Experiment, 1908–1922*. New York: Columbia University Press, 1970.

Granoff, Albert L. "To America with Love." AJA Small Collection 4215, Box 379.

Green, Louis. Untitled family history. TJHS Box 3A165, Folder 2.

Greene, Ward. "Notes for a History of the Klan." *American Mercury* 5 (June 1925): 240–243.

Greenstein, Howard R. *Turning Point: Zionism and Reform Judaism.* Chico, Calif.: Scholars Press, 1981.

Gurwitz, Alexander Ziskind. "Memories of Two Generations," vol. 2, tr. Amram Prero [1932]. TJHS Box 3A187.

Harelik, Mark. *The Immigrant.* New York: Broadway Play Publishing, 1989.

———. *The Legacy.* New York: Broadway Play Publishing, 1997.

Harris, Leon. *Merchant Princes: An Intimate History of Jewish Families Who Built Great Department Stores.* New York: Kodansha International, 1994 [1979].

Hart, Jan Siegel. *Hanna, the Immigrant,* illustrations by Charles Shaw. Austin: Eakin Press, 1991.

———. *The Many Adventures of Minnie,* illustrations by J. Kay Wilson. Austin: Eakin Press, 1992.

———. *More Adventures of Minnie,* illustrations by Diego Vela. Temple, Tex.: Hart Publishing, 1994.

Henry, Julius. "The Making of An Abolitionist." *American Jewish Archives* 13 (November 1961): 169–170.

Hertzberg, Steven. *Strangers Within the Gate City: The Jews of Atlanta, 1845–1915.* Philadelphia: Jewish Publication Society of America, 1978.

Hest, Amy. *The Private Notebook of Katie Roberts, Age 11,* illustrations by Sonja Lamut. Cambridge, Mass.: Candlewick Press, 1995.

Hill, Marilynn Wood. "A History of the Jewish Involvement in the Dallas Community." Master's thesis, Southern Methodist University, 1967.

Hordes, Stanley M. *To the End of the Earth: A History of the Crypto-Jews of New Mexico.* New York: Columbia University Press, 2005.

Horowitz, Henry Jacob. "Just a Reflection," *Western States Jewish History* 30 (July 1998): 316.

Hyman, Harold M. *Oleander Odyssey: The Kempners of Galveston, Texas, 1854–1980s.* College Station: Texas A&M University Press, 1990.

Ignatiev, Noel. *How the Irish Became White.* New York: Routledge, 1995.

Jackson, Kenneth T. *The Ku Klux Klan in the City, 1915–1930.* New York: Oxford University Press, 1967.

Jacobs, Mike. *Holocaust Survivor: Mike Jacobs' Triumph Over Tragedy, a Memoir,* ed. Ginger Jacobs. Austin: Eakin Press, 2001.

Jacobs, Wilbur R. *The Frontier in American History.* Tucson: University of Arizona Press, 1992.

Jacobus, Dorothy. "Growing Up in Dallas" (November 1977). TJHS Box 3A170, Folder 3.

James, Marquis. *The Raven: A Biography of Sam Houston.* New York: Blue Ribbon Books, 1929.

"'Jewish Role in Desegregating Dallas, The': Meeting of the Dallas Jewish Historical Society, January 6, 1998." Dallas: Dallas Jewish Historical Society, 1998. Videotape, Dallas Public Library.

Johnson, Lady Bird. *A White House Diary*. New York: Holt, Rinehart and Winston,
1970.

Joseph, Ernest, "Rope Walker's Tombstone," Address to Texas Kallah (February
23, 1976). TJHS Box 3A170, Folder 1.

Joseph, Harriet Denise. "The Brownsville Jewish Community: From Generation
to Generation." Paper presented at Texas State Historical Association Annual
Meeting, Austin (March 1990). TJHS Box 3A169, Folder 6.

Joseph, Samuel. *History of the Baron de Hirsch Fund: The Americanization of the Jewish
Immigrant*. Philadelphia: Jewish Publication Society, 1935.

Kahn, Ava F., ed. *Jewish Life in the American West: Perspectives on Migration, Settlement, and Community*. Los Angeles: Autry Museum of Western Heritage, 2002.

———. *Jewish Voices of the California Gold Rush: A Documentary History, 1849–1880*.
Detroit: Wayne State University Press, 2002.

Kahn, Ava F. and Ellen Eisenberg. "Western Reality: Jewish Diversity During the
'German' Period." *American Jewish History* 92 (2007): 455–479.

Kahn, Sharon. *Fax Me a Bagel*. New York: Scribner, 1998.

———. *Never Nosh a Matzo Ball*. New York: Berkley Prime Crime, 2002.

Kariel, Audrey Daniels. "The Jewish Story and Memories of Marshall, Texas." *Western States Jewish Historical Quarterly* 14 (April 1982): 195–206.

Kempner, I. H. *Recalled Recollections*. Dallas: Egan Press, 1961.

Kempner, Isaac Herbert. "My Memories of Father." *American Jewish Archives* 19
(April 1967): 41–59.

Kessler, Jimmy. *Henry Cohen: The Life of a Frontier Rabbi*. Austin: Eakin Press, 1997.

Kilgore, Linda Elaine. "The Ku Klux Klan and the Press in Texas, 1920–1927." Master's thesis, University of Texas at Austin, 1964.

Klein, Kerwin Lee. "Reclaiming the 'F' Word, or Being and Becoming Postwestern." *Pacific Historical Review* 65 (May 1996): 179–216.

Kohlberg, Walter K., tr. *Letters of Ernst Kohlberg, 1875–1877*. El Paso: Texas Western
Press, 1973.

Koppman, Lionel. "What I Remember" (May 12, 1985). AJA Biographies File.

Korn, Bertram Wallace. *The Early Jews of New Orleans*. Waltham: American Jewish
Historical Society, 1969.

———. *Jews and Negro Slavery In the Old South, 1789–1865*. Elkins Park, Penn.: Reform Congregation Keneseth Israel, 1961.

Landa, Harry. *As I Remember*. San Antonio: Carleton, 1945.

Larralde, Carlos Montalvo. "Chicano Jews in South Texas." PhD dissertation, University of California at Los Angeles, 1978.

Leeson, Daniel N. "In Search of the History of the Texas Patriot Moses A. Levy."
Western States Jewish History 21 (July 1989): 291–306 and 22 (October 1989): 22–
37.

LeMaster, Carolyn Gray. *A Corner of the Tapestry: A History of the Jewish Experience in Arkansas, 1820s–1990s.* Fayetteville: University of Arkansas Press, 1994.

Levy, William. "A Jew Views Black Education: Texas—1890." *Western States Jewish Historical Quarterly* 8 (July 1976): 351–360.

Liebman, Seymour B. *The Enlightened: The Writings of Luis de Carvajal, El Mozo.* Coral Gables: University of Miami Press, 1967.

———. *The Jews in New Spain: Faith, Flame and the Inquisition.* Coral Gables: University of Miami Press, 1970.

Limerick, Patricia Nelson. *Legacy of Conquest: The Unbroken Past of the American West.* New York: Norton, 1987.

———. "What on Earth is the New Western History?" In Limerick, Milner, and Rankin, *Trails: Toward A New Western History,* 81–88.

Limerick, Patricia Nelson, Clyde A. Milner II, and Charles E. Rankin, eds. *Trails: Toward a New Western History.* Lawrence: University Press of Kansas, 1991.

Lipson-Walker, Carolyn. "'Shalom Y'all': The Folklore and Culture of Southern Jews." PhD dissertation, Indiana University, 1986.

Maas, Elaine H. "Jews." In von der Mehden, *The Ethnic Groups of Houston,* 136–156.

MacLean, Nancy. *Behind the Mask of Chivalry: The Making of the Second Ku Klux Klan.* New York: Oxford University Press, 1994.

Marchiafava, Louis J. and David Courtwright. Interview with Robert I. Kahn, August 6, 1975. TJHS Box 3A174, Folder 7.

Marcus, Jacob Rader. *To Count a People: American Jewish Population Data, 1585–1984.* Lanham: University Press of America, 1984.

Marcus, Stanley. *Minding the Store: A Memoir.* Boston: Little, Brown and Company, 1974.

Marinbach, Bernard. *Galveston: Ellis Island of the West.* Albany: State University of New York Press, 1983.

Marks, Marguerite Meyer. "Integration of the Jew and the Non-Jew in Dallas." TJHS Box 3A170, Folder 3.

———. "Memoirs of My Family" (1984). TJHS Box 3A166, Folder 6.

Marlow, Judith Geller. "My Wandering Roots." In Geller, *Mazkeres Ahavah: Remembrance of Love,* 121–124.

Mayfield, Billie Jr. *Chroniclings of Billie.* Houston: Southwestern Press, 1916.

McDonald, Archie P., ed. *Hurrah for Texas! The Diary of Adolphus Sterne, 1838–1851.* Austin: Eakin Press, 1986.

Meinig, D. W. *Imperial Texas: An Interpretive Essay in Cultural Geography.* Austin: University of Texas Press, 1969.

Miller, Lauraine. "The Zale Story: Diamonds for the Rough." In Weiner and Roseman, *Lone Stars of David,* 148–161.

Moore, Deborah Dash. *To the Golden Cities: Pursuing the American Jewish Dream in Miami and L.A.* New York: Free Press, 1994.

Morse, Arthur. *While Six Million Died: A Chronicle of American Apathy.* New York: Random House, 1968.

N. W. Ayer & Son's American Newspaper Annual.

Nathan, Anne and Harry I. Cohen. *The Man Who Stayed in Texas: The Life of Rabbi Henry Cohen.* New York: Whittlesey House, 1941.

Olan, Levi. "Levi Olan: Oral History Interviews Conducted by Gerald D. Saxon on February 4 and April 6, 1983" (1983). Dallas Public Library.

Ornish, Natalie. *Pioneer Jewish Texans.* Dallas: Texas Heritage Press, 1989.

Panitz, Esther. "In Defense of the Jewish Immigrant (1891–1924)." *American Jewish Historical Quarterly* 55 (September 1965): 57–97.

Parker, Susanne. "Shema Israel: The Reform Jewish Movement in Marshall" (1983). TJHS Box 3A172, Folder 6.

Phillips, Michael. *White Metropolis: Race, Ethnicity, and Religion in Dallas, 1841–2001.* Austin: University of Texas Press, 2006.

Pollard, Clarice F. "WAACS in Texas during the Second World War." *Southwestern Historical Quarterly* 93 (July 1989).

Preuss, Karl. "Rabbi David Jacobson and the Integration of San Antonio." In Bauman and Kalin, *The Quiet Voices,* 135–151.

Rabinowitz, Dorothy. *New Lives: Survivors of the Holocaust Living in America.* New York: Alfred A. Knopf, 1977.

Ratkin, Gary Alan. "The Jews in Houston and Galveston, Texas during the Civil War" (May 1963). TJHS Box 3A172, Folder 1.

Ravitch, Diane. "The Educational Critic in New York." In Rosenberg and Goldstein, *Creators and Disturbers,* 388–400.

Rochlin, Harriet and Fred Rochlin. *Pioneer Jews: A New Life in the Far West.* Boston: Houghton Mifflin, 1984.

Rockoff, Stuart. "Deep in the Heart of Palestine: Zionism in Early Texas." In Weiner and Roseman, *Lone Stars of David,* 93–107.

Rogoff, Leonard. *Homelands: Southern Jewish Identity in Durham and Chapel Hill, North Carolina.* Tuscaloosa: University of Alabama Press, 2001.

Romanofsky, Peter. "'To Rid Ourselves of the Burden': New York Jewish Charities and the Origins of the Industrial Removal Office, 1890–1901." *American Jewish Historical Quarterly* 64 (June 1975): 331–343.

Rosenbaum, Glen. "Portrait of a Judge." *The Houston Lawyer* 35 (November 1997): 51–55.

Rosenbaum, Milton. "Remembering Fort Worth." TJHS Box 3A171, Folder 2.

Rosenberg, Bernard and Ernest Goldstein, eds. *Creators and Disturbers: Reminiscences By Jewish Intellectuals of New York.* New York: Columbia University Press, 1982.

Rosinger, Samuel. "Deep in the Heart of Texas." In Chyet, *Lives and Voices,* 114–153.

———, ed. *The Kallah: An Annual Convention of Texas Rabbis, Year Book 5696.* 1935.

Ruby, Lois. *Swindletop.* Austin: Eakin Press, 2000.

Sachar, Howard M. *A History of the Jews in America.* New York: Knopf, 1992.

Sajowitz, William. "History of Reform Judaism in San Antonio, Texas, 1874–1945." Master's thesis, Hebrew Union College–Jewish Institute of Religion, 1945.

Santos, Richard G. "Chicanos of Jewish Descent in Texas." *Western States Jewish Historical Quarterly* 15 (July 1983): 327–333.

———. *Silent Heritage: The Sephardim and the Colonization of the Spanish North American Frontier, 1492–1600.* San Antonio: New Sepharad Press, 2000.

Saunders, Jake and Howard Waldrop. *The Texas-Israeli War: 1999.* New York: Del Rey, 1974.

Schechter, Abraham, ed. *The Kallah: An Annual Convention of Texas Rabbis.* [Houston], 1928.

Schechter, Cathy. "Forty Acres and a Shul: 'It's Easy as Dell.'" In Weiner and Roseman, *Lone Stars of David,* 255–267.

Schlam, Helena Frenkil. "The Early Jews of Houston." Master's thesis, Ohio State University, 1971.

Schloff, Linda Mack. *And Prairie Dogs Weren't Kosher: Jewish Women in the Upper Midwest Since 1855.* St. Paul: Minnesota Historical Society Press, 1996.

Schmier, Louis. *Reflections of Southern Jewry: The Letters of Charles Wessolowsky, 1878–1879.* Macon: Mercer University Press, 1982.

Schooler, Lionel M. "Mitchell (Michael) Louis Westheimer (1831–c.1910)." TJHS Box 3A167, Folder 5.

Schutze, Jim. *The Accommodation: The Politics of Race in an American City.* Secaucus: Citadel Press, 1986.

Shankman, Arnold. *Ambivalent Friends: Afro-Americans View the Immigrant.* Westport, Conn.: Greenwood Press, 1982.

Sharfman, I. Harold. *Jews on the Frontier.* Chicago: Henry Regnery Company, 1977.

Smither, Harriet. "Diary of Adolphus Sterne." *Southwestern Historical Quarterly* 30 (October 1926): 139–155. [Continued intermittently in subsequent issues over about a year.]

Stone, Bryan Edward. "Edgar Goldberg and the *Texas Jewish Herald*: Changing Coverage and Blended Identity." *Southern Jewish History* 7 (2004): 71–108.

———. "On the Frontier: Jews without Judaism." In Weiner and Roseman, *Lone Stars of David,* 18–32.

———. "'Ride 'Em, Jewboy': Kinky Friedman and the Texas Mystique." *Southern Jewish History* 1 (1998): 23–42.

———. "'Texas News for Texas Jews': Edgar Goldberg and the *Texas Jewish Herald.*" *The (Houston) Jewish Herald-Voice Rosh Hashanah Edition* (September 1995): 6–23. Reprinted as "Edgar Goldberg and Forty Years of the *Texas Jewish Herald.*" *Western States Jewish History* 30 (July 1998): 290–314.

Stringer, Tommy. "A Most Unlikely Canaan: A Brief History of the Corsicana Jewish Community." TJHS Box 3A170, Folder 1.

———. "The Zale Corporation: A Texas Success Story." PhD dissertation, University of North Texas, 1985.

Tefteller, Carol. "The Jewish Community in Frontier Jefferson." *Texas Historian: Publication of the Junior Historians of Texas* 35 (September 1974): 2–9.

Temple Mizpah: 50 Years Remembered. Abilene: Temple Mizpah, 1992.

Texas Almanac 2006–2007. Dallas: *Dallas Morning News,* 2005.

"Texas Declaration of Independence, The. March 2, 1836." In Wallace, *Documents of Texas History,* 99.

Toll, William. *The Making of an Ethnic Middle Class: Portland Jewry over Four Generations.* Albany: State University of New York Press, 1982.

Toro, Alfonso. *The Carvajal Family,* tr. Frances Hernández. El Paso: Texas Western Press, 2002 [1943].

Trupin, Sophie. *Dakota Diaspora: Memoirs of a Jewish Homesteader.* Berkeley: Alternative Press, 1984.

Turner, Elizabeth Hayes. *Women, Culture, and Community: Religion and Reform in Galveston, 1880–1920.* Chapel Hill: University of North Carolina Press, 1997.

Turner, Frederick Jackson. "The Significance of the Frontier in American History." In Jacobs, *The Frontier in American History,* 1–38.

Union of American Hebrew Congregations, *Statistics of the Jews of the United States.* Cincinnati: Union of American Hebrew Congregations, 1880.

Viener, Saul. "Surgeon Moses Albert Levy: Letters of a Texas Patriot." *Publications of the American Jewish Historical Society* 46 (September 1956): 101–113.

von der Mehden, Fred R., ed. *The Ethnic Groups of Houston.* Houston: Rice University Studies, 1984.

Wagner, Frank. Untitled biography of David Hirsch. TJHS Box 3A165, Folder 4.

Walker, Stanley. *Texas.* New York: Viking, 1962.

Wallace, Ernest, ed. *Documents of Texas History.* Austin: Steck Company, 1963.

Webb, Clive. *Fight Against Fear: Southern Jews and Black Civil Rights.* Athens: University of Georgia Press, 2001.

Weiner, Deborah R. *Coalfield Jews: An Appalachian History.* Urbana: University of Illinois Press, 2006.

Weiner, Hollace Ava. *Jewish Stars in Texas: Rabbis and Their Work.* College Station: Texas A&M University Press, 1999.

———. "The Mixers: The Role of Rabbis Deep in the Heart of Texas." *American Jewish History* 85 (September 1997): 289–332.

———. "Rabbi Sidney Wolf: Harmonizing in Texas." In Bauman and Kalin, *The Quiet Voices,* 121–134.

———. "Removal Approval: The Industrial Removal Office Experience in Fort Worth, Texas." *Southern Jewish History* 4 (2001): 1–44.

———. "Tied and Tethered (*"Geknippt und Gebinden"*): Jews in Early Fort Worth." *Southwestern Historical Quarterly* 57 (January 2004): 388–413.

Weiner, Hollace Ava and Kenneth D. Roseman, eds. *Lone Stars of David.* Waltham: Brandeis University Press, 2007.

Weiner, Phyllis. "Freida Weiner." TJHS Box 3A167, Folder 3.

Weissbach, Lee Shai. *Jewish Life In Small-Town America: A History.* New Haven: Yale University Press, 2005.

White, Richard. *"It's Your Misfortune and None of My Own": A New History of the American West*. Norman: University of Oklahoma Press, 1991.

Whitfield, Gary P. "Confederate Stories: The Sanger Brothers of Weatherford, Dallas, and Waco." In Weiner and Roseman, *Lone Stars of David*, 33–49.

Whitfield, Stephen J. "Commercial Passions: The Southern Jew as Businessman." *American Jewish History* 71 (March 1982): 342–357.

Williams, Amelia W. and Eugene C. Barker, eds. *The Writings of Sam Houston, 1813–1863*. Austin: University of Texas Press, 1938.

Winegarten, Ruthe and Cathy Schechter. *Deep in the Heart: The Lives and Legends of Texas Jews, a Photographic History*. Austin: Eakin Press, 1990.

Winks, Robin W., ed. *Detective Fiction: A Collection of Critical Essays*. Englewood Cliffs: Prentice-Hall, 1980.

Wise, Stephen S. "The Shame of Houston." *Opinion: A Journal of Jewish Life and Letters* (February 1944): 5.

Wisehart, M. K. *Sam Houston, American Giant*. Washington, D.C.: Robert B. Luce, 1962.

Wisenberg, S. L. *The Sweetheart is In: Stories*. Evanston, Ill.: Triquarterly Books, 2001.

Wolin, Penny Diane. *The Jews of Wyoming: Fringe of the Diaspora*. Cheyenne: Crazy Woman Creek Publishing, 2000.

Wolitz, Seth L. "Bifocality in Jewish Identity in the Texas-Jewish Experience." In Gilman and Shain, *Jewries at the Frontier*, 185–208.

World Almanac and Book of Facts, 2003. New York: World Almanac Books, 2003.

Wyman, David S. *The Abandonment of the Jews: America and the Holocaust, 1941–1945*. New York: Pantheon Books, 1984.

Zimmerman, Sheldon. Speech to the Dallas Jewish Historical Society, April 14, 2002. Videotape in author's collection.

INDEX

A. Harris and Co., 194–195, 200, 203
Abilene, Tex., 180, 217
Abolitionism, 48, 50
Acculturation, 84, 100, 133, 148, 150, 218, 224–225, 236; and authenticity, 9–10, 16, 233; risk in frontier, 26, 40, 54; in Europe, 31–32; and Zionism, 81, 96, 186; Klan and, 123, 132–133, 145–146; and Reform Judaism, 158, 160–161
Adath Yeshurun (Houston), 105–106, 147–148, 151, 152
Adler, Cyrus, 2, 82
African Americans, 29; and Jews, 46–49, 50–51, 61, 134–136, 193–195, 197, 208, 210, 212; violence against, 98–99, 124, 128. See also Civil rights; Slavery
Agriculture: 76–81; appeal of, 40, 76; colonies, 76–77, 78–81; land ownership, 76–78; ranching, 77–78; Jewish Agric. and Industrial Aid Soc., 79–80; Tyler Comm., 79–80
Agudas Achim (Austin), 176
Agudas Achim (San Antonio), 151, 152, 156

Agudath Jacob (Waco), 151, 157
Ahavath Sholom (Fort Worth), 151
Aikman, Duncan, 126
Alabama, 70, 136
Alamo, 33, 147
Alaska, 7
Alexander, Charles C., 126–127
Altman, Jack, 185
American Assoc. of Univ. Women, 178
American Council for Judaism, 162–163, 164, 168, 186
American Hebrew (New York), 115, 116
American Israelite (Cincinnati), 41–42, 49, 50, 60, 61, 62, 64–65, 78, 88, 99, 104, 105, 108, 152
American Jewish Committee, 107, 111, 115, 173, 175
American Jewish Congress, 168
American Jewish Year Book, 43n7
American Party, 137
Americanization. See Acculturation
Amsterdam, 59
Andres, Harry and Chaya, 184
Angelina Co., Tex., 28

Judaism, Orthodox. *See* Orthodox Judaism

Judaism, Reform. *See* Reform Judaism

Judaism: authenticity of, 8–10, 11, 16, 42, 70; rituals of, 33, 155, 157, 161, 166, 168–169; circumcision, 57, 58–59, 60–61, 64–65; preservation of, 58–59, 70; schools, 64, 95, 149, 151, 152, 154, 156, 159, 191, 216; scholarship, 65, 152–153; confirmation, 105–106; denominations, 156–157; univeralism, 159–160, 170. *See also* Hebrew; Identity; Yiddish

Juneteenth, 50

Kahn, Julius, 4

Kahn, Robert, 159–160, 163–165, *165*, 167–168, 176

Kahn, Sharon, 226–228, 230–233, *231*

Kallah of Texas Rabbis, 152–153

Kashrut, 60, 88, 150, 151, 152, 158, 180, 182, 215, 216

Kaufman, David S., 35

Kellerman, Faye, 227

Kemelman, Harry, 227

Kempner, Harris, 48–49, 77, 90, 93n69, 158

Kempner, Isaac, 77, 90, 91, 97, 158

Kennedy, John F., 176, 205, 209

Kermin, Joseph, 188

Kerrville, Tex., 227

Keystone, W. Va., 45

Kiev, 82, 86

King, Martin Luther, Jr., 209, *209*, 210

Kirwin, James, 132, 138

Klan. *See* Ku Klux Klan

Klein, Kerwin Lee, 13

Klein, Nathan, 176

Kohlberg, Ernst, 52–54, *53*, 67, 191

Kokernot, David, 33

Kol Halev (Austin), 216

Koppman, Lionel, 134

Kosher. *See* Kashrut

Kosse, Tex., 62

Kramer, Arthur, 200

Kraus, Adolf, 115

Kruger's Jewelry, 194

Ku Klux Klan, 20, 118, 120–134, 136–142, 144–146, 195, 196, 214; Jewish opposition to, 106, 128, 130–134, 138–139, 144; State Fair Klan Day, *120*, 121–123, 127–128, 132; and Jews, 122–124, 126–127, 130–131, 145–146; in politics, 122, 123, 129–130, 136–140, 141, 142, 144–146; origins, 124–125; anti-Semitism of, 125, 126–127, 132; "100% Americanism," 125, 131–132, 141; in Tex., 125–130; as social regulator, 126–127, 128; use of violence, 127–128; boycotts against Jews, 128–129, 130, 134; dissolution of, 144–145. *See also* Anti-Semitism

La Bahía (Goliad, Tex.), 26

Labatt, Abraham C., 29

Laird, L. A. L., 37

Landa, Helena, 61

Landa, Joseph, 48, 61

Landes, H. A., 88–89

Landman, Minnie, 76

Laramie, Wyo., 15

Laredo, Tex., 51, 62, 135, 157, 181–182

Leavitt, Israel, 45

Lechenger's, 172

Leeser, Isaac, 40–41, 42, 45, 54, 56

Lefkowitz, David, 132–133, 163, 186, 200, 207

Legacy, The (Harelik), 223, 225–226

Leichtman, Carrie Chazan, 134

LeMaster, Carolyn Gray, 14

Leon and H. Blum, 45

Leonard, Oscar, 90–91, 107

Leshin, Julius, 135–136

Levi, Leo N., 84, 113

Levine's, 194

Levy, Abe, 180

Levy, Albert Moses, 33

Levy, Hannah, 59

Levy, Lewis A., 59–60, *60*, 76–77, 78

Levy, Mary A., 59, *60*

CPSIA information can be obtained
at www.ICGtesting.com
Printed in the USA
FSHW012134240919
62353FS